Tobacco Regulation, Economics, and Public Health, Volume I

Samuel C. Hampsher-Monk ·
James E. Prieger · Sudhanshu Patwardhan

Tobacco Regulation, Economics, and Public Health, Volume I

Clearing the Air on E-Cigarettes and Harm Reduction

Samuel C. Hampsher-Monk
Santa Clarita, CA, USA

Sudhanshu Patwardhan
Chilworth, Hampshire, UK

James E. Prieger
School of Public Policy
Pepperdine University
Malibu, CA, USA

ISBN 978-3-031-41311-7   ISBN 978-3-031-41312-4   (eBook)
https://doi.org/10.1007/978-3-031-41312-4

© The Editor(s) (if applicable) and The Author(s), under exclusive license to Springer Nature Switzerland AG 2024

This work is subject to copyright. All rights are solely and exclusively licensed by the Publisher, whether the whole or part of the material is concerned, specifically the rights of translation, reprinting, reuse of illustrations, recitation, broadcasting, reproduction on microfilms or in any other physical way, and transmission or information storage and retrieval, electronic adaptation, computer software, or by similar or dissimilar methodology now known or hereafter developed.

The use of general descriptive names, registered names, trademarks, service marks, etc. in this publication does not imply, even in the absence of a specific statement, that such names are exempt from the relevant protective laws and regulations and therefore free for general use.

The publisher, the authors, and the editors are safe to assume that the advice and information in this book are believed to be true and accurate at the date of publication. Neither the publisher nor the authors or the editors give a warranty, expressed or implied, with respect to the material contained herein or for any errors or omissions that may have been made. The publisher remains neutral with regard to jurisdictional claims in published maps and institutional affiliations.

This Palgrave Macmillan imprint is published by the registered company Springer Nature Switzerland AG
The registered company address is: Gewerbestrasse 11, 6330 Cham, Switzerland

Paper in this product is recyclable.

Funding Disclosure

This book was funded with a grant from the Foundation for a Smoke-Free World, an independent, U.S. nonprofit 501(c)(3) grantmaking organization with the purpose of improving public health by ending combustible tobacco use. Through September 2023, the Foundation received charitable gifts from PMI Global Services Inc. ("PMI"). Independent from PMI since its founding in 2017, the Foundation operates in a manner that ensures its independence from PMI and any commercial entity. The contents, selection, and presentation of facts, as well as any opinions expressed herein are the sole responsibility of the authors and under no circumstances shall be regarded as reflecting the positions of the Foundation for a Smoke-Free World, Inc.
We enjoyed complete editorial discretion throughout the conception, design, research, writing, and publishing of this book. None of the Foundation's staff reviewed any portion of the manuscript prior to its publication.
-The authors.

In grateful memory of Mark Kleiman.

For Amanda, Melanie, Pooja, Seth, Kaia, Jenna, Alex, Grant, Kabir, Saachi, and a billion people around the world still using combustible tobacco.

Foreword

The regulation of e-cigarettes shows the wisdom of economist Thomas Sowell's observation: "There are no solutions. There are only trade-offs."[1] The e-cigarette is an innovation that is disrupting tobacco markets. Given that tobacco use is estimated to cause over 8 million deaths each year across the world, why isn't tobacco market disruption the solution to a major public health problem?

E-cigarettes contain nicotine, the chemical that makes tobacco addictive. However, contrary to a misperception common among the general public and even among some healthcare professionals, nicotine is not the chemical in tobacco smoke that causes cancer or the other serious health consequences of smoking. E-cigarettes are disrupting tobacco markets because they contain nicotine, but the nicotine content is also the source of health trade-offs between smokers and vapers. Smokers can benefit by using e-cigarettes to cut down or quit using combustible cigarettes, but other groups can be harmed by e-cigarettes. Never-smokers who start vaping e-cigarettes can become addicted, although even there one must recognize that some, perhaps many, of them would have become addicted to cigarettes in the absence of e-cigarettes. Smokers of combustible cigarettes may maintain their nicotine addiction by vaping e-cigarettes

---

[1] Thomas, S. *A Conflict of Visions: Ideological Origins of Political Struggles.* William Morrow & Co, 1986.

in addition to smoking, instead of quitting entirely. There also might be adverse health consequences to vaping other than nicotine addiction.

Economists and public health professionals tend to view the trade-offs created by e-cigarettes differently. Economists recognize that people make trade-offs every day between their health and their consumption of goods and enjoyment of activities that they value. Almost none of us is as healthy as we could be, because personal health is not our only goal in life. The economic approach is to conduct cost-benefit analysis (or other formal approaches from the field of welfare economics, as the authors discuss in Vol. III, Chapter 2) of e-cigarette regulations to judge whether the consequences of reduced smoking are more valuable than the consequences of increased vaping. In other policy contexts, many public health professionals *do* recognize trade-offs. For example, many support policies that reduce the harms associated with injection drug use, such as needle exchange programs and clean injection sites. But among public health professionals, tobacco harm reduction remains controversial; the authors discuss the extent of the polarization and examine the reasons for it in Vol. II, Chapter 3. In a recent editorial in the American Journal of Public Health, 15 past Presidents of the Society of Nicotine and Tobacco Research concluded that "vaping can benefit public health, given substantial evidence supporting the potential of vaping to reduce smoking's toll."[2] However, in the same issue, other public health professionals argued that regulating e-cigarettes involves "an intergenerational trade-off" between helping older smokers addicted to nicotine versus "uncertain health risks for younger individuals."[3] Evidence on the health risks of using e-cigarettes, real and imagined, is reviewed in Vol II, Chapter 1.

---

[2] Balfour, D.J.K., Benowitz, N.L., Colby, S.M., Hatsukami, D.K., Lando, H.A., Leischow, S.J., Lerman, C., Mermelstein, R.J., Niaura, R., Perkins, K.A., Pomerleau, O.F., Rigotti, N.A., Swan, G.E., Warner, K.E., West, R. Balancing Consideration of the Risks and Benefits of E-Cigarettes [published correction appears in Am J Public Health. 2022 Apr;112(4):e6]. Am J Public Health. 2021;111(9):1661–1672. https://doi.org/10.2105/AJPH.2021.306416.

[3] Samet, J.M., Barrington-Trimis, J. E-Cigarettes and Harm Reduction: An Artificial Controversy Instead of Evidence and a Well-Framed Decision Context. Am J Public Health. 2021;111(9):1572–1574. https://doi.org/10.2105/AJPH.2021.306457.

To shed light on the controversial regulatory trade-offs, it is interesting to imagine an alternative, or counter-factual, history of e-cigarette regulation in the U.S. Soon after e-cigarettes began to be sold in U.S. markets, in 2009 the FDA denied their import on the grounds that e-cigarettes were an unapproved medical device that delivered nicotine to treat the withdrawal symptoms of nicotine addiction. The FDA lost the legal battle; the courts ruled that e-cigarettes could not be regulated as medical devices unless they were marketed with a therapeutic purpose. Because of this ruling and the 2009 Tobacco Control Act's restrictions on tobacco product health claims, e-cigarette manufacturers avoided making claims about cessation or any health benefits in their advertising. It is interesting to consider how different this could have been. In an alternative history, regulators and manufacturers could have made different strategic choices. Vol. II, Chapter 2 of this book reviews evidence that e-cigarettes are effective smoking cessation aids. Vol. II, Chapter 1 reviews evidence that vaping e-cigarettes is much less harmful than smoking combustible cigarettes. Could the manufacturers have made the case to the FDA to regulate e-cigarettes as an approved over-the-counter medical device for smoking cessation, and/or as a modified risk tobacco product for smokers to switch to? Could they still? In the real world, e-cigarette manufacturers frequently relied on what economists call 'image advertising' that associated their products with attractive settings and attractive young people. In a counterfactual world, e-cigarette manufacturers might instead have used advertising mainly to inform the large market of millions of established smokers about how e-cigarettes could help smokers quit and reduce risks to their health. In essence, if they had been allowed to do so, the e-cigarette manufacturers would have run a large and continuing anti-smoking campaign without taking a dollar from public funding available for tobacco control efforts.[4] At the same time, the content and targeting of the e-cigarette advertisements might have avoided appealing to young people. E-cigarettes would have seemed more like a medical product that treats a health problem faced by older people than a cool new product for the young. Compared to the actual history of e-cigarette regulation,

---

[4] Research on smoking cessation pharmaceutical product advertising illustrates the potential gains (Avery, R., Kenkel, D., Lillard, D., Mathios, A. Private Profits and Public Health: Does Advertising of Smoking Cessation Products Encourage Smokers To Quit? J Pol Econ. 2007;115:447-481. https://doi.org/10.1086/520065)

this optimistic alternative history shows how regulation could have helped adult smokers while avoiding the trade-off of increased youth vaping.

The issues raised by e-cigarette regulation are complex, including interactions between health and regulatory science, economics, policy, law, and marketing. The many interdisciplinary questions surrounding e-cigarettes and their impact on public health and consumer behavior are all explored in this text. As such, this book is a valuable resource for policymakers and others wrestling with the tradeoffs involved in e-cigarette regulation in the real world. The polarized debate about e-cigarettes puts regulators and social scientists in a difficult position. It is easy to conclude that the health consequences of vaping are uncertain, but that does not answer the harder questions about how to regulate e-cigarettes. The health consequences of smoking are well-documented and large. Regulating or banning e-cigarettes on the precautionary principle that they might cause harm (discussed in Vol. II, Chapter 3) ignores the harms of smoking that could be prevented if smokers switch to vaping. Based on their review of the scientific literature, the authors conclude that "the available evidence is more than sufficient to inform the development of optimal regulations....in the interests of the whole public." In particular, the authors explore in Vol. III, Chapter 2 how regulation could help adult smokers while mitigating the possible harms resulting from increases in youth vaping. Even readers who disagree about the best solutions to tobacco control and e-cigarette regulation will agree that this book provides a careful review of the evidence and thoughtful analysis of the policy trade-offs.

Donald Kenkel, Ph.D.
Brooks School of Public Policy
Cornell University
Ithaca, USA

ACKNOWLEDGEMENTS

A book such as this one is, by necessity, a collective enterprise. A great many individuals helped formulate the ideas presented herein, define the scope, develop the structure, provide source material, and enhance the analysis. Friends and colleagues have read drafts and provided welcome criticism and suggestions, all of which improved the text immeasurably. The authors are indebted to the following individuals in particular. This is by no means an exhaustive list. To anyone we have omitted to thank, our sincerest apologies. The oversight is ours alone. We also own the opinions and any errors in the text; none of those should be ascribed to those we thank below.

First, thanks are due to the Foundation for a Smoke-Free World, Inc. ("FSFW"), a U.S. nonprofit 501(c)(3) private foundation, which funded the production of this book with a grant. FSFW allowed us complete editorial discretion from inception to publication. The contents, selection, and presentation of facts, as well as any opinions expressed herein, are ours alone.

Particular thanks are also due to the staff at Palgrave Springer; Bronwyn Geyer, Wyndham Hacket Pain, Geetha Chockalingam, Susan Westendorf, Matthew Savin, and Meera Seth, for your interest in the topic, and especially for your patience with us while we fit the pieces together.

We owe a special debt of gratitude to Prof. Don Kenkel for writing the foreword; a difficult task at the best of times, made harder by the

xiv ACKNOWLEDGEMENTS

burden of competing priorities; teaching, publishing, public speaking engagements, and international travel.

This book would not have been possible without Lowry Heussler's humor, wisdom, dedication, and countless hours reading and re-reading drafts, providing comments and suggestions, all of which helped make the book before you what it is. Thanks also to Eliza Hunt, who balances appropriate skepticism with cautious optimism; your clarity of vision and perspective have improved the text immeasurably. Thanks to Lucy Evans and Rachel Ashton for providing editorial and referencing support on the science and public health sections. Special thanks to Sarah Cooney on publication planning.

We benefited greatly from in-depth discussions with Annie Kleykamp, Sally Satel, and Marewa Glover that helped refine the focus of this book. And thank you to Ian Irvine and David Sweanor, not only for your thoughtful insights and suggestions, but also for your example. It is not always easy to participate in the debate about tobacco control and harm reduction with grace and poise, and there are many who would do well to learn from your example.

We also owe a debt of gratitude to the many scholars and researchers who, whether they agree with our analysis or not, have helped build the knowledge base, providing much needed rigor and analysis, often in the face of considerable pressures to the contrary. In this regard special thanks are due to Clive Bates, for convening academics, authors, practitioners, regulators, and other stakeholders and creating a "safe space" in which rigorous and analytical discussion of the nuances of the emerging literature on Harm Reduction can take place, including occasional, but always respectful, disagreement. This book, indeed the development of the discourse, would not be possible without the thoughtful analyses and careful writing, much cited herein, of a great many individuals to whom we owe a considerable debt of gratitude. Our citation of published work should not be construed as the cited authors' endorsement of our thesis (nor our theirs), explicit or implicit. Nonetheless, our respectful thanks are warranted.

We also thank Elise Rasmussen, Gerry Stimson, Paddy Costall, Jessica Harding, Grzegorz Krol, and Dave MacKintosh for providing a platform at their global events for us to introduce the book's topic during the various stages of the book's evolution. Our special thanks go to Fiona Patten for putting a spotlight on the book at the Global Forum on Nicotine.

To Amanda Hampsher-Monk, Melanie Prieger, and Pooja Patwardhan, thanks (with apologies) for accommodating the late nights and working weekends necessary to complete this text, and for putting up with our borderline obsession with the issue, resulting in our annoying tendency to bring every conversation back to nicotine and tobacco.

CONTENTS

1	Introduction	1
1	*The Problem with Tobacco Control*	1
2	*The Need for Alternative Nicotine*	7
3	*What are E-cigarettes?*	12
4	*Friend or Foe?*	12
5	*A Polarized Discourse*	16
6	*The Challenge of Regulating E-cigarettes*	19
7	*What are the Goals of this Book?*	20
8	*What this Book is Not*	21
9	*Why did We Write this Book Now?*	22
10	*Who is this Book for?*	24

2	Who Is (Still) Smoking?	31
1	*A Brief History of Tobacco and Tobacco Control*	31
	1.1 The Birth of a Monster	31
	1.2 Marketing Tobacco in the Twentieth Century	35
	1.3 Understanding the Risks	36
	1.4 Reframing Smoking as a Public Health Issue	40
	1.5 Industry Obstruction	41
2	*Smoking Around the World*	44
	2.1 Prevalence	47
	2.2 Trends and Projections in Smoking	51
3	*Smoking-Related Disparities*	56
	3.1 Socioeconomic Disparities	58

xvii

xviii CONTENTS

	3.2	*Education-Based Smoking Disparities*	63
	3.3	*Smoking Among Ethnic & Racial Minorities*	64
	3.4	*Smoking in LGBTQ+ Communities*	67
	3.5	*Intersectionality*	68
4		*Smoking-Related Harms*	69
5		*Tobacco Control in the Twenty-First Century*	70
	5.1	*Approaches to Tobacco Control*	70
	5.2	*Policy Sharing and International Cooperation*	79
6		*Tobacco Control Successes*	82
7		*Why Are There Still Smokers?*	87
	7.1	*Uptake and Progression to Current Smoking*	87
	7.2	*Barriers to Cessation*	89

3 E-cigarettes: The Technology, the Market, and the Practice of Vaping — **147**

1		*Alternative Nicotine*	147
	1.1	*Nicotine ≠ Tobacco*	147
	1.2	*What Are Alternative Nicotine Products?*	149
	1.3	*A Lexicon of Alternative Nicotine*	151
	1.4	*What's in a Name?*	153
2		*The Technology of E-cigarettes*	155
	2.1	*Precursors to Modern E-cigarettes*	155
	2.2	*The Evolution of the Modern E-cigarette*	157
3		*The Market for E-cigarettes*	158
	3.1	*First Movers; 2003–2012*	158
	3.2	*Enter: Transnational Tobacco Companies; 2012–Present*	160
	3.3	*Global Market Trends*	166
	3.4	*U.S. E-cigarette Market Trends*	167
4		*The Practice of Vaping*	176
	4.1	*Measuring E-cigarette Consumption*	177
	4.2	*Estimating the Prevalence of E-cigarette Use*	178
	4.3	*Who Vapes?*	183
	4.4	*Why Do People Vape?*	194
	4.5	*Why Don't More Smokers Switch to E-cigarettes?*	202
	4.6	*What Does Vaping Feel Like, Compared with Smoking?*	204
	4.7	*How Is Vaping Perceived?*	205

Index — **255**

List of Figures

Chapter 2

Fig. 1 Global smoking prevalence of adults (15+) by region (2000–2020) — 48

Fig. 2 Global smoking prevalence of adults (15+) by income level (2000–2020) — 49

Fig. 3 Age standardized prevalence of current cigarette smoking among adults (15+) — 53

Fig. 4 Countries with the highest and lowest prevalence of adult smoking (15+) (2020) — 55

Chapter 3

Fig. 1 The evolution of the e-cigarette — 158

Fig. 2 U.S. e-cigarette sales, 2008–2021 — 168

Fig. 3 Prevalence of current smoking and e-cigarette use in the U.S. by age (2021) — 180

Fig. 4 Prevalence of current smoking and e-cigarette use in Great Britain by age (2021) — 181

Fig. 5 Prevalence of current smoking and e-cigarette use in Canada by age (2021) — 182

Fig. 6 Smoking status among current adult e-cigarette users (past-30-day use) in Great Britain, 2013–2022 — 184

Fig. 7 Past-30-day e-cigarette and smoking status of U.S. middle- and high-school students — 186

xix

Fig. 8   Reasons for e-cigarette and tobacco use among middle-
and high-school students who reported ever using
e-cigarettes, 2019   199

CHAPTER 1

Introduction

1   THE PROBLEM WITH TOBACCO CONTROL

Tobacco control is often hailed as one of the most successful public health victories of the twentieth century. During the 1960s, more than 40% of adults in countries such as the U.S., Australia, Canada, and the U.K. smoked. Beginning in the previous decade, however, a statistically robust set of epidemiological studies had begun to link smoking to adverse health effects. In response to growing awareness about the dangers of tobacco smoking, and accelerated by increasingly stringent tobacco control policies, the public began increasingly to turn away from cigarettes. By 1990, smoking rates in these countries had dropped to between 25% and 30%. Today between 10% and 15% of adults in these countries currently smoke.

Keystone studies such as Doll & Hill,[1] Wynder & Graham,[2] and Hammond & Horn[3] provided the world with the first robust statistical evidence documenting the harms of smoking in the 1950s. In reaction to these studies and subsequent influential reports by esteemed government agencies such as those by the Royal College of Physicians in 1962[4] and the U.S. Surgeon General in 1964,[5] governments around the world embarked on implementation of a series of tobacco control policies intended to encourage smoking cessation and discourage uptake. Initially, these focused on increasing public awareness of the risks associated with smoking, in the hopes that doing so would motivate smokers to quit or at least cut down on smoking. Public campaigns in print media, on posters,

© The Author(s), under exclusive license to Springer Nature Switzerland AG 2024
S. C. Hampsher-Monk et al., *Tobacco Regulation, Economics, and Public Health, Volume I*, https://doi.org/10.1007/978-3-031-41312-4_1

billboards, radio, television, and latterly online, as well as mandated health warning labels on packaging, sought to educate the public about the dangers of smoking. Still, for most societies, at least until the 1990s, smoking was firmly embedded within the private sphere. If an individual consumer wanted to smoke and understood the risks, the decision to do so was considered a personal one.

In the 1990s, as scientific understanding of the harms posed by second-hand smoke grew, smoking was reframed as a public health issue. The new justification provided by these negative social externalities accelerated the implementation of more robust control measures, including increased tobacco taxes, more stringent marketing restrictions and, especially, smoke-free laws. Despite, or perhaps ultimately because of, the best efforts of many large tobacco companies to refute and suppress the evidence that their products killed and sickened their users, growing public hostility to tobacco companies energized support for tobacco control, prompting governments to adopt further measures to encourage smokers to quit and dissuade others from starting. These measures sought to make the use of combustible tobacco less acceptable, accessible, affordable, and attractive. Restrictions on depictions of tobacco use in film and television and restrictions on who could purchase cigarettes (age limits), where sales could occur (bans on vending machines for cigarettes), and in what quantity (pack sizes) followed. In recent years, the use of graphic health warnings covering large portions of cigarette packs has become widespread (outside the U.S.) and, in an increasing number of countries, "plain pack" rules ban brand identifiers from tobacco packaging.

Of all tobacco control measures, however, taxation was and continues to be likely the most effective method of reducing smoking. Tobacco taxes are not new. Tobacco has been taxed in Great Britain since the seventeenth century, and in the U.S. the federal government began taxing tobacco during the Civil War (1861–1865). However, over time these taxes have increased significantly. The evidence for the efficacy of tobacco taxes is well established. A 10% increase in the price of cigarettes leads to a reduction in the quantity demanded of between three and five percent.[6] Advocates argue that taxes are especially effective at discouraging consumption by young people, who tend to be more price-sensitive because they have below-average income.[7] The same is true for at least some socio-economically disadvantaged groups, among whom smoking is often concentrated.[8] However, that fact also means that tobacco taxes are regressive, since they fall disproportionately on those least able to pay.

Where tobacco taxes were designed to internalize the external costs that smoking created for society, research suggests that modern tobacco taxes impose far higher costs on the consumer than the consumer's behavior imposes on the rest of society. Thus, taxes today are sometimes viewed as a paternalistic intervention designed to save smokers from their own poor choices.[9,10]

The timelines and details of tobacco control policies adopted by different governments vary significantly. For example, in 2002 there were only two nations that required graphic health warnings on tobacco packs, and as late as 2008 only twenty-four nations required health warnings to cover 50% of the total pack size. By 2022, that figure had grown to 122 countries and 134 countries required graphic warning labels on tobacco packaging.[11] Policy sharing between nations and international treaties between states, including the EU's Tobacco Products Directive and the WHO's Framework Convention on Tobacco Control (FCTC), have accelerated the adoption of ostensibly similar packages of tobacco control policies across different jurisdictions. Today, visitors to countries as far apart as Malaysia, Ghana, Norway, Argentina, New Zealand, and Canada will find broad similarities in the way cigarettes are regulated: Combustible cigarettes may not be sold to those under 18 and smoking in indoor public places is tightly restricted. Purchasers of cigarettes in each of these nations (and many others) are confronted with pictographic health warnings that cover at least half of the package. Tobacco advertising promotion and sponsorship on digital and print media are banned. And, of course, cigarettes are highly taxed relative to other goods to reduce demand and fund education and programs to encourage cessation.[12]

Adoption of robust tobacco control policies lowers the prevalence of smoking, both relative to other locations and to historical rates prior to the adoption of the current restrictions. The fact that the nations with the best track records in cessation have adopted the most comprehensive tobacco control regulations and that the adoption of those regulations coincided with increased cessation all speaks to the success of tobacco control. Tobacco control efforts have not only achieved a decline in tobacco prevalence but have also effectively transformed public knowledge, beliefs, and attitudes about tobacco. Stigma is not usually discussed as a positive factor (at least outside of a subset of strong proponents of tobacco control), but it is a powerful force. In the twentieth century, tobacco companies sought to market their products by associating smoking with sophistication, vitality, and independence. Today, however, throughout much of the world, smokers are heavily stigmatized. They are stereotyped as lacking self-control and having poor hygiene. Smoking is increasingly associated with poverty and lack of education. Among academics they are viewed as the poster children for consumer irrationality. Surveys from different countries in recent years report decreased approval for smoking coinciding with the introduction of tobacco control policies.[13]

However, while educating consumers about the risks of smoking and reducing the appeal, accessibility, and affordability of tobacco help some smokers quit, they do not help *all* smokers to quit. Smoking remains the most significant avoidable cause of morbidity and premature mortality globally. Around the world, there are approximately one billion smokers and approximately eight million people die each year from illnesses directly attributed to smoking.[14] Annually, in the U.S. alone, it is estimated that there are more than 480,000 deaths due to smoking,[15] more than are caused by HIV, overdoses, alcohol, road traffic accidents, and firearms combined, and more than the population of Miami, Florida.

No country in the world has eliminated smoking. Even in nations where smoking prevalence is dropping, metrics such as spending on tobacco, absolute consumption, and frequency suggest that smoking may not be declining as much. Moreover, as discussed in Chapter 2, smoking rates and related harms are often and increasingly concentrated among historically disadvantaged communities including those suffering from mental health disorders, housing insecurity, unemployment or underemployment, and LGBTQ+ groups. In Australia, Canada, New Zealand, and the U.S., rates of smoking are significantly higher among indigenous communities than the general population. Such disparities present a particular moral imperative for tobacco control to transcend one-size-fits-all policy approaches and tailor interventions to the communities most in need.

Moreover, while the global prevalence of smoking is in decline, in many less-developed countries the number of smokers continues to increase. This growth is driven by increasing disposable income, general population growth, and the intensive marketing activity of the tobacco industry. With the prominent exception of South Africa, the countries of Sub-Saharan Africa, for example, have enjoyed significantly lower rates of smoking relative to the nations of Europe and the Americas, but the policy framework for tobacco control in those countries is often underdeveloped. Cameroon, Cape Verde, Guinea, and Malawi have no minimum age for purchasing tobacco. These and some other Sub-Saharan African nations, including Côte d'Ivoire, Ghana, and Guinea-Bissau, also have some of the worst records of taxing tobacco.[16] The fight to end the global "tobacco epidemic" is far from over.

The harms associated with tobacco smoking are reasonably well understood. But it bears repeating that smoking can damage every organ in the human body. The lungs, heart, and vascular system are particularly badly affected. Smokers' risk of lung cancer is 25 times those of non-smokers, though smokers are at elevated risk of cancers throughout the body. Smoking causes and exacerbates other lung diseases including asthma, emphysema, bronchitis, and Chronic Obstructive Pulmonary Disease (COPD)—of which smokers are more than 12 times as likely to die compared to non-smokers. Rates of heart disease among smokers are between two- and four-times background rates. Smoking damages the blood vessels, making them thicker and narrower, increasing the risks of blood clots and stroke. Smoking is also a primary risk factor for diabetes, which is 40% more common among active smokers than non-smokers.[17]

In the U.S., for every smoking-related death, at least 30 people are living with smoking-related illnesses.[18] Smokers surviving heart attacks may have to live with artificial heart pumps for the remainder of their lives. Those suffering damage to the kidneys may need constant dialyses to avoid renal failure. Smoking-attributed strokes have caused paralysis, rendering the afflicted with a lifelong disability. Survivors of smoking-attributed cancers have had voice boxes and parts of their digestive tract removed rendering them unable to speak, incontinent, and having to be fed through a tube. Vascular damage resulting from smoking often necessitates amputations. Smoking also causes macular degeneration and cataracts leading, in some cases, to blindness. In addition, smoking decreases immunological response making smokers more susceptible to infections, diseases and causes chronic inflammation and rheumatoid arthritis. Smoking has also been found to reduce fertility in both men and women.

While the worst effects of tobacco smoke are borne by long-term and heavy users, second-hand and side-stream smoke[19] presents real dangers to those who spend time in the vicinity of smokers. In the U.S., more than 41,000 deaths each year are attributed to secondhand smoke exposure. Globally, the figure is more than twenty times higher.[20] Babies born to smoking mothers are disproportionately born prematurely, and many of those begin life in incubators and suffer lifelong medical complications. Smoking also increases the risk of miscarriage, stillbirth, and Sudden Infant Death Syndrome (SIDS).

There are also economic costs to consider. A recent estimate puts the global costs of smoking at around US$1.85 trillion, which is about 1.8% of the global GDP.[21] The CDC estimates that, in the U.S. alone, smoking-related illnesses cost over $240 billion in direct medical care and $372 billion in lost productivity in 2018.[22] At the individual level, money spent on tobacco is, of course, money not spent on other goods and services for the consumer and the household's dependents. That cost is increased greatly by taxation. Consider, for example, the financial reality of smoking in Australia, where a pack of 20 cigarettes costs more than AUD35 (about USD24!). Here, a full-time worker earning minimum wage would earn AUD812.60 per 38-hour work week (as of July 2022). A pack-a-day smoker would spend an eye-watering AUD245.00 or 30% of pre-tax weekly earnings on cigarettes. In New York, a full-time minimum-wage worker earns USD600 per week before taxes. Here, the average pack of 20 cigarettes costs USD12.85 at the time of writing, thanks to the highest cigarette taxes in the U.S. A pack-a-day habit would cost a minimum-wage worker 15% of his pre-tax income. In addition, smokers may pay higher costs for life and health insurance policies. For some, these outlays may induce cessation, or at least a reduction in smoking, but for those who are unable to quit or reduce smoking, the effect on their ability to pay for necessities is severe.

For those who continue to smoke, there are also social costs to consider. Just as taxes incentivize quitting but add to the economic harm smoking caused to those who continue the practice, the policy-induced stigma of smoking may create a powerful incentive for some smokers to quit but imposes a social cost on those who continue to smoke. That cost may be particularly pronounced among some of the most vulnerable segments of the population.[23] This stigma can backfire. Social disapproval may perversely incentivize experimentation by some groups of consumers. In segments of society suffering from low education and income, high rates of disabling mental illness, and general despair sustained by historical marginalization and exploitation, smoking may not only be a coping mechanism but a gesture of defiance signifying group membership and representing a powerful expression of self-identity. Thus, the stigmatization of smokers may incentivize uptake by some youth and impede cessation among some current smokers.

The persisting disparities in smoking-related health outcomes, and indeed the persistence of smoking in the general population suggests the need for another strategy to supplement, without replacing, the tried and tested formula of traditional tobacco control. As the adage suggests, the definition of insanity is repeatedly doing the same thing and expecting different results. In the past, increasing the public's awareness of smoking harms and increasing the price of tobacco or otherwise reducing its appeal or accessibility paid dividends in terms of cessation. But many people today continue to smoke, despite understanding the damage that cigarettes cause despite high tobacco taxes and other restrictions on sales and consumption, and despite access to behavioral support, pharmacotherapies, and nicotine replacement therapies (NRTs). To reiterate, these policies and programs have borne fruit and should continue. Nor should we oppose the implementation of those policies in contexts where they have not yet been implemented. However, not all of today's smokers should be expected to quit by simply pushing the same practices that have, for them, proven inadequate thus far.

2 THE NEED FOR ALTERNATIVE NICOTINE

Michael Russell, a British psychiatrist and researcher who is widely regarded as a father of Tobacco Harm Reduction is credited with the observation that "People smoke for nicotine but they die from the tar . . . it's not the nicotine that kills half of all long-term smokers, it's the delivery mechanism." Russell pioneered the methodology for measuring toxicant exposure from cigarette smoking and environmental tobacco smoke, which led to the discovery that so-called "low-tar" cigarettes were not less harmful than traditional products. He was also instrumental in demonstrating the efficacy for cessation of nicotine chewing gum (developed in Sweden by Ove Ferno) and the subsequent development of nicotine nasal spray.[24] While nicotine is addictive, it is tar, the particulate matter created in the process of tobacco combustion, that is responsible for the horrendous morbidity and mortality associated with smoking. Nicotine is not entirely benign; it is infamously addictive. It may also adversely affect brain development in young people, leading to reduced cognitive ability and behavioral abnormalities.[25] Nicotine also causes short-term increases in heart rate and blood pressure, though it is unclear to what extent these acute effects lead to negative cardiovascular health outcomes in the long term. And, crucially, nicotine

8   S. C. HAMPSHER-MONK ET AL.

itself does not cause cancer or lung disease directly. Certainly, nicotine in combustible tobacco products has kept people using products that do cause cancers, pulmonary and cardiovascular disease, but those are the result of combustion, not nicotine per se. Given the right delivery mechanism, even long-term use of nicotine products can result in few side effects, and even fewer serious ones. Nicotine replacement therapy (NRTs) have been widely available since the 1990s and initial offerings— transdermal patches—were quickly followed by gums and other products. NRTs have helped millions of people stop smoking, and stay quit. Many former smokers continue to use nicotine replacement, instead of tapering down completely, to help minimize nicotine cravings that might otherwise put them at risk of relapse.

The value of non-combustible nicotine products is rooted in a simple truth: Quitting is hard. Mark Twain is often claimed to have said, "Giving up smoking is the easiest thing in the world—I should know, I've done it thousands of times." The quotation is probably misattributed,[26] but it conveys the truth that most quit attempts end in failure. The fact that so many smokers report wanting to quit is encouraging. But a *desire* to quit, even accompanied by motivation to *try*, is seldom sufficient. Data from the U.S. shows that roughly three in four smokers express a desire to quit, and more than one in two smokers attempts to quit each year. However, fewer than 10% of those attempts are successful. Other countries report even lower figures.[27,28] And if half of smokers attempt to quit each year, that means that half do not even try. Motivation is clearly an important factor contributing to smoking cessation. Twain, again (this time for real): "When they used to tell me I would shorten my life ten years by smoking...they little knew how trivial and valueless I would regard a decade that had no smoking in it!"[29] Despite having ample motivation, successful smoking cessation is hindered by the widespread availability of tobacco products, the influence of smoking among family members, friends, and colleagues, the lack of effective cessation support, and the reluctance of smokers to seek available help.

To assist smokers interested in quitting, many nations offer behavioral support, including group-based behavioral support, individual therapies (both in person and remote), and telephone-, text-, and web-based support. Like tobacco control policies, the availability, affordability, and efficacy of these offerings vary by context. Differences in funding for and the availability of services as well as differences in participation criteria all inform efficacy and differences in those criteria lead to wide variations

1 INTRODUCTION 9

in successes across contexts. But even when these therapies are available, many smokers are unwilling to frame their smoking as a disease in need of medical treatment. And many others report a fear of failure as an important obstacle to preventing or delaying engagement with supports that could otherwise facilitate cessation. Moreover, behavioral therapy does little to address what is for many the primary obstacle for smoking cessation: nicotine dependence. For those with pharmacological nicotine dependence, abstinence is necessarily accompanied by withdrawal symptoms. Mood swings, insomnia, headaches, anxiety, and weight gain all contribute to what Nobelist Tom Schelling described as "the intolerable feeling of being deprived of a cigarette." Such symptoms typically taper off after a few weeks, but some people may experience symptoms for months or longer.[30] To help such smokers achieve cessation, many countries offer pharmacotherapies, mainly varenicline and bupropion, which have been clinically demonstrated to help smokers manage nicotine withdrawal. Alternatively, nicotine replacement therapies including patches, lozenges, gum, inhalators, and sprays may be used to eliminate the need for smokers to eschew nicotine as a precondition for going smoke-free. Over-the-counter NRTs treat withdrawal symptoms without the commitment required by behavioral therapy options, nor to frame their nicotine dependence as a medical problem in need of a physician-prescribed treatment. Still, the overwhelming majority of quit attempts involve no support at all. While those that are supported by NRTs or behavioral therapy tend to be more successful than those that are unassisted—a combination of both is better still[31]—even under these circumstances, the success rates are still low. Under optimal conditions, NRTs may increase the odds of successful quitting by between 50 and 70%[32] compared to an unassisted approach, but given that the success rate of unassisted attempts is so low to begin with, such efforts still fail far more smokers than they help. Whatever resources smokers engage to support a quitting attempt, relapse is the most common outcome.

Why, if NRTs deliver nicotine, is their efficacy so low? The reasons are both physiological and psychological. While NRTs do deliver nicotine, they do so in smaller quantities and at a slower rate than cigarettes. As such, NRTs do not provide the characteristic "hit" associated with smoking. Secondly, NRTs do not replicate the tactile, psychological, and social characteristics of smoking. These are rewards in themselves, reinforcing smoking behaviors. The absence of these features makes traditional NRTs an imperfect analogue for combustible cigarettes.

Persistent smoking among individuals who are aware of the risks and desire to quit, but are unable yet to do so, highlights the shortcomings of conventional policies, programs, and products in effectively addressing their needs. Neither traditional approaches to tobacco control nor the provision of conventional cessation therapies seem sufficient to eliminate smoking. Even in the countries that might be considered emblems of success in tobacco control, having achieved significant reductions in rates of adult smoking (U.K., Canada, New Zealand, and Australia typically score well on metrics measuring successful implementation of tobacco control policies) smoking is projected to remain stubbornly above 10% through at least 2025.[33] What should be done for the remainder? Focusing on preventing the uptake of smoking among young people is certainly valuable; studies show that those that start smoking in adolescence smoke for longer and find it more difficult to quit,[34] and few smokers initiate at all after their mid-20s. But ignoring older smokers seems not so much a strategy as a capitulation. Is that assessment fair? After all, the combination of policies, programs, and products that helped others quit is still available to those who continue to smoke. In response, it seems fitting to repeat that, as a group, many of these smokers have been exposed to that combination and if it were going to be effective for this group, it would have been.

What more can be done to reduce smoking more effectively? Conventional wisdom might suggest more of the same: turn the screws. Keep ramping up taxation on combustible tobacco as Australia, New York, and many other jurisdictions are doing. Alternatively, incrementally increase the minimum age at which people are allowed to purchase tobacco. New Zealand and the UK have considered rolling age-restrictions which would mean that those born after the mid 2000s would never reach the legal age for tobacco purchases. Regulators could mandate that no combustibles are allowed to contain levels of nicotine that would sustain addiction—a proposal that has received support from the Food and Drug Administration, which regulates tobacco products in the U.S. Such proposals are effectively prohibitions on cigarettes, and as such they face a common liability in the form of illicit trade.

The twentieth century has provided at least three opportunities to learn that prohibitions on temptation goods do not work.[35] While intuitively appealing, banning popular risky products like cocaine, cannabis and even alcohol does not eliminate use but creates an illicit, unregulated market without product safety oversight. Prohibitions that lead to illicit markets sacrifice an opportunity to restrict sales to adults and forgo the public revenue generated by taxation that could otherwise support education and cessation services. Enforcing prohibitions necessitates increased public expenditure to detect, prosecute, and sanction violations. Illicit trade in tobacco products (ITTP) has been a boon for organized criminal groups also engaged in human trafficking, arms dealing, and selling illicit drugs, and has even been used to fund terrorist groups. Additional enforcement tends to make these problems worse: creating additional incentives for the use of violence by those eager to evade law enforcement and protect illicit revenue streams. Enforcing prohibitions, law enforcement can reasonably be expected to target consumers in an attempt to get to suppliers, eroding community-police relations and criminalizing consumers leading to arrests, prosecution, and mass incarceration which damages the social fabric of communities with intergenerational consequences that tend, predictably, to be disproportionately borne by historically disadvantaged communities. These unintended consequences are not exclusive to prohibitions. Higher prices driven by tobacco taxes increase potential rewards for those who can evade the tax. The greater the group of people for whom access to the regulated market is barred, the greater the potential demand for unregulated products. Removing desirable features of products also creates opportunities for purveyors of illicit analogues to distinguish their products while driving demand to the illicit markets.

If smoking cessation cannot be coerced, nor the market for combustible tobacco be eliminated by force, what options remain? One answer is to replace cigarettes with something better. If a product could approximate the user experience of smoking, delivering acceptable quantities of nicotine in a format that replicates the pharmacological profile of smoking without exposing the user to the byproducts of combustion, and satisfy the psychosocial aspects that reinforce smoking behavior, some smokers—even those who have demonstrated an inability or an unwillingness to quit smoking—might be persuaded to switch. Those substitutions could represent a significant reduction in the harms to which consumers and those in their vicinity are exposed.

3 WHAT ARE E-CIGARETTES?

This book takes a close look at the promise of e-cigarettes to re-invigorate tobacco control and efforts to facilitate cessation from smoking. So what are e-cigarettes? Most important is what they are not: E-cigarettes do not burn tobacco. Instead, they aerosolize a liquid containing nicotine, a humectant (a miscible agent such as propylene glycol or vegetable glycerin), and (optionally) flavorings. The e-liquid is absorbed by a wick (typically silica or cotton) and heated to below the point of combustion and aerosolized in an atomizer.[36] Aerosolization occurs when the liquid solution (e-liquid) comes into contact with a metal coil that is heated by passing an electric current through it. This is similar to the manner in which water is vaporized upon contact with a hot pan, hence the term "vaping" for using e-cigarettes in common usage (although aerosol is not merely water vapor). The aerosol is then inhaled by the user. Chapter 3 explores the evolution of the product category. The first products, called cig-a-likes, were closed-tank systems resembling combustible cigarettes in dimensions and appearance. Second-generation systems were rechargeable and typically contained a larger refillable tank. Over time, these have given way to "mods" which more closely resemble flashlights than cigarettes. These devices allow the user to modify (hence the name) the power of the device, change components and adjust the wick size to create more or less aerosol as desired. Pod devices such as Juul, Vuse, and other devices deploying refillable pod-based technology represent a fourth generation of e-cigarettes. These rechargeable devices resemble a USB flash drive and utilize disposable pods of e-liquids containing nicotine salt[37] (unlike earlier generation products, which used free-base nicotine). These devices typically have lower power than mod devices, and produce less aerosol, but the use of nicotine salts means that the consumer usually inhales more nicotine per puff than they would with a commensurate inhaled volume of aerosol from a free-base e-liquid.

4 FRIEND OR FOE?

E-cigarettes have surged in popularity in recent years. In the U.K., for example, the prevalence of e-cigarette use increased from less than 2% in 2012 to more than 7% in 2021.[38] In 2021 the global e-cigarette market was valued at over \$20 billion.[39] However, unlike NRTs, which have received widespread endorsement from the medical and public health community, e-cigarettes are highly controversial. To date, nowhere in the world is there a commercially available e-cigarette that is sold as a medical device or pharmaceutical approved by a regulator. So, for now at least, e-cigarettes represent a distinct category from NRTs. There is a general consensus that e-cigarettes are safer than combustible cigarettes, however, there is fierce disagreement about how much safer they are. Given how dangerous combustible tobacco is, merely being safer is a low bar for a new product to hurdle. While some public health agencies consider e-cigarettes to be safer by a margin that is sufficient to warrant their endorsement as cessation aids, others disagree. Some advocates have claimed that e-cigarettes are "safe" and, falsely, that e-cigarette aerosol contains only water and nicotine. Some skeptics have claimed, again almost surely falsely, that e-cigarettes are as dangerous or more so than cigarettes.

A balanced analysis of the evidence, presented in Volume II, Chapter 1, suggests that e-cigarettes are not risk-free but that they are significantly safer than combustibles. Emissions tests show that e-cigarette aerosol may contain chemicals capable of harming humans, but also that, by category and quantity, these chemicals are significantly less in e-cigarette aerosol than in cigarettes' smoke. Clinical studies demonstrate that former smokers who have switched to e-cigarettes display fewer biomarkers for toxicant exposure as well as improved lung and cardiovascular function, suggesting that e-cigarettes are significantly safer than smoking. The U.K.'s Royal College of Physicians reported in 2016[40] that e-cigarettes were unlikely to represent more than 5% of the risks posed by combustibles. This oft-cited figure was intended not as a precise point comparator—as the RCP stated the ultimate risks are unknown (indeed they may ultimately be much lower than that), but based on the available toxicological and clinical evidence the Royal Colege of Physicians and Public Health England adopted the figure as a communication device to inform decision-makers both at the regulatory and consumer level. Updates have affirmed this assessment, drawing on chemical analyses of e-liquids, laboratory-based emissions tests, in vitro toxicological studies, and short-term clinical trials as these have emerged. Similar opinions have been offered by the National Academy of Sciences.

As the evidence explored in Volume II, Chapter 2 suggests, e-cigarettes seem to be more effective than conventional NRTs at supporting smoking cessation. This conclusion is supported strongly by clinical trials, and to a lesser extent by observational cohort and longitudinal studies. The evidence from the latter is not uniformly in favor of a positive effect of e-cigarette use on cessation, which will require careful discussion in Volume II, Chapter 2 of correlation versus causality and the many confounding factors that bedevil observational studies. There are also data to suggest that smokers who do not quit smoking outright but use both combustibles and e-cigarettes for a period (i.e., "dual users") smoke less than they otherwise would. Given severity of smoking-related harms, any reduction—even with a transient period of dual use—might reasonably be considered a good thing if it ultimately leads to complete smoking cessation. The economic literature confirms, with few exceptions, that these products are economic substitutes for combustible tobacco: Increasing the price of combustible cigarettes relative to e-cigarettes increases demand for the latter, and vice versa. Furthermore, as discussed throughout this book (Volume III, Chapters 1 and 2 in particular), regulatory decisions may increase or decrease such substitutions variously, by establishing or protecting, or restricting and eliminating advantages (perceived or otherwise) that e-cigarettes have over combustibles. Price, characteristics such as flavor and nicotine levels, and marketing and sales restrictions may all be designed to either encourage or discourage smokers' substitutions toward these safer alternatives.

Yet e-cigarette regulation is not that simple. In contrast to the well-established evidence base linking combustible tobacco to numerous health risks, we do not yet have robust long-term data detailing the effects of vaping on the human body. Because e-cigarettes simply have not been around long enough, and because we lack long-term human-subject trials, we cannot ascertain the *ultimate* risks of e-cigarette use with anything close to statistical certainty. While e-cigarette emissions contain less of the toxic and carcinogenic chemicals present in tobacco smoke, several chemicals of concern may be present, some of which are not found in tobacco smoke. At the individual level, the consequences of e-cigarette use are dependent on a number of variables including (at least) the frequency of use, types of products used, and the technique deployed by the consumer. Variations in these modalities further impede the precision with which the safety of e-cigarettes as a category can be determined. The picture is further complicated by the fact that, at both the individual and population levels, the value or risk of e-cigarette use depends largely on the circumstances of the users. Most e-cigarette users are former and current smokers, which makes it difficult to differentiate the causal relationship between e-cigarette use and a given comorbidity from the residual effects of historical smoking. Among current smokers, replacing some combustible tobacco use with vaping likely represents a reduction in harm, and replacing all smoking with vaping likely represents a greater benefit. But it is also relevant to assess whether the uptake of vaping prolongs overall nicotine use or lessens the likelihood of forgoing nicotine entirely. Compared with smokers who, absenting e-cigarettes, might successfully quit next year, we do not know that a lifetime of e-cigarette use, or long-term dual use would not represent a net increase in lifetime risk, even if e-cigarettes were significantly less risky than smoking in the short term.

In terms of risk-characterization, it is important that some people who use e-cigarettes have no history of smoking. Among non-smokers, e-cigarettes offer none of the benefits of smoking cessation and all of the risk of nicotine addiction, leading to long-term exposure to other potential harms (whatever those turn out to be). If e-cigarettes lead people toward future smoking who would not otherwise have done so, then the risks posed by e-cigarettes would be especially severe. Studies have indeed reported that e-cigarette use is associated with higher odds of smoking initiation. However, as Volume II, Chapters 1 and 2 explain, it is far from clear that this association is causal, and there are good reasons to suggest that much of it is not. Like smoking, vaping is a risky activity. Risk-prone individuals who are more likely to engage in one risky behavior tend to be more likely than average to engage in another. In other words, teens who vape are more likely than their peers to have become smokers in the absence of e-cigarettes. This "common liability" undercuts the conclusion that e-cigarettes drive youth smoking by leading to sample-selection biases in observational studies. Even if smoking follows vaping among some individuals, it does not mean that vaping *causes* smoking.

If e-cigarette use *were* causing smoking, we would expect to see national smoking rates increase as the use of e-cigarettes became more popular. In fact, we see the opposite.[41] In the U.S., Canada, and the U.K.—to take just three examples, while e-cigarettes have gained in popularity the rates of smoking have approached their lowest recorded levels, since peaking in the mid-twentieth century. Recent data suggests that, in some contexts including the U.S., the use of e-cigarettes among youth has also declined dramatically since 2019.[42] That does not negate concerns regarding the possibility that e-cigarettes could entice another generation toward nicotine dependence, and there remains considerable uncertainty regarding the ultimate consequences of e-cigarette use. So, regulators must find a way to balance the known opportunity for smoking cessation with the possible risks. The tension in the discourse is between skeptics arguing that interventions should be dictated by the possibility of risk (precaution) and harm reduction advocates defending these products on the basis of epistemic probabilism[43]—the notion that judgment should be informed by what is most probably true given the present state of knowledge. Skeptics call for the traditional tools of tobacco control (taxes, advertising, and marketing restrictions, age limits, etc.) to be applied to e-cigarettes just as they are to combustible tobacco products. Advocates of Tobacco Harm Reduction, call for somewhat less stringent restrictions, citing the evidence that restrictions themselves are not risk-free, and that if e-cigarettes are less risky than combustibles, then applying the same restrictions would violate the principle of proportionality and discourage substitutions which would otherwise reduce smoking-related harms.

5 A Polarized Discourse

E-cigarettes are, as explored in Volume II, Chapter 1, a deeply polarizing issue in public health. On one hand, advocates of e-cigarette-led smoking cessation can face systematic "de-platforming," and are often maligned as tools of the tobacco industry. Harm reduction advocates often find themselves unable to publish in certain peer-reviewed journals; are routinely denied public research funding and are barred from public conferences. On the other hand, those concerned with plausible, if unproven risks, have been chastised for inadvertently playing into the hands of the tobacco industry establishment, and perpetuating a stigmatizing regulatory infrastructure that reinforces structurally predetermined health inequalities. Caught in the middle, regulators have faced litigation from both sides for at once failing to act on their legislative mandate and overstepping their remit.

In one sense, the vitriol is perplexing: Both advocates and skeptics share a common goal to minimize the harms of smoking. Moreover, e-cigarettes' safety, riskiness, and efficacy for cessation are empirical questions which could, one day at least, be answered via scientific investigation. While there was once a lack of data in that regard, there is an increasingly robust evidence base on which to draw conclusions about how e-cigarettes help or hinder the goals of smoking cessation, and how regulation could help increase the benefits and mitigate the risks. However, a new problem has emerged. There are now so many studies that it sometimes seems as if researchers can find a peer-reviewed source to support virtually any claim regarding e-cigarettes. Disputes about the quality of the data, how it should be interpreted, who should get to produce and report data, and how regulation should respond to uncertainty all drive polarization of the debate about e-cigarettes. There are philosophical questions to consider too: Should addiction count as a harm in itself, or must it serve as a conduit for additional social, medical, or economic harms to qualify? How should near-term consequences be weighed against long-term ones? How should the interests of one group (adult smokers) be weighed against the interests of another (adolescent non-smokers)?

The problem with the discourse on e-cigarettes is not polarization per se. After all, free inquiry is vital for scientific investigation and free speech and a healthy debate are central characteristics of liberal democracies. The problem is that polarization blinds decision-makers, including private consumers, health professionals, and government officials, to the more nuanced middle-ground. In truth, e-cigarettes are neither wholly good nor wholly bad. There are both risks and benefits. Regulation is the best tool we have to ensure that the risks are minimized and the benefits are maximized. Consumer decisions respond to regulation and the pronouncements of their governments but, like the products they are concerned with, regulators' choices and pronouncements are themselves not risk-free. Absent or inadequate regulation can allow runaway experimental use of e-cigarettes by non-smokers and fail to provide safeguards that make the products safer for consumers. Equally, overly stringent restrictions not only forgo the benefit of assisting smoking cessation, but inadvertently increase demand for combustible tobacco and nudge consumers toward unregulated e-vapor products. Such products are almost certainly riskier than regulated ones, and unregulated markets forgo an opportunity to age-gate sales. Meanwhile, in response to restrictions on e-cigarettes, reductions in smoking cessation harm not only adult smokers but those around them subject to second-hand smoke, as well as future generations who might otherwise have never had smoking modeled to them.

If the possibility of e-cigarette risks justifies a policy response of some kind, we should also acknowledge that there are risks inherent in some of those responses; both the opportunity costs and the unintended consequences of interventions restricting access, and that these risks should also factor into the decision-making process. A narrow fixation on the

18   S. C. HAMPSHER-MONK ET AL.

possible harms that e-cigarette use may result in (youth nicotine addiction for example) ignores the opportunity (reduction in smoking harms). Similarly, focusing only on the opportunity may allow avoidable harms to manifest. Those navigating that dichotomy must not lose sight of the distinction between possible risks and demonstrable risks. To do so is to become detached from the evidence base. Once that happens, decisions become mere expressions of subjective value judgments.

If the current discourse on e-cigarettes generates more heat than light, that is, in no small part, a legacy of the despicable conduct of Transnational Tobacco Companies (TTCs). It took a congressional inquiry to uncover that the industry suppressed the truth about how harmful cigarettes were and disseminated false information in an effort to keep profiting from smoking. As a direct consequence of that deception, the public is justifiably skeptical about any products associated with the tobacco industry. And, as discussed in Chapter 3, tobacco companies are increasingly invested in e-cigarettes, as well as other alternative nicotine products. But if that legacy results in a skepticism toward a genuinely safer alternative to cigarettes, and if TTCs are denied an opportunity to change for the better then, as a result of the TTC's past health fraud, the health of the public will be harmed twice.

Fortunately, regulators tasked with weighing the pros and cons of e-cigarettes have at their disposal an increasing body of information regarding the risks and benefits and tradeoffs. One important area in which the evidence base has begun to develop relates to the consequences (intended and otherwise) of policy decisions. The world's governments have taken radically different approaches to regulating e-cigarettes; ranging from outright prohibitions and product bans to the active endorsement of e-cigarettes for the purposes of smoking cessation. Just as the passage of time provides an opportunity to better understand the safety of e-cigarettes and their efficacy as cessation aids, it also provides opportunity to interrogate the consequences of regulatory decisions, on which the suitability of e-cigarettes as a cessation aid is largely dependent. Even while the scientific evidence continues to develop, the evidence is more than sufficient to model the effects of e-cigarette policies at the population level. As public health researchers, medical experts, epidemiologists, and population scientists investigate with ever-increasing precision the conditions under which e-cigarettes serve the goal of smoking cessation; and electrical engineers, chemists, and toxicologists work to increase the safety and efficacy of e-cigarettes via product innovation; social scientists, especially policy analysts and health economists, can help demonstrate which policies, programs and interventions are most effective to encourage substitutions by current smokers and discourage uptake by non-smokers. This book explains the current state of evidence on these topics, why the science is contested, and why the risks of e-cigarettes are often overstated. Certainly, there are risks, but as Abrams and colleagues have summarized,[44] many of the risks can be mitigated through appropriate regulation. That regulation must be informed by an accurate assessment of the evidence, clearly communicated to all stakeholders.

6 THE CHALLENGE OF REGULATING E-CIGARETTES

Still, significant challenges remain. E-cigarettes are a heterogenous mix of products. Differences in design, power output, temperature, components, materials, ingredients, nicotine concentration, and other product characteristics can all influence health outcomes. These characteristics are changing constantly as commercial innovations respond to consumer demand, competition among producers, and regulatory decisions. Similarly, consumption patterns are constantly evolving. Consumers are influenced by public knowledge and attitudes, and also respond to regulatory decisions and the emerging evidence base communicated (most often imperfectly) by the media. These feedback loops mean that the parameters of optimal policy toward e-cigarettes are not fixed, and decisions which benefitted the public in one context and at one time may not do so in another time and place, forcing regulators to periodically reevaluate their cost–benefit analyses.

Misinformation, and indeed willfully distributed disinformation about e-cigarettes, have brought about widespread misunderstandings about the safety and efficacy of e-cigarettes for the purposes of smoking cessation. These not only afflict the general public, perpetuating smoking among those who might otherwise be convinced to switch to a safer alternative, but some of the public health agencies and medical professionals who are in a position to inform consumers' choices. As discussed in Chapter 3 of Volume II, elected officials (and by extension the agencies accountable to them) care as much about what the public *believes* as what the public (correctly) *knows*, and so there is a danger that sentiment and not science steers the public discourse. In this regard, the public discourse on e-cigarettes has much in common with other areas of public policy and politics where objectivity may be abandoned in favor of rhetoric. Recall for example, discussion of "alternative facts" during the Trump Administration in the U.S. and the growing general distrust of experts there and in the U.K.[45] If facts are no longer universal, but merely something to be accumulated in defense of a subjective preference, and if technical expertise is something that can be refuted on the basis of sentiment, then public decision-making might as well be reduced to a screaming match.

Nonetheless, e-cigarettes are an emotive topic. Fear, especially in the face of uncertainty, is powerful, and the known unknowns raise the stakes, both for advocates (on either side of the debate) and regulators charged with interpreting the apparently conflicting evidence and adjudicating between competing interests: What if we encourage the uptake of e-cigarettes trying to reduce the harm of tobacco but find that e-cigarettes carry a specific and horrific risk of harm which takes decades to materialize? What if the use of e-cigarettes causes smokers who would have quit (eventually, anyway) in the absence of e-cigarettes, to instead continue using a product that is, while safer than smoking, more dangerous than counterfactual abstinence? What if regulators discourage smokers from the most effective method of smoking cessation for fear of risks that fail to materialize, consigning millions to the morbidity and mortality caused by smoking?

7   What are the Goals of this Book?

E-cigarette regulation is not a dichotomous choice between fully enforced prohibitions and the unrestrained free market. There are a multitude of intermediary alternatives, and that is where the most promising options lie. The consequences, whether intended and unintended, of current different regulatory approaches, are examined in Volume III, Chapter 1. Chapter 2 of Volume III sketches a vision for optimal e-cigarette regulation that would balance the pursuit of benefits with the avoidance of risks. On the one hand, lighter-touch regulation of e-cigarettes would encourage substitutions that support smoking cessation by those unable to quit via other means. On the other, risks that may arise include uptake by non-smokers (especially youth), protracted dual use instead of complete substitution away from cigarettes, and perhaps even long-term exclusive use by those who, having successfully quit smoking, could be encouraged to quit e-cigarettes too without risk of relapse to combustible cigarettes. To some extent, the benefits and risks trade off against each other, since many of the features of e-cigarettes and e-cigarette regulations which appeal to current smokers also appeal to non-smokers and youth. Making e-cigarettes cheaper, for example, increases demand across the population. Flavors may help keep adult users from returning to combustibles, but they also appeal to non-smokers. Higher nicotine content may help satisfy former smokers' dependence on nicotine, but that also increases the dependence potential for non-smokers experimenting with e-cigarettes.

These tradeoffs have led to the perception that regulators must pick a side by choosing to either help smokers quit or to protect the well-being of non-smokers. Thus, the discourse on e-cigarettes has become deeply polarized with two groups both claiming "evidence-based approaches" while calling for radically different regulatory policies.[46,47,48] These volumes explain the origins and consequences of that polarization and argues that ultimately the apparent dichotomy is a false one. Some of the tradeoffs can be mitigated, and where tradeoffs are inevitable, the available evidence is more than sufficient to inform the development of optimal regulations. This book presents and contextualizes the available evidence describing how it can, and should, be used to optimize e-cigarette regulation in the interests of the whole public. Fully considered, optimal regulation bears little resemblance to the regulations, and lack thereof, which have defined the e-cigarette market to date throughout much of the world. This book helps explain what the unintended consequences of sub-optimal e-cigarette regulations are, and how they can be avoided.

8 What this Book is Not

Voicing anything less than full-throated opposition to e-cigarettes is likely to attract hostility and criticism. While, as discussed in Volume II, Chapter 2, harm reduction is part of mainstream public health science in other areas, tobacco harm reduction has been framed as a cynical ploy by Big Tobacco to hook another generation on its products, profiting from addiction to the detriment of public health. There is no suggestion here that e-cigarettes are without risks. The authors do not endorse vaping for non-smokers. Youth, in particular, should be discouraged from experimenting with nicotine products. Smokers who can quit without using e-cigarettes should certainly be encouraged to do so, and e-cigarettes should not replace demonstrably effective programs for supporting cessation. Having quit combustible tobacco, those e-cigarette users who can reduce or quit e-cigarette use should also be encouraged to do so, so long as that does not result in increased smoking or relapse.

However, none of these goals supports the bans on e-cigarettes and other restrictions that are being increasingly adopted throughout the world. Framing e-cigarettes only as a public health hazard is a dangerous oversimplification; regulating e-cigarettes purely to minimize their use forgoes their demonstrated benefit. E-cigarettes are not absolutely safe, but whatever the risks turn out to be there is no indication that they would be anything other than significantly safer than their analog, combustible cigarettes. Plausible risks withstanding, their use for the purposes of smoking cessation by those who are unable to quit with other means should be encouraged, but that does not mean that concerns about the effects of e-cigarettes use (both direct and indirect) on non-smokers should not be taken seriously.

9   Why did We Write this Book Now?

As e-cigarettes grow in popularity, so do calls for more stringent regulations. Faced with immediate and pressing concerns such as youth vaping, policy analysts often focus on short-term wins, and are encouraged by any evidence that an intervention could help address the fears of vocal constituents alarmed by often inaccurately reported data. For regulators unsure how to respond, policy sharing often seems like a smart approach. But the preference for "evidence-based practices" often means that first movers' policy choices are replicated purely on the basis that they have been tried before. This is evident both at the national scale in federal jurisdictions such as the U.S. and Canada, and at the international scale in the EU. In recent years many governments of nations at all levels of development have looked to the example of the U.S. authorities and the advice of the WHO to inform their own policy decisions. Examples include citing concerns about the so-called e-cigarette and vaping product-associated lung injuries (EVALI) and the "epidemic" in youth vaping. Encouraged by the American regulators' indictments against e-cigarettes and bolstered by lavish funding from western philanthropists, governments of many developing countries (including Vietnam, Malaysia, and Thailand) have pursued restrictions that, in many cases, surpass the example of the U.S. regulator.

1 INTRODUCTION 23

But the concerns about e-cigarettes posed by EVALI turned out to be misplaced; it was an additive in illicit THC products, not regulated nicotine e-liquids, that caused those lung injuries. The "epidemic" in youth vaping has also been exaggerated, as discussed in Volume II, Chapter 1, by a failure to distinguish between infrequent use indicative of experimentation and more frequent use associated with dependency. European markets for example suggest that youth vaping rates can be kept much lower than the rates seen in America and Canada, without sacrificing the benefits of adult smoking cessation. Moreover, where teen vaping is most prevalent, teen smoking rates have never been lower. Even in the most pessimistic outlook, this is a serious silver lining. The latest population data from the U.S. suggest that youth vaping is in decline. Of course, the fact that youth vaping rates have declined may be cited in support of recently adopted e-cigarette restrictions. But, as Chapter 1 of Volume III explores, the unintended effects of those regulations are also becoming clear: Not only does reducing the accessibility, appeal, and affordability of e-cigarettes reduce smoking cessation but taxes, flavor and product bans and minimum age restrictions have been found to lead young e-cigarette users toward combustible tobacco, exposing them to greater harm than vaping.

In light of this evidence, it is far from clear that other nations should emulate the U.S. approach. There is an alternative. In the U.K. and New Zealand, national governments are embracing e-cigarettes to further reduce the prevalence of smoking, while enacting and enforcing age restrictions and other policies that limit youth access. Given the passage of enough time the epidemiological data, currently absent, may begin to speak for itself. Perhaps the rates of smoking and related harms in countries integrating commercial e-cigarettes into their tobacco control plans will fall so low that other countries will be forced to acknowledge the success of this approach and countries currently enacting prohibitions and product bans will be forced to contend with the unintended consequences of their approaches. Alternatively, perhaps, prohibitions and product bans will turn out to be more effective for e-cigarettes than they have been for every other temptation good. Perhaps those countries designing e-cigarette regulations to support smoking cessation will see such massive increases in nicotine addiction or other harms resulting from the use of e-cigarettes that the net effect will outweigh the public health victory of additional smoking cessation. That seems unlikely. In the 20 years of accumulated data there is no evidence that e-cigarette use leads to end-point

24   S. C. HAMPSHER-MONK ET AL.

harms at the population level that come close to outweighing the benefit they deliver in terms of supporting quit attempts. In either case, time will tell. But with more than 20,000 smoking-related deaths each day, time is not a luxury we can afford.

10   Who is this Book for?

This book is for the health economists, behavioral and social scientists, policy analysts, and regulatory scientists interested in the present and future possible implications of e-cigarettes on public health. Ultimately, the book is also intended to benefit policymakers, who have the challenging responsibility of designing regulations to maximize public welfare, despite having limited knowledge about the definitive risks and benefits associated with these products. We also hope that the former group of academics and scientists will find the book useful to communicate to the latter group of policymakers.

Optimal regulations balance support for smoking cessation with protections for non-smokers. Many of these tradeoffs can be mitigated, and where they cannot be mitigated, the analysis herein outlines an approach that balances risks and benefits in the public interest. Implementing optimal e-cigarette regulation will involve a broad range of participants to continue to develop the evidence base, construct, implement, evaluate and (where necessary) correct policies and regulations, and educate the public in general and nicotine consumers in particular. Volume III, Chapter 4 explores the role for public health agencies, the research community, industry, healthcare providers, and the media. Chapter 10 also asks, "What if we're wrong?" What if new evidence emerges detailing a novel and specific harm resulting from vaping? Or what if, in response to the proposed regulations, enough non-smokers initiate e-cigarette use that the calculation about public harm shifts? The scientific method requires that hypotheses be adapted in response to contradictory evidence. The same holds in social and regulatory sciences. So, in this scenario, we would need to adapt the policies accordingly. For this reason, it is advisable to retain the possibility for a dynamic response in policy design so that interventions may be updated incrementally in response to emerging evidence. By the same standard, however, on the basis of the available evidence, many contemporary e-cigarette regulations must also be replaced. We hope this book provides both a greater perspective and a higher resolution focus on the pathways by which this may be achieved.

This book is also for practitioners working diligently to run programs and interventions that encourage and support smoking cessation. These pages do not negate that work and are not intended to suggest that e-cigarettes and other non-combustion nicotine products can or should replace those interventions. We do however suggest that by making regulated alternatives available to participants in these programs, the success of these interventions may be increased.

We write, also, for the friends and families of those who smoke and use e-cigarettes. Children, parents, siblings, partners, friends, and colleagues can play a fundamental role in encouraging and supporting smokers' decisions to quit combustible tobacco, especially if they are equipped with the right information. This book is also for those who may be curious about vaping. We aim to provide an accurate assessment of the risks that e-cigarettes pose and a reminder that these products are not intended for youth or non-smokers. We also hope to provide context for these concerns; while any vaping among minors should be discouraged, e-cigarette use is significantly less harmful than smoking.

Finally, this book is for approximately 1 billion people around the world who continue to smoke, with the hope that, directly or indirectly, the discussion presented helps illuminate a path away from the associated morbidity and mortality, and for those using e-cigarettes to quit or reduce smoking, with the hope that the text helps ensure that the products which aid smoking cessation may continue to be available.

Notes

1. Doll, R., Hill, A.B. Smoking and Carcinoma of the Lung Preliminary Report. Br Med J. 1950;2(4682):739–748. https://doi.org/10.1136/bmj.2.4682.739.
2. Wynder, E.L., Graham, E.L. Tobacco Smoking as a Possible Etiologic Factor in Bronchiogenic Carcinoma: A Study of Six Hundred and Eighty-Four Proved Cases. J Am Med Assoc. 1950;143(4):329–336. https://doi.org/10.1001/jama.1950.02910390001001.
3. Hammond, E.C., Horn, D. Smoking and Death Rates: Report on Forty-Four Months of Follow-up of 187,783 Men. 2. Death Rates

by Cause. J Am Med Assoc. 1958 Mar 15;166(11):1294–1308. https://doi.org/10.1001/jama.1958.02990110030007.

4. Royal Collage of Physicians. Smoking and Health RCP, London, 1962. https://www.rcplondon.ac.uk/projects/outputs/smoking-and-health-1962.

5. United States: Department of Health, Education, and Welfare: Public Health Service: Surgeon General's Advisory Committee on Smoking and Health. "Smoking and Health: Report of the Advisory Committee to the Surgeon General of the Public Health Service," 1 January, 1964. https://www.govinfo.gov/app/details/GPO-SMOKINGANDHEALTH.

6. Health, National Center for Chronic Disease Prevention and Health Promotion (US) Office on Smoking and *Preventing Tobacco Use Among Youth and Young Adults.* Centers for Disease Control and Prevention (US), 2012. https://www.ncbi.nlm.nih.gov/books/NBK99237/.

7. Gallet, C.A., List, J.A. Cigarette Demand: A Meta-Analysis of Elasticities. Health Econ. 2003;12(10):821–835. https://doi.org/10.1002/hec.765..

8. Farrelly, M.C., Bray, J.W., Pechacek, T., Woollery, T. Response by Adults to Increases in Cigarette Prices by Sociodemographic Characteristics. South Econ J. 2001;68(1):156–165. https://doi.org/10.1002/j.2325-8012.2001.tb00404.x.

9. Gruber, J. Smoking's Internalities. Regulation 2002;25:52–57.

10. Viscusi, W.K. The New Cigarette Paternalism. Regulation 2002;25:58–64.

11. Canadian Cancer Society, Cigarette Package Health Warnings: International Status Report, Seventh Edition, October 2021.

12. Unless otherwise noted, we use the term "cessation" to refer specifically to abstinence from using cigarettes.

13. Rennen, E., Nagelhout, G.E., van den Putte, B., Janssen, E., Mons, U., Guignard, R., Beck, F., de Vries, H., Thrasher, J.F., & Willemsen, M.C. Associations between Tobacco Control Policy Awareness, Social Acceptability of Smoking and Smoking Cessation. Findings from the International Tobacco Control (ITC) Europe Surveys. Health Educ Res. 2014 Feb;29(1):72–82. https://doi.org/10.1093/her/cyt073.

14. World Health Organisation. (2022). Fact Sheets: Tobacco, World Health Organisation Newsroom, accessed 3 May 2023, available at: https://www.who.int/news-room/fact-sheets/detail/tobacco.
15. U.S. Department of Health and Human Services. The Health Consequences of Smoking—50 Years of Progress: A Report of the Surgeon General. Atlanta: U.S. Department of Health and Human Services, Centers for Disease Control and Prevention, National Center for Chronic Disease Prevention and Health Promotion, Office on Smoking and Health, 2014.
16. Chaloupka, F., Drope, J., Siu, E., Vulovic, V., Stoklosa, M., Mirza, M., Rodriguez-Iglesias, G., Lee, H. Tobacconomics Cigarette Tax Scorecard. Chicago, IL: Health Policy Center, Institute for Health Research and Policy, University of Illinois Chicago, 2020. https://www.tobacconomics.org.
17. U.S. Centers for Disease Control and Prevention. (October 29, 2021). Health Effects of Cigarette Smoking. CDC.gov. https://www.cdc.gov/tobacco/data_statistics/fact_sheets/health_effects/effects_cig_smoking/index.htm.
18. U.S. Centers for Disease Control and Prevention. (July 29, 2022). Diseases and Death. CDC.gov. https://www.cdc.gov/tobacco/data_statistics/fact_sheets/fast_facts/diseases-and-death.html.
19. While second-hand smoke refers to smoke expelled by a smoker, side-stream smoke refers to emissions from smoldering cigarettes. These are collectively known in the public health literature as "environmental smoke".
20. Yousuf, H., Hofstra, M., Tijssen, J., et al. Estimated Worldwide Mortality Attributed to Secondhand Tobacco Smoke Exposure, 1990–2016. JAMA Netw Open. 2020;3(3):e201177. https://doi.org/10.1001/jamanetworkopen.2020.1177.
21. Vulovic, V. Economic Costs of Tobacco Use. A Tobacconomics Policy Brief. Chicago, IL: Tobacconomics, Health Policy Center, Institute for Health Research and Policy, University of Illinois at Chicago, 2019. https://www.tobacconomics.org.
22. CDC Tobacco Free. Economic Trends in Tobacco. Centers for Disease Control and Prevention. Published September 9, 2022. Accessed February 20, 2023. https://www.cdc.gov/tobacco/data_statistics/fact_sheets/economics/econ_facts/index.htm.

23. Graham, H. Smoking, Stigma and Social Class. J Soc Policy. 2012;41(1):83–99. https://doi.org/10.1017/S0047279411000033X.
24. Jarvis, M. Michael Russell. The Guardian. https://www.theguardian.com/science/2009/aug/04/obituary-michael-russell. Published August 4, 2009. Accessed February 20, 2023.
25. Treur, J.L., Munafò, M.R., Logtenberg, E., Wiers, R.W., Verweij, K.J. Using Mendelian Randomization Analysis to Better Understand the Relationship Between Mental Health and Substance Use: A Systematic Review. Psychol Med. 2021;51(10): 1593–1624.
26. Twain was indeed a smoker, but he probably never said those words. The quip is more likely to belong to W. C. Fields who delivered a version of it in a 1938 radio broadcast, "The Temperance Lecture" on the topic of drinking.
27. Etter, J.F., Perneger, T.V., Ronchi, A. Distributions of Smokers by Stage: International Comparison and Association with Smoking Prevalence. Prev Med. 1997;26(4):580–585. https://doi.org/10.1006/pmed.1997.0179.
28. Li, L., Li, H., Zhang, Y., Zheng, C., Xu, H., Cheng, Z. Exploring the Degree of Nicotine Dependence and Willingness to Quit Smoking in Chinese Smoking Patients with Stroke: A Cross-Sectional Survey. Medicine (Baltimore). 2021;100(49):e27715. https://doi.org/10.1097/MD.0000000000027715.
29. The Letters Of Mark Twain, Volume 4, 1886–1900 Mark Twain (Samuel Clemens) August 21, 2006 [EBook #3196] Letter to Joseph Twichell, 19 Dec 1870.
30. Hughes, J.R. Tobacco Withdrawal in Self-Quitters. J Consult Clin Psychol. 1992;60(5):689–697. https://doi.org/10.1037//0022-006x.60.5.689.
31. Wadgave, U., Nagesh, L. Nicotine Replacement Therapy: An Overview. Int J Health Sci (Qassim). 2016;10(3):425–435. Accessed 20 February 2023. https://www.ncbi.nlm.nih.gov/pmc/articles/PMC5003586/.
32. Stead, L.F., Perera, R., Bullen, C., Mant, D., Lancaster, T. Nicotine Replacement Therapy for Smoking Cessation. Cochrane Database Syst Rev. 2008;(1):CD000146. https://doi.org/10.1002/14651858.CD000146.pub3.
33. Age-standardized Estimates of Current Tobacco Use, Tobacco Smoking and Cigarette Smoking (Tobacco Control:

Monitor). Accessed 20 February 2023. https://www.who.int/ data/gho/data/indicators/indicator-details/GHO/gho-tobacco-control-monitor-current-tobaccouse-tobaccosmoking-cigarrettesm oking-agestd-tobagestdcurr.

34. Park, S.H. Smoking and Adolescent Health. Korean J Pediatr. 2011 Oct;54(10):401–404. https://doi.org/10.3345/kjp.2011. 54.10.401.

35. The tragedy is that we seem to have to learn that lesson anew with each temptation good.

36. While the term "vaping" is used to describe e-cigarette use, derived from the "vapor" produced by the device, e-cigarettes technically do not produce vapor, but aerosol.

37. See Chapter 3 for a discussion of salt nicotine and free-base nicotine.

38. Action on Smoking and Health (ASH). Use of e-cigarettes (vapes) among adults in Great Britain. 2021. Accessed 20 February 2023. https://ash.org.uk/uploads/Use-of-e-cigarettes-vapes-among-adults-in-Great-Britain-2021.pdf.

39. Global E-Cigarette Market (2022 to 2027) - Industry Trends, Share, Size, Growth, Opportunity and Forecasts - ResearchAnd-Markets.com. Published April 1, 2022. Accessed 20 February 2023. https://www.businesswire.com/news/home/202204010 05272/en/Global-E-Cigarette-Market-2022-to-2027---Industry-Trends-Share-Size-Growth-Opportunity-and-Forecasts---Resear chAndMarkets.com.

40. Royal College of Physicians. Nicotine without smoke: Tobacco harm reduction. London, RCP; 2016. https://www.rcplondon. ac.uk/projects/outputs/nicotine-without-smoke-tobacco-harm-reduction.

41. Levy, D.T., Warner, K.E., Cummings, K.M., Hammond, D., Kuo, C., Fong, G.T., ... Borland, R. Examining the Relationship of Vaping to Smoking Initiation Among US Youth and Young Adults: A Reality Check. Tob Control. 2019;28(6):629–635.

42. Park-Lee, E. Notes from the Field: E-Cigarette Use Among Middle and High School Students—National Youth Tobacco Survey, United States. MMWR Morb Mortal Wkly Rep. 2021;70. https:// doi.org/10.15585/mmwr.mm7039a4.

43. Pettigrew, R. Epistemic Utility Arguments for Probabilism. In Zalta EN (Ed) *The Stanford Encyclopedia of Philosophy*. Metaphysics

Research Lab, Stanford University; 2019. Accessed 20 February 2023. https://plato.stanford.edu/archives/win2019/entries/epistemic-utility/.

44. Abrams, D.B., Glasser, A.M., Villanti, A.C., Pearson, J.L., Rose, S., Niaura, R.S. Managing Nicotine Without Smoke to Save Lives Now: Evidence for Harm Minimization. Prev Med. 2018;117:88–97. https://doi.org/10.1016/j.ypmed.2018.06.010.

45. In 2017, Lord Chancellor Michael Gove asserted that "the people of this country have had enough of experts."

46. Eisenkraft Klein, D., Hawkins, B., Schwartz, R. Understanding Experts' Conflicting Perspectives on Tobacco Harm Reduction and E-cigarettes: An Interpretive Policy Analysis. *SSM-Qual Res Health*. 2022;2:100197. https://doi.org/10.1016/j.ssmqr.2022.100197.

47. Smith, M.J., Baxter, A.J., Skivington, K., McCann, M., Hilton, S., Katikireddi, S.V. Examining the Sources of Evidence in E-cigarette Policy Recommendations: A Citation Network Analysis of International Public Health Recommendations. PLOS ONE. 2021;16(8):e0255604. https://doi.org/10.1371/journal.pone.0255604.

48. Hawkins, B., Ettelt, S. The Strategic Uses of Evidence in U.K. E-Cigarettes Policy Debates. Evid Policy: J Res, Debate Pract. 2019;15(4):579–596. https://doi.org/10.1332/174426418X15212872451438.

CHAPTER 2

Who Is (Still) Smoking?

Tobacco is...the single most preventable cause of illness and death in the world...killing more people than AIDS, malaria and tuberculosis combined.
—World Health Organization[1]

Although this book is about e-cigarettes, the utility of e-cigarettes as a public health intervention is inextricably linked with smoking. Behaviors surrounding the use of e-cigarettes hinge on a plethora of personal preferences, values, knowledge, beliefs, and attitudes and respond not only to contemporary regulations but also to the historical, economic, cultural, sociological, and political legacy of tobacco control. It is therefore necessary to preface the topic of e-cigarettes with the broader context of tobacco usage.

1 A BRIEF HISTORY OF TOBACCO AND TOBACCO CONTROL

1.1 The Birth of a Monster

Tobacco has been used for ceremonial and ritualistic purposes by indigenous peoples in North and Central America for hundreds and perhaps thousands of years. From the first contact with those populations, European sailors and explorers brought tobacco and the practice of smoking it back to Europe, where it was perceived to have medicinal properties. In 1560, Jacques Nicot, from whose cognomen we derive the word

© The Author(s), under exclusive license to Springer Nature Switzerland AG 2024
S. C. Hampsher-Monk et al., *Tobacco Regulation, Economics, and Public Health, Volume I*, https://doi.org/10.1007/978-3-031-41312-4_2

31

"nicotine," sent snuff to the Spanish royal family, believing that it could treat migraines. Eleven years later, Nicolás Monardés outlined 36 conditions, including cancer, which he believed could be treated by smoking tobacco.[2] And in 1595, Anthony Chute published a pamphlet titled *Tobaco*[3] arguing that pipe-smoking had health-giving properties.

Seen as an exotic curio, tobacco initially sold for its weight in silver in Elizabethan England.[4] Due to its increasing popularity, and an apparent inability to cultivate it in Europe, tobacco quickly became a valuable overseas cash crop, providing economic fuel for European imperialism. Slave labor enabled the cultivation of tobacco and the intercontinental trade.[5] Between 1525 and 1866, an estimated 12.5 million Africans were shipped across the Atlantic in bondage to live a life of servitude in the tobacco, cotton, and sugar plantations of European colonies.[6] Tobacco was so important to the economies of the British colonies in North America that it was often used as currency, sometimes qualifying as legal tender.[7] Annual exports from the Virginia colony of Jamestown to England increased from 200,000 pounds in 1624 to 3 million pounds in weight in 1638. By the 1680s, Jamestown alone was shipping more than 25 million pounds of tobacco to Europe.[8]

As Jacob Sullum has argued,[9] the stigmatization of tobacco and people who smoke tobacco[10] has long been a part of the history of tobacco. While such stigma has flourished under the modern tobacco control efforts beginning in the last third of the twentieth century, both the stigma associated with smoking and concerns about smoking-related health risks have far earlier origins. Early modern writings voicing concerns about smoking were often explicitly paternalistic and even culturally imperialistic in tone. For example, in 1526, Fernandez de Oviedo y Valdes complained of the "evil practices" of "the Indians," namely the inhaling of tobacco smoke.[11] Other opponents of tobacco framed their objections in similar terms. In *A Counterblaste to Tobacco* (1604), James I wrote, "Shall we…abase ourselves so farre, as to imitate these beastly Indians?… Why doe we not as well imitate them in walking naked as they doe?…yea why doe we not denie God and adore the Devill as they doe?".[12]

It was not only on cultural and spiritual grounds that tobacco was opposed. While scientific evidence of smoking-related harms would not be properly developed until the twentieth century, many earlier writers seem to have been well aware that tobacco was addictive and injurious to health. James I observed how many of his subjects were unable to quit smoking any more than "an old drunkard can abide to be sober," and famously opined that tobacco was "hateful to the nose, harmful to the brain, [and] dangerous to the lungs," providing some of the earliest evidence that smoking was thought to be dangerous as well as addictive.[13] Francis Bacon similarly observed that tobacco "conquers men with a secret pleasure" and, "those accustomed thereto can later hardly be restrained therefrom."[14] Cotton Mather in 1726 observed the "extreme hazard" of becoming a "slave to the Pipe...such slavery is below the dignity of a rational creature; and much more of a gracious Christian."[15]

The religious and moral objections to tobacco resulted in some of the earliest tobacco control regulations.[9] In New England in the 1630s, Massachusetts banned the sale of tobacco and smoking in public, and Connecticut also passed an early smoke-free law and restricted the sale of tobacco to adults in 1647. Tobacco was banned in Bavaria, Saxony, and Zurich in the 1650s and 1660s. Elsewhere, a more heavy-handed approach was evident: Smoking was a capital offense in the Ottoman Empire under Sultan Murad IV. In 1664 Russia's Tsar Michael Romanov ordered that smokers be flogged or have their noses slit. In China, those found selling tobacco were put to death by decapitation.[16] Despite the horrific penalties, use of tobacco continued.

Most rulers opted for a more pragmatic approach. In 1604, James I levied a tax of 6 shillings and 10 pence per pound of tobacco, and in 1619 made the tobacco trade a royal monopoly. Several Italian republics also established tobacco monopolies, a model that persisted until late into the twentieth century. In France, Louis XIII also imposed a tobacco tax of thirty sols per pound in 1629.

Contemporary sources indicate, however, that concerns for the harms of smoking remained. In 1699 a court physician of Louis XIV noted "All other pleasures bring satiety, which weakens their ill effects; tobacco alone becomes a fatal, insatiable necessity...a permanent epilepsy."[4] Addiction was, however, not the only problem: John Hill's 1761 study of snuff users asserted that that they risked nasal cancer,[17] and in 1795 Samuel Thomas von Sömmerring reported cancers of the lip in pipe smokers.[18] As today, lawmakers hoped that taxation would reduce demand for tobacco, but they also quickly became accustomed to, and dependent on, the revenues generated by tobacco taxes. Two centuries after France enacted a tobacco tax, Napoleon III famously remarked, "I will certainly forbid it at once— as soon as you can name a virtue that brings in as much revenue."[19]

Until the nineteenth century, pipe-smoking and snuff were the predominant modes of consuming tobacco. However, European colonialism and conflict between colonial powers led to the adoption of cigar-smoking which was a common practice among indigenous populations in South America. Cigars were more practical than pipe-smoking, especially following the introduction of the phosphorous friction match in 1827. The uptake of cigar-smoking was initially concentrated in the upper classes. Despite economies of scale, nineteenth-century tobacco was still relatively expensive and cigars were beyond the reach of the European working classes. However, in 1880, the invention of the Bonsack rolling machine launched mass production of cigarettes by substantially lowering costs. The resulting decline in prices led to a significant uptick in consumption. Per-capita consumption of cigarettes rose from about 0.4 per adult in 1870, to 8.2 in 1880 and 35.5 in 1890—almost a 100-fold increase over twenty years.[20]

The rapid rise in cigarette smoking caught the attention of the medical establishment and those concerned for public health on both sides of the Atlantic. In 1836, Samuel Green wrote "that thousands and tens of thousands die of diseases of the lungs generally brought on by tobacco smoking, is a fact as well known in the whole history of disease. How is it possible to be otherwise? Tobacco is a poison."[21] In 1849, Joel Shew listed oral cancer as a consequence of tobacco chewing and smoking, and noted that it is "beyond doubt, chronic throat disease which is so prevalent at this day, is often caused, in great part, by the use of tobacco."[22] Dr. John Lezars also observed in 1859 that smoking led to cancers of the tongue and lip.[23] In 1868, *The Lancet* reported that "it is improper to subject the organism to the action of tobacco at all, during its period of development and especially before and during the establishment of puberty."[24] However, the editors were opposed to prohibition, seemingly attributing health harms to additives or paper wrapping. The journal emphasized the importance of ensuring that "pure tobacco" was available to the poorest.[25]

Smoking among children, however, was a growing concern. In 1891, Manchester's Medical Officer estimated that 80% of boys in Lancashire smoked cigarettes.[25] In England, several societies were set up in the latter half of the ninetieth century to deter children from smoking, including the British Lads Anti-Smoking Union, the Hygienic League and Union for the Suppression of Cigarette-Smoking by Juveniles. The Primitive Methodist Anti-Cigarette League handed out certificates to minors pledging to abstain from smoking tobacco until the age of 21. Several town councils also discussed the possibility of using local by-laws to enforce a ban on sales to minors.[25] However, it would be another 99 years before the sale of tobacco to all minors was banned in the U.K.

The U.S. saw greater legislative action against smoking, then as today often focusing on concerns for children. By the late 1890s, the tobacco industry was attracting public criticism for offering prizes and giveaways as incentives for purchases.[9] Social reform groups, including the Women's Christian Temperance Union and the National Anti-Cigarette League (subsequently the International Anti-Cigarette League), promoted tobacco control legislation. The cigar industry, fearing that cigarettes would take market share, served as an unlikely ally. Twenty-six U.S. states passed laws banning the sale of cigarettes to minors by 1890. Other states went further. Between 1890 and 1927, 15 states banned cigarette sales,[26] although by the 1930s all such bans had succumbed to a combination of industry pressure and the lure of taxation.[27]

1.2 Marketing Tobacco in the Twentieth Century

During both world wars, tobacco was issued as part of the daily rations provided to servicemen; the medical establishment believed that the benefit to morale outweighed any concerns for health. Tobacco advertisements exploited the association between military service and smoking, suggesting that smoking was patriotic.[28] But soldiers returning from service were often nicotine-dependent and modeled smoking to their families. As military conflict consumed generations of working-age men, women were increasingly engaged in the labor market, ushering in a new era of female emancipation and economic empowerment. Again, the tobacco industry seized upon this opportunity to market directly to women, leveraging themes of individual empowerment and economic independence ("You've come a long way, baby"—Virginia Slims), while suggesting that smoking conveyed sophistication, sexuality ("Blow some my way."—Chesterfields), and health ("Reach for a Lucky instead of a sweet."—American Tobacco). For many women, smoking became a "symbol of emancipation" and a "temporary substitute for the ballot."[29] In response to this cultural shift, leveraged by tobacco industry advertising, smoking rates among women increased rapidly. Female consumers represented just 5 percent of U.S. tobacco consumption in 1924, but this increased to 14 percent in just seven years.[9] This change in the gender

36   S. C. HAMPSHER-MONK ET AL.

composition of consumption was not due to any decline in the smoking rate of men, indicating the rapidity with which smoking among U.S. women rose in the inter-war years.

Meanwhile, from the 1930s, the tobacco industry ran ad campaigns in prominent medical journals including the *New England Journal of Medicine* and the *Journal of the American Medical Association*, sponsored events at medical conventions and targeted physicians' private practices, offering free product samples and industry-produced reports. The aim was not to make doctors smoke (though many did) but to leverage public trust in the medical profession to foster brand loyalty and, later, to use doctors to sow doubt regarding any causal link between smoking and disease.[30] In 1937, for example, Philip Morris advertisements featured "doctors reports" purporting that switching to Philip Morris products lessened or eliminated "irritation." R.J. Reynolds claimed that their products burned more slowly, decreasing the absorption of nicotine. From 1946 to 1951, Reynolds' Camels were marketed with claims that these were the "cigarette of choice" for doctors.[31] Product placement was also a major marketing tactic. Tobacco companies partnered with Hollywood to portray their products as glamorous.[32]

The tobacco industry, however, did not go unchallenged. In response to a complaint bought by the Federal Trade Commission questioning the health claims in cigarette advertisements, Reynolds replaced references to "all physicians surveyed" to "113,597 physicians."[33] Indicating industry executives' concerns about potential litigation, Reynolds noted in correspondence with their advertising agency that they should avoid claiming that Camels are recommended by physicians or that Camels are good for health.[34] Given the implicit messaging in contemporaneous advertisements, that nuance went largely overlooked. In 1949, Reynolds claimed that "noted throat specialists" had concluded after a scientific investigation that there was "not one single case of throat irritation" from smoking Camels.[35] Of course, even if true, "throat irritation" was hardly the issue.

1.3   Understanding the Risks

As previously discussed, mouth and lung cancers were already widely attributed to tobacco use by the nineteenth-century medical establishment. By the second and third decades of the twentieth century, the medical community was well on the way to understanding the role of cigarette smoking in cancers of the lung. As early as 1912, Isaac Adler linked lung cancer with smoking in a published clinical report on 374 cases of primary carcinoma and sarcoma.[36] In 1925, reporting on the San Francisco Cancer Survey, Fredrick Hoffman made reference to the "inherent risk of excessive habits of smoking with particular reference to cancer of the buccal cavity, the throat and the oesophagus."[37] Three years later, The *New England Journal of Medicine* published a paper by Herbert L. Lombard and Carl B. Doering reporting the excess death rates of smokers for many types of cancer, including lung cancer. The authors noted, that "heavy smoking is more common in the cancer group than among the controls."[38]

The first robust statistical evidence for the association between smoking and lung cancer can be traced to a 1929 study by a German researcher, Fritz Lickint.[39] Lickint noted the disproportionate number of heavy smokers among cancer patients, and the concentration of such cases among males, who made up the majority of German smokers.[40] Unfortunately, that research did not gain the attention of international audiences. Robert Proctor explains that the war-time disintegration in international cooperation, subscription cutbacks, and boycotts of German publications meant that this important finding was largely overlooked.[41] In hindsight, the association with Nazism may have been sufficient to erase this important evidence from history.

In 1950, Richard Doll and Bradford Hill of the British Medical Research Council (BMRC) published the first sophisticated statistical analysis showing an association between lung cancer and smoking.[42] Three years later, the BMRC announced a direct causal link between smoking and lung cancer, and in 1962, a report by the Royal College of Physicians (RCP) reiterated the BMRC's conclusion adding that smoking probably contributes to heart disease.[43] Across the Atlantic in 1958, Hammond and Horn[44] published evidence documenting an "extremely high association" between smoking and excess deaths (form coronary disease and cancers including lung cancer) among U.S. males. The Surgeon General's first Smoking and Health report in 1964 further linked smoking with lung cancer and heart disease and concluded that smoking also caused laryngeal cancer and chronic bronchitis.[45] This emerging evidence would fundamentally change public perceptions of smoking and pave the way for the now familiar tobacco control policies.

Despite the evidence, the British government's response was initially muted.[46] Practical and structural reasons may explain this hesitancy. Ministers were not accustomed to considering risk, particularly voluntarily chosen risk, as part of their public health remit. An unresolved tension between the science of genetics highlighting inherited traits and the novel statistical approach emphasizing relative risks meant that the Ministry of Health was initially uncertain as to the nature of the evidence offered by Doll & Hill's work.[47] There were also cultural concerns. As strange as it may seem today, smoking was still considered a purely private matter, and state-sanctioned interventions seemed like overreach at a time when rationing and other painful memories of World War II were still recent.

There were economic considerations, too, since, public funds were in short supply during the austerity of the 1950s, and the Treasury had grown accustomed to tobacco tax revenue. In 1950, tobacco taxes accounted for 16% of the U.K. government's revenue.[48] Moreover, the public costs associated with the still-new national health service (NHS) were significant. Regulators were eager to avoid swamping the National Health Service with demand from worried smokers.[49,50] Ian Macleod, Minister of Health remarked in 1956, "the Welfare State and much else is based on tobacco smoking."[51] British regulators continued to endow individual citizens with responsibility for smoking behavior, but opted to embark on media campaign to educate the public about the evidence on the harms of smoking.[50] The Ministry of Health argued, in 1960, that newspapers, magazines, radio, and television were more effective methods of transmitting the emerging evidence than local health authorities. Government announcements and scientific papers could serve as important sources on this subject.[52] In 1962, the Royal College of Physicians' report *Smoking and Health* emphasized the importance of mass media in disseminating research findings and introduced possible future interventions.[50]

Of course, the tobacco industry did not intend to go quietly into the night. In the U.S., the Tobacco Industry Research Committee was formed in 1953 and the Tobacco Institute in 1958 to undermine, refute, challenge, and discredit the emerging scientific evidence that smoking was harmful, and continue to frame smoking as a matter of personal choice. Yet, tobacco executives were evidently concerned. Industry advertising switched focus from advertisements using physicians to make health claims, which it was thought could attract unwanted attention of those concerned with public health, to a strategy that involved touting the supposed benefits of their products' features, such as filter tips, which were widely adopted in the 1950s.[53] Filter tips may have given the illusion that modern cigarettes were safer, but this was false, as was well understood by the tobacco companies at least by the 1960s.[54]

In the 1950s and 60s, TV served as an important medium for cigarette companies to advertise their products. The tobacco industry sponsored, and paid to have their products placed in popular shows, including those designed for children such as *The Flintstones*.[55] Following the 1964 U.S. Surgeon General's report on smoking[56] which highlighted the evidence that smoking causes cancer and other diseases, federal legislation mandated that U.S. cigarette packs carry warning labels, and by 1969 in print cigarette advertisements were required to carry warning labels too.[57] Tobacco advertising also met increasing resistance in the U.K., where the 1964 Cohen Report on Health Education,[58] highlighted tobacco industry "propaganda," and called for tobacco advertising to be countered through the same mediums.[50] The Health Education Council (HEC) and Action on Smoking and Health (ASH) U.K. were established in 1968 and 1971 respectively for this purpose. Government spending on anti-tobacco messaging expanded rapidly in the 1970s, funding increasingly professionalized and evidence-based campaigns with themes such as preventing smoking among pregnant women, reducing second-hand smoke exposure, and preventing teenagers from initiating tobacco use.[50] In 1962 the RCP recommended more stringent regulation of cigarettes with restrictions on sale, advertising, and public consumption. Following Labour's victory in the 1964 General Election, physician Kenneth Robinson became Britain's Health Minister. Soon thereafter, cigarette advertising on TV was banned before 9 p.m., and print media and billboard advertising were also restricted.[50]

In the U.S., a group of anti-smoking advocates known (also) as Action on Smoking and Health lodged a complaint with the Federal Communications Commission in 1967 arguing that TV and radio stations advertising cigarettes should provide free time for anti-smoking public health messages. As a result, between 1967 and 1970 anti-smoking messages received about US$75 million (roughly $4.415 billion in today's money) in free airtime. A significant decline in cigarette consumption followed. However, tobacco industry spending on advertising and promotions increased rapidly from the mid-1970s in an attempt to offset the effects of anti-tobacco public health messaging. In 1974 the industry spent the equivalent of $1.75 billion in 2022 dollars. Two years later this figure had jumped to US$3.34 billion, and by 1985 the industry was

40 S. C. HAMPSHER-MONK ET AL.

spending $6.85 billion on advertising.[59,60] While there were state-funded anti-tobacco media campaigns in Minnesota (1984) Arizona (1995), California (1989), Florida (1997), and Oregon (1996), the national anti-smoking media campaigns did not make a comeback until 2000 when the American Legacy Foundation launched its "truth" campaign.

1.4 Reframing Smoking as a Public Health Issue

The emergence of the scientific evidence that smoking poses a risk to bystanders precipitated a seismic shift in tobacco control, helping regulators and activists reframe smoking as a public health issue. In the U.S., several publications, including *The Health Consequences of Involuntary Smoking: A Report of the Surgeon General*[61]; the National Research Council reported *Indoor Pollutants*[62] and *The Airliner Cabin Environment: Air Quality and Safety*[63] reported the association between cardiovascular health risks and second-hand smoke. This evidence focused the public's attention on the risks of environmental smoke and galvanized non-smoker's rights groups and public opinion in general in support of smoking bans. Arizona implemented a limited smoke-free law in 1973, and by 1986, 4 states and the District of Columbia had passed legislation restricting public smoking in some circumstances. However, it was not until 1998 that California became the first state to adopt smoke-free policies for all restaurants and bars. Still, in 1988 federal law banned smoking on domestic flights shorter than 2 hours. This was extended to all commercial U.S. flights in 1990. The publication of *The Respiratory Health Effects of Passive Smoking: Lung Cancer and Other Disorders by the EPA* in 1992,[64] further reiterated the public health risk posed by second-hand smoke, and may be credited with numerous subsequent state and local smoke-free laws. By the late 2000s, comprehensive smoke-free laws had passed in some 30 U.S. states, prohibiting smoking in most workplaces and all public places, including previously exempted bars and restaurants.[65]

Similarly, in the U.K., publications by the RCP[66] and the ISCSH[67] emphasized the risks of second-hand smoke. By the late 1990s, with smoking rates now below 30%, the weight of public opinion was increasingly against smoking and the government faced growing calls for smoke-free legislation, including from the British Medical Association (BMA).[68] By then, smoking had already been banned in many offices and enclosed public places such as cinemas and on public transport. However, smoking in pubs, bars, and restaurants was still permitted. Still, Britain's New Labour government continued to favor industry self-regulation, with fears about profits and job losses in the tobacco and hospitality industry preventing the 1999 Health and Safety Commission's Approved Code of Practice on passive smoking at work from being implemented. Instead, the Department of Health sought to partner with industry stakeholders to implement a voluntary agreement, leading to the Public Places Charter (1999). Perhaps unsurprisingly, the effects of this voluntary charter were limited; the proportion of smoke-free venues only increased by 1% to 2%.[69]

While Department of Health economists may have been unconvinced about the benefit of smoke-free laws on smoking prevalence, they did see the potential for significant health gains if those laws could discourage uptake especially among the youngest workers, who were between 16 and 18 years old. In March 2005, a *British Medical Journal* report published the most authoritative data yet on the impact of passive smoking, suggesting it killed 11,000 a year in the U.K.[70] Later that year, the Scottish Parliament passed the U.K.'s first comprehensive smoke-free legislation and England and Wales adopted similar legislation in 2007. Elsewhere, other countries were even quicker to adopt smoke-free laws. Ontario, Canada banned smoking in public spaces and workplaces in 1994 and Italy introduced a comprehensive smoking ban in 2003. The Netherlands banned smoking in public buildings and public transport in 1988, expanding the scope to include non-hospitality workplaces in 2004. New Zealand restricted smoking in schools and workplaces beginning in 1990, but extended this to all indoor public workplaces and hospitality venues after 2004; Ireland also banned smoking in all workplaces in 2004. Australia phased in bans on smoking in workplaces and public spaces by 2006.

1.5   Industry Obstruction

As is now widely known, the tobacco industry fought (and has continued to oppose) restrictions on cigarettes often via fraudulent and duplicitous means with the goal of protecting their market. In 1954, the tobacco industry paid hundreds of American newspapers to publish the *Frank Statement to Cigarette Smokers*[71] which stated that the public's health was the industry's primary concern and promising industry-wide change.

But over the course of the next five decades, the tobacco industry consistently misled the public about the harms of its products. Instead of changing, the industry chose to refute, suppress, and deny the scientific evidence regarding the harms their products caused, even while those harms were understood by executives. This deliberate attempt to mislead the public attenuated the decline in smoking rates and exacerbated the enormous damage that smoking causes. As described by Naomi Oreskes in *Merchants of Doubt: How a Handful of Scientists Obscured the Truth on Issues from Tobacco Smoke to Global Warming*,[72] the tobacco industry sought to create the perception that there was still some scientific debate about the risk of smoking. Thus, an internal memo within the tobacco industry declared that "doubt is our product."[73] The industry spent vast sums to publicly question the scientific evidence causally linking smoking with cancer and falsely suggested that the evidence for toxicity of tobacco smoke were inadequate. In a 1971 television interview the president of Philip Morris denied that smoking poses a health risk to pregnant women and babies.[74] In April 1994, the top tobacco executives swore under oath to a congressional committee hearing that they believed that "nicotine is not addictive."[75] The CEOs of Reynolds and Lorillard testified to Congress that their companies did not manipulate the levels of nicotine in their products to get or keep smokers addicted to their products.[76] As the public attention turned to the dangers of second-hand smoke, the tobacco industry again refuted the evidence.[77, 78] Perhaps worst of all, the industry consistently marketed its products to children, knowing that new smokers would be needed to replace the attrition rate caused by smoking-related mortality and that those who start smoking in adolescence would be less likely to quit.[79]

Time and again industry promises were proven to be false, and companies' own documents show that industry executives knew them to be false.[80] In 1994, suspicions that tobacco companies' misconduct crossed the line from unethical to criminal were borne out by a leak of 4,000 pages of damning internal tobacco industry documents proving that the industry knew the dangers of smoking, worked to suppress this information, and continued to mislead consumers. University of California professors published excerpts from these papers and an analysis of them in *The Cigarette Papers*.[80] Two years later, another trove of industry documents was made public in the findings preceding the Tobacco Master Settlement Agreement (TMSA). The TMSA settlement was between state Attorneys General from 46 U.S. states,[81] five territories and the District of

Columbia and the four largest cigarette manufacturers in the U.S. (named "Original Participating Manufacturers" [OPMs]): Philip Morris Inc, R.J. Reynolds, Brown & Williamson and Lorillard. The plaintiffs agreed to drop their lawsuits against the industry for the healthcare costs incurred as a result of industry duplicity. In exchange, the OPMs agreed not to: "take any action, directly or indirectly, to target Youth within any Settling State in the advertising, promotion or marketing of Tobacco Products, or take any action the primary purpose of which is to initiate, maintain or increase the incidence of Youth smoking within any Settling State; disband Tobacco-related Organizations [Tobacco Institute, the Center for Indoor Air Research, and the Council for Tobacco Research] and restrict the creation of, and participation with trade associations; make publicly available a trove of industry documents from the discovery phase drawing attention to the industry's attempts to mislead the public; create and fund a National Public Education Foundation to reduce youth smoking and reduce smoking-related disease; and make annual payments in perpetuity to states, calculated on the basis of OPMs relative market share in 1997." The payments would amount to over US$200 billion between 1998 and 2023. While smoking has continued to decline in the U.S. in the years since the TMSA, the settlement has been criticized for being too lenient[82] and states have been criticized for using their allocated funds to fill holes in their general funds. By one estimate, less than 3 cents in every dollar paid out is spent on tobacco prevention programs.[83]

In the 2000s, the industry was again in hot water—this time over its fraudulent use of descriptors such as "light," "mild," and "low tar." Since the mid-twentieth century, the industry had explicitly and implicitly suggested that the use of filters would make their products less toxic. In the 1970s, filter tips were adapted to include small "ventilation" holes in cigarette filters which, under machine testing conditions, diluted the smoke with air. Industry-funded studies claimed that these so-called "light," "mild," and "low-tar" cigarettes were safer than conventional cigarettes. Because they were perceived as less harmful, health-conscious smokers switched to these products instead of quitting or reducing smoking.[84] But in the real-world, smokers using such products adapted by inhaling more deeply and blocking the holes with their fingers, rendering these products just as harmful. The use of "mild," light," and "low-tar" descriptors was banned by the EU in 2001 and has since been banned elsewhere, including in Australia (2006), Malaysia (2013), and the Philippines (2014). In 2009, the U.S. Supreme Court upheld a 2006 ruling that multinational tobacco companies had violated the Racketeer Influenced and Corrupt Organizations Act, defrauding the public about the safety of these products, and the use of descriptors such as "mild," light," and "low tar" was banned in the U.S. Three years earlier another U.S. judge wrote that the tobacco industry had deceptively marketed its lethal products, pursuing profit with no regard for public wellbeing. But it would be 2017 before the tobacco companies began to run court-ordered advertisements in TV and newspapers, on cigarette packs and on websites acknowledging the harms of smoking, the addictiveness of cigarettes and nicotine, the lack of evidence that "low-tar," "light," "mild," and "natural" cigarettes confer any reduction in risk; admitting that the industry manipulated the design of cigarettes to optimize nicotine delivery and acknowledging the harms of second-hand smoke exposure.

2   SMOKING AROUND THE WORLD

Understanding what factors contribute to smoking behaviors is vital in evaluating the effect of tobacco control policies. However, the ostensibly simple question "how common is smoking?" can be deceptively difficult to answer. Smoking is typically measured in prevalence—the portion of a given community who smoke. But what behavior patterns qualify a person as "a smoker"? Lifetime use of a combustible tobacco product? Current use? If it is the latter, how frequently and for how long must a person smoke to be included in the category? Even among people who currently smoke on a regular basis, not everyone does so on a daily basis, and those that do may use different quantities over the course of a day or week. In the U.S. in 2016, 28% of smokers consumed 20–29 cigarettes per day, but 25% consumed less than 10.[85] The frequency of smoking for the average smoker in a given community also varies significantly between nations. For example, in 2012, daily smokers in Canada averaged 27.6 cigarettes per day, whereas in France, for example, the average was 14.4.[86] Given this variation we might also be interested in the total consumption of tobacco by a community. Cigarette sales and shipment data may help illuminate the total volume of legal cigarette sales. For example, in 2021 the U.K. released 23.7 billion cigarettes for consumption.[87] But such figures can be hard to conceptualize. To help, consider the population of British smokers in 2020 (approximately 6.6 million)[88] giving a share of 3,591 cigarettes per every adult smoker or just under 10 cigarettes per day. Estimates for total consumption must also account for sale to visitors, consumption of tobacco purchased elsewhere or outside of the study window, and illicit trade. Failing to account for these factors risks over-estimating, or under-estimating consumption.

To measure the prevalence of smokers in a population, researchers typically depend on self-reported survey data. However, these are again imperfect. Researchers must try to accommodate for the fact that stigma may lead smokers to consciously underreport smoking. Individuals may also misestimate their own use. Respondents are prone to rounding up or down which results in estimates clustering around rounded numbers such as those ending in zero or five. This is referred to as digit bias. Survey administrators may try to overcome bias, for example by checking blood, saliva, or urine samples for the presence of cotinine, a metabolite of nicotine; by collecting consumption data in real-time with electronic data entry systems; or by collecting the cigarette butts of study participants. However, such methodologies are resource-intensive and are accordingly relatively uncommon. Further, unless carefully administered under controlled conditions, cotinine testing provides little insight into the type of nicotine product used, when and in what quantity.

Typically, adults are categorized as "smokers" if they have smoked 100 or more cigarettes in their lifetime and also currently smoke cigarettes.[89] "Current smoking" leaves some room for interpretation. The qualifier may result in irregular or non-daily smokers being discounted. This is a particular concern for countries such as Brazil, India, Indonesia, Thailand, and Mexico where non-daily smoking is an established pattern.[90] "Current smoking" also fails to disclose recent increases or decreases in frequency. For example, if 90% of smokers dropped from 20 cigarettes per day to 5 cigarettes per day, as a result of a particular intervention, the exclusive use of the "current smoker" categorization would risk overlooking that achievement.

Until the mid-2000s, national-level data collection on the prevalence of smoking was largely limited to population surveys conducted in high-income nations. These included the National Health Interview Survey, National Adult Tobacco Survey, and National Youth Tobacco Survey in the U.S.; the Canadian Tobacco and Nicotine Survey and Canadian Student Tobacco Survey (formerly Youth Smoking Survey); Brazil's Pesquisa Nacional de Saúde (National Health Survey); The Korea Health and Nutritional Examination Survey (South Korea); the New Zealand Health Survey; Australia's National Drug Strategy Household Survey; the Health Survey for England and the Smoking and Alcohol

46   S. C. HAMPSHER-MONK ET AL.

Toolkit Study (U.K.). These cross-sectional studies provide a snapshot of smoking behavior at a given moment in time by taking a representative sample of a given population. Repeated cross-sectional studies take a fresh sample each time they are carried out. In contrast, longitudinal studies follow the same sample of people over time to see how behaviors change. Examples of longitudinal studies include the U.S.' Population Assessment of Tobacco and Health (PATH) Study, the U.K.'s Adult Tobacco Policy Survey, New Zealand's SoFIE-Health longitudinal survey, and France's CONSTANCE population-based cohort study. Cross-sectional studies are more common and tend to be larger in scale and scope. Longitudinal studies are smaller and focused on a more specific topic, but better at supporting causal inferences. Chapter 3 will explore this topic more fully.

Different survey methodologies, inclusion criteria, and implementation timelines can make comparison of different national-level survey data difficult. A multiplicity of population-based surveys and monitoring systems also imposes a resource burden, especially for smaller and less affluent countries. Harmonization of surveys helps reduce this burden while ensuring that improved data collection and analysis, and dissemination of findings remain possible. Recognizing the need for standardization of methodologies to support the generation of comparable data within and across countries, concerted efforts have been made over the past twenty years to develop international surveys on smoking. The Global Tobacco Surveillance System (GTSS), developed by the WHO alongside the U.S. Centers for Disease Control, and the Canadian Public Health Association, presents data from four global tobacco surveys to "monitor key articles of the World Health Organization's (WHO) Framework Convention on Tobacco Control (FCTC) and components of the WHO MPOWER technical package."[91] The four studies operating under the GTSS are the Global Youth Tobacco Survey (GYTS)[92]; the Global School Personnel Survey (GSPS)[93]; the Global Health Professions Student Survey (GHPSS)[94]; and the Global Adult Tobacco Survey (GATS).[95] Several nations are conspicuously absent from these studies, including Australia, Canada, France, Germany, Ireland, Israel, Japan, Norway, Sweden, the U.K., and the U.S. These countries operate their own surveys, however (once again) differences in the methodologies used by population surveys mean that there is some variation between estimates of smoking rates. For example, in the U.S., reporting on data from the National Health Interview Survey, the CDC reports that 12.5% of

U.S. adults aged 18 and over was a current smoker in 2020, whereas the WHO[96] estimate was 19.1%; in Australia, the National Drug Strategy Household Survey (NDSHS) reports that in 2019 11.2% of Australians were daily smokers, whereas the WHO estimate for current smoking prevalence in Australia in 2019 was 14%.[97]

2.1   Prevalence

2.1.1   Global Prevalence of Tobacco Use

In 1998, the WHO developed guidelines for monitoring the tobacco epidemic.[98] The WHO and the World Bank provide comprehensive estimates of smoking prevalence using standardized methodologies (questions, timeframes, definitions, age ranges, etc.) as discussed. According to the WHO's 2021 global report on trends in prevalence of tobacco use[99] around the world in 2020, 1.3 billion people above the age of 15, 22.3% of the global population, used tobacco. According to the report, this figure is projected to fall by 236 million by 2025, at which point a projected 20.5% of males and 6.6% of females over the age of 15 will use tobacco. These figures exclude use of tobacco by those under the age of 15 which, while markedly less frequent than use by older adolescents and adults, is not zero. Between 2020 and 2021 142 countries surveyed school-aged children on the use of tobacco. The results, tabulated by the WHO suggest that, 7.4% of girls and 12.9% of boys aged 13–15 use tobacco of any kind (excluding ENDS), amounting to a further 25 million boys and 13.4 million girls.

As evidenced by these statistics, tobacco use is more common among males than females. The WHO estimates for 2020 suggest that, globally, 36.7% of male adults but only 7.8% of female adults is a current tobacco user. As a global average, tobacco use tends to peak in males in the 45–54 age range, whereas in females use peaks slightly later; between 55 and 64. The highest rates of tobacco use are found in the nations of southeast Asia, Europe, and the Western Pacific, and tobacco use is least prevalent in the populations of African nations. Note that these data include non-combustible (oral) tobacco products. While less common in High-Income Countries (HICs), oral tobacco products are widely used in parts of the world, including snus in Norway and Sweden and products such as gutkha, zarda and paan in South Asia. Between 2010 and 2020 the WHO estimates that 24.7% of males and 11.6% of females over 15 use oral tobacco. Worldwide, the prevalence of smokeless tobacco use is much lower: 8.5% of males and 3.4% of females. Still by those estimates 240 million men and 96 million women around the world use smokeless tobacco.

2.1.2 Global Prevalence of Smoking

Smoking is the most common form of tobacco use worldwide. The WHO[99] places the global prevalence of smoking at 991 million for 2020 (17% of those over the age of 15). As with tobacco use in general, smoking is more common among males than females: 28.9% of males aged (15 +) were smokers in 2020 compared to 5.2% of women. Regionally, the highest smoking rates are found in Southeast Asia, Europe, and Central Asia, where close to one in four adults currently smokes (See Fig. 1). The prevalence of smoking has declined in all WHO regions since 2000, with the fastest decline evident in South Asia. Globally, the pace of the decline appears to have slowed in recent years, with the global prevalence unchanged between 2018 and 2020. Smoking rates remain higher in Europe, Asia, and North America, and lower in Africa and Latin America. Exceptions to these regional trends are discussed below.

Countries can also be grouped by level of development to examine how common smoking is (see Fig. 2). In 2000, the prevalence of smoking was bifurcated across middle-income countries (MICs); countries with

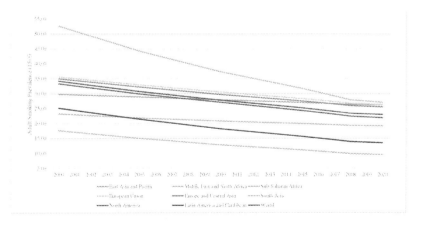

Fig. 1 Global smoking prevalence of adults (15+) by region (2000–2020) (*Source* Authors' elaborations of World Bank World Development Indicators[100])

lower-middle income exhibited higher rates, and upper-middle-income countries exhibited lower rates compared with other MICs. Over the time series, the difference between MIC groups has attenuated. Low-income countries (LICs) continue to exhibit lower prevalence of smoking than MICs.

There are often wide discrepancies in the prevalence of smoking between genders, which vary from region to region. In the Western Pacific for example, 43.1% of males smoke, while only 2.7% of females do so. Likewise, in Southeast Asia, the ratio of male smokers to female is more than 15:1.[99]

The results from surveys of school students aged 13–15 in 159 countries show that, in addition, approximately 21.4 million adolescents—15.2 million boys and 6.3 million girls (7.9% and 3.5% of the respective populations) are current smokers.[99] The nations of Southeast Asia contribute 29% of the global total of smoking in this age range, and LMICs represent 46% of the global youth smoking.[99] In all WHO regions the prevalence of adolescent smoking is more common among males than females. Only in the Americas is it close: here 7.4% of boys and 7.1% of girls report current smoking. [99]

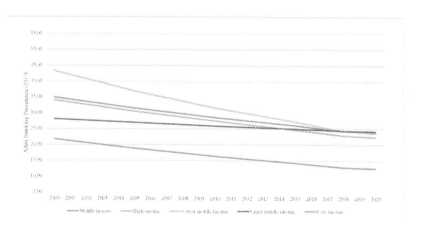

Fig. 2 Global smoking prevalence of adults (15+) by income level (2000–2020) (*Source* Authors' elaborations of World Bank World Development Indicators[101])

50   S. C. HAMPSHER-MONK ET AL.

2.1.3   Smoking Rates in Various Countries

African nations exhibit markedly lower smoking prevalence rates compared with many other nations. According to WHO estimates for 2020,[102] the prevalence of adult smoking in Benin, Ghana, Ethiopia, and Nigeria is less than 5%, many other African nations as well as and some South or Central American nations including Panama, El Salvador, Colombia, Haiti, Barbados, Peru, and Costa Rica have smoking rates below 10%, Chile and South Africa are notable exceptions, here the latest estimates place smoking prevalence at approximately 30% and 20% respectively. The countries with the highest rates of smoking tend to be clustered in Southeast Asia, Pacific, and Europe. In Indonesia, for example, approximately 32.2% adults smoke. In Laos it is more than 26%. In Kiribati more than 40% smoke, and in Papua New Guinea it is 39.3%. Meanwhile, smoking rates for adults exceed 30% in much of Europe including France, Greece, Hungary, and Serbia, while in Bulgaria close to 40% of adults smoke.[102]

Few European nations have rates lower than 20%, notable exceptions being the countries of Scandinavia, Iceland, and the U.K.[102] The nation with the highest rate of smoking is the Pacific Island nation Nauru where 43.8% of adults currently smokes. Of course, population size matters. Nauru is home to just over 10,000 people. In contrast, while the prevalence of smoking is lower in countries such as China; where about 23.5% of adults currently smoke, and India; where 8% do so,[103,104] these countries' massive populations make them important targets for global public health.

These national-level estimates mask important disparities in smoking rates between sub-national groups. As mentioned, smoking is almost uniformly concentrated among males, but gap between the sexes varies widely across national contexts. The largest gender differences in smoking rates are to be found in some African, Middle Eastern, and Southeast Asian countries. In Gambia, Algeria, Bangladesh, Eritrea, Malaysia, Lesotho, Egypt, Sri Lanka, and Azerbaijan there are more than 50 male smokers for every female smoker.[102] Conversely, relatively small gender differences are found in Denmark, Croatia, Spain, Sweden, and France. In these countries, male smoking is less than 10 percentage points higher than smoking among females.[102] Very rarely are smoking rates higher for women than men. According to the WHO data for 2020, Montenegro is the only national population for which this is true.[102] Cultural gender norms and social stigma may contribute to these discrepancies,[105] though these cultural factors may also lead women who do smoke to underreporting it. Countries with strong gender equality tend to have smaller gaps between male and female smoking,[106] but the tobacco industry has also used themes of female empowerment and emancipation to market cigarettes to women.[107]

As well as how many people in a community smoke (prevalence), it is important to measure the intensity of smoking in a community. Interestingly there are marked differences between the consumption of cigarettes by smokers in different national contexts. In 2012 North America, East Asia, and Oceana smokers typically consumed 20–25 cigarettes per day; Canada (27.6 cigarettes per day), South Korea (25), Russia (24.4), Japan (23.8), the U.S. (22.5), China (22.3), Australia (20.1), and New Zealand (20.1) are examples.[108] In Southeast Asia, the frequency with which smokers smoke appears to be somewhat lower: India (8.2), Indonesia (11), and Thailand (12.5). Of course, these are just averages; individual smokers may smoke significantly more or less frequently. Numerous studies report that, in addition to exhibiting a lower smoking prevalence, those women who do smoke also smoke fewer cigarettes per day than their male counterparts. This has been reported in the U.K.,[109] and throughout the EU.[110]

2.2   Trends and Projections in Smoking

2.2.1   Trends in Global Smoking Prevalence

Worldwide in the year 2000, 26.9% of people aged 15 and older (1.129 billion) were estimated to be current tobacco smokers. By 2020 this figure had fallen to 17% (991 million).[99] Relative to the 2000 rates, the global decline in smoking has been more marked among females than males. Globally, smoking among females aged 15 and older declined from 10.4% (216 million) in 2000 to 5.2% (151 million) in 2020. Among males, in 2000 the prevalence of smoking stood at 43.5% (912 million), declining to 28.9% (840 million) in 2020. Regionally, between 2000 and 2020, the largest reductions in smoking prevalence have occurred in Southeast Asia. Here the prevalence of adult smoking declined by 55% from 29.3% in 2000 to 13.1% in 2020. Africa and the Americas have also seen aggregate reductions of more than 40%, while the nations of Europe, the Eastern Mediterranean, and Western Pacific have fared somewhat worse with relative reductions of 27, 28 and 17% respectively.[111]

In most regions, aggregated national smoking rates for females are declining faster than smoking among males. For example, between 2000 and 2020 female smoking in Southeast Asia declined by 82%, whereas among males it declined by a relatively less impressive 50%.[99] Similar stories play out in Africa (58% reduction among females versus 40% among males), Americas (45% vs. 41%), the Eastern Mediterranean (56% vs. 24%), and Western Pacific (44% vs. 15%). Only in Europe did the decline in male smoking outpace the decline among females (30% vs. 22%).[99]

In absolute terms, despite the reduction in smoking prevalence, the number of smokers in Africa rose between 2000 and 2020 from 48 to 49 million.[99] Similarly in the Eastern Mediterranean and Western Pacific regions, the absolute numbers of smokers rose in the same time period, adding 16 million and 19 million smokers respectively, largely as a result of population growth. Economic development may afford greater purchasing power for citizens of many lower and middle-income countries (LMICs). That could lead to greater smoking, unless taxation increases beyond the pace at which incomes wise.[112] This contrasts with data from many High-Income Nations (HICs), where increased affluence tends to be associated with a reduction in smoking. The tobacco industry is well aware of this bifurcated response and can be expected to target its marketing toward growth areas, including LMICs and sub-national populations where smoking is concentrated. Thus, the absolute number of male smokers in Africa and the Eastern Mediterranean regions is expected to increase by a combined 6 million smokers between 2020 and 2025[113] (Fig. 3).

2.2.2 Projections of Global Smoking Prevalence

Globally, the prevalence of smoking is projected to decline further from 17% of adults (over 15 years of age) to 15.4% by 2025; a reduction of 35 million, bringing the projected total down to 956 million.[99] The largest declines will be seen in the Americas (where there will be 10 million fewer smokers in 2025 relative to 2020), Southeast Asia (11 million fewer smokers), and Europe (12 million fewer smokers). The Western Pacific is also forecast to see 6 million fewer smokers by 2025, however Africa and the countries of the Eastern Mediterranean will add 2 million and 3 million smokers respectively. Given the gender disparity in smoking it is unsurprising that the majority of the global reduction will be seen among men (22 million vs.12 million) however relative to gender-specific

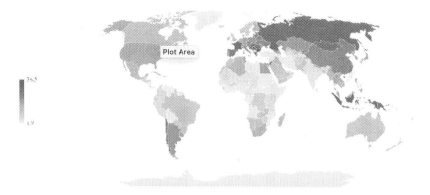

Fig. 3 Age standardized prevalence of current cigarette smoking among adults (15+) (*Note* The highest rates of age-standardized adult smoking are found in the Eastern Mediterranean region of Europe, Southeast Asia, and some Pacific island nations. The lowest rates are typically found in African countries. Exceptions to these regional trends are discussed in the text. *Source* WHO[114])

prevalence, the decline in smoking among women will be more marked. Relative to 2020 rates, female smoking will decline by 13.5% through 2025, relative to an 8.7% decline among men.

2.2.3 Projections of Smoking in Various Countries

Comparing WHO estimates for the prevalence of current tobacco smoking among adults in 2020 and the projected prevalence for 2025,[99] 38 nations are forecast to see reductions of greater than 15%. The nations forecast to make the largest reductions in adult smoking prevalence are: Peru (30%); Cote D'Ivoire (29%); Tanzania and Sierra Leone (26%); and Uganda and India (25%). However, 44 nations will see reductions of less than 5%: Four countries (Brunei, Egypt, France, and Singapore), will see no decline, and 11 nations are projected to see their rates of adult smoking increase. These include The Bahamas (−0.94% reduction), The Congo (−10.87%), Croatia (−2.44%), Indonesia (−2.48%), Jordan (−2.59%), Marshall Islands (−1.72%), Oman (−2.78%), Portugal (−0.39%), Moldova (−3.94%), Saudi Arabia (−0.79%), Slovakia (−0.32%).

Interestingly, while in some countries there is little difference in the projections for each sex, in other nations, wide discrepancies exist. For example, in Armenia, Brazil, Germany, Chile, Poland, and Uganda, the projections for the decline in male adult smoking are within a percentage point of those for females. In other countries the reduction is heavily slanted to one sex. In Turkey, Benin, Cote D'Ivoire, Portugal, and Tanzania projected declines in female smoking are more than 10 percentage points lower than those forecast for men. Conversely, in many other nations, notably in Sri Lanka, Bangladesh, Congo, Eritrea, and Malaysia, the forecast decline in female adult smoking far outstrips the projected decline among males. Indeed, in the Congo, Egypt, Indonesia, and the Bahamas, while increases in male smoking prevalence are forecast, reductions in female smoking prevalence are also due. The extent to which the latter offset the former will depend on the absolute prevalence of smoking in each group.

As evident in Fig. 4, the Eastern Mediterranean region of Europe, Southeast Asia, and Pacific are home to some of the countries with the highest rates of smoking, and many of the lowest national prevalences are found in African countries. Note also that, while countries with both the highest and the lowest rates of smoking exhibit a disparity in the rates between men and women, the countries with the highest rates tend to exhibit high rates for both men and women (Indonesia and Timor-Leste being notable exceptions). In contrast the nations with the lowest national adult smoking prevalence figures typically exhibit almost no smoking among females.

2.2.4 Trends and Projections for Smoking-Related Morbidity and Mortality

While the smoking trends are evidently moving in the right direction *en masse*, the absolute numbers of smokers around the world and the risk that smoking poses to those who do smoke continue to be enormous. According to the latest WHO figures more than 8 million people die each year as a result of tobacco use, and 1.2 million non-smokers die as the result of exposure to second-hand smoke.[115] These are astonishing numbers, representing 15% of all deaths in 2017.[116] But, again, the share of deaths for which smoking is responsible is not evenly distributed. In some countries in 2017 including the U.K., Ireland, Poland, and Turkey more than one in five deaths was caused by tobacco. In China in 2019 it was 1 in 4. Of course, those figures are higher for nations where deaths resulting from smoking belie otherwise healthy populations. A better gauge for the lethality of smoking is the rate of smoking-related

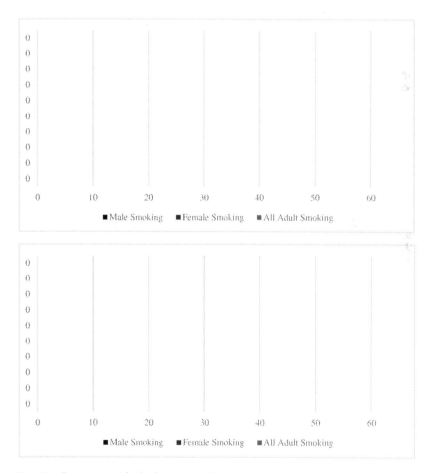

Fig. 4 Countries with the highest and lowest prevalence of adult smoking (15+) (2020) (*Source* WHO[101])

deaths per capita. On this metric, the worst affected areas closely track the nations with the greatest smoking prevalence: In 2019 Russia, China, Ukraine, Pakistan, Myanmar, Mongolia, Cambodia, and Indonesia all saw in excess of 125 smoking-related deaths for every 100 thousand citizens. In the same year, Micronesia, Narau, The Solomon Islands, and Kiribati saw more than 350 such deaths per 100 thousand.[86]

Fortunately, as the prevalence of smoking has declined, the incidence of smoking-related deaths has also fallen.[86] In 1990 there were 146 smoking-related deaths per 100,000 worldwide. By 2017 that figure had declined to 90 per 100 thousand. The U.S., Canada, Brazil, India, Ireland, New Zealand, South Korea, the Netherlands, and the U.K. all saw smoking-related deaths decline from in excess of 150 per 100 thousand in 1990, to below 100 per 100 thousand by 2019; and Canada, New Zealand South Korea and Brazil declined to fewer than 75 deaths per 100 thousand. The majority of these deaths afflict people above the age of 70, though about a quarter affect those between the ages of 50 and 69. But smoking-related deaths have not declined in all contexts: Montenegro, Lesotho, Azerbaijan, Egypt, Dominican Republic, Afghanistan, Guinea, Mali, and Sao Tome & Principe have all seen the frequency of smoking-related deaths increase since the early 1990s, against the global trend. In other Lower- and Middle-Income Countries (LMICs) we may expect more smoking-related deaths in the near future, as population growth and aging offset the decline in smoking-related *rates*. In the twentieth century it is estimated that smoking led to approximately 100 million premature deaths, most of which were concentrated in today's wealthy nations.[117] However, smoking declines in HICs will likely continue to outpace the declines in LMICs, shifting the burden of smoking-related harm toward LMICs. Without accelerated progress, tobacco products are projected to cause 1 billion deaths this century.[118]

3   SMOKING-RELATED DISPARITIES

Reviewing the national-level data on smoking prevalence reminds us that there are wide differences in the smoking rates between national populations. Interestingly, the highest rates of smoking are frequently concentrated among middle-income nations while lower rates are found in both low- and high-income nations. If smoking prevalence is charted on the y axis and countries ranged by national income on the x axis, a bell-shaped trend emerges. This feature of the cigarette epidemic[119] may be explained by two mechanisms operating simultaneously. In low-income nations a price-effect dominates; that is to say, a lack of disposable income inhibits smoking. Given that disposable incomes in LMICs tend to be lower there may, historically, have been less incentive for the industry to market its products in the poorest nations. If so, poorer nations may have been insulated, to some extent, from the effects of tobacco marketing which has driven demand for tobacco in wealthier nations. But, as a perverse consequence of economic development, rising levels of disposable income might now drive increased levels of smoking in such context. The industry might also be expected to target "growth markets" further increasing the uptake of tobacco products in LMICs, especially since, having had relatively low rates of smoking historically, and other pressing public health concerns including infectious disease control and the provision of adequate nutrition and clean water, many of the world's poorest countries lack robust tobacco control measures that have been successfully implemented in wealthier nations. This makes LMICs an important target for tobacco control efforts. But if purchasing power increases the demand for tobacco, why do we see lower rates in wealthier nations?

The answer lies in the observation that different populations are at different points in the evolution of the tobacco epidemic. The tobacco epidemic has been described as having four distinct phases[120]: Initially, smoking is rare among both men and women. In the second phase, smoking rates rise, initially led by men and higher SES individuals with women and lower SES individuals lagging by several years. In the third stage, smoking peaks and begins to decline, again led by males and higher SES individuals, but latterly with other groups too. Finally, in the fourth stage, aided by tobacco control policies, smoking rates decline among all groups, approaching some stable minimum.[121] Although that chronology is consistent, different nations are at different phases of the epidemic: in many HICs, a significant decline is well underway, while in some LMICs the epidemic is either plateauing or, worse, may yet peak. Even in the final phase, the decline in smoking does not extend to the elimination of smoking. Thus, even in nations that have achieved some of the largest reductions in smoking in the last two decades, smoking rates remain consistently above 10%,[102] eluding the goal of a smoke-free generation. This narrative goes some way to explain the differences in smoking prevalence between sub-national populations. In nations situated earlier in the tobacco epidemic, smoking is associated with high socioeconomic status (indicative of greater disposable income). Conversely, in nations situated in the latter stages of the epidemic, smoking tends to be concentrated in lower SES groups.[119] That pattern appears to be consistent across a wide range of national context, transcending economic, cultural, social, and political differences.[122]

Social gradients in smoking affect not only the prevalence, but also the constituents of uptake and cessation, as well as smoking-related harms.

Disparities signal the need for policies and interventions that recognize that people who smoke are not a homogenous group but have numerous complex and person-specific factors affecting their smoking and quitting behavior, in light of which the one-size-fits-all model traditionally adopted is likely to be severely limited in efficacy. Instead, interventions should be tailored to the communities in which smoking and smoking-related harms are concentrated.[123]

As national surveys have become increasingly sophisticated, a more nuanced picture has emerged: Smoking is not only concentrated among the poorer members of wealthy societies, but also among other historically disadvantaged groups too: some racial and ethnic minorities, those with lower rates of educational attainment, the incarcerated and formerly incarcerated; those facing housing insecurity; those living with long-term mental illness, and the LGBTQ + community. The evidence on these disparities is still emerging, but there is strong evidence of the effects of intersectional disadvantage on smoking-related harm: that is those suffering from one disadvantage may be more likely to experience another, creating a compounding effect. A 2019 study of more than 275,000 Americans, comparing the odds of current smoking with unemployment, poverty, lack of educational attainment, disability, and psychological distress found that disparities in smoking prevalence were successively larger with each additional disadvantage faced, and were expressed in both higher smoking initiation odds and lower smoking cessation odds.[124] Similarly, in Sweden, the highest rates of smoking are found among those facing multiple disadvantages: 54% of young-middle aged, immigrant males, with low educational attainment who lived alone smoked, compared to just 6% of native higher educated Swedish women aged 65–84 living with others.[125] The compounding effect of multiple disadvantages has also been reported in the U.K.[126]

3.1 Socioeconomic Disparities

In HICs, lower-income groups frequently exhibit higher levels of smoking than wealthier groups. A 2019 report by ASH (U.K.) *Health Inequalities and Smoking*[127] found that, whereas 10.2% of those in managerial and professional occupations were smokers, 18.5% of those in long-term unemployment, and 25.4% of those working routine and manual jobs were smokers. The report also highlights that while the rates of quitting attempts appear to be common across socioeconomic groups, those from more disadvantaged backgrounds appear less likely to succeed[128]; a fact that may be explained by higher levels of Nicotine dependence in disadvantaged groups, evidenced by more frequent smoking and the consumption of greater quantities of nicotine per cigarette.[129] The association between smoking and socioeconomic disadvantage is also evident in the U.S. where smoking rates are negatively correlated with income. More than one in five Americans living in households with annual incomes lower than US$35,000 smoked in 2020, compared to one in ten living in households with income between $75,000 and $100,000, and fewer than one in 16 with household incomes above $100,000.[130,131] As in the U.K., "blue-collar" workers (those in manual occupations such as agriculture, manufacturing, construction, mining, or maintenance) have been found to be less likely to quit relative to "white-collar" workers (those in occupations including management, administration, sales, law, business, medicine, etc.). The former group also tends to start smoking at a younger age and smoke more heavily.[132] Exposure to second-hand smoke is also higher among lower-income Americans. This may be explained, at least in part, by the fact that historically, smoke-free work environments have been more common for white-collar occupations than blue-collar ones.[117] Moreover, because people tend to live with others of similar socioeconomic status and smoking is more common in lower SES communities, it stands to reason that non-smokers from lower SES would be more likely than non-smokers from other backgrounds to be exposed to second-hand smoke at home. Indeed, data for 2017–2018 show that Americans living below the poverty line were more than twice as likely as all others to be exposed to second-hand smoke.[133]

In Japan too, smoking is more common among those with lower incomes. A 2005 study[134] found that men from the highest income quartile were only 60% as likely to smoke as men from the lowest income quartile. For women, the comparable figure was 29%. And in South Korea, among both men and women, smoking is correlated with income: Data from 1999–2016 shows that, consistently, for both men and women, higher earners are significantly less likely to smoke than lower earners.[135] Similar findings have been reported in Brazil,[136] China, Ghana, India, and South Africa.[137]

However, the concentration of smoking among a nation's poor is by no means universal. A 2021 study of socioeconomic status and tobacco consumption in Low and Middle-Income Countries (LMICs and MICs) found that in Russia, and Mexico, current smoking is actually concentrated among the wealthy.[137] Another study found that smoking was also concentrated among the wealthy in Georgia, Mexico, and Mauritania.[138]

Other studies have documented gender differences in the socioeconomic disparities related to smoking. A 2018 study of Jordan, Lebanon, Syria, and Palestine using national cross-sectional survey data found that in Jordan, Syria, and Palestine only the richest men were less likely to smoke, while in Lebanon there is a strong negative association between income and smoking prevalence, regardless of gender. Conversely, among women in Syria and Jordan, the wealthiest women are more likely to smoke than less affluent counterparts, whereas in Lebanon, the wealthiest women exhibit the lowest smoking prevalence.[139] In Europe, current smoking appears to be more prevalent among poorer women, while in Southeast Asia and the Western Pacific, wealthier women smoked more.[138] There is also evidence that the socioeconomic disparities in smoking may themselves be concentrated among the lowest income countries.[140] Collectively, these studies suggest that the relationship between socioeconomic status and smoking in poorer countries is heterogeneous and may be different among LMICs to the prevailing trends evident in wealthier nations. Perhaps, just as different nations may be at different phases of the tobacco epidemic, different sub-national-level social groups may also be at different points in the chronology leading to differences between genders and income levels for smokers within a single national context.

Understanding *that* lower SES individuals smoke more[141] is not synonymous with understanding *why* they continue to smoke at higher rates. The influences on smoking behavior are numerous and include macro-level influences of policies, economics, law, and media; meso-level influences such as environmental considerations of occupation and education and neighborhood (product availability, consumption cues, etc.); micro-level influences such as familial and fraternal relationships and finally at the individual level, knowledge beliefs and attitudes, personal values, conceptions of self-identity, psychology, and physiology. These different levels of influence interact with each other, but crucially the combination of all of these influences affects different communities and even different individuals differently. An examination of how knowledge beliefs and attitudes, behavioral conditioning, and social and environmental factors may contribute to nicotine dependence[142] may be helpful.

Many smokers cite stress management as a leading motivation for smoking.[143] Individuals from lower SES communities may be more likely to experience stress[144] be it financial, social or trauma-related. COVID-19 provides a recent example of how the experience of stress brought on by existential threat, social isolation, and economic hardship may have increased smoking among those worst affected.[145] In fact, the past-year prevalence of quitting attempts in the U.S. experienced a year-on-year drop from 2019–2020 (65.2% to 63.2%, respectively).[146] The use of nicotine may be particularly important among those with depression, anxiety, and other psychiatric disorders. It is evident that lower SES individuals are more likely to experience a range of mental health disorders,[147] although it is not clear whether this relationship is causal.[148] Stress exacerbates some of these conditions. Nicotine-dependent people may experience stress relief when smoking. The pleasure hormone dopamine is thought to antagonize cortisol—the stress hormone. But that is not to say that, on balance, nicotine helps these conditions—instead nicotine addiction may, on aggregate, exacerbate stress even if the consumption of nicotine is experienced as a salve in the short term. Smoking may exacerbate these conditions by exposing the smoker to additional health, social and economic harms that offset any short-term psychological benefit that nicotine confers. But behavioral conditioning nevertheless contributes to the perceived benefit of nicotine on stress. Although a person unaccustomed to nicotine will likely derive little stress relief from initial use, those accustomed to nicotine experience nicotine consumption as relief from withdrawal symptoms including agitation, restlessness, anxiety, and difficulty concentrating.[149] It is understandable then that, among initiated smokers, smoking quickly becomes associated with stress relief, and certainly once accustomed to smoking, withdrawal symptoms exacerbate underlying stress impeding successful cessation.

Social support[150] improves a smoker's chances of quitting. The resources enjoyed by wealthier individuals (disposable income and free time) may make accessing health information, behavioral therapy, and cessation aids easier than it is for lower SES smokers.[151] Indeed, a lack of economic resources has been associated with reduced odds of successful smoking cessation, even though lower SES smokers may in fact be more likely to want to quit (perhaps as a result of the burden placed on them by tobacco taxation) those that do try to quit tend to be less likely to succeed.[152] Tobacco use disorder[153] is categorized as a mental health condition, one which should be treated with medical products including approved NRTs, pharmacological therapies including Varenicline and Bupropion, and behavioral therapy. But barriers to access may inhibit the uptake of these products by lower SES smokers. Transaction costs may prevent lower SES individuals from accessing cessation treatments, even where they are available. Meanwhile the traditional public health focus on education and taxation and the framing of smoking as a dangerous, irresponsible, and unhygienic vice stigmatizes people who smoke.,[154,155] That stigma may encourage some to quit, but it increases the smoking-related harms experienced by those that do not.,[156,157] Though taxation is demonstrably effective at reducing demand on aggregate, and may even reduce socioeconomic disparities in smoking (if the incentive it provides is more keenly felt by those with less disposable income), taxes increase the harms placed on those who cannot or will not quit. Tobacco taxation also incentivizes illicit trade. Proximity to illicit tobacco markets, and a motivation to patronize them, are both concentrated in poorer communities,[158] off-setting to some extent the intended benefit of taxation and attenuating smoking cessation in these groups. Where law enforcement activities are funded on a local basis, economically disadvantaged communities may have fewer resources to spend enforcing tobacco control laws, leaving opportunities for violations to go unsanctioned.

Social and physical environmental factors operative in lower SES communities may also contribute to the concentration of smoking in that group.[122] Environmental cues, such as seeing people smoke, and seeing tobacco products advertised and sold reinforce smoking behaviors.[159] Not coincidentally, smoking rates are influenced by occupational and domestic settings: people who live and work with people who smoke are more likely to smoke themselves; a higher relative frequency of social ties to and interactions with other smokers may reinforce smoking behaviors.[160] At the neighborhood level, the persistence of smoking in a locale incentivizes the sale of tobacco products,[161] protecting smoking as a social norm. Further, Lee et al.[162] point to industry documents as evidence that tobacco marketing specifically targets demographic groups including those defined by race,[163] ethnicity,[164] mental health status,[165] gender,[166,167] and sexual orientation.[168] Product prices (both licit and illicit) may reflect local economic conditions giving communities where smoking is concentrated continued access to tobacco products priced at levels not seen in more affluent communities, further reinforcing smoking in communities where it is already concentrated. Conversely, a declining rate of smoking in more affluent communities reduces the incentive for the local economy to offer those products and makes local ordinances against tobacco sales and advertising more viable. Relatedly, in more affluent groups where a critical mass of members has quit, peer pressure may switch from reinforcing smoking to reinforcing quitting.

There may be an element of groupthink at work too. Like smoking behavior, quitting behaviors are informed by consumers' internal and external identities.[169] The recent decline in smoking prevalence has occurred when the middle and upper-middle classes of many nations entered a period of post-affluence in which, material needs having been largely met, consumerism was replaced with other values including a pursuit of purpose, quality of life, free time, and general well-being.[170] In that context, the emphasis on personal health can be associated with upward class mobilization. However, perversely, other socioeconomic groups may have responded by framing smoking as an indicator of own-group membership. For example, in the U.K., some smokers view smoking as a signifier of working-class identity and an expression of defiance toward middle-class values.[171] In such groups, smoking cessation may be framed as a betrayal of one's group.[171]

3.2 Education-Based Smoking Disparities

A negative association between educational attainment and smoking has been reported in many national contexts including the U.S.,[172] U.K.,[173] Japan,[174] Malaysia,[175] and Finland.[176] This is perhaps unsurprising given that educational attainment is a proxy for socioeconomic status, and fits with the notion that those with greater resources will have greater access to quality information informing health decisions.[177] The broader positive effect of education on health awareness has been well established,[178] and health education in particular improves understanding of the beneficial consequences of healthy behaviors, encouraging the same.[179] Meanwhile, it is also established that a lack of education may make people less receptive and less responsive to health messaging about smoking.[180]

The concentration of smoking among lower-educated groups has been observed since the mid-twentieth century,[181] and the evidence is overwhelming[182]: lower educational attainment is associated with increased risk of smoking initiation and, among smokers, heavier use, and reduced likelihood of cessation.[183] For example, in the U.S. between 1974 and 1985 a large and increasing gap in smoking status across education levels is evident. The annual decline in smoking prevalence among college is approximately five times greater relative to those with less than a high-school education,[184] and the education gap has since expanded further: By 2018, U.S. adults without a high-school education were six times more likely to smoke relative to those with an advanced degree,[185] and in some groups the gap may be higher still. In 2020, 32.0 percent of U.S. adult smokers aged 25 and older have no education beyond a general educational development (GED) certificate. Just 5.6 percent of adult smokers aged 25 and older have a college education and only 3.5 percent have a graduate degree.[131] While smoking rates are concentrated among less educated Americans, the odds of successful smoking cessation are also elevated among those with higher educational attainment.[186] Similar findings have been widely reported elsewhere. In India, a 2012 study[187] reported that the Odds Ratio (OR) of using tobacco was significantly higher among illiterate respondents as compared to the college-educated (male OR = 4.23, female OR = 8.15). In China, a 2018 study[188] found that those with high-school or college education were significantly less likely to smoke, compared to those with no formal education, and those that did smoke were less likely to be addicted. In South Korea too, smoking prevalence is lower among men and women with undergraduate or post-graduate degrees than those who have only a GED or less.[135] Studies from Brazil[136] Ghana,[189] Vietnam,[190] and Nepal[191] also report that the number of years spent in education is negatively associated with the likelihood of smoking.

There is, however, some disagreement about whether the effect is causal. A causal association between low educational attainment and increased smoking risk is certainly possible.[192] However, at least some of the education differential in smoking may be attributed to social and environmental effects in place prior to school entry. Thus, while Gilman et al.[193] find that lower educational attainment was associated with more pack-years of smoking, fewer quit attempts, a lower likelihood of cessation, and a higher risk of smoking frequency/intensity, other factors operating at the family level may contribute to the relationship between education and smoking behaviors.

3.3   Smoking Among Ethnic & Racial Minorities

As discussed, the origins of the tobacco industry were marked by colonialization and slave labor. In more recent decades, the tobacco industry has exploited the traditional and ceremonial use of tobacco among some indigenous populations, leveraging the autonomy afforded to tribal nations and exploiting race-based messaging to target historically marginalized racial and ethnic groups to promote commercial tobacco products and increase sales.[194] Since members of non-majority groups often face systemic marginalization in political, economic, and social systems, these groups may be "left behind" by programs and policies that are not designed with them in mind. Given this history, and the structural disadvantages these groups often face, it is especially appropriate to focus on the racial and ethnic disparities in smoking-related harms.

In 2007 the UN highlighted the need for nation states to improve their data collection regarding indigenous peoples. More than 90 countries are home to indigenous populations, accounting for approximately 5% of the world's population.[195] However, the data on smoking rates in these communities is often inconsistently collected. In some countries collecting and reporting community-level data by ethnicity is prohibited.[196] With the exception of Australia, Canada, New Zealand, and the U.S. there is often a notable lack of evidence on the disparity in smoking-related harms faced by indigenous populations. However, in these countries at least[197] smoking appears to be concentrated in indigenous communities including the Alaskan Native and American Indian populations in the U.S., First Nation's and Inuit communities in Canada, Aboriginal and Torres Strait Islander peoples in Australia, and the Maori and Pacific Islander communities in New Zealand.[198]

According to data from the Australian Bureau of Statistics'[199] National Aboriginal and Torres Strait Islander Health Survey 2018–2019, Aboriginal and Torres Strait Islander are almost three times more likely to smoke than the WHO estimated rates for all Australians. This disparity appears to be independent of socioeconomic background.[200] In Canada too, rates of smoking among indigenous peoples are significantly higher than background rates. Data from the Canadian Community Health Survey (2010–2013) report that smoking rates among the Métis, First Nations, and Inuit were 1.7, 1.9, and 2.4 times higher than among non-indigenous adult Canadians.[201] The disparity appears to be particularly pronounced among youth. In 2012 for example 11% of Canadians aged 15–19 were current smokers, but 31% of Métis youth, 33% of First Nations youth, and 56% of Inuit youth were current smokers. Canada's indigenous youth appear to start smoking an average of seven years earlier than non-indigenous youth, and the smoking cessation is also less marked in these groups.[202] The government of Canada connects these inequities to unaddressed legacy of intergenerational trauma stemming from colonial policies and practices including the reservation system, confiscation of lands belonging to indigenous peoples and their forced relocation, as well as the banning of indigenous languages and cultural practices, and the imposition of the residential school system.[203] The 2020/21 New Zealand Health Survey reports that the rate of current smoking in New Zealand was 10.9%: but, again, this masks a significant disparity between New Zealanders of European or Asian ethnicity (among whom smoking rates were 8.3% and 3.9% respectively) and Māori and Pacific Islanders, among whom smoking rates stood at 22.3% and 16.4%.[204] In the U.S., CDC data[205] report that American Indians/Alaska Natives (AI/ANs) have the highest current smoking prevalence of any racial/ethnic group: 27.1% of American Indian/Alaska Native American adults over 18 was a current smoker in 2020, compared with a background rate of 12.5%. According to the CDC, the ceremonial, spiritual, and religious role that tobacco plays in many Native American cultures may transfer to commercial tobacco products, affecting attitudes, beliefs, and behaviors around smoking.[206] The tobacco industry has used the traditional role of tobacco to market products to these communities.[207] Further, federal and state tobacco laws often do not apply on tribal lands, meaning that tobacco products sold on reservations are typically not subject to state and national taxes, which reduces costs, forgoing an opportunity to reduce smoking rates.[208] Data also shows that AI/AN people are less likely to be covered by smoke-free rules.[209,210] The higher rates of smoking among AI/AN people result in these communities facing higher health risks related to tobacco use.[211,212,213] Greater prevalence of smoking among indigenous populations relative to the general population have also been reported among the Adivasi in India,[214] the Austronesian minority of Taiwan,[215] and among the indigenous populations of Russia, Panama,[216] and Greenland.[217] However not all nations with distinct indigenous ethnic groups appear to host such disparities. In particular there appears to be no disparity between the rates of smoking among the Saami and the majority populations of Norway, Sweden, and Finland.[218]

In addition to the above, some countries that collect data on smoking rates disaggregating by race and/or ethnicity have found marked differences between sub-national-level populations. In England for example, in 2019, data from the Annual Population Survey (APS) reports higher rates of smoking among mixed-race adults (19.5%), relative to White ethnic groups (14.4%), Chinese (6.7%), Asian (8.3%), and Black (9.7%) Britons. The pace of change in smoking rates may also vary between different racial and ethnic communities. Among White Britons, smoking rates declined by 29% between 2012 and 2019, but the comparable decline was only 26% among Black Britons, 24% among Asian Britons, and 22% among Mixed-race Britons.[219] Meanwhile in the U.S., while rates of smoking are similar for Black and White Americans,[220] African Americans tend to be less successful in quitting attempts than other racial groups, and suffer higher rates of smoking-related morbidity and mortality relative to White smokers.[221] Smoking rates have also been reported to be higher among non-White Brazilians than their White counterparts.[136]

3.4 Smoking in LGBTQ+ Communities

Historically, much of the data collected on smoking prevalence has not been disaggregated by sexual orientation or gender identity. However, in recent years, some national surveys, predominantly in North American and Western European countries have begun to investigate smoking-related disparities between members of the LGBTQ+ community and heterosexual or cis-gendered majorities. Consistently, such studies report that Gay, Lesbian, Bisexual, Transgender, and Queer (LGBTQ+) individuals appear to smoke with greater frequency than heterosexual counterparts. This may be attributed to the unique stresses their sexual identification places upon these individuals,[222] driven by discrimination, prejudice, and homo/transphobia. "Minority stress"[223] has been linked to anxiety, depression, substance abuse, and suicide.[224] In the U.S., CDC data[220] for 2020 reports that while 12.3% of Heterosexual adults were current smokers, 16.1% of those identifying as Lesbian, Gay, or Bisexual smoked. Transgender and gender expansive (TGE) adults are twice as likely to smoke cigarettes than cisgender individuals.[225] LGB adolescents are not only more likely to smoke, but also more likely to start smoking at a younger age and more likely to exhibit a higher frequency of smoking relative to heterosexual peers.[226] Similarly in the U.K., ASH also reported that in 2019, Lesbian and Gay adults were significantly more likely to smoke relative to Heterosexual adults (23.1% Vs. 15.9%).[227] Smoking has also been found to be concentrated in LGBTQ communities in Sweden,[228] Canada,[229] Brazil,[230] New Zealand,[231] and Spain.[232] However, some studies have found that, after adjusting for

68   S. C. HAMPSHER-MONK ET AL.

other covariates the association between minority sexual identity and smoking disappears.[233,234]

3.5   Intersectionality

The literature also reports smoking to be concentrated among those experiencing physical[235,236] or mental disability[237]; psychiatric disorders, including depression[238] and anxiety;[237,239] Substance Use Disorder;[239] unemployment;[239] and homelessness[240]; social isolation[241,242] and a history of incarceration.[243] Taken together, while the categories and extent of the disparities vary by context, smoking and related harms are consistently concentrated among groups facing social, economic, and health-related disadvantages. In many instances, these disadvantages cooccur and may be mutually reinforcing, leading to the concentration of smoking, and related harms, in complex and inter-relating ways. Researchers have therefore begun to examine the intersectionality of smoking-related disparities. For example, according to Glover et al.,[244] "smoking cessation rates among rainbow communities are much lower for members who additionally belong to an ethnic minority group."[245] Similarly, a meta-analysis by Shokoohi et al.[246] suggests that the intersection of sexual orientation and gender/sex may contribute to higher rates of cigarette use. Other disadvantages including income and socioeconomic status[247] may further intersect with sexual and ethnic minority group membership, with implications for smoking and related harms. For example, in the U.S. recent reductions in smoking rates have been concentrated among highly educated non-Hispanic Whites, but progress has been slower both among less highly educated Americans in general, and among even highly educated African Americans and Hispanic/Latinos[248] providing further evidence of the effects of intersectional disadvantage. Thus, Glover and colleagues[249] conclude that intersecting disadvantages reinforce the association between socioeconomic inequality and smoking prevalence, suggesting the need for greater data disaggregation and for public health interventions to be more targeted to specific groups. The social justice imperative to address these disparities remains regardless of whether these disadvantages are causally linked to smoking-outcomes, or whether they cooccur with other factors which are the root-cause of smoking.

4 SMOKING-RELATED HARMS

The medical consequences of tobacco smoking have been increasingly well-documented since epidemiological studies established the link between cigarette smoking and lung cancer in the 1950s and 1960s.[42] By the 1990s, a causal relationship had been demonstrated between smoking and a wide range of cancers, cardiovascular disease, chronic obstructive pulmonary disease, inflammatory conditions, and metabolic disorders.[250] The diseases caused by smoking include cancer, heart disease, stroke, lung disease, diabetes, and chronic obstructive pulmonary disease (COPD), emphysema and chronic bronchitis, certain eye diseases, and problems of the immune system.[251] WHO estimates that smoking causes eight million deaths each year,[252] of which around 80% occur in LMICs.[253] Moreover, for every person who dies from a smoking-related disease, there are 30 more living with tobacco-related illnesses.[254]

Smoking-related morbidity and mortality impose huge costs both on people who smoke, and on society in general. By one recent estimate, the economic cost of smoking around the world exceeded US$1.85 trillion, or around 1.8% of global GDP.[255] These costs can be subdivided into direct & indirect, internal & external costs, tangible & intangible, and avoidable & unavoidable costs. Direct costs include the value of goods and services consumed as a result of tobacco use and related illness; indirect costs include the value of lost productivity from tobacco-related illness and premature death. Internal costs are borne by the consumer (consumers own medical expenses), external costs are borne by others, for example medical expenses incurred due to exposure to second-hand smoke. Healthcare costs and productivity losses are relatively easy to measure. These are therefore considered tangible costs. Other factors, including the loss of life, reduction in health, sickness, and pain are far more difficult to quantify economically. This difficulty often leads them to be underestimated, but these are obviously important considerations for welfare calculation. For the purposes of welfare decisions, it is also important to consider that there are both avoidable costs and unavoidable costs. Avoidable costs such as the health expenses to be incurred from the uptake of smoking in the future may be reduced by present interventions. In contrast, the consequences of former smoking are "locked in," and are therefore, to some extent, unavoidable.

As with so many aspects of smoking, the economic costs vary widely between national contexts due to differences in consumption patterns, regulatory costs, tobacco tax generation, income, healthcare costs, productivity, etc.[256] HICs, with relatively higher healthcare costs and wages, incur especially high tangible costs. According to one estimate,[257] in both the Americas and Europe, the total economic cost of smoking is 2.5% of Gross Domestic Product (GDP) whereas in LMICs the costs range from 1.1% to 1.7%.

There are also opportunity costs to consider. At the personal level, tobacco consumption expenses are significant. Of course, if the decision-maker is rational and well informed, then the notion of revealed preference from microeconomics indicates that buying tobacco is perceived to be the best use of those funds. However, there are reasons to believe (discussed later in the book) that consumers' purchasing decisions regarding tobacco are not fully rational, and in any event the thorny question of intra-household negative spillovers remains. At the societal level, enforcing tobacco regulations means that there is less public capital to spend on other areas of law enforcement. Land dedicated to tobacco production sacrifices an opportunity for food production or other uses. Tobacco cultivation, curing, and processing also produces waste and pollution from smoke generated in flu-curing, and from the use of fertilizers and pesticides in cultivation, etc. These pollutants endanger public and environmental health, not least by harming biodiversity, with key pollinators especially badly affected by pesticides. Meanwhile, clearing land (old growth forests in particular) for monocrop tobacco cultivation and wood-cutting for the purposes of curing tobacco contributes to deforestation, both of which reduces the ecosystem services that uncultivated land might otherwise deliver.[254]

5   Tobacco Control in the Twenty-First Century

5.1   Approaches to Tobacco Control

Since the 1960s, many governments around the world have adopted an array of increasingly robust policies and programs designed to encourage their citizens to quit, or at least reduce, smoking, and to discourage non-smokers from starting. These policies include, in no particular order, taxes, mass media campaigns, bans on advertising and sponsorship, minimum legal sale age restrictions, bans on vending machine sales, smoke-free restrictions, plain packaging laws, mandated health warnings, purchase size-limits, and flavor bans. The tactics, timelines for deployment and the stringency of these restrictions all vary between contexts, but a multifaceted strategy is evident. That strategy has sought to increase the public's awareness of risk; decrease the affordability, access, appeal, and acceptability of smoking to discourage uptake and motivate cessation; and support quitting attempts with pharmacological and behavioral therapies, as well as Nicotine Replacement Therapies.

5.1.1   Increase Awareness of Risk

Anti-smoking Mass Media Campaigns (MMCs) have been a hallmark of tobacco control in many countries since the 1970s. MMCs have used television, radio, print, and digital media, to educate smokers about the harms of smoking (both for the user and for those around them) and to encourage quitting and discourage uptake. Examples include the American Legacy Foundation's *Truth Campaign* in the U.S., and the U.K.'s *Stoptober* which was credited with generating an additional 350,000 quit attempts.[258] Between 2002 and 2009 the adult smoking prevalence in the U.K. fell by almost 20% and, according to one study, MMCs were responsible for 13.5% of this decline.[259] According to a report by the U.S. surgeon general, MMCs can be one of the most effective ways of changing attitudes to smoking, by evoking strong negative emotional responses.Large well-funded and sustained campaigns utilizing targeted evidence-based messages appear to be particularly effective.[260] However, the impact of MMCs is generally mixed perhaps due to variations in the type of message, format, and mechanism used.

Health Warnings on tobacco packages offer another means of communicating the risk of smoking. Text warnings have been mandated in the U.K. since 1971 and in the U.S. since 1965. Since the 2000s, the use of graphic pictorial warnings has also taken off around the world. As of 2022, 67 countries require graphic warning labels to cover at least 50% of packaging for combustible tobacco products, and 20 countries require those labels to cover more than 75% of the packages surface.[261] In the EU, the passage of the Tobacco Products Directive 2014/40/EU (TPD2) required tobacco sold in member states to have graphic warnings covering at least 65% of tobacco packaging after 2016. Studies suggest that both large text warnings and pictorial warnings improve smokers' awareness of risks,[262] and motivation to quit.[263,264,265,266,267] Pictorial warnings appear to elicit stronger responses than text-only warnings.[268] But it is less clear if health warnings actually succeed in reducing smoking at the population level, not least because other interventions have occurred simultaneously making it difficult to disentangle the causal effects and attributing them to a specific policy.[268,269] There is some evidence that pictorial warnings increase the likelihood of quit attempts,[270] though the evidence for pictorial warnings having a positive effect on smoking prevalence is at best mixed.[270]

Even with the health warnings in place, the design of tobacco packs themselves may be a driver of smoking by contributing to brand awareness and appeal. From the 2010s, several countries have adopted standardized packaging laws for tobacco products, mandating the use of specific colors and fonts and removing characterizing brand signifiers and logos in an attempt to make cigarettes less appealing. Australia became the first country in the world to adopt plain packaging in 2012. Others have followed, including France and the U.K. in 2017; and New Zealand Norway and Ireland in 2018. By 2022 plain pack laws were also in effect in Thailand, Uruguay, Saudi Arabia, Slovenia, Turkey, Israel, Canada, Singapore, Belgium, and the Netherlands. Advocates eagerly report that plain packaging rules appear to reduce the appeal of tobacco[271] and may even increase motivation to quit.[272] But, once again, while these outcomes are often cited to credit these interventions with success, there is less evidence that plain pack-rules contribute to the more salient goal of reducing the prevalence of smoking in the long term.[273]

5.1.2 Reduce Affordability

Relative to many other goods, demand for tobacco is quite inelastic,[274] meaning that the quantity demanded is relatively insensitive to changes in its price. That makes sense, considering that nicotine is addictive and that cigarettes are the main form for delivering it. As such, some dependent users will swallow the price increase resulting from taxation instead of quitting, and may not even be reducing their consumption much. Taxes on tobacco, as with other goods not produced in perfectly competitive markets with infinitely elastic supply curves, are not passed through to consumers dollar for dollar.[275,276] This means that the consumer may incur less of an economic cost than the architects of a tax intended. In some cases there is also evidence for "overshifting" whereby sales prices increase by more than the value of a tax, as can happen in markets where producers enjoy market power. In the case of tobacco manufacturers, it is claimed that overshifting of taxes for premium brands allows them to keep prices of other brands artificially low or to preemptively soften the blow of future tax increases.[277] These supply-side responses to taxation may reduce the reduction in demand that policymakers expect from a novel or increased tax.

Regardless, demand overall is inelastic and so taxation does effectively reduce demand for combustible tobacco.[278] Estimates for the price elasticity of tobacco vary, but a review of more than 100 econometric studies conducted in 2011 by the International Agency for Research on Cancer[279] concluded increasing the price of tobacco by 50% reduces consumption by about 20%, corroborating the World Bank's estimate of tobacco price elasticity (-0.4).[278] Many countries have successfully used price increases to reduce smoking. In the U.K., for example, a report by HMRC found that between 1982 and 2009, a 10% increase in the price of duty-paid cigarettes produced a 10% reduction in consumption, implying an unusually large demand elasticity.[280] However, the report notes that some of that demand merely shifted to hand-rolled tobacco, which was not taxed as stringently during that period. Similarly, in France, following a series of tax increases enacted between 1990 and 2005, cigarette consumption has halved.[281] Similar reductions have been noted in other countries adopting a similar strategy including South Africa.[282]

In addition to national taxes, many regional and municipal governments levy their own tobacco taxes. Taxes may be applied on an *ad valorem* basis as a feature of a product's price (i.e., as a percentage of the value of the sale), or on a specific excise base (i.e. on a fixed rate basis per sales unit). Value Added Tax (VAT) or Sales Tax may be implemented in addition to the specific tobacco levy. The value of tobacco taxes varies dramatically from context to context. Chaloupka et al. (2020)[283] ranked 185 countries based on, among other criteria, the total tax share as a percentage of cigarette prices. Only four countries received the highest score for tax share (those in which tax represented more than 75% of the price of cigarettes). Those were Andorra (79.34% total tax share, 75.03 percent excise tax share), Argentina (76.22%, 71.20%), Egypt (77.19%, 77.19%), and Mauritius (83.54%, 70.50%). But 45 countries, including many in the African continent, received a score of zero meaning that taxes represented less than 35% of cigarette prices.

Unsurprisingly, higher taxes lead to higher prices, and once again there are significant differences between countries: Chaloupka et al. also examined the price of a 20-cigarette pack of the most-sold brand in international dollars, adjusted for purchasing power parity (PPP) in 2018 and found the highest prices in Sri Lanka (about US$22.17),

Turkmenistan ($18.81), Saudi Arabia ($17.68), Singapore ($16.87), and Jamaica ($16.59). Conversely, the lowest prices were found in Paraguay ($0.80), Iraq ($1.24), Democratic Republic of the Congo ($1.28), Cambodia ($1.42), and Afghanistan ($1.50).

In 2018, the WHO reported that only 14% of the global population lived in countries where tobacco taxes made up at least 75% of the cost of tobacco,[284] moreover the WHO has argued that in many contexts, taxes have not increased in line with inflation and rising incomes, reducing their relative effect over time.[285]

The effect of price changes is also not uniform across the consumer base. As stated, price-sensitive groups may be especially responsive to tobacco taxation because they have relatively less spending power. Teenagers and young adults for example may be between two and three times more susceptible to taxation relative to older adults.[286,287,288,289,290,262] Since smokers who initiate use in adolescence tend to smoke more heavily and are less likely to quit,[291,292,293] reducing youth smoking is especially important. Lower SES smokers may also be above-averagely responsive to taxation.[287,294,295] To the extent that tobacco taxes are more keenly felt among some of the most important targets for tobacco control, taxation may help redress the persisting socioeconomic disparities in smoking. However, those that are unable to quit will be forced to pay more, reducing the resources they have for other things including healthcare, nutrition, and education. Thus, one of the concerns raised about tobacco taxes is that they are regressive.[296] That regressivity has also been justified by appealing to the welfare gains that are experienced by groups in which higher taxation prompts smoking cessation.[297] Another concern is that, while taxes may encourage some users to quit, they also steer demand, or some portion of it, to the illicit market[298] bringing about other harms which will be discussed in Volume II, Chapter 3.

5.1.3 Reduce Acceptability

In addition to reducing the affordability of smoking, tobacco control has also sought to reduce the social acceptability of smoking, leveraging social stigma as a tool to discourage smoking. This strategy has been especially important given the evidence that smoking not only harms the direct use, but those in their vicinity. Smoke-free laws are now commonplace throughout the world.[299] At least 93 countries have some restrictions on smoking in indoor workplaces, and many others have enacted smoke-free laws in specific settings such as educational and healthcare facilities, hospitality venues, and public transport. Most smoke-free laws, however, are relatively recent developments.[300] The stated aim of the smoke-free laws was to protect the non-smoking public from the well-documented harms of second-hand smoke.[301] To this end at least the bans, where enforced, appear to be effective. Following the U.S.' comprehensive smoke-free laws in 2006–2007 reported reductions in exposure of second-hand smoke by hospitality workers declined by up to 93%.[302] Smoke-free legislation in the U.K. also appears to have reduced children's exposure to second-hand smoke by almost 80%[303] and, as a consequence, significant reductions in prenatal mortality, and childhood asthma hospital admissions have been reported.[304,305,306,307] The law also appears to have incentivized smokers to quit. Data from the Smoking Toolkit Study reports that an additional 300,000 quit attempts were stimulated in England by the ban.[308] Similar observations have been made in Scotland.[309] However the evidence that the ban actually resulted in reduced smoking prevalence is less clear.[310]

5.1.4   Reduce Appeal

Several policies, including advertising bans, marketing restrictions, prohibitions on promotions and sponsorships and bans on product placements have been designed to reduce the appeal of smoking. Advertising bans have been a central component of tobacco control in many countries since the 1960s. In the U.K., for example, advertising tobacco products on television was banned in 1965, and in the EU in 1989. The U.K. also banned print media and billboard advertising as well as sponsorship in 2003. A report by the U.S. surgeon[311] general describes a causal relationship between advertising and promotion and the uptake of smoking in young people. Banning advertising reduces the desirability of smoking, reducing both the uptake by young people and consumption of adults. According to the World Bank, comprehensive advertising bans may reduce smoking by up to 7%.[286] The adoption of comprehensive ad bans in Norway, Finland, and France appears to have resulted in a significant reduction in the sale of tobacco products.[312] Point-of-sale promotions and product displays have been exempted from advertising bans in several contexts. Today only 33 countries explicitly ban all POS displays.[313] Studies have concluded that exposure to point-of-sale promotions increases smoking.[314] Studies from Iceland and Ireland are among those suggesting that closing this loophole helps de-normalize smoking.[315] Product placement in films, TV programs, and computer games remains one of the least controlled areas of tobacco advertising. Product placement models smoking behaviors to consumers of these media.[316]

Several countries including the U.S., U.K., Canada, Brazil, and EU have banned the use of characterizing flavors in combustible cigarettes which increase the product's appeal, especially to uninitiated users.[317] Menthol was typically exempt from many flavor bans, but in recent years the U.K., Canada, Brazil, Ethiopia, Senegal, and the EU, extended their flavor bans to include Menthol. And in August 2022, the U.S. FDA announced a new product standard that would prohibit menthol in cigarettes and cigars, closing a loop which had been left open by the exemption in the 2009 Tobacco Control Act.[318] Also in 2022, the FDA announced its intention to reduce the nicotine content of cigarettes.[318] To date, no country has adopted a Very Low Nicotine Content (VLNC) standard so it remains to be seen how consumers will respond. The FDA, in 2018, projected[319] that a potential nicotine limit could prevent 33 million from becoming regular smokers, drastically reducing the smoking rate and saving more than 8 million lives. However, concerns have also been raised that the VLNC rule might lull smokers into a false sense of security. Many smokers falsely believe that smoking VLNC cigarettes would be less likely to cause cancer than traditional cigarettes,[320] and fears have been raised that smokers might even increase smoking in compensatory response.[321] Some survey respondents have reported that they would be less likely to quit following the implementation of a VLNC product standard, believing (falsely) that the compliant products would be less dangerous.[322] There are also concerns that the removal of nicotine from cigarettes would create an unmanageable illicit market frequented by those unwilling to quit or switch to a regulated nicotine product.[323]

5.1.5 Reduce Access to Tobacco

Age limits for tobacco sales or purchases have been in effect, in some locales, for over 100 years. Today very few countries allow sales of tobacco products to minors.[324] Increasing the minimum age at which tobacco may be purchased has been demonstrated to reduce smoking among teenagers. For example, in the U.K., the age restriction was raised from 16 to 18 in 2007, and was associated with a steep decline in smoking among 11–15 year olds[325] and 16–17 year olds.[326] However, the effects of minimum legal sales age (MLSA) restrictions vary with enforcement,[327,328] and proxy purchasing and illicit sales to minors undermine efficacy.[329,330] Other attempts and suggestions to reduce access to tobacco include prohibitions on vending machines,[331] limits on pack sizes,[332] and prohibitions on the sale of individual cigarettes.[333]

5.1.6 Support Cessation

In addition to discouraging uptake, and encouraging cessation, various efforts have been made to increase the success rates of quitting attempts, including the provision of behavioral therapies and psychological support; pharmacotherapies and Nicotine Replacement Therapies. A global smoking cessation landscape analysis performed in 2018 found 89 distinct cessation aids (including NRT, non-medically licensed nicotine products, and services such as acupuncture, hypnotherapy, quitting competitions, health-care provider advice, and self-help).[334] The scientific literature concerning the efficacy of all forms of cessation aids is covered in Volume II, Chapter 2, and in the Appendix summarizing the Cochrane reviews on smoking cessation interventions; here they are only briefly introduced.

5.1.7 Behavioral Therapies and Support

Examples of behavioral therapy include advice from healthcare professionals, telephone quit lines, online counseling, and in-person one-to-one or group-based counselling. Collectively these services are referred to as Stop Smoking Services (SSS). The U.K. was an early adopter of SSS, making them available on the National Health Service (NHS) nationwide in 2000–2001.[335] An investigation into the efficacy of English Stop Smoking Services in 2010[336] found that four weeks after treatment, 53% of clients were recorded as CO-validated quitters. However, at 12 months, only 14.6% of clients were CO-validated as abstinent. More recent evaluations of smoking cessation interventions have confirmed over time, significant proportions of those who are initially successful quitters relapse.[337] The study also identifies nuances in the efficacy of SSS: group interventions appear to be more effective than one-to-one interventions; the intensity of the intervention also appears to be integral to its effectiveness (although it may act in conjunction with other specific service characteristics); older smokers are more likely to quit successfully than young smokers; and men appear to be more successful at quitting than women, despite the fact that more women engage the smoking cessation services. The literature also highlights that barriers to accessing smoking cessation services including factors such as cost, timing, lack of childcare, lack of appropriate information, perceived ineffectiveness, and negative publicity impede utilization and subsequent real-world effectiveness of stop smoking services.[338]

5.1.8 *Pharmacotherapies*

The efficacy of behavioral support for smoking cessation appears to be increased by the concurrent use of pharmacological therapies such as varenicline (Chantix/Champix) and bupropion (Zyban/Wellbutrin). According to a 2021 evidence synthesis by the U.S. Agency for Healthcare Research and Quality,[339] the use of a combination of pharmacotherapy and behavioral interventions increases smoking abstinence by 83 percent among adults compared with groups receiving the usual minimal support. However, varenicline is generally considered to be more effective than bupropion. Many studies suggest that using pharmacotherapies helps smokers to achieve cessation. However, the success rate of unassisted quitting attempts is well below 10%,[340] so even doubling the baseline success rate (about what is found for varenicline) leaves most attempts by far failing. Furthermore, the use of pharmacotherapies is relatively uncommon,[341] and so altogether the effect of pharmacotherapies at the population level is disappointing. Even in the U.K., where such products are available on the NHS, the estimated effect on smoking prevalence for which NHS SSS is responsible is 0.1–0.3% above the background rate.[342,343] Young smokers, in particular, appear to be less likely to use pharmacotherapies,[344] and there is evidence that even when they are used by this population, success rates are especially disappointing.[345]

5.1.9 *Nicotine Replacement Therapies*

Nicotine replacement therapies (NRTs) represent another branch of support for smoking cessation. In the U.S., the Food and Drug Administration (FDA) has approved five such NRTs, including nicotine patch, gum, lozenge, inhaler and nasal spray, alongside the two pharmacotherapies discussed above.[346] Outside of the U.S., nicotine sublingual tablets and nicotine mouth spray (Nicorette Quickmist) may also be available.[347] Thus, compared with quitters in the U.S., those in the U.K. have greater access to a wider choice of NRTs, including mouth spray (Nicorette Quickmist) and an inhaler (Voke) licensed for general sales by the MHRA.

To the casual observer there seems to be a reasonably diverse range of cessation aids. However, while 70% of smokers report wanting to quit, and upwards of 50% may try to in a given year, most attempts do not make use of available treatments.[348] Among U.S. smokers who make a quit attempt, only 29.1% use NRT, only 7.9% use varenicline, and 2.4% use bupropion.[349] And for those who do use these products, the resulting abstinence rates are, though an improvement on unassisted quitting, still not spectacular; as the evidence discussed in Volume II, Chapter 2 shows, the use of cessation supports is associated with at most a doubling of the chances of long-term abstinence relative to "cold turkey." These data suggest that the needs of many people, even those who are motivated to quit smoking, are not currently met by traditional support.

NRTs may be especially inadequate for some key groups including, for example, women who smoke during pregnancy. Even in places such as the U,K. where a wide range of tobacco control measures have already been implemented, rates of smoking by expectant mothers often remain high. In this group especially, disappointingly low uptake and success of smoking cessation treatments remains a particularly urgent problem,[350] and there is limited clinical trial data on the safety of some valuable pharmacotherapies (varenicline for example) in this context.[351] Fears about side effects, and the high failure rate may impede uptake of NRTs. Most smoking cessation medications have an efficacy of under 20% at six months,[352] though varenicline is slightly higher. However, compared to NRT or bupropion, varenicline may be associated with higher incidence of some side effects such as nausea.[353,354] That could reduce the efficacy of varenicline by limiting the frequency and or duration of use. Studies have reported that significant portions of patients stop treatment early due to those side effects.[355,356] According to Patwardhan & Rose, clinicians prescribe varenicline for only 7.9% of quit attempts, thus "there is a "gap" in our current selection of smoking cessation medications," which is to say there is an urgent need for a cessation aid that is more effective and has fewer side effects than the current offerings.[352]

5.2 Policy Sharing and International Cooperation

While there are social, political and economic differences between populations which may limit the degree to which policy success may be exported between contexts, experiences from one group may still be instructive for regulators in others, eager to build on their neighbors' successes and avoid any unintended consequences. As national tobacco control gained pace, policy sharing has accelerated the rate of uptake of tobacco control policies, with "first movers" exporting their approaches elsewhere, and policy analysts simulating the effects of policies *ex ante*, based on the outcomes from one locale, prior to implementation in another.

International governance has played a major role in encouraging the uptake of "tried and tested" policies among nation states. The European Union (EU) Tobacco Products Directive (TPD) for example, sought to standardize, at least to some degree, tobacco control policies across European nations. But the best example of an international governing body advancing policy sharing in the realm of tobacco control is, of course, the WHO's landmark Framework Convention on Tobacco Control (FCTC). At the time of writing, 182 countries are signatories to the FCTC, covering 90% of the world's population.[357,358] Adopted in 2003, the FCTC, emphasizes the importance of demand reduction strategies, in contrast to many national tobacco control efforts focusing on supply. The FCTC recognizes that, due to global supply chains, multinational corporatism, trade liberalization and international trade and movement, tobacco is necessarily a globalized epidemic. In response, tobacco control efforts must also be international in nature. Signatories are committed to protecting current and future generations from the health, social, environmental, and economic harms of tobacco by implementing a framework of tobacco control measures designed to "continually and substantially" decrease the prevalence of smoking, and the public's exposure to tobacco smoke. In 2008, the WHO introduced a package of technical measures under the acronym MPOWER[359] guiding signatories' interventions:

- *Monitor tobacco use.* Data collection and sharing is encouraged to help study patterns and determinants of tobacco use and associated harms, to inform the design and implementation of effective strategies.
- *Protect people from tobacco smoke.* Comprehensive smoke-free laws are encouraged to protect non-smokers from harm discourage initiation by non-smokers and encourage cessation.
- *Offer help for those seeking to quit.* Tobacco use should be treated with more comprehensive behavioral therapy and pharmacotherapies including NRTs and medications such as Bupropion and Varenicline.
- *Warn about the dangers of tobacco.* The use of health warning labels and mass media campaigns is encouraged, along with the use of mass media to disseminate anti-tobacco messaging.

- *Enforce bans on advertising, promotion, and sponsorship.* Comprehensive advertising, promotion, and sponsorship (TAPS) bans are required.
- *Raise taxes on tobacco.* Signatories are called to use a simple tax structure leveraging specific excise taxes in a manner that adjusts for inflation and economic growth to increase tobacco prices.

In 2019 a review[360] of the global evidence on the implementation and effectiveness of the FCTC in its first ten years concluded that FCTC has successfully increased the implementation of tobacco control measures, with tangible improvements regarding prevalence, consumption along with other benefits following its implementation. According to one study,[361] between 2007 and 2014, almost 22 million premature smoking-attributable deaths were averted via the implementation of demand-reduction measures adopted by countries following FCTC guidelines. Moreover, more robust implementation of key measures outlined in the FCTC has been associated with the largest reductions in smoking prevalence and tobacco consumption.[362,363,364]

However, implementation of the FCTC has varied both between countries and across domains. Chung-Hall et al.[360] report "significant and rapid progress" on the adoption of comprehensive smoke-free laws (Article 8), pictorial health warnings on cigarette packages (Article 11), mass media education campaigns (Article 12), and minimum legal sale age restrictions (Article 16). The number of Parties submitting implementation reports (in accordance with Article 21) has also increased steadily. However, more moderate progress has been made on the implementation of tobacco taxation (Article 6), contents and emissions disclosures (Article 10), Tobacco Advertising Promotion and Sponsorship (TAPS) bans (Article 13), Cessation services (Article 14), measures to counter illicit tobacco trade (Article 15), and tobacco-related research, surveillance and information exchange (Article 20). Across these domains, the authors characterize progress as "slow" and "often limited [by] partial implementation": Relatively few countries have taken steps to protect tobacco control policies from industry interference (Article 5), regulate the contents and emissions of tobacco products (Article 9), promote economically viable alternatives for tobacco farmers (Article 17), address the health and environmental impacts related to the cultivation and manufacture of tobacco (Article 18), allow for legislative action against the tobacco industry (Article 19), and facilitate international cooperation (Article 22).

6 TOBACCO CONTROL SUCCESSES

Though the timelines and details of implementation vary among nations and (in federalist countries) states and provinces, jurisdictions with the most robust implementation of MPOWER measures tend to exhibit the most significant decreases in smoking prevalence.[362] Data from 126 countries collected between 2005 and 2014 demonstrates that nations that had put into effect three additional top-tier FCTC measures saw an average reduction of 4.71 percentage points in the prevalence of smoking.[365] In 2020 fully 150 countries showed declines in tobacco use, and 60% of these countries, representing 41% of the world's population, were on track to meet or exceed the target 30% reduction between 2010 and 2025 set by the WHO's Non-Communicable Diseases Global Action Plan (NCD GAP). Tobacco use is now only rising in six countries: Egypt, Jordan, Lebanon, Oman, the Democratic Republic of Congo, and Moldova (though a further 29 countries have insufficient data to establish a trend). Encouragingly, the reduction in smoking rates appears to be driven by both declining initiation rates among youth[366] and increased quit rates, at least in some contexts,[367] though, sadly, declining prevalence among older smokers may result from the premature death of many smokers.

The simultaneous implementation of multiple tobacco control policies and the myriad variables affecting smoking behaviors across populations makes it difficult to quantify the causal effect of a particular policy on smoking behavior in a given context. However, the literature generally concurs that taxes, smoke-free policies, health warnings, tobacco advertising, promotion and sales (TAPS) bans, and cessation interventions are some of the most effective strategies to reduce tobacco consumption and prevalence. Data form high-income countries (HICs) also speaks to the efficacy of mass media campaigns and restrictions on youth access. However, as Chung-Hall et al.[360] argue, tobacco industry interference, poor enforcement, a lack of more detailed guidelines to implementation and lack of financial support provide significant, if not always insurmountable, obstacles inhibiting more robust implementation.

Increasing the financial cost of smoking via taxation appears to be an especially powerful strategy for behavior change, and has been recognized accordingly by the WHO.[368] Price and tax increases are among most implemented strategy highlighted by the FCTC.[360] In low and middle-income countries (LMIC), a 10% price rise has been associated with a reduction in consumption of between 5 and 8%. The decline in high-income nations is around 4%.[369] Tobacco taxes have been associated with reduced consumption by continuing smoker, as well as increased cessation and decreased prevalence.[370] The U.K.'s HMRC estimated in 2014 that increasing tobacco taxes by 5% above inflation would reduce the smoking prevalence by 0.7 percentage points.[371] Tobacco taxes appear to be especially effective in price-sensitive groups, making them an important tool for limiting youth uptake and consumption,[372,373,374] and for targeting lower socioeconomic groups where smoking is concentrated, imposing a correspondingly greater health burden associated with smoking.[375]

Smoke-free laws have also been widely implemented following the FCTC, helping protect the public against second-hand smoke exposure. To that end smoke-free laws do appear to be effective. A 2016 Cochrane review[376] of 77 studies on the topic conducted in 21 countries found that consistently, the introduction of national smoke-free legislation was followed by improvements in cardiovascular health outcomes; in particular, reduced admissions for acute coronary syndrome were reported. Reduced smoking-related mortality was also consistently reported at the national level. Such findings are evident in the U.K., following the introduction of smoke-free legislation in 2007/2008, following which there was a marked reduction in hospital admissions for smoking-related conditions,[377] acute coronary syndrome in particular, as well as reduced mortality from smoking-related illnesses.[378] However, the Cochrane authors find less consistent evidence for other health outcomes including respiratory and perinatal health, and on the topic of whether or not smoke-free laws influenced smoking prevalence and other metrics of tobacco consumption the evidence was found to be inconsistent at best. Comprehensive public use bans may "de-normalize" smoking, leveraging social pressure to encourage reductions in use and, perhaps, cessation. A general reduction in consumption has been reported in England, following the introduction of smoke-free legislation, along with (albeit less significantly) increased quitting.[379] In particular, smokers reported decreasing consumption while socializing in public, and were motivated both by the inconvenience and conspicuousness of having to go outdoors to smoke and by the public disapproval that doing so attracted them.[380] Cancer Research U.K. has also reported that 20% of smokers directly credit the smoking ban with helping them reduce daily cigarette consumption and 14% of ex-smokers cited bans as having significantly aided their decision to quit.[381]

Article 11 of the FCTC advises states to include health warning labels and standardized packaging for tobacco projects, both of which have been associated with non-behavioral reactions (e.g. decrease in appeal). HWLs and plain packaging have been disproportionately implemented in high-income countries,[382,383] though evidence from lower and middle-income countries is sparser; a 2016 systematic review[384] found only two such articles, in India[385] and Brazil,[386] with findings similar to those of HICs. A Cochrane review[387] summarizes the evidence and, once again, the utility of the intervention is more pronounced with regard to non-behavioral outcomes (risk awareness, perception, etc.) as opposed to actual quitting attempts/successes. The former outcomes are also better studied. With regard to an effect on prevalence, the Cochrane review found only one report of GHW resulted in a decline in smoking prevalence and just 0.5 percentage points at that. The study was also judged to be of low quality. The Cochrane review also reports mixed evidence on whether GHWs increased quitting attempts or contributed to a decline in consumption at the individual level, and there were no studies investigating the effect on cessation, uptake, or relapse.[388] Such findings have led some researchers to conclude that, even where GHWs do increase "quitting cognitions" and "health concerns," additional measures would be necessary to reduce smoking behavior.[389]

Anti-tobacco awareness media campaigns (Article 12) have been credited with some success in curbing uptake, reducing consumption, and promoting cessation. A 2017 Cochrane review found that comprehensive tobacco programs which incorporate mass media awareness campaigns can be associated with reduced smoking behaviors in adults.[390] However, measuring the effectiveness of mass media campaigns can be challenging due to variations in the intensity and duration of the campaign, and the cooccurrence of secular trends and events influencing smoking behaviors. Positive associations have been identified between U.K. government expenditure on anti-tobacco mass media campaigns and increased success rates of quit attempts,[391] while the suspension of public tobacco control mass media campaigns in 2012 was associated with decreased demand for cessation support systems (quit-line calls and smoking cessation websites).[392] As discussed, anti-tobacco media campaigns were originally conceived to counter tobacco advertising. Marketing restrictions such as those described in Article 7 were credited with a 23.5% reduction in per-capita consumption of tobacco in a 2008 review of 30 countries.[393] Unfortunately, this remains one of the lesser-implemented articles.[394]

Article 16 calls on states to introduce minimum age sale restrictions for minors under the age to a minimum of 18. Today few countries allow minors to purchase tobacco and, in many countries, including the U.S., tobacco 21 laws prevent adults between 18 and 20 from purchasing tobacco. In 2015 a report published by the U.S. Institute of Medicine[395] concluded that a tobacco 21 law in the U.S. would reduce the initiation rate by 25% among 15–17 year olds, avoiding an estimated 50,000 cases of lung cancer and preventing 223,000 smoking-related premature deaths each year. The authors noted that a tobacco 25 law would have a still-greater effect though would be challenged politically. The U.S. adopted a tobacco 21 age restriction in 2019, hoping to discourage uptake among young people (the vast majority of smoking initiation occurs before age 21[396,397]). While age limits may make it harder for young people to obtain cigarettes, the ultimate effect of MLSAs is undermined by violations, social distribution, and illicit trade, and the effects of the laws can be disappointing and short-lived.[398] Accordingly, a 2019 literature review of 52 articles examining tobacco age restrictions reported mixed effects on youth smoking rates, with reductions highly dependent on enforcement capacity and activities.[399] U.S. data suggest that, as a consequence of the focus on youth smoking prevention, the age of smoking initiation has become older in recent years, emphasizing the need for additional focus on prevention targeted to young adults.[400]

Despite the adoption of the FCTC in 2003, interrupted time series and event modelling suggests that there has not been a substantial decrease in global cigarette consumption.[401] While per-capita cigarette consumption has decreased in high-income and European countries, event modeling reports that annual cigarette consumption has increased in low and middle-income and Asian countries by over 500 cigarettes per adult compared to a counterfactual event model.[402] Poor implementation, especially in LMICs where the majority of the world's smoking-related harms are concentrated has led to criticism of the convention.[403] Beaglehole & Bonita (2022) cite the slow rate of change in global rates of tobacco use, and the concentration of related harms in low and middle-income countries to argue that tobacco control is not working for most of the world.[404] The overwhelming majority of countries is not on target to achieve the target 30% reduction in prevalence by 2030.[405] Progress has

86 S. C. HAMPSHER-MONK ET AL.

also been too slow in addressing non-communicable diseases (Sustainable Development Goal 3.4).[406] Thus, the authors argue, "The FCTC is no longer fit for purpose."[403]

That assessment is based, in part, on the observation that both the WHO and the FCTC ignore the important contributions of non-combustible alternative nicotine products and the increasing evidence that these can increase substitutions away from combustibles. "The missing strategy ... is harm reduction."[384] Tobacco harm reduction can be defined as efforts to encourage those who cannot or will not quit smoking to switch to less risky alternative sources of nicotine.[407] But while harm reduction has been rejected by the WHO and the Conference of Parties,[408] it was explicitly enshrined in the FCTC: Article 1, (d) defined "tobacco control" as "a range of supply, demand *and harm reduction strategies* that aim to improve the health of a population by eliminating or reducing their consumption of tobacco products and exposure to tobacco smoke" (emphasis added).[409] Deborah Arnott and colleagues point out that the FCTC itself contains no prohibition on harm reduction but instead encourages FCTC signatories to develop their own regulations in line with their own laws, legal frameworks, and public health objectives.[410] Many of those may be inappropriate, as will be argued in Volume III, Chapters 1 and 2, but the prima facie rejection of Harm Reduction seems at odds with the FCTC.

Relatedly, there may be a case for revising the FCTC to better reflect the emerging evidence on the utility of Harm Reduction strategies, as has been suggested by Derek Yach,[411] who was instrumental in the original development of the FCTC. But that does not, in itself, imply that the FCTC should be replaced outright, or that the current convention would not be more effective with more thorough implementation, as Arnott and colleagues suggest.[410] Indeed, as this book will explore, the availability of safer commercial sources of non-combustible nicotine may complement many of those same policies, making them more effective tools with which to achieve target reductions in smoking prevalence and related instances of non-communicable disease. Before turning to the topic of e-cigarettes and their role in smoking cessation, it is worth exploring further why greater declines in smoking have not been achieved.

7 Why Are There Still Smokers?

7.1 Uptake and Progression to Current Smoking

Without new smokers, cessation and smoking-related mortality would eventually result in the elimination of smoking at the population-level. Novel uptake impedes the decline. Perhaps because tobacco control has focused on prevention,[412] declines in smoking behaviors tend to be concentrated among younger age groups.[413] The focus on prevention has a practical significance: given the addictive nature of nicotine, it may be easier to persuade a person not to start smoking, than it is to persuade them to stop. If so, prioritizing prevention may make for an efficient allocation of finite resources. But the focus on prevention is problematic, not only because it risks leaving the populations where smoking-related harms are concentrated with inadequate support, but also since smoking in older adults harms younger generations by exposing them to second-hand smoke and by modeling smoking behavior to them, perpetuating uptake and progression to current smoking.[414]

Young people tend to make up the vast majority of new smokers. In the U.S., over 90% of smokers tried their first cigarette before the age of 18;[413] Similar figures have been reported for Europe.[415] Youth experimentation, peer pressure, and in-home exposure (parental modeling) are among the main drivers of youth smoking. There has been a general decline in risky behaviors among youth in recent decades,[416] but experimentation remains, to some extent, central to the adolescent experience. Qualitative studies have highlighted the importance of identity construction and social factors in understanding smoking in young people; youth is a time of social and occupational transition.[417] Young people, with identities and related behaviors still forming, may be particularly susceptible to social conformity and peer pressure. An unwillingness to be left out is therefore a key factor determining experimental smoking in school-aged children.[418] Accordingly, in the U.S. in 2019, just 4% of early teens with non-smoking friends reported having tried cigarettes, compared to 35% of young teens with smoking friends.[419] The positive association between parental smoking and youth smoking uptake has also been well-documented.[418,419] Children are three times more likely to experiment with smoking if, in a two-parent household, both parents smoke.[420] As such, it is unsurprising that youth in communities with higher smoking rates appear more likely to experiment, and latterly transition to current use, perpetuating many of the historical disparities in smoking over time.

But parental modeling can be a positive force too: A Dutch study[421] suggests that the children of parents who successfully quit are less likely to subsequently smoke in adolescence. The downside is that, where quitting is concentrated in higher SES groups, parental modeling may leave residual harms concentrated in disadvantaged communities.

Recent research suggests that certain genes may make carriers more susceptible to nicotine addiction and to other chemical constituents in cigarettes, accelerating the transition from experimentation to frequent use. West et al.[149] suggest that genetic factors may account for between 30 and 50% of smoking initiation, and Vink et al. 2005[422] estimate that genetics may account for 70–80% of cigarette addiction. That does not mean that carriers of those genes will necessarily smoke or use nicotine, but rather that for those with such a disposition, the tendency to become nicotine-dependent may be greater. Research also supports the suggestion that smoking is associated with personality, in particular trait-impulsivity: A meta-analysis of 97 studies found a strong association between impulsivity on the one hand and smoking status and severity of nicotine addiction on the other.[423] A disposition toward novelty seeking and reward dependence also appears to be predictive of lower likelihood of cessation.[424] Those reward components are at odds with the known risks, hence the literature refers to cognitive dissonance; the experience of internally inconsistent thoughts, beliefs, and attitudes, such as the *knowledge* that smoking is dangerous and the simultaneous *belief* that smoking will not be personally harmful. The creation of rationalizing narratives may help smokers reconcile cognitive dissonance. "I'll quit before smoking damages my health," "Life is horrible, and this is my only pleasure," or "I've tried and failed to stop, so there's no use in trying again," being three fraught but common examples. These defenses deter cessation and impede engagement with available resources, especially if the rationalizing narrative involves justifying smoking today, on the promise that quitting tomorrow will be possible. Rationally, that belief contradicts the evidence that smoking for a longer duration increases smoking-related harms. But the human brain has evolved to give greater weight to what is happening right now than to potential future events. Future discounting, or present bias, may be explained by evolutionary psychology in terms of the tradeoff between growth and reproduction during hard times. Our earliest ancestors faced daily existential threats, so tough actions undertaken in the present were likely to fail to produce dividends in the distant future. Thankfully, most of us today have good reason to believe that we will survive long enough to profit from our present actions, and so have developed the capacity to incur discomfort in the present in pursuit of future benefit. But humans still grapple with the atavistic propensity, perhaps especially when they are under stress and feel there is little hope for the future. In the context of smoking, future discounting may lead smokers to ignore, or discount known future harms, even when those are understood at a conceptual level.

7.2 Barriers to Cessation

There are many remaining barriers to cessation, including dependence, the need for something more than awareness and motivation, a lack of substitutes that are both enjoyable to use and effective, shortcomings with current tobacco control efforts, perverse response to stigma, and the entanglement of the government with the tobacco industry in some countries.

7.2.1 Nicotine Dependence
Among the most important barriers to smoking cessation is nicotine dependence. Exposure to nicotine activates nicotinic acetylcholine receptors (nAChRs) in the brain, resulting in the release of dopamine—the pleasure hormone. However, over time, repeated exposure to nicotine reduces the body's sensitivity to nicotine, meaning greater volumes of nicotine are required to satisfy cravings. Meanwhile, abstinence results in cravings, characterized by accompanying irritability, insomnia, anxiety, headaches, and weight gain. Avoidance of these symptoms stimulates usage, perpetuating consumption which in turn reinforces smoking in a positive feedback loop ultimately leading toward nicotine dependence.[425] Nicotine dependence is, however, only a partial explanation for the continuation of smoking, since there are evidently millions of smokers who successfully abandon nicotine entirely, albeit not without considerable effort.

7.2.2 Awareness of Harms Is Not Enough
The logic that educating smokers of the risks would increase cessation is intuitive, and is supported by the evidence that marked reductions in smoking prevalence coincided with increased public awareness of the risks of smoking in the latter decades of the twentieth century.[426] The provision of tobacco-related health information has been hailed as a driver

of behavioral change, taking as fundamental the premise that rational, informed consumers would cease smoking. However, in nations as diverse as Japan,[427] Greece,[428] and the U.S.,[429] most current smokers exhibit a reasonably sophisticated awareness of the risks of smoking, even if they tend to underestimate the extent of those risks.[430] It is also noteworthy that some smokers actually *over*estimate those risks, yet continue the behavior nonetheless.[431] Ignorance of the risks therefore also seems insufficient to explain the persistence of smoking. And while for many smokers in the late twentieth century, simply learning about the risks of cigarette smoking was enough to encourage them to quit, that strategy alone seems less likely to pay dividends for many of today's smokers.

7.2.3 *Motivation Is Not Enough*

Perhaps, if awareness of risks is insufficient, additional motivation might help. As discussed, tobacco control has sought to motivate quitting attempts by making cigarettes less available, attractive, affordable, and appealing. Such policies do succeed in motivating some quitting attempts. And of those, a desire to quit is certainly a necessary component for success. Concerns for health, family, price, and peer judgment are often cited as principal motivations for smoking cessation.[432] But, like knowledge, motivation alone is often insufficient, as evident in the high frequency of quitting attempts coupled with the low rates of success[433] and high rates or subsequent relapse.[434] In the U.S., between 30 and 50% of smokers attempt to quit each year, but only 7.5% succeed in the long term.[435] Worse, the number of quit attempts is negatively associated with success: the more failed attempts one makes, the less likely one is to succeed next time.[436] Successful cessation therefore requires not only motivation, but also a mechanism.

7.2.4 *A Lack of Effective Substitutes*

In randomized controlled trials, pharmacological cessation treatment or NRTs used in conjunction with behavioral counseling have been shown to be the most effective method for sustained smoking cessation.[437] But, even the most successful behavioral support programs fail more smokers than they help. There are many possible explanations. For one thing, many support systems often have significant access barriers.[438] Levesque and colleagues[439] describe how health literacy, knowledge of the available options, trust in the provision of care, ability to physically reach support options, and ability to pay all inform engagement. Such considerations may be used to inform service delivery, for example by ensuring that available options are well publicized, staff are professional and non-judgmental, services are located in communities most in need and integrated with other healthcare services and, subsidized to the fullest possible extent. However, even with such dimensions considered, the medical cessation supports still require the smoker to frame their nicotine dependence as an illness, and require the smoker to commit themselves to a medical course of action, which many are unwilling to do. The available cessation supports also force people who smoke to embark on a course of action with cessation as an explicit end. That such programs require the smoker to make a private or, in the context of group therapy, a public commitment to cessation, and confront the possibility of failure is often a discouraging impediment.[440] Where commercially available, NRTs forgo some of these barriers, but the efficacy of these interventions is often undermined by insufficient or inappropriate dosage, early termination of use and irregular use.[441] Inadequate information on withdrawal symptoms, concerns over product safety, and unrealistic expectations were often cited as the reason for misuses of these therapies.[442] And NRTs offer a poor approximation of the aesthetic, behavioral, psychological, and physiological components of smoking, limiting their desirability and utility for smoking cessation (see Volume II, Chapter 2).

7.2.5 Shortcomings of Tobacco Control Policy

There are further reasons why traditional tobacco control might leave behind some people who smoke.

First, where authority for tobacco control is devolved to the regional or even local level, it can result in a patchwork of regulatory conditions. Regulatory gradients between neighboring jurisdictions create opportunities for consumers to subvert restrictions. This is particularly evident in federal systems. Notably, in the U.S., tobacco taxes are devolved to the state level. But a lack of standardization between states results in broad and significant variations across state borders. When one state has higher taxes, or more stringent regulations than its neighbor, demand migrates across the jurisdictional boundary. Thus, residents of one state subject to higher tobacco taxes, more restrictive flavor bans, or tighter minimum sale age restrictions can simply bypass these restrictions by traveling, in many cases, just a few miles. The silver lining is that this patchwork creates valuable data with which analysis can illuminate the degree to which, and under what conditions interventions are effective.

Second, a lack of enforcement capacity often renders tobacco controls toothless. In 2020, the FDA for example, has a total of over 18,000 employees nationwide,[443] but its Office of Criminal Investigations has only 300 agents as of 2016.[444] Today, most of their casework involves combating the opioid crisis, not enforcement of tobacco laws. This makes it difficult to detect a sufficiently high portion of violations so as to present a meaningful deterrent. Compared with other illicit markets, the sanctions for illicit trade in tobacco are often mild. A low likelihood of violation detection, coupled with relatively lenient sanctions may lead illicit actors to view prosecution as little more than a mildly inconvenient cost of doing business. In the absence of effective deterrents, there is little to curb the illicit trade which follows tobacco taxes and other policies that remove desirable product characteristics from the market place. Concerns regarding illicit trade in tobacco products (ITTP) have been dismissed as a talking point of the tobacco industry,[445] but it and its resulting harms are significant. According to recent estimates, more than one in every ten cigarettes smoked around the world is illicit.[446] But in many countries, including the U.S., ITTP may represent more than 20% of the tobacco market.[447]

ITTP denies the government of revenue, robbing it of resources used to fund tobacco control and offer cessation programs, products, and services. Globally, eliminating ITTP could generate close to $50 billion per year in government revenue.[447] ITTP also subverts the effect of tobacco taxation which reduces the demand for tobacco; ITTP therefore perpetuates smoking. Goodchild et al. (2022)[447] estimate that, in countries where ITTP represents more than 15% of the tobacco market (including countries such as the U.S., Brazil, Canada, Turkey, U.K., Mexico, and India) eliminating ITTP would be followed by an average reduction in cigarette consumption of 4.1% and an average reduction in smoking prevalence of a 2.2%. Furthermore, because illicit vendors have no incentive to conduct age-checks, ITTP provides young people a means to access to tobacco.[448] Moreover, while all cigarettes are harmful, counterfeit tobacco products have been found to be more so[449,450] and, relatedly, smokers of illicit cigarettes often have worse health than other smokers.[451]

The potential for ITTP to fund organized criminal organizations, often violent ones, is another concern.[452,453,454] There have been cases in which profits from ITTP have been used to finance terrorist organizations including al Qaeda, Hezbollah, Hamas, ISIL, FARC, and other terrorist groups.[455,456,435] Greater enforcement might seem like the obvious solution. But that too has costs: Not only is enforcement capital expensive, but enforcement against the supply side of illicit markets makes those markets more violent.[457,458,459,460] By raising costs, enforcement shifts the supply curve up, increasing the revenue that can be generated by those who are able to evade capture and prosecution. By "raising the stakes" supply-side enforcement incentivizes more sophisticated and more violent methods by illicit market actors eager to protect their interests. Further, enforcement is rarely solely concentrated on the supply-side. In an effort to reach the suppliers, law enforcement typically interacts first with the demand side, thus criminalizing individuals in the communities where illicit trade is concentrated which are often historically disadvantaged.[461] This contributes to the erosion of civil liberties, mass incarceration, police brutality and breakdown in community-police relations evident as a result of the failed "war on drugs."

7.2.6   Perverse Response to Stigma

While tobacco control has succeeded in stigmatizing smoking as an irrational, deviant, and unhygienic habit over which smokers have little or no control,[462] many smokers nevertheless find smoking to be enjoyable.[463] Smokers may find value in the increased concentration or lessened anxiety they perceive themselves to derive from nicotine use. They may appreciate the opportunity smoking provides to step out away from work or study and value it for the lubricant it provides for social exchange. While non-smokers may be reluctant to acknowledge such benefits, the inconvenience of the reality that many smokers find cigarettes to be enjoyable or valuable does not make it any less true. Given the subjectivity of preferences and benefits, perceived or otherwise, characterizing smoking simply as irrational is inappropriate. Ignoring smokers' own experiences and values not only insults the individuals who choose to smoke but, by doing so, alienates them from the medical and regulatory community which, in theory at least, should be trying to protect them.[464] Is it surprising that, having been ostracized, smokers are reluctant to listen to tobacco control advocates or engage their proffered services? The stigmatization of smoking may pay dividends by encouraging some smokers to quit, but for others, perversely, stigma may undermine smokers' willingness to heed medical advice and engage support for quitting.

7.2.7 The Nexus of Government and the Tobacco Industry

Finally, the role of the tobacco industry as a major player in tobacco policy design and implementation has been—and, in some cases, remains— undeniable. In many countries, government monopolies provided perverse incentives inhibiting policy to accelerate the decline in smoking. Even after these monopolies disbanded, many governments continue to hold stakes in the largest companies, such as Japan's Ministry of Finance which, in 2022, owns a 33% stake in Japan Tobacco[465]—the world's fifth largest tobacco company.

Even where there were no such monopolies, it has been argued that corporate finance and the revenue generated by the industry through taxation give the tobacco companies powerful influence over policy-makers and elected officials.[466] Industry capital also allowed the tobacco industry to spend vast resources to challenge policies in court that threatened their interests. In the U.S., tobacco industry interest groups spent over US$28 million on the federal level in 2020. In 2021, there were 236 registered federal lobbyists (individuals or groups), of whom nearly 80% were previous employees of the government who took advantage of the revolving door between industry and government; such individuals are likely to maintain contact with important decision-makers.[467] At the state level, Altria (formerly Philip Morris U.S.) registered over 300 of such groups spanning all 50 states, followed by Reynolds American with 201 groups registered across 49 states.[467] It is noteworthy, though, that companies' concerns over the demonstrated harms of illicit tobacco continue to go unheard.[468] Some consider these as protectionist claims made by the industry to prevent further regulation,[469] but the fact that such concerns are consistently dismissed is at odds with the claim that tobacco companies wield significant power over regulators.

This chapter has explored why smoking continues to be a public health emergency. Tobacco control deserves to be credited with significant successes, first in educating the public about the risks of smoking and the benefits of quitting, and second by motivating cessation via policies designed to reduce the accessibility, affordability, acceptability, and appeal of tobacco products. However, while these policies have all helped some smokers quit, they have not helped all smokers quit. Sporadic implementation of traditional tobacco control policies, a lack of enforcement, and the inevitability of unintended consequences (including illicit market activity) all undermine the efficacy of tobacco control. Moreover, while many former smokers have been persuaded to quit by policies that educated them about the risks of smoking, and reduced the access, appeal, accessibility, and affordability of combustible tobacco, the fact that smoking remains and that many people who smoke today exhibit a relatively sophisticated awareness of the risks suggest that these strategies may be less effective in today's smokers than they have been in the past. For many smokers, successful cessation requires not only motivation but a mechanism. Behavioral therapy coupled with pharmacotherapy and NRTs seek to provide this mechanism, and there is good evidence that they have value. However, once again, that there are some smokers for whom these supports are beneficial does not invalidate the evidence that they fail more people than they help. Perhaps these offerings could be improved: reducing the barriers might make these interventions more widely accessible. But access is only part of the problem: These interventions still fail three of every four people who use them. NRTs offer a poor approximation of the smoking experience, failing to replicate the pharmacokinetic, psychosocial, and behavioral aspects of smoking. To be truly effective a substitute must not only be safer but must also be equally or more enjoyable than smoking. The remainder of this book explores whether and under what conditions e-cigarettes might qualify for this purpose.

Notes

1. Tobacco EURO. Accessed 20 February 2023. https://www.who.int/europe/health-topics/tobacco.
2. Kozlowski, L., Henningfield, J., Brigham, J. *Cigarettes, Nicotine, Health: Biobehav Approach.* https://doi.org/10.4135/9781452232669.
3. Chute, A. *Tobaco.* London: Printed for William Barlow, 1595.
4. Coti, E.C. *A History of Smoking.* London: George Harp, 1931.
5. Kulikoff, A. Land and Labor in the Household Economy, 1680–1800. In *Tobacco and Slaves: The Development of Southern Cultures in the Chesapeake*, 1680–1800 University of North Carolina Press, 1986. pp. 45–77. http://www.jstor.org/stable/10.5149/9780807839225_kulikoff.6.
6. Trans-Atlantic Slave Trade—Database. Accessed 20 February 2023. https://www.slavevoyages.org/voyage/database.

7. Salmon, E.J., Salmon, J. Virginia Humanities. (n.d.). Tobacco in Colonial Virginia, Virginia Humanities Encyclopedia, available at: https://encyclopediavirginia.org/entries/tobacco-in-colonial-virginia/.
8. Nash, G., Roy Jeffrey, J., Howe, J.R., Davis, A.F., Frederick, P., Wrinkler, A.M. *The American People* Addison-Wesley; 4th edition. August 1997.
9. Sullum J. *For Your Own Good: The Anti-smoking Crusade and the Tyranny of Public Health*. New York: Free Press, 1998.
10. Despite (or perhaps because of) the ubiquity of the term "smoker" there are growing calls to abandon the term on the basis that it may perpetuate harmful stigma and negative stereotypes. Williamson et al. (Changing the Language of How We Measure and Report Smoking Status: Implications for Reducing Stigma, Restoring Dignity, and Improving the Precision of Scientific Communication, 2020) and Dr. Nora Volkow—Director of the National Institute on Drug Abuse—(Stigma and the toll of addiction, 2020) encouraging person-first language (e.g., "people who smoke") rather than commonly used labels (e.g., "smokers") to promote greater respect and convey dignity for people who smoke. Despite these well-meaning concerns, we do use the terms "smoker" and "smokers" in this book. By doing so, we do not mean to suggest that the act of smoking defines the identity of the individual. We prefer to show our respect for the dignity of individuals who consume cigarettes not by using the wordy and inelegant "people who smoke" construction but instead by devoting these pages to discussing how their lives can best be improved.
11. Gonzalo Fernández de Oviedo y Valdés. (1555). Natural History of the West Indies.
12. James 1st. *A Counterblaste to Tobacco*. Robert Barket London, 1604.
13. James 1st. *A Counterblaste to Tobacco*. Robert Barket London, 1604.
14. Bacon, F., Rawley, W. *Historia vitae et mortis*. Printed by Iohn Haviland for William Lee, and Humphrey Mosley London. 1623.
15. Mather, C. Manuductio ad ministerium. Directions for a candidate of the ministry. Printed for Thomas Hancock. Boston, 1726.

16. Goldberg, R., Mitchell, P. *Drugs Across the Spectrum*. Raymond Goldberg 13, Cengage Learning, 8th Ed. 2018. 1337557366.
17. Hill, J. Cautions Against Immoderate Use of Snuff. Founded on the Known Qualities of the Tobacco Plant; and the Effects it Must Produce when this Way Taken into the Body: and Enforced by Instances of Persons Who have Perished Miserably of Diseases, Occasioned, or Rendered Incurable by its Use. London: R. Baldwin and J. Jackson; 1761, available at: http://resource.nlm.nih.gov/2166041R.
18. Von Soemmering, S.T. *DeMorbis Vasorum*. Varrentrapp u. Wenner, Frankfurti, 1795.
19. Gately, I. *Tobacco: A Cultural History of How an Exotic Plant Seduced Civilization*. New York: Grove, 2001.
20. Troyer, R.J. Markle, G.E. *Cigarettes: The Battle over Smoking*. New Brunswick: Rutgers University Press, 1983 p. 34.
21. Green, S. *Smoking*. New London: New England Almanack and Farmers' Friend, 1836. pp. 25–26.
22. Shew, J. *Tobacco: Its History, Nature, and Effects on the Body and Mind*. England: G. Turner Pub Co. Stoke, 1849.
23. Lizars, J. The Use and Abuse of Tobacco. Philadelphia (PA) Lindsay & Blakinston, 1859, available at https://medicolegal.tripod.com/lizars1859.htm.
24. Ed. James Wakley. *The Lancet*, 1868. vol. 2, p. 642.
25. Welshman, J. Images of Youth: The Issue of Juvenile Smoking, 1880–1914. Addiction. 1996;91(9):1379–1386. https://doi.org/10.1046/j.1360-0443.1996.919137913.x.
26. Proctor, R.N. Why Ban the Sale of Cigarettes? The Case for Abolition. Tob Control. 2013 May;22(suppl 1):i27–30. https://doi.org/10.1136/tobaccocontrol-2012-050811.
27. Linder, M. "Inherently Bad, and Bad Only": A History of State-level Regulation of Cigarettes and Smoking in the United States Since the 1880s. University of Iowa, 2012, available at: http://ir.uiowa.edu/cgi/viewcontent.cgi?article=1001&context=books.
28. Smith, E.A., Malone, R.E. "Everywhere the Soldier Will Be": Wartime Tobacco Promotion in the U.S. Military. Am J Public Health. 2009;99(9):1595–602. https://doi.org/10.2105/AJPH.2008.152983.
29. Atlantic Monthly. (April 16, 1916:574,575).

30. Pearl, R. Tobacco Smoking and Longevity. Science. 1938;87(2253):216–217. https://doi.org/10.1126/science.87.2253.216.
31. Gardner, M.N., Brandt, A.M. "The Doctors' Choice is America's Choice": The Physician in US Cigarette Advertisements, 1930–1953. Am J Public Health. 2006 Feb;96(2):222–232. https://doi.org/10.2105/AJPH.2005.066654.
32. UCSF Center for Tobacco Control Research and Education. Smoke Free Movies, 1920s–1950s, available at: https://smokefreemovies.ucsf.edu/history/1920s-1950s.
33. See letters from Tiemann Helen, secretary to William Esty, to the RJR Advertising Department dated January 9, 1946. (Bates No. 502597537, available at http://legacy.library.ucsf.edu/tid/ijs78d00) and December 26, 1945 (Bates No. 502597519. Available at http://legacy.library.ucsf.edu/tid/qis78d00).
34. Smither, W.T. "Memorandum of Visit to William Esty." June 10, 1946. Bates No. 501889543. http://legacy.library.ucsf.edu/tid/guv29d00.
35. Reynolds, R.J. "How Mild Can a Cigarette Be?" July 1949. Bates No. 502471375, available at http://legacy.library.ucsf.edu/tid/nfj88d00; Reynolds, R.J. "How Mild Can a Cigarette Be?" July 1949, Bates No. 502598073. http://legacy.library.ucsf.edu/tid/ztr78d00.
36. Adler, I. Primary Malignant Growths of the Lungs and Bronchi: A Pathological and Clinical Study. New York: Longmans, Green; 1912, available at: https://wellcomecollection.org/works/zeh7vspv.
37. Hoffman, F.L. San Francisco Cancer Survey: Third Preliminary Report (Fifth and Sixth Quarterly Reports). Prudential Press, 1928, available at: https://wellcomecollection.org/works/p24qjef9/items?canvas=7.
38. Lombard, H.L., Doering, C.R. Cancer Studies in Massachusetts: Habits, Characteristics and Environment of Individuals With and Without Cancer. N Engl J Med. 1928;198(10):481–487. https://doi.org/10.1056/NEJM192804261981002.

39. Lickint, F. Tabak and Tabakrauch als aetiologischer Faktor des Carcinoms [Tobacco and Tobacco Smoke as Etiological Factors for Cancer]. Krebsforsch Z. 1929;30:349–365.
40. Gourd, K. Fritz Lickint. Lancet Respir Med. 2014 May;2(5):358–359. https://doi.org/10.1016/S2213-2600(14)70064-5. Epub 2014 Apr 10. PMID: 24,726,404.
41. Proctor, R.N. Commentary: Schairer and Schöniger's Forgotten Tobacco Epidemiology and the Nazi Quest for Racial Purity. Int J Epidemiol. 2001 Feb;30(1):31–34. https://doi.org/10.1093/ije/30.1.31.
42. Doll, R., Hill, A.B. Smoking and Carcinoma of the Lung; Preliminary Report. Br Med J. 1950;2(4682):739–748. See also: Royal College of Physicians. Smoking and Health London: Royal College of Physicians, 1962; US Public Health Service. Smoking and health: Report of the Advisory Committee to the Surgeon General of the Public Health Service. Atlanta, GA: US Public Health Service, 1864.
43. Royal College of Physicians. Smoking and Health. Pitman Medical Publishing Co. Ltd, 1962, available at: https://www.rcplondon.ac.uk/projects/outputs/smoking-and-health-1962.
44. Hammond, E.C., Horn, D. Smoking and Death Rates: Report on Forty-four Months of Follow-up of 187,783 Men. 2. Death Rates by Cause. J Am Med Assoc. 1958 Mar 15;166(11):1294–1308. https://doi.org/10.1001/jama.1958.02990110030007.
45. United States Public Health Service. (1964). Smoking and Health: Report of the Advisory Committee to the Surgeon General of the Public Health Service. Washington, DC: US Department of Health, Education, and Welfare.
46. Webster, C. Tobacco Smoking Addiction: A Challenge to the National Health Service. Br J Addict. 1984 Mar;79(1):7–16. https://doi.org/10.1111/j.1360-0443.1984.tb00243.x.
47. Parascandola, M. Cigarettes and the US Public Health Service in the 1950s. Am J Public Health. 2001 Feb;91(2):196–205. https://doi.org/10.2105/ajph.91.2.196.
48. Berridge, V. Post War Smoking Policy in the U.K. and the Redefinition of public health. 20 Century Br Hist. 2003;14(1):61–82. https://doi.org/10.1093/tcbh/14.1.61.
49. Cantor, D. Representing 'the Public': Medicine, Charity and Emotion in Twentieth-Century Britain. In Sturdy S (Ed.),

Medicine, Health and the Public Sphere in Britain, 1600–2000 London: Routledge; 2002. pp. 145–168.

50. Berridge, V., Loughlin, K. Smoking and the New Health Education in Britain 1950s–1970s. Am J Public Health. 2005;95:956–964. https://doi.org/10.2105/AJPH.2004.037887.

51. Letter from Ian Macleod to John Boyd Carpenter 29 January 1954. Ministry of Health papers.MH 55/1011.

52. National Archives. Ministry of Health papers. Paper to Mr Galbraith on smoking and lung cancer. 15 March 1960. MH55/2226.

53. Centers for Disease Control and Prevention (US); National Center for Chronic Disease Prevention and Health Promotion (US); Office on Smoking and Health (US). (2010). How Tobacco Smoke Causes Disease: The Biology and Behavioral Basis for Smoking-Attributable Disease: A Report of the Surgeon General. Atlanta (GA): Centers for Disease Control and Prevention (US), p. 2. The Changing Cigarette.

54. Department of Health and Human Services, Public Health Service, National Institutes of Health. *Smoking and Tobacco Control Monograph No. 13: Risks Associated with Smoking Cigarettes with Low Machine Measured Yields of Tar and Nicotine.* Bethesda, Maryland: National Cancer Institute, 2001.

55. UCSF Center for Tobacco Control Research and Education. How long has Big Tobacco bought its way on screen? available at: https://smokefreemovies.ucsf.edu/sites/smokefreemovies.ucsf.edu/files//sfm_ad113.pdf.

56. US Department of Health E, and Welfare. Smoking and Health: Report of the Advisory Committee to the Surgeon General of the Public Health Service. Washington, DC, 1964.

57. United States Congress, Public Health Cigarette Smoking Act of 1969, Pub. L. 91–222, Apr 1, 1970, 84 Stat. 87.

58. Bartlet, S.H. Health Education—The Cohen Committee, Public Health. 1964 Jul;78:248–251. https://doi.org/10.1016/s0033-3506(64)80030-5.

59. Ibrahim, J.K., Glantz, S.A. The rise and fall of tobacco control media campaigns, 1967 2006. Am J Public Health. 2007 Aug;97(8):1383–1396. https://doi.org/10.2105/AJPH.2006.097006.

60. Author's calculations of 2005 U.S. dollar values provided by Ibrahim and Glantz, 2007.
61. Koop, C.E. The Health Consequences of Involuntary Smoking: A Report of the Surgeon General, 1986 Corporate Authors(s): United States, Public Health Service. Office of the Surgeon General.; United States. Office on Smoking and Health. DHHS publication; no. (CDC) 87–8398; Health consequences of smoking. 1986. https://stacks.cdc.gov/view/cdc/20799.
62. National Research Council (US) Committee on Indoor Pollutants. *Indoor Pollutants*. Washington (DC): National Academies Press (US), 1981.
63. National Research Council (US) Committee on Airliner Cabin Air Quality. *The Airliner Cabin Environment: Air Quality and Safety*. Washington (DC): National Academies Press (US), 1986.
64. U.S. EPA. Respiratory Health Effects of Passive Smoking (Also Known as Exposure to Secondhand Smoke or Environmental Tobacco Smoke ETS). U.S. Environmental Protection Agency, Office of Research and Development, Office of Health and Environmental Assessment, Washington, DC, EPA/600/6-90/006F, 1992.
65. Institute of Medicine (US) Committee on Secondhand Smoke Exposure and Acute Coronary Events. *Secondhand Smoke Exposure and Cardiovascular Effects: Making Sense of the Evidence*. Washington (DC): National Academies Press (US), p. 5. The Background of Smoking Bans, 2010. https://www.ncbi.nlm.nih.gov/books/NBK219563/.
66. Royal College of Physicians. Health or Smoking? Follow-up Report of the Royal College of Physicians. Royal College of Physicians of London Pitman, 1983;0272797456.
67. ISCSH. ISCSH. Independent Scientific Committee on Smoking and Health. Fourth Report, HMSO, London, 1988.
68. Gulland, A. BMA Steps Up Call for Ban on Smoking in Public Places BMJ. 2002;325:1058. https://doi.org/10.1136/bmj.325.7372.1058/a.
69. Institute for Government. The Ban on Smoking in Public Places, 2007. www.instituteforgovernment.org.uk/sites/default/files/smoking_in_public_places.pdf.
70. Passive Smoking May Kill 30 People a Day in the UK. BMJ. 2005 Apr 9;330(7495):0. PMCID: PMC556050.

71. The "Frank Statement" was published in various periodicals, including *The Tobacco Leaf*, January 1954. http://www.pmdocs.com/PDF/2015002376.PDF, marked Bates No. 2015002376.
72. Oreskes, N., Conway, E.M. *Merchants of Doubt: How a Handful of Scientists Obscured the Truth on Issues from Tobacco Smoke to Global Warming.* New York: Bloomsbury Press, 2011.
73. Michaels, D. *Doubt Is Their Product: How Industry's Assault on Science Threatens Your Health* (pp. 3–4). Oxford University Press, 2008.
74. Cullman, J. Face the Nation, 1971. https://www.youtube.com/watch?v=VpwcF3Malj8.
75. Hearing on the Regulation of Tobacco Products House Committee on Energy and Commerce Subcommittee on Health and the Environment, 14 April 1994, available at: https://senate.ucsf.edu/tobacco-ceo-statement-to-congress.
76. Hilts, P.J. Tobacco Chiefs Say Cigarettes Aren't Addictive. *The New York Times* 1994, April 15, available at: https://www.nytimes.com/1994/04/15/us/tobacco-chiefs-say-cigarettes-aren-t-addictive.html.
77. This time, however, they were on firmer ground given the weak evidence base at the time. For example, the influential study mentioned earlier from the Environmental Protection Agency purporting to show the dangers of environmental smoke was savaged by a federal court for its "disturbing" cherry-picking of evidence to reach its desired conclusion. [See: Prieger JE. (2021). Smoke or Vapor? Regulation of Tobacco and Vaping. In Hoffer A, Nesbit T (Eds.), *Regulation and Economic Opportunity: Blueprints for Reform*. The Center for Growth and Opportunity, Utah State University].
78. Bero, L. Implications of the Tobacco Industry Documents for Public Health and Policy. Annu Rev Public Health. 2003;24:267–288. https://doi.org/10.1146/annurev.publhealth.24.100901.140813. Epub 2001 Nov 6. PMID: 12415145.
79. Perry, C.L. The Tobacco Industry and Underage Youth Smoking: Tobacco Industry Documents From the Minnesota Litigation. *Arch Pediatr Adolesc Med.* 1999;153(9):935–941. https://doi.org/10.1001/archpedi.153.9.935.

2 WHO IS (STILL) SMOKING? 103

80. Glantz, S.A., Slade, J., Bero, L.A., Hanauer, P., & Barnes, D.E., (Eds.). *The Cigarette Papers*. Berkeley: University of California Press, c1996–1996. http://ark.cdlib.org/ark:/13030/ft8 489p25j/.
81. Florida, Minnesota, Texas and Mississippi had already reached independent settlements with the industry.
82. Twombly, R. J Natl Cancer Inst. 2004 May 19;96(10):730–732. https://doi.org/10.1093/jnci/96.10.730. https://www.jncicancerspectrum.oxfordjournals.org.
83. Jones, W.J. Silvestri, G.A. The Master Settlement Agreement and its Impact on Tobacco Use 10 Years Later: Lessons for Physicians about Health Policy Making. Chest. 2010 Mar;137(3):692–700. https://doi.org/10.1378/chest.09-0982. PMID: 20202950; PMCID: PMC3021365.
84. Benson, P. Safe Cigarettes. Dialect Anthropol, 2010;34(1):49–56.
85. CDC. Smoking is Down, but Almost 38 Million American Adults Still Smoke. *CDC News Room*. 2018 https://www.cdc.gov/media/releases/2018/p0118-smoking-rates-declining.html.
86. Our World in Data. (n.d.). Smoking, Our World in Data. https://ourworldindata.org/smoking.
87. Von Gelder, K. Total quantity of cigarettes released for consumption in the United Kingdom (UK) from 2011 to 2022 (in billion sticks). *Statista*, 2023. https://www.statista.com/statistics/603 088/total-cigarettes-released-for-consumption-united-kingdo m-uk/.
88. Office of National Statistics. Adult Smoking Habits in the UK: 2021. https://www.ons.gov.uk/peoplepopulationandcommu nity/healthandsocialcare/healthandlifeexpectancies/bulletins/ adultsmokinghabitsingreatbritain/2021#:~:text=In%202021% 2C%20the%20proportion%20of,14.0%25%20of%20the%20popu lation.
89. Bondy, S.J., Victor, J.C., Diemert, L.M. Origin and Use of the 100 Cigarette Criterion in Tobacco Surveys. Tob Control. 2009;18(4):317–323. https://doi.org/10.1136/tc.2008. 027276.
90. Levy, D., Zavala-Arciniega, L., Reynales-Shigematsu, L.M., Fleischer, N.L., Yuan, Z., Li. Y., Romero, L.M.S., Lau, Y.K., Meza, R., Thrasher, J.F. Measuring Smoking Prevalence in a Middle

Income Nation: An Examination of the 100 Cigarettes Lifetime Screen. Glob Epidemiol. 2019;1:100016. https://doi.org/10.1016/j.gloepi.2019.100016.

91. CDC. (n.d.), GTSS Data Sources, Centers for Disease Control and Protection. https://www.cdc.gov/tobacco/global/gtss/index.htm.

92. GYTS examines patterns of tobacco use, cessation, exposure to secondhand smoke, accessibility of tobacco, exposure to marketing and use of e-cigarettes among school students aged 13–15 in more than 180 countries. The survey uses a standardized methodology to sample and select participating schools and cohorts, and process and evaluate data. The survey is funded by the Canadian Public Health Association, National Cancer Institute, United Nations Children Emergency Fund, and the World Health Organization's Tobacco Free Initiative.

93. Since 2000 the GSPS has documented patterns of tobacco use, as well as knowledge beliefs and attitudes of school personnel toward tobacco and monitored the existence and efficacy of tobacco control policies in schools. The survey runs in more than 80 countries.

94. GHPSS was developed by the World Health Organization, CDC, and the Canadian Public Health Association to collect data on tobacco use and cessation counseling among health professional students in all WHO member states. It is a school-based survey of third-year students pursuing advanced degrees in medicine and/or healthcare. Survey topics include prevalence of cigarette smoking and other tobacco use, knowledge, beliefs and attitudes about tobacco use, exposure to secondhand smoke, desire for smoking cessation, and training received regarding patient counseling on smoking cessation techniques.

95. The Global Adult Tobacco Survey (GATS) is a nationally representative household survey of adults 15 years of age or older, monitoring tobacco use and tracking tobacco control indicators.

96. While not all countries are included in the WHO's GATS, the WHO still collects data and produces estimates.

97. Note that the National Drug Strategy Household Survey (NDSHS) reports daily smoking—which likely excludes regular but non-daily smokers included in the WHO figure.

2 WHO IS (STILL) SMOKING? 105

98. Guidelines for controlling and monitoring the tobacco epidemic. Geneva, World Health Organization, 1998.
99. WHO. WHO Global Report on Trends in Prevalence of Tobacco Use 2000–2025, fourth edition. ISBN: 9789240039322, 2021.https://www.who.int/publications/i/item/978924003 9322.
100. The World Bank, World Development Indicators: Prevalence of current tobacco use (% of adults). The World Bank Group Data-Bank. https://databank.worldbank.org/reports.aspx?dsid=2&ser ies=SH.PRV.SMOK.
101. The World Bank, World Development Indicators: Prevalence of current tobacco use (% of adults). The World Bank Group Data-Bank. https://databank.worldbank.org/reports.aspx?dsid=2&ser ies=SH.PRV.SMOK.
102. WHO Age-standardized estimates of current tobacco use, tobacco smoking and cigarette smoking. Data by country. https://apps.who.int/gho/data/node.main.TOBAGESTD CURR?lang=en.
103. Note that while smoking is relatively low in India, the WHO estimates that close to 1 in 3 Indian adults uses tobacco, many in the form of smokeless tobacco products.
104. World Population Review. (n.d.). Smoking Rates by Country 2018, World Population Review. https://worldpopulationreview. com/country-rankings/smoking-rates-by-country.
105. Lee, C., Gao, M., Ryff, C.D. Conscientiousness and Smoking: Do Cultural Context and Gender Matter? Front Psychol. 2020 Jul 7;11:1593. https://doi.org/10.3389/fpsyg.2020. 01593. PMID: 32733344; PMCID: PMC7358448.
106. Hitchman, S.C., Fong, G.T. Gender Empowerment and Female-to-Male Smoking Prevalence Ratios. Bull World Health Organ. 2011;89(3):195–202. https://doi.org/10.2471/BLT. 10.079905.
107. Centers for Disease Control 2001 Surgeon General's Report Highlights: Marketing Cigarettes to Women, U.S. Surgeon General's Office, 2001. https://www.cdc.gov/tobacco/sgr/ 2001/highlights/marketing/index.htm.
108. Our World in Data. (n.d.). Smoking, Our World in Data. https:// ourworldindata.org/smoking.

109. Peters, S.A., Huxley, R.R., Woodward, M. Do Smoking Habits Differ Between Women and Men in Contemporary Western Populations? Evidence from Half a Million People in the UK Biobank Study. BMJ Open. 2014 Dec 30;4(12):e005663. https://doi.org/10.1136/bmjopen-2014-005663.
110. Eurostat. (2019). Tobacco Consumption Statistics, Eurostat, webpage, accessed 3 May 2023. https://ec.europa.eu/eurostat/statistics-explained/index.php?title=Tobacco_consumption_statistics#Level_of_cigarette_consumption.
111. These data predate the COVID-19 pandemic, which is now understood to have affected behaviors around tobacco use and smoking. Interestingly, surveys of tobacco use in the COVID era have found evidence that the pandemic's economic, social, and psychological effects have led to different responses among different groups: in some contexts, smoking has increased, perhaps as the result of a reduction in access to, or the provision of cessation services and (in some contexts) nicotine replacement therapies. The experience of stress, exacerbated by economic uncertainty and social isolation, increased free time and, in some circumstances, increased spending power could have contributed to greater smoking. Conversely, a focus on health, and lung health in particular, increased proximity to non-smoking family, and economic uncertainty could have encouraged others to quit or reduce use.
112. Nargis, N., Stoklosa, M., Shang, C., Drope, J. Price, Income, and Affordability as the Determinants of Tobacco Consumption: A Practitioner's Guide to Tobacco Taxation. Nicotine & Tobacco Research. 2021 Jan;23(1):40–47. https://doi.org/10.1093/ntr/ntaa134.
113. WHO Global Report on Trends in Prevalence of Tobacco Use 2000–2025, fourth edition. Geneva: World Health Organization; 2021. Licence: CC BY-NC-SA 3.0 IGO.
114. The Global Health Observatory. (n.d.), Age-standardized Estimates of Current Tobacco Use, Tobacco Smoking and Cigarette Smoking (Tobacco control: Monitor), World Health Organisation. https://www.who.int/data/gho/data/indicators/indicator-details/GHO/gho-tobacco-control-monitor-current-tobaccouse-tobaccosmoking-cigarrettesmoking-agestd-tobagestdcurr.

115. WHO. (2022). Tobacco Fact Sheet. *World Health Organisation*, accessed 3 May 2023. https://www.who.int/news-room/fact-sheets/detail/tobacco#:~:text=Tobacco%20kills%20more%20t han%208,%2D%20and%20middle%2Dincome%20countries.
116. Institute for Health Metrics and Evaluation (IHME). (2019). Cause and Risk Summary, IHME, University of Washington, 2020.
117. Jha, P. Avoidable Global Cancer Deaths and Total Deaths from Smoking. Nat Rev Cancer. 2009;9(9):655. https://www.nature.com/articles/nrc2703.
118. Jha, P., Peto, R. Global Effects of Smoking, of Quitting, and of Taxing Tobacco. N Engl J Med. 2014;370(1):60–68. https://www.nejm.org/doi/10.1056/NEJMra1308383.
119. Lopez, A.D., Collishaw, N, Piha, T. A Descriptive Model of the Cigarette Epidemic in Developed Countries. Tob Control. 1994;3:242–247.
120. Huisman, M., Kunst, A.E., Mackenbach, J.P. Educational Inequalities in Smoking Among Men and Women Aged 16 Years and Older in 11 European Countries. Tob Control. 2005;14:106–113.
121. This trends broadly matches E.M. Rogers model for the diffusion of innovation, see: Rogers EM. *Diffusion of Innovations*. New York: Free Press, 1995.
122. Östergren, O. The Social Gradient in Smoking: Individual Behaviour, Norms and Nicotine Dependence in the Later Stages of the Cigarette Epidemic. Soc Theory Health. 2021. https://doi.org/10.1057/s41285-021-00159-z.
123. Kock, L., Brown, J., Hiscock, R., Tattan-Birch, H., Smith, C., Shahab, L. Individual-level Behavioural Smoking Cessation Interventions Tailored for Disadvantaged Socioeconomic Position: A Systematic Review and Meta-regression. Lancet Public Health. 2019 Dec;4(12):e628–e644. https://doi.org/10.1016/S2468-2667(19)30220-8. PMID: 31812239; PMCID: PMC7109520.
124. Leventhal, A.M., Bello, M.S., Galstyan, E., Higgins, S.T., Barrington-Trimis, J.L. Association of Cumulative Socioeconomic and Health-Related Disadvantage with Disparities in Smoking Prevalence in the United States, 2008 to 2017. JAMA Intern Med. 2019;179(6):777–785. https://doi.org/10.1001/jamain ternmed.2019.0192.

125. Fisk A.S., Lindström, M., Perez-Vicente, R., et al. Understanding the Complexity of Socioeconomic Disparities in Smoking Prevalence in Sweden: A Cross-sectional Study Applying Intersectionality Theory. BMJ Open. 2021;11:e042323. https://doi.org/10.1136/bmjopen-2020-042323.

126. Sharma, A., Lewis, S., Szatkowski, L. Insights into Social Disparities in Smoking Prevalence using Mosaic, a Novel Measure of Socioeconomic Status: An Analysis Using a Large Primary Care Dataset. BMC Public Health 2010;10:755. https://doi.org/10.1186/1471-2458-10-755.

127. ASH UK. (2019). Health Inequalities and Smoking. *Action on Smoking and Health.* https://ash.org.uk/wp-content/uploads/2019/09/ASH-Briefing_Health-Inequalities.pdf.

128. Caleyachetty, A., Lewis, S., McNeill, A. et al. Struggling to Make Ends Meet: Exploring Pathways to Understand Why Smokers in Financial Difficulties are Less Likely to Quit Successfully. Eur J Public Health. 2012;22(suppl 1):41–48. https://doi.org/10.1093/eurpub/ckr199.

129. Fidler, J., Jarvis, M., Mindell, J. & West, R. Nicotine Intake in Cigarette Smokers in England: Distribution and Demographic Correlates. Cancer Epidemiol. Biomarkers Prev. 2008;17:3331–3336. https://doi.org/10.1158/1055-9965.EPI-08-0296.

130. In 2022, the average household income was around US$87,500.

131. Cornelius, M.E., et al. Tobacco Product Use Among Adults—United States, 2020. MMWR Morb Mortal Wkly Rep. 2022;71:397–405. https://doi.org/10.15585/mmwr.mm7111a1. Current smoking is defined as persons who reported having smoked 100 cigarettes during their lifetimes and, at the time of the survey, reported smoking every day or some days.

132. Ham, D.C., et al. Occupation and Workplace Policies Predict Smoking Behaviors: Analysis of National Data from the Current Population Survey. J Occup Environ Med. 2011 Nov;53(11):1337–1345.

133. Shastri, S.S., Talluri, R., Shete, S. Disparities in Second-hand Smoke Exposure in the United States: National Health and Nutrition Examination Survey 2011–2018. JAMA Intern Med. 2021;181(1):134–137. https://doi.org/10.1001/jamainternmed.2020.3975.

134. Fukuda, Y., Nakamura, K., Takano, T. Socioeconomic Pattern of Smoking in Japan: Income Inequality and Gender and Age Differences. Ann Epidemiol. 2005;15:365–372. https://doi.org/10.1016/j.annepidem.2004.09.003.

135. Kim, Y.N., Cho, Y.G., Kim, C.H., Kang, J.H., Park, H.A., Kim, K.W., et al. Socioeconomic Indicators Associated with Initiation and Cessation of Smoking Among Women in Seoul. Korean J Fam Med. 2012;33:1–8. https://doi.org/10.4082/kjfm.2012.33.1.1.

136. Garcia, G.A.F., SIlva, E.K.P.D., Giatti, L., Barreto, S.M. The Intersection Race/Skin Color and Gender, Smoking and Excessive Alcohol Consumption: Cross Sectional Analysis of the Brazilian National Health Survey, 2013. Cad Saude Publica. 2021 Dec 1;37(11):e00224220. https://doi.org/10.1590/0102-311X00224220.

137. Rossouw, L. Socioeconomic Status and Tobacco Consumption: Analyzing Inequalities in China, Ghana, India, Mexico, the Russian Federation and South Africa. Tob Prev Cessat. 2021 Jun 25;7:47. https://doi.org/10.18332/tpc/137085.

138. Harper, S., McKinnon, B. Global Socioeconomic Inequalities in Tobacco Use: Internationally Comparable Estimates from the World Health Surveys. Cancer Causes Control. 2012 Mar;23 suppl 1:11–25. https://doi.org/10.1007/s10552-012-9901-5.

139. Abdulrahim, S., Jawad, M. Socioeconomic Differences in Smoking in Jordan, Lebanon, Syria, and Palestine: A Cross-Sectional Analysis of National Surveys. PLoS ONE. 2018;13(1):e0189829. https://doi.org/10.1371/journal.pone.0189829.

140. Sreeramareddy, C.T., Harper, S., Ernstsen, L. Educational and Wealth Inequalities in Tobacco use Among Men and Women in 54 Low-income and Middle-income Countries. Tob Control. 2018;27:26–34. https://doi.org/10.1136/tobaccocontrol-2016-053266.

141. Hiscock, R., Bauld, L., Amos, A., Fidler, J.A., Munafo, M. Socioeconomic Status and Smoking: A Review. Ann N Y Acad Sci. 2012;1248(1):107–123. https://doi.org/10.1111/j.1749-6632.2011.06202.x.

142. Benowitz, N.L. Nicotine addiction. N Engl J Med. 2010;362(24):2295–2303. https://doi.org/10.1056/NEJ Mra0809890.
143. Nichter, M., Nichter, M., Carkoglu, A. Tobacco Etiology Research Network. Reconsidering Stress and Smoking: A Qualitative Study Among College Students. Tob Control. 2007 Jun;16(3):211–214. https://doi.org/10.1136/tc.2007.019869.
144. Thoits, P.A. Personal Agency in the Stress Process. J Health Soc Behav. 2006;47(4):309–323. https://doi.org/10.1177/002214 650604700401.
145. Rosoff-Verbit, Z., Logue-Chamberlain, E., Fishman, J., Audrain-McGovern, J., Hawk, L., Mahoney, M., Mazur, A., Ashare, R. The Perceived Impact of COVID-19 among Treatment-Seeking Smokers: A Mixed Methods Approach. Int J Environ Res Public Health. 2021 Jan 9;18(2):505. https://doi.org/10.3390/ijerph 18020505.
146. Bandi, P., Asare, S., Majmundar, A., et al. Changes in Smoking Cessation–Related Behaviors Among US Adults During the COVID-19 Pandemic. JAMA Netw Open. 2022;5(8):e2225149. https://doi.org/10.1001/jamanetworkopen.2022.25149.
147. Lorant, V., Deliège, D., Eaton, W., Robert, A., Philippot, P., Ansseau, M. Socioeconomic Inequalities in Depression: A Meta-Analysis. Am J Epidemiol. 2003;157(2):98–112. https://doi. org/10.1093/aje/kwf182.
148. Reiss, F. Socioeconomic Inequalities and Mental Health Problems in Children and adolescents: A Systematic Review. Soc Sci Med. 2013;90:24–31. https://doi.org/10.1016/j.socsci med.2013.04.026.
149. West, R. Tobacco Smoking: Health Impact, Prevalence, Correlates and Interventions. Psychol Health. 2017;32(8):1018–1036. https://doi.org/10.1080/08870446.2017.1325890.
150. Soulakova, J.N., Tang, C.Y., Leonardo, S.A., Taliaferro, L.A. Motivational Benefits of Social Support and Behavioural Interventions for Smoking Cessation. J Smok Cessat. 2018 Dec;13(4):216–226. https://doi.org/10.1017/jsc.2017.26.
151. Christiansen, B., Reeder, K., Hill, M., Baker, T.B., Fiore, M.C. Barriers to Effective Tobacco-dependence Treatment for the Very Poor. J Stud Alcohol Drugs. 2012 Nov;73(6):874–884. https:// doi.org/10.15288/jsad.2012.73.874.

152. Siahpush, M., Yong, H.H., Borland, R., Reid, J.L., Hammond, D. Smokers with Financial Stress are More Likely To Want to Quit But Less Likely to Try or Succeed: Findings from the International Tobacco Control (ITC) Four Country Survey. Addiction. 2009;104(8):1382–1390. https://doi.org/10.1111/j.1360-0443.2009.02599.x.

153. American Psychiatric Association. Diagnostic and Statistical Manual of Mental Disorders. 5. Arlington, VA: American Psychiatric Press (DSM-5), 2013.

154. Goldstein, J. The Stigmatization of Smokers: An Empirical Investigation. J Drug Educ. 1991;21(2),167–182. https://doi.org/10.2190/Y71P-KXVJ-LR9H-H1MG.

155. Stuber, J., Galea, S., Link, B.G. Smoking and the Emergence of a Stigmatized Social Status. Soc Sci Med. 2008;67(3):420–430. https://doi.org/10.1016/j.socscimed.2008.03.010.

156. Williamson, T.J., Riley, K.E., Carter-Harris, L., Ostroff, J.S. Changing the Language of How We Measure and Report Smoking Status: Implications for Reducing Stigma, Restoring Dignity, and Improving the Precision of Scientific Communication. Nicotine Tob Res. 2020 Dec 12;22(12):2280–2282. https://doi.org/10.1093/ntr/ntaa141.

157. Volkow, N.D. Stigma and the Toll of Addiction. N Engl J Med. 2020 Apr 2;382(14):1289–1290. https://doi.org/10.1056/NEJMp1917360.

158. National Academies Press. Understanding the U.S. Illicit Tobacco Market: Characteristics, Policy Context, and Lessons from International Experiences. National Research Council, Committee on the Illicit Tobacco Market: Collection and Analysis of the International Experience, 2015.

159. Piasecki, T.M., Fiore, M.C., McCarthy, D.E., Baker, T.B. Have We Lost Our Way? The Need for Dynamic Formulations of Smoking Relapse Proneness. Addiction. 2002;97(9):1093–1108. https://doi.org/10.1046/j.1360-0443.2002.00216.x. See also Rosenthal, D.G., Weitzman, M., Benowitz, N.L. Nicotine Addiction: Mechanisms and Consequences. Int J Ment Health. 2011;40(1):22–38.

160. Hitchman, S.C., Fong, G.T., Zanna, M.P., Thrasher, J.F., Laux, F.L. The Relation Between Number of Smoking Friends, and

Quit Intentions, Attempts, and Success: Findings from the International Tobacco Control (ITC) Four Country Survey. Psychol Addict Behav. 2014 Dec;28(4):1144–1152. https://doi.org/10.1037/a0036483.

161. Lee, J.G., Henriksen, L., Rose, S.W., Moreland-Russell, S., Ribisl, K.M. A Systematic Review of Neighborhood Disparities in Point-of-Sale Tobacco Marketing. Am J Public Health. 2015 Sep;105(9):e8–18. https://doi.org/10.2105/AJPH.2015.302777.

162. Lee, J.G., Henriksen, L., Rose, S.W., Moreland-Russell, S., Ribisl, K.M. A Systematic Review of Neighborhood Disparities in Point-of-Sale Tobacco Marketing. Am J Public Health. 2015 Sep;105(9):e8–18. https://doi.org/10.2105/AJPH.2015.302777.

163. Yerger, V.B., Przewoznik, J., Malone, R.E. Racialized Geography, Corporate Activity, and Health Disparities: Tobacco Industry Targeting of Inner Cities. J Health Care Poor Underserved. 2007;18(4, suppl):10–38. https://doi.org/10.1353/hpu.2007.0120.

164. Cruz, T.B., Wright, L.T., Crawford, G. The Menthol Marketing Mix: Targeted Promotions for Focus Communities in the United States. Nicotine Tob Res. 2010;12(suppl 2):S147–S153. https://doi.org/10.1093/ntr/ntq201.

165. Apollonio, D.E., Malone, R.E. Marketing to the Marginalised: Tobacco Industry Targeting of the Homeless and Mentally ill. Tob Control. 2005;14(6):409–415. https://doi.org/10.1136/tc.2005.011890.

166. Amos, A., Greaves, L., Nichter, M., Bloch, M. Women and Tobacco: A Call for Including Gender in Tobacco Control Research, Policy and Practice. Tob Control. 2012;21(2):236–243.

167. Morrow, M., Barraclough, S. Gender Equity and Tobacco Control: Bringing Masculinity into Focus. Glob Health Promot. 2010;17(1 suppl):21–28.

168. Stevens, P., Carlson, L.M., Hinman, J.M. An Analysis of Tobacco Industry Marketing to Lesbian, Gay, Bisexual, and Transgender (LGBT) Populations: Strategies for Mainstream Tobacco Control and Prevention. Health Promot Pract. 2004;5(3, suppl):129S–134S.

169. Tombor, I., Shahab, L., Herbec, A., Neale, J., Michie, S., West, R. Smoker Identity and Its Potential Role in Young Adults' Smoking Behavior: A Meta-ethnography. Health Psychol. 2015 Oct;34(10):992–1003. https://doi.org/10.1037/hea0000191.
170. Etzioni, A. The Post Affluent Society. Rev Soc Econ. 2004;62:407–420. https://doi.org/10.1080/003467604200 0253990.
171. Thirlway, F. How Will e-cigarettes Affect Health Inequalities? Applying Bourdieu to Smoking and Cessation. Int J Drug Policy. 2018;54:99–104.
172. Agaku, I.T., et al. Disparities in Current Cigarette Smoking Among US Adults, 2002–2016. Tob Control. 2020.
173. Sanderson, E., Davey Smith, G., Bowden, J., et al. Mendelian Randomisation Analysis of the Effect of Educational Attainment and Cognitive Ability on Smoking Behaviour. Nat Commun. 2010;10:2949. https://doi.org/10.1038/s41467-019-10679-y.
174. Tomioka, K., Kurumatani, N., Saeki, K. The Association Between Education and Smoking Prevalence, Independent of Occupation: A Nationally Representative Survey in Japan. J Epidemiol. 2020 Mar 5;30(3):136–142. https://doi.org/10.2188/jea.JE2 0180195.
175. Lim, K.H., Jasvindar, K., Cheong, S.M., et al. Prevalence of Smoking and Its Associated Factors with Smoking Among Elderly Smokers in Malaysia: Findings from a nationwide Population-based Study. Tob Induced Dis. 2016;14:8. https://doi.org/10. 1186/s12971-016-0073-z.
176. Ruokolainen, O., Härkänen, T., Lahti, J., Haukkala, A., Heliö-vaara, M., Rahkonen, O. Association between Educational Level and Smoking Cessation in an 11-year Follow-up Study of a National Health Survey. Scand J Public Health. 2021;49(8):951–960. https://doi.org/10.1177/1403494821993721.
177. Link, B.G., Phelan, J. Social Conditions as Fundamental Causes of Disease. J Health Soc Behav. 1995;35:80. http://www.jstor.org/stable/2626958?origin=crossref.
178. Glanz, K., Rimer, B.K., Viswanath, K. *Health Behavior and Health Education: Theory, Research, and Practice.* New York: John Wiley and Sons, 2008.

179. Grossman, M. The Correlation between Health and Schooling. In: Nestor E Terleckyj (Ed.), *Household Production and Consumption* (pp. 147–247). New York: Columbia University Press, 1976.
180. Berger, M.C., Leigh, J.P. Schooling, Self-Selection, and Health. J Hum Resour.1989;24:433–455.
181. Phelan, J.C., Link, B.G., Tehranifar, P. Social Conditions as Fundamental Causes of Health Inequalities: Theory, Evidence, and Policy Implications J Health Soc Behav. 2010 Mar 8;51(suppl 1):S28–S40. https://doi.org/10.1177/0022146510383498.
182. Gugushvili, A., Zhao, Y., Bukodi, E. Intergenerational Educational Mobility and Smoking: A Study of 20 European Countries using Diagonal Reference Models. Public Health. 2020;181:94–101. https://doi.org/10.1016/j.puhe.2019.12.009.
183. Gage, S.H., Davey Smith, G., Bowden, J., Munafò, M.R. Investigating Causality in Associations Between Education and Smoking: A Two-Sample Mendelian Randomization Study. Int J Epidemiol. 2018;47:1131–1140.
184. Pierce, J.P., Fiore, M.C., Novotny, T.E., et al. Trends in Cigarette Smoking in the United States. Educ Differ Are Increasing JAMA. 1989;261:56–60.
185. U.S. Department of Health and Human Services, n.d U.S. Department of Health and Human Services Office of Disease Prevention and Health Promotion. Healthy People 2020-Tobacco Use. https://www.healthypeople.gov/2020/topics-obj ectives/topic/tobacco-use/objectives.
186. Babb, S., Malarcher, A., Schauer, G., et al. Quitting Smoking Among Adults - United States, 2000–2015. MMWR Morb Mortal Wkly Rep. 2017;65:1457–1464. https://doi.org/10. 15585/mmwr.mm6552a1.
187. Prabhakar, B., Narake, S.S., Pednekar, M.S. Social Disparities in Tobacco use in India: The Roles of Occupation, Education and Gender. Indian J Cancer. 2012 Oct-Dec;49(4):401–409. https://doi.org/10.4103/0019-509X.107747.
188. Wang, Q., Shen, J.J., Sotero, M., Li, C.A., Hou, Z. Income, Occupation and Education: Are they Related to Smoking Behaviors in China? PLoS ONE. 2018;13(2):e0192571. https://doi. org/10.1371/journal.pone.0192571.
189. Nketiah-Amponsah, E., Afful-Mensah, G., Ampaw, S. Determinants of Cigarette Smoking and Smoking Intensity Among Adult

Males in Ghana. BMC Public Health. 2018;18:941. https://doi. org/10.1186/s12889-018-5872-0.

190. Nguyen, C.V. Demographic and Socio-economic Determinants of Smoking Bevaiour: Evidence from Vietnam. Econ Bull. 2012;32(3):2301–2312.

191. Khanal, V., Adhikari, M., Karki, S. Social Determinants of Tobacco Consumption among Nepalese Men: Findings from Nepal Demographic and Health Survey 2011. Harm Reduct J. 2013;10(1):40. https://doi.org/10.1186/1477-7517-10-40.

192. Gage, S.H., Bowden, J., Davey Smith, G., Munafò, M.R. Investigating Causality in Associations between Education and Smoking: A Two-sample Mendelian Randomization Study. Int J Epidemiol. 2018 Aug 1;47(4):1131–1140. https://doi.org/10.1093/ije/dyy131.

193. Gilman, S.E., Martin, L.T., Abrams, D.B., Kawachi, I., Kubzansky, L., Loucks, E.B., Rende, R., Rudd, R., Buka, S.L. Educational Attainment and Cigarette Smoking: A Causal Association? Int J Epidemiol. 2008 Jun;37(3):615–624. https://doi. org/10.1093/ije/dym250.

194. Lempert, L.K., Glantz, S.A. Tobacco Industry Promotional Strategies Targeting American Indians/Alaska Natives and Exploiting Tribal Sovereignty. Nicotine Tob Res: Off J Soc Res Nicotine Tob. 2019;21(7):940–948. https://doi.org/10.1093/ntr/nty048.

195. WHO Dept Economic and Social Affairs. Indigenous Peoples & the Covid-19 Pandemic: Considerations, 2020. https://www. un.org/development/desa/indigenouspeoples/wp-content/upl oads/sites/19/2020/04/COVID19_IP_considerations.pdf.

196. Glover, M., Patwardhan, P., Selket, K. Tobacco Smoking in Three "left behind" Subgroups: Indigenous, the Rainbow Community and People with Mental Health Conditions. Drugs Alcohol Today. 2020;20(3):263–281. https://doi.org/10.1108/DAT-02-2020-0004.

197. Heris, C.L., Chamberlain, C., Gubhaju, L., Thomas, D.P., Eades, S.J. Factors Influencing Smoking Among Indigenous Adolescents Aged 10–24 Years Living in Australia, New Zealand, Canada, and the United States: A Systematic Review. Nicotine Tob Res. 2020 Nov;22(11):1946–1956. https://doi.org/10.1093/ntr/ntz219.

198. Ball, J., Stanley, J., Wilson, N., Blakely, T., Edwards, R. Smoking prevalence in New Zealand from 1996–2015: A Critical Review of National Data Sources to Inform Progress Toward the Smokefree 2025 Goal. N Z Med J. 2016;129:11–22.

199. Australian Bureau of Statistics. (2018–2019). National Aboriginal and Torres Strait Islander Health Survey. ABS. https://www.abs.gov.au/statistics/people/aboriginal-and-torres-strait-islander-peo ples/national-aboriginal-and-torres-strait-islander-health-survey/latest-release.

200. Heris, C., Guerin, N., Thomas, D., Chamberlain, C., Eades, S. and White, V.M. Smoking Behaviours and Other Substance use Among Indigenous and Non-Indigenous Australian Secondary Students, 2017. Drug Alcohol Rev. 2021;40:58–67. https://doi.org/10.1111/dar.13130.

201. Public Health Agency of Canada. *Key Health Inequalities in Canada: A National Portrait*. Ottawa: Public Health Agency of Canada, 2018.

202. Jetty, R. Canadian Paediatric Society, First Nations, Inuit and Métis Health Committee, Ottawa, Ontario. Tobacco use and Misuse among Indigenous Children and Youth in Canada. Paediatr Child Health. 2017 Oct;22(7):395–405. https://doi.org/10.1093/pch/pxx124.

203. Health Canada. (2019). Infographic: Inequalities in Smoking in Canada, Government of Canada. https://www.canada.ca/en/public-health/services/publications/science-research-data/ine qualities-smoking-infographic.html.

204. Minstry of Health. (2021). Annual Update of Key Results 2020/21: New Zealand Health Survey, New Zealand Ministry of Health. https://www.health.govt.nz/publication/annual-upd ate-key-results-2020-21-new-zealand-health-survey.

205. Cornelius, M.E., Loretan, C.G., Wang, T.W., Jamal, A., Homa, D.M. Tobacco Product Use Among Adults—United States, 2020. MMWR Morb Mortal Wkly Rep. 2022;71:397–405.

206. U.S. Department of Health and Human Services. Tobacco Use Among U.S. Racial/Ethnic Minority Groups—African Americans, American Indians and Alaska Natives, Asian Americans and Pacific Islanders, Hispanics: A Report of the Surgeon General. Atlanta, Georgia: U.S. Department of Health and Human Services, Centers for Disease Control and Prevention, National

Center for Chronic Disease Prevention and Health Promotion, Office on Smoking and Health, 1998.

207. Minnesota Dept Health Traditional Tobacco and American Indian Communities in Minnesota. https://www.health.state.mn.us/communities/tobacco/traditional.

208. U.S. Department of Health and Human Services. (2014). The Health Consequences of Smoking—50 Years of Progress: A Report of the Surgeon General. Atlanta: U.S. Department of Health and Human Services, Centers for Disease Control and Prevention, National Center for Chronic Disease Prevention and Health Promotion, Office on Smoking and Health.

209. U.S. Department of Health and Human Services. Smoking Cessation. A Report of the Surgeon General. Atlanta, GA: U.S. Department of Health and Human Services, Centers for Disease Control and Prevention, National Center for Chronic Disease Prevention and Health Promotion, Office on Smoking and Health, p. 57, 2020.

210. O'Donald, E.R., Miller, C.P., O'Leary, R., Ong, J., Pacheco, B., et al. Active smoking, secondhand smoke exposure and serum cotinine levels among Cheyenne River Sioux communities in context of a Tribal Public Health Policy. Tob Control. 2020 June;29(5):570–576. Public Health Law Center. Smoke-free Tribal Housing Policies.

211. Odani, S., Armour, B.S., Graffunder, C.M., Garrett, B.E., Agaku, I.T. Prevalence and Disparities in Tobacco Product Use Among American Indians/Alaska Natives—United States, 2010–2015. Morbidity and Mortality Weekly Report, 2017;66(50):1374–1378.

212. Substance Abuse and Mental Health Services Administration. Results from the 2018 National Survey on Drug Use and Health: Detailed Tables. Rockville, MD: Substance Abuse and Mental Health Services Administration, Center for Behavioral Health Statistics and Quality, 2019.

213. Espey, D.K., Jim, M.A., Cobb, N., et al. Leading Causes of Death and All-Cause Mortality in American Indians and Alaska Natives. Am J Public Health. 2014;104(suppl 3):S303–S311.

214. Subramanian, S.V., Smith, G.D., Subramanyam M. Indigenous Health and Socioeconomic Status in India. PLoS Med.

2006;3(10):e421. https://doi.org/10.1371/journal.pmed.003 0421.

215. Tsai, L.T., Lo, F.E., Yang, C.C., Lo, W.M., Keller, J.J., Hwang, C.W., Lin, C.F., Lyu, S.Y., Morisky, D.E. Influence of Socioeconomic Factors, Gender and Indigenous Status on Smoking in Taiwan. Int J Environ Res Public Health. 2016;13(11):1044. https://doi.org/10.3390/ijerph13111044.

216. Quintana, H., Roa, R. Tobacco Use and Access Among 13 to 15 Year Olds in Kuna Yala, an Indigenous Region of Panama. Tob Control. 2021;e2:e158–61. https://doi.org/10.1136/tob accocontrol-2020-055736.

217. Pedersen, J.M. Substance Abuse among Greenlandic School Children. Arct Med Res. 1992;51(2):67.

218. Spein, A.R., Kvernmo, S.E., Sexton, H. The north Norwegian Youth Study: Cigarette Smoking among Ethnically Diverse Adolescents. Ethn Health. 2002;7(3):163–179. Spein AR, Sexton H, Kvernmo S. Predictors of Smoking Behaviour among Indigenous Sami Adolescents and Non-indigenous Peers in North Norway. Scand J Public Health. 2004;32(2):118–129.

219. ONS. Cigarette Smoking Among Adults: Percentage Of Adults Who Smoked Cigarettes, by Ethnicity, 2021. https://www.eth nicity-facts-figures.service.gov.uk/health/alcohol-smoking-and-drug-use/adult-smokers/.

220. CDC. (n.d.). Cigarettes and Smoking in the United States by Race, CDC Tobacco Campaign. https://www.cdc.gov/tobacco/ campaign/tips/resources/data/cigarette-smoking-in-united-sta tes.html#by_race.

221. U.S. Department of Health and Human Services. (2019). Office of Disease Prevention and Health Promotion. Healthy People 2020. http://healthypeople.gov. Updated 11 October.

222. Hoffman, L., Delahanty, J., Johnson, S.E., Zhao, X. Sexual and Gender Minority Cigarette Smoking Disparities: An Analysis of the 2016 Behavioral Risk Factor Surveillance System data. Prev Med. 2018;113:109–115. https://doi.org/10.1016/ j.ypmed.2018.05.014.

223. Meyer, I.H. Prejudice, Social Stress, and Mental Health in Lesbian, Gay, and Bisexual Populations: Conceptual Issues and Research Evidence. Psychol Bull. 2003;129:674–697. https:// doi.org/10.1037/0033-2909.129.5.674.

224. Glover, M., Patwardhan, P., Selket, K. Tobacco Smoking in Three "Left Behind" Subgroups: Indigenous, the Rainbow Community and People with Mental Health Conditions. Drugs Alcohol Today. 2020;20(3):263–281. https://doi.org/10.1108/DAT-02-2020-0004.

225. Tan, A., Gazarian, P., Darwish, S., Hanby, E., Farnham, B., Koroma-Coker, F., Potter, J., Ballout, S. Smoking Protective and Risk Factors Among Transgender and Gender-Expansive Individuals (Project SPRING): Qualitative Study Using Digital Photovoice. JMIR Public Health Surveill. 2021;7(10):e27417. https://doi.org/10.2196/27417.

226. Corliss, H.L., Wadler, B.M., Jun, H.J., Rosario, M., Wypij, D., Frazier, A.L., Austin, S.B. Sexual-orientation Disparities in Cigarette Smoking in a Longitudinal Cohort study of Adolescents. Nicotine Tob Res. 2013 Jan;15(1):213–222. https://doi.org/10.1093/ntr/nts114.

227. UK Content Delivery Network and ASH UK. Smoking: LGBT people, UK Content Delivery Network, 2019. https://cdn.ash.ten4dev.com/uploads/HIRP-LGBT-community.pdf.

228. Lindström, M., Axelsson, J., Modén, B., et al. Sexual Orientation, Social Capital and Daily Tobacco Smoking: A Population-based Study. BMC Public Health. 2014;14:565. https://doi.org/10.1186/1471-2458-14-565.

229. Azagba, S., Asbridge, M., Langille, D., Baskerville, B. Disparities in Tobacco Use by Sexual Orientation Among High School Students. Prev Med. 2014;69:307–311. https://doi.org/10.1016/j.ypmed.2014.07.042.

230. Fontanari, A.M.V., Churchill, S., Schneider, M.A., Soll, B., Costa, A.B., Lobato, M.I.R. Tobacco use among transgender and gender non-binary youth in Brazil. Cien Saude Colet. 2021;26(suppl 3):5281–5292. Published 2021 Nov 15. https://doi.org/10.1590/1413-812320212611.3.35272019.

231. Health Promotion Agency. Sexual Attraction and Substance Use, New Zealand Health Promotion Agency, 2019. https://www.hpa.org.nz/sites/default/files/Sexual%20attraction%20and%20substance%20use%20-%20findings%20from%20the%20Youth%20Insights%20Survey%202016-2018.pdf.

232. Perales, J., Checa, I., Espejo, B. Current Active and Passive Smoking among Adults Living with Same Sex Partners in Spain. Gac Sanit. 2018 Nov–Dec;32(6):547–552. https://doi.org/10.1016/j.gaceta.2017.03.006.

233. Hoffman, L., Delahanty, J., Johnson, S.E., Zhao, X. Sexual and gender Minority Cigarette Smoking Disparities: An analysis of 2016 Behavioral Risk Factor Surveillance System data. Prev Med. 2018 Aug;113:109–115. https://doi.org/10.1016/j.ypmed.2018.05.014.

234. Shahab, L., Brown, J., Hagger-Johnson, G., et al. Sexual Orientation Identity and Tobacco and Hazardous Alcohol Use: Findings from a Cross-sectional English Population Survey. BMJ Open. 2017;7:e015058. https://doi.org/10.1136/bmjopen-2016-015058.

235. Emerson, E. Smoking among Adults With and Without Disabilities in the UK. J Public Health. 2018 Dec;40(4):e502–e509. https://doi.org/10.1093/pubmed/fdy062.

236. CDC. Smoking in Adults. CDC Disability and Health, 2020. https://www.cdc.gov/ncbddd/disabilityandhealth/smoking-in-adults.html.

237. Jamal, A., Phillips, E., Gentzke, A.S., Homa, D.M., Babb, S.D., King, B.A., Neff, L.J. Current Cigarette Smoking Among Adults—United States, 2016. MMWR Morb Mortal Wkly Rep. 2018 Jan 19;67(2):53–59. https://doi.org/10.15585/mmwr.mm6702a1.

238. Han, B., Volkow, N.D., Blanco, C., Tipperman, D., Einstein, E.B., Compton, W.M. Trends in Prevalence of Cigarette Smoking Among US Adults with Major Depression or Substance Use Disorders, 2006–2019. JAMA. 2022. https://doi.org/10.1001/jama.2022.4790.

239. Lin, S.C., Gathua, N., Thompson, C., Sripipatana, A., Makaroff, L. Disparities in Smoking Prevalence and Associations with Mental Health and Substance Use Disorders in Underserved Communities Across the United States. Cancer. 2022. https://doi.org/10.1002/cncr.34132.

240. Soar, K., Dawkins, L., Robson, D., Cox, S. Smoking amongst Adults Experiencing Homelessness: A Systematic Review of Prevalence Rates, Interventions and the Barriers and Facilitators

to Quitting and Staying quit. J Smok Cessat. 2020;15(2):94–108. https://doi.org/10.1017/jsc.2020.11.

241. Dyal, S.R., Valente, T.W. A Systematic Review of Loneliness and Smoking: Small Effects, Big Implications. Subst Use Misuse. 2015;50(13):1697–1716. https://doi.org/10.3109/10826084.2015.1027933.

242. Yang, J., Yockey, R.A., Chu, Y., Lee, J.G.L. The Influence of Loneliness on the Smoking and Physical Activity of Community-Dwelling Older Adults: Results from the Health and Retirement Study. Am J Health Promot. 2022;36(6):959–966. https://doi.org/10.1177/08901171221081136.

243. Spaulding, A.C., Eldridge, G.D., Chico, C.E., Morisseau, N., Drobeniuc, A., Fils-Aime, R., Day, C., Hopkins, R., Jin, X., Chen, J., Dolan, K.A. Smoking in Correctional Settings Worldwide: Prevalence, Bans, and Interventions. Epidemiol Rev. 2018;40(1):82–95. https://doi.org/10.1093/epirev/mxy005.

244. Glover, M., Patwardhan, P., Selket, K. Tobacco Smoking in Three "Left Behind" Subgroups: Indigenous, the Rainbow Community and People with Mental Health Conditions. Drugs Alcohol Today. 2020;20(3):263–281. https://doi.org/10.1108/DAT-02-2020-0004.

245. See also Eliason, M.J., Dibble, S.L., Gordon, R., Soliz, G.B. The Last Drag: An Evaluation of an LGBT-Specific Smoking Intervention. J Homosex 2012;59(6):864–878.

246. Shokoohi, M., Salway, T., Ahn, B. Disparities in the Prevalence of Cigarette Smoking Among Bisexual People: A Systematic Review, Meta-analysis and Meta-regression. Tob Control. 2021;e2:e78–86. https://doi.org/10.1136/tobaccocontrol-2020-055747.

247. Amroussia, N., Pearson, J.L., Gustafsson, P.E. What Drives Us Apart? Decomposing Intersectional Inequalities in Cigarette Smoking by Education and Sexual Orientation Among U.S. Adults. Int J Equity Health. 2019;18(1). https://doi.org/10.1186/s12939-019-1015-1.

248. Nguyen-Grozavu, F.T., Pierce, J.P., Sakuma, K.K., Leas, E.C., McMenamin, S.B., Kealey, S., Benmarhnia, T., Emery, S.L., White, M.M., Fagan, P., Trinidad, D.R. Widening Disparities in Cigarette Smoking by Race/Ethnicity across Education Level in the United States. Prev Med. 2020;139:106220. ISSN 0091–7435. https://doi.org/10.1016/j.ypmed.2020.106220.

249. Glover, M., Patwardhan, P., Selket, K. Tobacco Smoking in Three "Left Behind" Subgroups: Indigenous, the Rainbow community and People with Mental Health Conditions. Drugs Alcohol Today. 2020;20(3):263–281. https://doi.org/10.1108/DAT-02-2020-0004.
250. Doll, R., Peto, R., Wheatley, K., Gray, R., Sutherland, I. Mortality in Relation to Smoking: 40 years' Observations on Male British Doctors. BMJ 1994;309(6959):901–911. Peto, R. Smoking and Death: The Past 40 Years and the Next 40. BMJ 1994;309(6959):937–939.
251. U.S. Department of Health and Human Services (USDHHS). (2014).The Health Consequences of Smoking—50 years of Progress. A Report of the Surgeon General.
252. WHO. (2022). Tobacco Fact Sheet. World Health Organisation, accessed 03 May 2023. https://www.who.int/news-room/fact-sheets/detail/tobacco#:~:text=Tobacco%20kills%20more%20than%208,%2D%20and%20middle%2Dincome%20countries.
253. GBD 2015 Risk Factors Collaborators. Global, Regional, and National Comparative Risk Assessment of 79 Behavioural, Environmental and Occupational, and Metabolic Risks or clusters of risks, 19902015: A Systematic Analysis for the Global Burden of Disease Study 2015. Lancet. 2016;388:1659–1724.
254. Tobacconomics. Economic Costs of Tobacco Use. Tobacconomics, 2019. https://tobacconomics.org/files/research/523/UIC_Economic-Costs-of-Tobacco-Use-Policy-Brief_v1.3.pdf.
255. Goodchild, M., Nargis, N., d'Espaignet, E. Global Economic Cost of Smoking-attributable Diseases. Tob Control. 2018;27:58–64.
256. U.S. National Cancer Institute and World Health Organization (NCI/WHO). The Economics of Tobacco and Tobacco Control. National Cancer Institute Tobacco Control Monograph 21, 2016.
257. Vulovic, V. Economic Costs of Tobacco Use. A Tobacconomics Policy Brief. Chicago, IL: Tobacconomics, Health Policy Center, Institute for Health Research and Policy, University of Illinois at Chicago, 2019. www.tobacconomics.org.
258. Brown, J., Kotz, D., Michie, S., et al. How Effective and Cost-effective was the National Mass Media Smoking Cessation Campaign 'Stoptober'. Drug Alcohol Depend. 2014;135:52–58.

259. Sims, M., Salway, R., Langley, T., et al. Effectiveness of Tobacco Control Television Advertising in Changing Tobacco Use in England: A Population-based cross-sectional Study. Addiction. 2014;109:986–994.
260. US Surgeon General. Preventing tobacco use among youth and young adults. A Report of the Surgeon General. Atlanta, GA: US Department of Health and Human Services, Centers for Disease Control and Prevention, National Center for Chronic Disease Prevention and Health Promotion, Office on Smoking and Health, 2012. www.surgeongeneral.gov/library/reports/preventing-youth-tobacco-use/index.html.
261. Tobacco Control Laws. (n.d.). Homepage, webpage, accessed May 03 2023. https://www.tobaccocontrollaws.org/.
262. Fathelrahman, A., Omar, M., Awang, R., et al. Smokers' Responses Towards Cigarette Pack Warning Labels in Predicting Quit Intention, Stage of Change, and Self-efficacy. Nicotine Tob Res. 2009;11:248–253.
263. Environics Research Group. The Health Effects of Tobacco and Health Warning Messages on Cigarette Packages – Survey of Adults and Adult Smokers: Wave 12 surveys. Prepared for Health Canada. Toronto, Canada: Environics Research Group, 2007.
264. Hammond, D., Fong, G., Borland, R., et al. Text and Graphic Warnings on Cigarette Packages: Findings from the International Tobacco Control Four Country Study. Am J Prev Med. 2007;32:202–209.
265. Environics Research Group. Canadian Adult and Youth Opinions on the Sizing of Health Warning Messages. Toronto, Canada: Environics Research Group, 1999.
266. Willemsen, M. The new EU Cigarette Health Warnings Benefit Smokers Who Want to Quit the Habit: Results from the Dutch Continuous Survey of Smoking Habits. Eur J Public Health. 2005;15:389–392.
267. Environics. (2001). Canadian Cancer Society Evaluation of New Warnings on Cigarette Packages. Environics, Focus Canada, 2001–2003.
268. Hammond, D. Health Warning Messages on Tobacco Products: A Review. Tob Control. 2011;20:327–323.
269. Hammond, D., Wakefield, M., Durkin, S., et al. Tobacco Packaging and mass Media Campaigns: Research Needs for Articles

11 and 12 of the WHO Framework Convention on Tobacco Control. Nicotine Tob Res. 2013;15:817–831.

270. Azagba, S., Sharaf, M. The Effect of Graphic Warning Labels on Smoking Behaviour: Evidence from the Canadian Experience. Nicotine Tob Res. 2013;15:708–717.

271. Moodie, C., Stead, M., Bauld, L., et al. *Plain Tobacco Packaging: A Systematic Review.* PHR/ePPI Centre, 2012. http://phrc.lshtm.ac.uk/papers/PHRC_006_Final_Report.pdf.

272. Durkin, S., Brennan, E., Coomber, K., et al. Short-term Changes in Quitting-related Cognitions and Behaviours After the Implementation of Plain Packaging with Larger Health warnings: Findings from a National Cohort Study with Australian Adult Smokers. Tob Control. 2015;24:26–32.

273. McNeill, A., Gravely, S., Hitchman, S.C., Bauld, L., Hammond, D., Hartmann-Boyce, J. Tobacco Packaging Design for Reducing Tobacco Use. Cochrane Database Syst Rev. 2017;(4):CD011244. https://doi.org/10.1002/14651858.CD011244.pub2.

274. Blecher, E., Bertram, M. The economics and control of tobacco, alcohol, food products, and sugar-Sweetened Beverages. In Vaccarella S, Lortet-Tieulent J, Saracci R, et al. (Eds.), *Reducing Social Inequalities in Cancer: Evidence and Priorities For Research.* Lyon (FR): International Agency for Research on Cancer; 2019. (IARC Scientific Publications, No. 168.) Chapter 11. https://www.ncbi.nlm.nih.gov/books/NBK566208/

275. The microeconomic underpinnings of tax pass through is discussed in Volume III, Chapter 2.

276. Hiscock, R., Branston, J.R., McNeill, A., et al. Tobacco industry Strategies Undermine Government tax Policy: Evidence from Commercial Data. Tob Control. 2018;27:488–497.

277. Ross, H., Tesche, J., Vellios, N. Undermining Government Tax Policies: Common Legal Strategies Employed by the Tobacco Industry in Response to Tobacco Tax Increases. Prev Med. 2017 Dec;105S(suppl):S19–S22. https://doi.org/10.1016/j.ypmed.2017.06.012.

278. World Bank. Public Health at a Glance: Tobacco. Washington DC: World Bank, 2003. http://web.worldbank.org/archive/website01213/WEB/0__CON-8.HTM. World Bank. Tobacco. www.worldbank.org/en/topic/health/brief/tobacco.

2 WHO IS (STILL) SMOKING? **125**

279. International Agency for Research on Cancer. Effectiveness of Tax and Price Policies for Tobacco Control. IARC Handbooks of Cancer Prevention. Tob Control. 2011;14. Lyon, France: IARC. www.iarc.fr/en/publications/pdfsonline/prev/handbook14/handbook14.pdf.

280. Czubek, M., Johal, S. *Econometric Analysis of Cigarette Consumption in the UK*. London: HM Revenue & Customs, 2010.

281. Jha, P., Peto, R. Global Effects of Smoking, of Quitting, and of Taxing Tobacco. N Engl J Med. 2014 Jan 2;370(1):60–68. https://doi.org/10.1056/NEJMra1308383.

282. Van Walbeek, C.P. Industry Responses to the Tobacco Excise Tax Increases in South Africa. S Afr J Econ 2006;74:110–122.

283. Chaloupka, F., Drope, J., Siu, E., Vulovic, V., Stoklosa, M., Mirza, M., Rodriguez Iglesias, G., Lee, H. Tobacconomics Cigarette Tax Scorecard. Chicago, IL: Health Policy Center, Institute for Health Research and Policy, University of I linois Chicago, 2020. www.tobacconomics.org.

284. World Health Organization. (2021). Countries Share Examples of How Tobacco Tax Policies Create Win-Wins for Development, Health and Revenues. World Health Organization, 12 April 2021. https://www.who.int/news-room/feature-stories/detail/countries-share-examples-of-how-tobacco-tax-policies-cre ate-win-wins-for-development-health-and-revenues.

285. World Health Organization. (2019). Report on the Global Tobacco Epidemic 2019: Offer Help to Quit Tobacco Use, Appendix IX, Table 9.6. Geneva, CH.

286. Jha, P., Chaloupka, F.J. *Curbing the Epidemic: Governments and the Economics of Tobacco Control*. Washington: World Bank, 1999.

287. Chaloupka, F.J., et al. The Taxation of Tobacco Products. In Jha P, Chaloupka F (Eds.), *Tobacco Control in Developing Countries*. Oxford: Oxford University Press, 2000.

288. Ross, H., Chaloupka, F.J. The Effects of Cigarette Prices on Youth Smoking. ImpacTEEN Research Paper Series, No. 7. February 2001.

289. Nikaj, S., Chaloupka, F. The Effect of Prices on Cigarette use among Youths in the Global Youth Tobacco Survey. Nicotine Tob Res. 2014;16(suppl 1):S16–23.

290. US Surgeon General. Preventing tobacco use among youth and young adults. A Report of the Surgeon General. Atlanta, GA:

US Department of Health and Human Services, Centers for Disease Control and Prevention, National Center for Chronic Disease Prevention and Health Promotion, Office on Smoking and Health, 2012. www.surgeongeneral.gov/library/reports/pre venting-youth-tobacco-use/index.html.

291. Taioli, E., Wynder, E.L. Effect of Age at which Smoking Begins on Frequency of Smoking in Adulthood. N Engl J Med. 1991;325(13):968–969.

292. Breslau, N., Fenn, N., Peterson, E.L. Early Smoking Initiation and Nicotine Dependence in a Cohort of Young Adults. Drug Alcohol Depend. 1993;33(2):129–137.

293. Breslau, N., Peterson, E.L. Smoking Cessation in Young Adults: Age at Initiation of Cigarette Smoking and Other Suspected Influences. Am J Public Health. 1996;86(2):214–220.

294. U.S. Department of Health and Human Services. (2000). Reducing Tobacco Use: a Report of the Surgeon General. Atlanta, US Department of Health and Human Services, Public Health Service, Centers for Disease Control, National Center for Chronic Disease Prevention and Health Promotion, Office of Smoking and Health.

295. Townsend, J.L., Roderick, P., Cooper, J. Cigarette Smoking by Socio-Economic Group, Sex, and Age: Effects of Price, Income, and Health Publicity. Br Med J. 1994;309:923–926.

296. Warner, K.E. The Economics of Tobacco: Myths and Realities. Tob Control. 2000;9:78–89. https://doi.org/10.1136/tc. 9.1.78.

297. Verguet, S., Kearns, P.K.A., Rees, V.W. Questioning the Regressivity of Tobacco Taxes: A Distributional Accounting Impact Model of Increased Tobacco Taxation. Tob Control. 2021;30:245–257.

298. National Research Council. Understanding the U.S. Illicit Tobacco Market: Characteristics, Policy Context, and Lessons from International Experiences. Washington, DC: The National Academies Press, 2015. https://doi.org/10.17226/19016.

299. Tobacco Control Lawes, Homepage, Tobacco Control Laws. https://www.tobaccocontrollaws.org.

300. Royal College of Physicians. *Going Smokefree: The Medical Case for clean Air in the Home, at Work and in public Places.* London: RCP, 2005.

2 WHO IS (STILL) SMOKING? 127

301. U.S. Department of Health and Human Services. The Health Consequences of Smoking—50 Years of Progress: A Report of the Surgeon General. Atlanta, GA: U.S. Department of Health and Human Services, Centers for Disease Control and Prevention, National Center for Chronic Disease Prevention and Health Promotion, Office on Smoking and Health, 2014.

302. Semple, S., van Tongeren, M., Galea, K.S., et al. UK Smoke-free Legislation: Changes in PM2.5 Concentrations in Bars in Scotland, England, and Wales. Ann Occup Hygiene. 2009;54:272–280.

303. Jarvis, M., Feyerabend C. Recent Trends in Children's Exposure to Second-hand Smoke in England: Cotinine Evidence from the Health Survey for England. Addiction. 2015;110:1484–1492.

304. Millett, C., Lee, J., Laverty, A., et al. Hospital Admissions for Childhood Asthma after Smokefree Legislation in England. Pediatrics. 2013;131:495–501.

305. Been, J., Nurmatov, U., Cox, B. et al. Effect of Smoke-free Legislation on Perinatal and Child Health: A Systematic Review And Meta-analysis. Lancet 2014;383:1549–1560.

306. Sims, M., Maxwell, R., Bauld, L., et al. Short term Impact of Smoke-free Legislation in England: Retrospective Analysis of Hospital Admissions for Myocardial Infarction. BMJ. 2010;340:c2161.

307. Tan, C., Glantz, S. Association between Smoke-free Legislation and Hospitalizations for Cardiac, Cerebrovascular, and Respiratory Diseases: A Meta-Analysis. Circulation. 2012;126:2177–2183.

308. Hackshaw, L., McEwen, A., West, R., et al. Quit Attempts in Response to Smokefree Legislation in England. Tob Control. 2010;12:160–164.

309. Mackay, D., Haw, S., Pell, J. Impact of Scottish Smoke-free Legislation on Smoking Quit Attempts and prevalence. PLoS One. 2011;6(11).

310. Lee, J., Glantz, S., Millett, C. Effect of smoke-free legislation on adult smoking Behaviour in England in the 18 months following implementation. PLoS One. 2011;6:e20933.

311. US Surgeon General. (2012). Preventing tobacco use among youth and young adults. A Report of the Surgeon General. Atlanta, GA: US Department of Health and Human Services,

Centers for Disease Control and Prevention, National Center for Chronic Disease Prevention and Health Promotion, Office on Smoking and Health. www.surgeongeneral.gov/library/reports/preventing-youth-tobacco-use/index.html

312. Joosens, L. (2000). *The Effectiveness of Banning Advertising of Tobacco Products*. Brussels: International Union against Cancer.

313. Tobacco Control Lawes, Advertising Regulations, Tobacco Control Laws. https://www.tobaccocontrollaws.org/legislation/find-by-policy?policy=advertising-promotion-sponsorship&matrix=apsRegulatedForms&handle=advertising-promotion-sponsorship&criteria=point-of-sale-product-display&status=P.

314. Robertson, L., McGee, R., March, L., et al. A Systematic Review on the Impact of Point-of-sale Tobacco Promotion on Smoking. Nicotine Tob Res. 2015;17:2–17.

315. McNeill, A., Lewis, S., Quinn, C., et al. Evaluation of the Removal of Point-of-sale Tobacco Displays in Ireland. Tob Control. 2011;20:137–143.

316. US Department of Health and Human Services. Preventing tobacco use among youth and young adults. A Report of the Surgeon General. Atlanta, GA: US Department of Health and Human Services, Centers for Disease Control and Prevention and Health Promotion, Office on Smoking and Health, 2012. www.cdc.gov/tobacco/data_statistics/sgr/2012/index.htm.

317. Carpenter, C.M., Wayne, G.F., Pauly, J.L., Koh, H.K., Connolly, G.N. New Cigarette Brands with Flavors that Appeal to Youth: Tobacco Marketing Strategies. Health Aff (Millwood). 2005 Nov–Dec;24(6):1601–1610. https://doi.org/10.1377/hlthaff.24.6.1601.

318. US Food and Drug Administration. (2022). FDA Proposes Rules Prohibiting Menthol Cigarettes and Flavored Cigars to Prevent Youth Initiation, Significantly Reduce Tobacco-Related Disease and Death, FDA. https://www.fda.gov/news-events/press-announcements/fda-proposes-rules-prohibiting-menthol-cigarettes-and-flavored-cigars-prevent-youth-initiation.

319. Apelberg, B.J., Feirman, S.P., Salazar, E., Corey, C.G., Ambrose, B.K., Paredes, A., Richman, E., Verzi, S.J., Vugrin, E.D., Brodsky, N.S., Rostron, B.L. Potential Public Health Effects of Reducing Nicotine Levels in Cigarettes in the United States. N Engl

J Med. 2018 May 3;378(18):1725–1733. https://doi.org/10. 1056/NEJMsr1714617.

320. Villanti, A.C., Byron, M.J., Mercincavage, M., et al. Misperceptions of Nicotine and Nicotine Reduction: the Importance of Public Education to Maximize the Benefits of a Nicotine Reduction standard. Nicotine Tob Res. 2019;21:S88–90. https://doi. org/10.1093/ntr/ntz103.

321. Henderson, K.C., Loud, E.E., Duong, H.T., et al. Perceptions of Nicotine Reduction Policy in the United States: A Qualitative Study. Nicotine Tob Res. 2022;24:ntac071. https://doi.org/10. 1093/ntr/ntac071.

322. Byron, M.J., Jeong, M., Abrams, D.B., Brewer, N.T. Public Misperception That Very Low Nicotine Cigarettes are Less Carcinogenic. Tob Control. 2018 Nov;27(6):712–714. https:// doi.org/10.1136/tobaccocontrol-2017-054124.

323. Hall, M.G., Byron, J.M., Brewer, N.T., Noar, S.M., Ribisl, K.M. Interest in Illicit Purchase of Cigarettes Under a Very Low Nicotine Content Product Standard. Nicotine Tob Res. 2019 Dec 23;21(suppl 1):S128–S132. https://doi.org/10.1093/ntr/ ntz159.

324. Most commonly, the laws are written to prohibit sale to minors. It is less common, but not uncommon, to additionally (or instead) criminalize the purchase of tobacco by a minor. That is, the legal onus is typically placed on the retailer, not the young would-be consumer.

325. Health and Social Care Information Centre. (2007). Smoking, drinking and drug use among young people in England in 2006. London: HSCIC. www.hscic.gov.uk/searchcatalogue?productid= 1303&q=title%3a%22Smoking%2c+Drinking+and+Drug+Use+ among+Young+People+in+England%22&sort=Relevance&size= 10&page=1#top.

326. Fidler, J.A., West, R. Changes in Smoking Prevalence in 16–17-year-old versus older Adults Following a Rise in Legal age of Sale: Findings from an English Population Study. Addiction. 2010;105:1984–1988.

327. Di Franza, J., Savageua, J., Fletcher, K. Enforcement of Underage Sales Laws as a Predictor of Daily Smoking Among Adolescents—A National Study. BMC Public Health. 2009;9:107.

328. Richardson, L., Hemsing, N., Greaves, L., et al. Preventing Smoking in Young People: A Systematic Review of the Impact of Access Interventions. J Environ Res Public Health. 2009;6:1485–1514.

329. Health and Social Care Information Centre. *Smoking, Drinking and Drug use among Young People in England in 2010*. London: HSCIC, 2011.

330. Dodds, B., Wood, L., Bainbridge, R., Grant, I., Robb, S. *Smoking among 13 and 15 year olds in Scotland 2013*. Edinburgh: NHS National Services Scotland, 2014.

331. Vuolo, M., Kelly, B.C., Kadowaki, J. Impact of Total Vending Machine Restrictions on US Young Adult Smoking. Nicotine Tob Res. 2016 Nov;18(11):2092–2099. https://doi.org/10.1093/ntr/ntw150.

332. Blackwell, A.K.M., Lee, I., Scollo, M., Wakefield, M., Munafò, M.R., Marteau, T.M. Should Cigarette Pack Sizes be Capped? Addiction. 2020 May;115(5):802–809. https://doi.org/10.1111/add.14770.

333. Stillman, F.A., Bone, L.R., Milam, A.J., Ma, J., Hoke, K. Out of View but in Plain Sight: the Illegal sale of Single Cigarettes. J Urban Health. 2014 Apr;91(2):355–365. https://doi.org/10.1007/s11524-013-9854-3.

334. Parthenon, E.Y. Smoking Cessation Products and Services Global Landscape Analysis, 2018. https://www.smokefreeworld.org/wp-content/uploads/2019/06/ey-p_smoking_cessation_landsc ape_analysis_key_findings.pdf.

335. West, R., May, S., West, M., et al. Performance of English Stop Smoking Services in First 10 years: Analysis of Service Monitoring Data. BMJ. 2013;347:f4921. https://doi.org/10.1136/bmj.f4921.

336. Bauld, L., Bell, K., McCullough, L., Richardson, L., Greaves, L. The Effectiveness of NHS Smoking Cessation Services: A Systematic Review. J Public Health, 2010 March;32(1):71–82. https://doi.org/10.1093/pubmed/fdp074.

337. Livingstone-Banks, J., Norris, E., Hartmann-Boyce, J., West, R., Jarvis, M., Chubb, E., Hajek, P. Relapse Prevention Interventions for Smoking Cessation. Cochrane Database of Systematic Reviews 2019;(10):CD003999. https://doi.org/10.1002/146 51858.CD003999.pub6.

2 WHO IS (STILL) SMOKING? **131**

338. Jones, E., Molyneux, A., Antoniak, M., et al. 'If someone could wave a Magic wand I'd never Smoke again...' - Barriers and Motivators to Accessing Smoking Cessation Services amongst Smokers in Deprived areas of Nottingham. Thorax. 2002;57:iii3–iii47.

339. Patnode, C.D., Henderson, J.T., Melnikow, J., et al. Interventions for Tobacco Cessation in Adults, Including Pregnant Women: An Evidence Update for the U.S. Preventive Services Task Force [Internet]. Rockville (MD): Agency for Healthcare Research and Quality (US); 2021 Jan. (Evidence Synthesis, No. 196). https://www.ncbi.nlm.nih.gov/books/NBK567066/.

340. Watkins, S.L., Thrul, J., Max, W., Ling, P.M. Real-world Effectiveness of Smoking Cessation Strategies for Young and Older Adults: Findings from a Nationally Representative Cohort. Nicotine Tob Res. 2020;22(9):1560–1568. https://doi.org/10.1093/ntr/ntz223.

341. Zhu, S.H., Cummins, S.E., Gamst, A.C., et al. Quitting Smoking Before and After Varenicline: A Population Study Based on Two Representative Samples of US Smokers. Tob Control. 2016;25:464–469. https://doi.org/10.1136/tobaccocontrol-2015-052332.

342. Milne, E. NHS Smoking Cessation Services and smoking Prevalence: Observational Study. BMJ 2005;330:760.

343. Bauld, L., Judge, K., Platt, S. Assessing the Impact of Smoking Cessation Services on Reducing Health Inequalities in England: Observational Study. Tob Control. 2007;16:400–404.

344. Tibuakuu, M., Okunrintemi, V., Jirru, E., et al. National Trends in Cessation Counseling, Prescription Medication Use, and Associated Costs Among US Adult Cigarette Smokers. JAMA Netw Open. 2019;2(5):e194585. https://doi.org/10.1001/jamanetworkopen.2019.4585.

345. Bailey, S.R., Crew, E.E., Riske, E.C., Ammerman, S., Robinson, T.N., Killen, J.D.. Efficacy and Tolerability of Pharmacotherapies to Aid Smoking Cessation in Adolescents. Paediatr Drugs. 2012 Apr 1;14(2):91–108. https://doi.org/10.2165/11594370-000000000-00000.

346. Cahill, K., Stevens, S., Lancaster, T. Pharmacological Treatments for Smoking Cessation. JAMA. 2014 Jan 8;311(2):193–194. https://doi.org/10.1001/jama.2013.283787.

347. Rigotti, N. Pharmacotherapy for Smoking Cessation in Adults, 2019. https://www.uptodate.com/contents/pharmacotherapy-for-smoking-cessation-in-adults.
348. CDC. Smoking Cessation Fast Facts, Centers for Disease Control and Prevention, 2022. https://www.cdc.gov/tobacco/data_stat istics/fact_sheets/cessation/smoking-cessation-fast-facts/index.html.
349. Babb, S., Malarcher, A., Schauer, G., et al. Quitting smoking among adults—United States, 2000–2015. MMWR Morb Mortal Wkly Rep. 2017;65:1457–1464.
350. Smokefree in Pregnancy Challenge Group. (2019). https://smo kefreeaction.org.uk/smokefree-nhs/smoking-in-pregnancy-cha llenge-group/press-releases/government-risks-missing-ambition-as-rates-of-smoking-during-pregnancy-not-falling-fast-enough/.
351. Tran, D.T., Preen, D.B., Einarsdottir, K., Kemp-Casey, A., Randall, D., Jorm, L.R., Choi, S., Havard, A. Use of Smoking Cessation Pharmacotherapies During Pregnancy Is Not Associated with Increased Risk of Adverse Pregnancy Outcomes: A Population-based Cohort Study. BMC Med. 2020;18(1):15. https://doi.org/10.1186/s12916-019-1472-9.
352. Patwardhan, S., Rose, J. Overcoming Barriers to Disseminate Effective Smoking Cessation Treatments Globally. Drugs Alcohol Today. 2020,20(3):235–247. https://doi.org/10.1108/DAT-01-2020-0001.
353. Tonstad, S., Davies, S., Flammer, M., et al. Psychiatric Adverse Events in Randomized, Double-Blind, Placebo-Controlled Clin ical Trials of Varenicline. Drug-Safety. 2010;33:289–301. https://doi.org/10.2165/11319180.
354. Medsafe. Update: Varenicline and Neuropsychiatric Adverse Reactions. Prescriber Update. 2017;38(4):59–60. https://www.medsafe.govt.nz/profs/PUArticles/December2017/Varenicline.htm.
355. Gonzales, D., Rennard, S., Nides, M., Oncken, C., Azoulay, S., Billing, C.B., Watsky, E.J., Gong, J., Williams, K.E., Reeves R. Varenicline. An $\alpha 4\beta 2$ Nicotinic Acetylcholine Receptor Partial agonist, vs Sustained- Release Bupropion and placebo

for Smoking Cessation, a randomized controlled trial. JAMA. 2006;296(1):47–55. https://doi.org/10.1001/jama.296.1.47.
356. Stahl, S.M., Pradko, J.F., Haight, B.R., Modell, J.G., Rockett, C.B., Learned-Coughlin, S. A Review of the Neuropharmacology of Bupropion, a Dual Norepinephrine and Dopamine Reuptake Inhibitor. Prim Care Companion J Clin Psychiatry. 2004;6(4):159–166.
357. WHO. (n.d.). FCTC Parties to the Convention, World Health Organisation. https://fctc.who.int/who-fctc/overview/parties.
358. While the vast majority of the world's nations have signed and ratified the FCTC, Andorra, Dominican Republic, Eritrea, Indonesia, Liechtenstein, Malawi, Monaco, Somalia, and South Sudan have done neither and, while they have signed the FCTC, Argentina, Cuba, Haiti, Morocco, Mozambique, Switzerland, and the U.S. have not ratified it.
359. WHO. (n.d.). MPOWER Measures of the FCTC, World Health Organisation. https://www.emro.who.int/tfi/mpower/index. html#:~:text=In%20line%20with%20the%20WHO,countries%20r educe%20demand%20for%20tobacco.
360. Chung-Hall, J., Craig, L., Gravely, S., et al. Impact of the Who FCTC Over the First Decade: A Global Evidence Review Prepared for the Impact Assessment Expert Group. Tob Control. 2019;28:s119–s128.
361. Levy, D.T., Yuan, Z., Luo, Y., et al. Seven Years of Progress in Tobacco Control: An Evaluation of the Effect of Nations Meeting The Highest Level Mpower Measures between 2007 and 2014. Tob Control. 2018;27:50–57. https://doi.org/10.1136/tobacc ocontrol-2016-053381.
362. Dubray, J., Schwartz, R., Chaiton, M., et al. The Effect of Mpower on Smoking Prevalence. Tob Control. 2015;24:540–542. https://doi.org/10.1136/tobaccocontrol-2014-051834.
363. Ngo, A., Cheng, K.W., Chaloupka, F.J., et al. The Effect of MPOWER Scores on Cigarette Smoking Prevalence and Consumption. Prev Med. 2017;105S:S10–14. https://doi.org/10.1016/j.ypmed.2017.05.006.
364. Gravely, S., Giovino, G.A., Craig, L., et al. Implementation of Key Demand-reduction Measures of the WHO Framework

Convention on Tobacco Control and Change in Smoking Prevalence in 126 countries: An Association Study. Lancet Public Health. 2017;2:e166–74. https://doi.org/10.1016/S2468-266 7(17)30045-2.

365. Gravely, S., Giovino, G.A., Craig, L., Commar, A., D'Espaignet, E.T., Schotte, K., Fong, G.T. Implementation of Key Demand-reduction Measures of the WHO Framework Convention on Tobacco Control and Change in Smoking Prevalence in 126 Countries: An Association Study. Lancet Public Health. 2017 Apr;2(4):e166–e174. https://doi.org/10.1016/S2468-2667(17)30045-2. Epub 2017 Mar 22. PMID: 29253448.

366. Ma, C., Xi, B., Li, Z., Wu, H., Zhao, M., Liang, Y., Bovet, P. Prevalence and Trends in Tobacco Use Among Adolescents Aged 13–15 Years in 143 Countries, 1999–2018: Findings from the Global Youth Tobacco Surveys. Lancet Child Adolesc Health. 2021 Apr;5(4):245–255. https://doi.org/10.1016/S2352-464 2(20)30390-4. Epub 2021 Feb 2. PMID: 33545071.

367. Méndez, D., Tam, J., Giovino, G.A., Tsodikov, A., Warner, K.E. Has Smoking Cessation Increased? An Examination of the US Adult Smoking Cessation Rate 1990–2014. Nicotine Tob Res. 2017 Dec;19(12):1418–1424. https://doi.org/10.1093/ntr/ntw239.

368. WHO. (2022). Tobacco, World Health Organisation webpage, accessed 28 March 2023. https://www.who.int/news-room/fact-sheets/detail/tobacco.

369. Bethesda MD. (2016). U.S. Department of Health and Human Services, National Institutes of Health, National Cancer Institute. The economics of tobacco and tobacco control, World Health Organization.

370. Le, T.T.T., Jaffri, M.A. The Association between Smoking Behaviors and Prices and Taxes per Cigarette Pack in the United States From 2000 Through 2019. BMC Public Health. 2022;22:856. https://doi.org/10.1186/s12889-022-13242-5.

371. Cancer Research UK. (2014). Cancer Research UK Briefing: Tobacco Taxation and Product Pricing. https://www.cancerresearchuk.org/sites/default/files/policy_apr2014_tobaccotaxationandproductpricing_briefing_cruk.pdf.

372. Ding, A. Youth are More Sensitive to Price Changes in Cigarettes Than Adults. Yale J Biol Med. 2003;76(3):115–124. PMID: 15369626; PMCID: PMC2582704.
373. Bader, P., Boisclair, D., Ferrence, R. Effects of Tobacco Taxation and Pricing on Smoking Behavior in High Risk Populations: A Knowledge Synthesis. Int J Environ Res Public Health. 2011;8(11):4118–4139. https://doi.org/10.3390/ije rph8114118.
374. Nazar, G.P., Sharma, N., Chugh, A., et al. Impact of Tobacco Price and Taxation on Affordability and Consumption of Tobacco Products in the South-East Asia Region: A Systematic review. Tob Induc Dis. 2021 Dec;19:97. https://doi.org/10.18332/tid/143179.
375. Blakely, T., Gartner, C. Tobacco Taxes Have Mixed Effects on Socioeconomic Disparities. Lancet Public Health. 2019 Dec;4(12):e595–e596. https://doi.org/10.1016/S2468-266 7(19)30223-3.
376. Frazer, K., Callinan, J.E., McHugh, J., van Baarsel, S., Clarke, A., Doherty, K., Kelleher, C. Legislative Smoking Bans for Reducing Harms from Secondhand Smoke Exposure, Smoking Prevalence and Tobacco Consumption. Cochrane Database Syst Rev. 2016;(2):CD005992. https://doi.org/10.1002/146 51858.CD005992.pub3.
377. Bauld, L. The impact of Smokefree Legislation in England: Evidence Review. University of Bath, 2011. https://assets.pub lishing.service.gov.uk/government/uploads/system/uploads/att achment_data/file/216319/dh_124959.pdf.
378. Hoffman, S.J., Tan, C. Overview of Systematic Reviews on the Health-related Effects of Government Tobacco Control Policies. BMC Public Health. 2015;15:744. https://doi.org/10.1186/s12889-015-2041-6.
379. Bauld, L. The Impact of Smokefree Legislation in England: Evidence Review. Department of Health (DH) 2011.
380. Hargreaves, K., Amos, A., Highet, G., Martin, C., Platt, S., Ritchie, D. and White, M. The Social Context of Change in Tobacco Consumption Following the Introduction of 'Smoke-free' England Legislation: A Qualitative, Longitudinal Study. Soc Sci Med. 2010;71:459–466.

381. Cancer Research UK. (2017). British Smokers Down by 1.9 Million Since the Ban [Press Release]. https://www.cancerresear chuk.org/about-us/cancer-news/press-release/2017-07-01-bri tish-smokers-down-by-19million-since-the-ban.

382. Stead, M., Moodie, C., Angus, K., Bauld, L., McNeill, A., Thomas, J., Hastings, G., Hinds, K., O'Mara-Eves, A., Kwan, I., Purves, R.I., Bryce, S.L. Is Consumer Response to Plain/Standardised Tobacco PACKAGING Consistent with Framework Convention on Tobacco Control Guidelines? A Systematic Review of Quantitative Studies. PLoS One. 2013 Oct 16;8(10):e75919. https://doi.org/10.1371/journal.pone. 0075919.

383. Pang, B., Saleme, P., Seydel, T., et al. The Effectiveness of Graphic Health Warnings on Tobacco Products: A Systematic Review on Perceived Harm and Quit Intentions. BMC Public Health. 2021;21:884. https://doi.org/10.1186/s12889-021-10810-z.

384. Hughes, N., Arora, M. Grills, N. Perceptions and Impact of Plain Packaging of Tobacco Products in Low and Middle Income Countries, Middle to Upper Income Countries and Low-income Settings in High-income Countries: A Systematic Review of the literature. BMJ Open. 2016;6:e010391. https://doi.org/10. 1136/bmjopen-2015-010391.

385. Arora, M., Tewari, A., Grills, N., et al. Exploring Perception of Indians about Plain Packaging of Tobacco Products: A Mixed Method Research. Front Public Health. 2013;1:35. https://doi. org/10.3389/fpubh.2013.00035.

386. White, C.M., Hammond, D., Thrasher, J.F., et al. The Potential Impact of Plain Packaging of Cigarette Products among Brazilian Young Women: An Experimental Study. BMC Public Health. 2012;12:737. https://doi.org/10.1186/1471-2458-12-737.

387. McNeill, A., Gravely, S., Hitchman, S.C., Bauld, L., Hammond, D., Hartmann-Boyce, J. Tobacco Packaging Design for Reducing Tobacco Use. Cochrane Database of Systematic Reviews 2017;(4):CD011244. https://doi.org/10.1002/14651858. CD011244.pub2.

388. McNeill, A., Gravely, S., Hitchman, S.C., Bauld, L., Hammond, D., Hartmann-Boyce, J. Tobacco Packaging Design for Reducing Tobacco Use. Cochrane Database Syst Rev. 2017

Apr 27;4(4):CD011244. https://doi.org/10.1002/14651858. CD011244.pub2.

389. Strong, D.R., Pierce, J.P., Pulvers, K., et al. Effect of Graphic Warning Labels on Cigarette Packs on US Smokers' Cognitions and Smoking Behavior After 3 Months: A Randomized Clinical Trial. JAMA Netw Open. 2021;4(8):e2121387. https://doi.org/10.1001/jamanetworkopen.2021.21387.

390. Bala, M.M., Strzeszynski, L., Topor-Madry, R. Mass Media Interventions for Smoking Cessation in Adults. Cochrane Database Syst Rev. 2017;(11):CD004704. https://doi.org/10.1002/146 51858.CD004704.pub4.

391. Kuipers, M.A.G., Beard, E., West, R., Brown, J. Associations Between Tobacco Control Mass media Campaign Expenditure and Smoking Prevalence and Quitting in England: A Time Series Analysis. Tob Control. 2018;27(4):455–462. https://doi.org/10.1136/tobaccocontrol-2017-053662.

392. Langley, T., Szatkowski, L., Lewis, S., McNeill, A., Gilmore, A.B., Salway, R., Sims, M. The Freeze on Mass Media Campaigns in England: A Natural Experiment of the Impact of Tobacco Control Campaigns on Quitting Behaviour. Addiction. 2014;109(6):995–1002. https://doi.org/10.1111/add.12448.

393. Blecher, E. The Impact of Tobacco Advertising Bans on Consumption in Developing Countries. J Health Econ. 2008 Jul;27(4):930–942. https://doi.org/10.1016/j.jhealeco.2008.02.010.

394. Chung-Hall, J., Craig, L., Gravely, S., et al. Impact of the WHO FCTC over the First Decade: A Global Evidence Review Prepared for the Impact Assessment Expert Group. Tob Control. 2019;28:s119–s128.

395. Bonnie, R.J., Stratton, K., Kwan, L.Y. (Eds.). Public Health Implications of Raising the Minimum age of Legal Access to Tobacco Products. Washington (DC): National Academies Press, 2015. https://www.ncbi.nlm.nih.gov/books/NBK310412/.

396. Freedman, K.S., Nelson, N.M., Feldman, L.L. Smoking Initiation among Young Adults in the United States and Canada, 1998–2010: A Systematic Review. Prev Chronic Dis. 2012;9:E05.

397. Marcon, A., Pesce, G., Calciano, L., Bellisario, V., Dharmage, S.C., Garcia-Aymerich, J., Gislasson, T., Heinrich, J., Holm, M., Janson, C., Jarvis, D., Leynaert, B., Matheson, M.C., Pirina, P.,

Svanes, C., Villani, S., Zuberbier, T., Minelli, C., Accordini, S. Ageing Lungs In European Cohorts Study. Trends in Smoking Initiation in Europe over 40 years: A Retrospective Cohort Study. PLoS One. 2018 Aug 22;13(8):e0201881. https://doi.org/10.1371/journal.pone.0201881.

398. Yörük, E.C. Yörük, B.K. Do Minimum Legal Tobacco Purchase Age Laws Work?. Contemp Econ Policy. 2016;34:415–429. https://doi.org/10.1111/coep.12153.

399. Kuijpers, T.G., Kunst, A.E., Willemsen, M.C. Policies That Limit Youth Access and Exposure to Tobacco: A Scientific Neglect of the First Stages of the Policy Process. BMC Public Health. 2019;19:825. https://doi.org/10.1186/s12889-019-7073-x.

400. Barrington-Trimis, J.L., Braymiller, J.L., Unger, J.B., McConnell, R., Stokes, A., Leventhal, A.M., Sargent, J.D., Samet, J.M., Goodwin, R.D. Trends in the Age of Cigarette Smoking Initiation Among Young Adults in the US From 2002 to 2018. JAMA Netw Open. 2020 Oct 1;3(10):e2019022. https://doi.org/10.1001/jamanetworkopen.2020.19022.

401. Hoffman, S.J., Poirier, M.J.P, Rogers, Van Katwyk, S., Baral, P., Sritharan, L. Impact of the WHO Framework Convention on Tobacco Control on Global Cigarette Consumption: Quasi-experimental Evaluations Using Interrupted Time Series Analysis and In-sample Forecast Event Modelling. BMJ. 2019;365:l2287.

402. Hoffman, S.J., Poirier, M.J.P., Rogers, Van Katwyk S., Baral, P., Sritharan, L. Impact of the WHO Framework Convention on Tobacco Control on Global Cigarette Consumption: Quasi-experimental Evaluations using Interrupted time Series Analysis and in-sample Forecast Event Modelling. BMJ. 2019;365:l2287.

403. Beaglehole, R., Bonita, R. Tobacco Control: Getting to the Finish Line. Lancet. 2022 May 14;399(10338):1865. https://doi.org/10.1016/S0140-6736(22)00835-2. PMID: 35569463.

404. Beaglehole, R., Bonita, R. The Lancet Tobacco Control: Far From The Finish Line. Lancet. 2022;398:1939.

405. WHO. (2021). WHO Global Report on Trends in Prevalence of Tobacco use 2000–2025. 4th edn. Geneva: World Health Organization.

406. Countdown NCD. NCD Countdown 2030: Pathways to Achieving Sustainable Development Goal target 3.4. Lancet. 2020;396:918–934.

407. Rodu, B., Godshall, W.T. Tobacco Harm Reduction: An Alternative Cessation Strategy for Inveterate Smokers. Harm Reduct J. 2006;3:37. https://doi.org/10.1186/1477-7517-3-37.
408. WHO. WHO Report on the Global Tobacco Epidemic 2021: Addressing New and Emerging Products. Geneva: World Health Organization, 2021.
409. WHO. FCTC, 2003.
410. Arnott, D., Lindorff, K., Goddard, A. Tobacco Control: The FCTC Provides the Route to the Finish Line. Lancet. 2022 Aug 6;400(10350):427. https://doi.org/10.1016/S0140-673 6(22)01334-4. Epub 2022 Jul 22. PMID: 35878621.
411. Yach, D. Time for a Rethink, Tobacco Reporter, 2023. https://tobaccoreporter.com/2023/02/20/time-for-a-rethink/.
412. Coop, K. Don't Forget the Smokers, Washington Post, 1998. https://www.washingtonpost.com/archive/opinions/1998/03/08/dont-forget-the-smokers/3560fbed-880a-45ff-8669-110fd8b63509/.
413. Barrington-Trimis, J.L., Braymiller, J.L., Unger, J.B., et al. Trends in the Age of Cigarette Smoking Initiation Among Young Adults in the US From 2002 to 2018. JAMA Netw Open. 2020;3(10):e2019022. https://doi.org/10.1001/jamanetworkopen.2020.19022.
414. Alcalá, H.E., Sharif, M.Z., Albert, S.L. Social Cohesion and the Smoking Behaviors of Adults Living with Children. Addict Behav 2016;53:201–205. ISSN 0306–4603, https://doi.org/10.1016/j.addbeh.2015.10.022.
415. Gallus, S., Lugo, A., Liu, X., Behrakis, P., Boffi, R., Bosetti, C., Carreras, G., Chatenoud, L., Clancy, L., Continente, X., Dobson, R., Effertz, T., Filippidis, F.T., Fu, M., Geshanova, G., Gorini, G., Keogan, S., Ivanov, H., Lopez, M.J., Lopez-Nicolas, A., Precioso, J., Przewozniak, K., Radu-Loghin, C., Ruprecht, A., Semple, S., Soriano, J.B., Starchenko, P., Trapero-Bertran, M., Tigova, O., Tzortzi, A.S., Vardavas, C., Vyzikidou, V.K., Colombo, P., Fernandez, E. Tack SHS Project Investigators. Who Smokes in Europe? Data From 12 European Countries in the TackSHS Survey (2017–2018). J Epidemiol. 2021 Feb 5;31(2):145–151. https://doi.org/10.2188/jea.JE20190344.

416. Arnett, J.J. Getting Better all the Time: Trends in Risk Behavior among American Adolescents since 1990. Arch Sci Psychol. 2018;6(1):87–95. https://doi.org/10.1037/arc0000046.

417. Fry, G., Grogan, S., Gough, B., Conner, M. Smoking in the Lived World: How Young People Make Sense of the Social Role Cigarettes play in their lives. Br J Soc Psychol. 2008;47(Pt 4):763–780.

418. Amos, A., Angus, K., Bostock, Y., Fidler, J., Hastings, G. A Review of Young People and Smoking in England. Public Health Res Consort, 2009.

419. Laverty, A.A., Filippidis, F.T., Taylor-Robinson, D., et al. Smoking Uptake in UK Children: Analysis of the UK Millennium Cohort Study. Thorax. 2019;74:607–610.

420. Leonardi-Bee, J., Jere, M.L., Britton, J. Exposure to Parental and Sibling Smoking and the Risk of Smoking Uptake in Childhood and Adolescence: A Systematic Review and Meta-analysis. Thorax. 2011 Oct;66(10):847–855. https://doi.org/10.1136/thx.2010.153379.

421. den Exter Blokland, E.A., Engels, R.C., Hale, W.W. 3rd, Meeus W, Willemsen MC. Lifetime Parental Smoking History and Cessation and Early Adolescent Smoking Behavior. Prev Med. 2004 Mar;38(3):359–368. https://doi.org/10.1016/j.ypmed.2003.11.008.

422. Vink, J.M., Willemsen, G., Boomsma, D.I. Heritability of Smoking Initiation and Nicotine Dependence. Behav Genet. 2005;35:397–406. https://doi.org/10.1007/s10519-004-1327-8.

423. Kale, D., Stautz, K., Cooper, A. Impulsivity Related Personality Traits and cigarette Smoking in Adults: A Meta-analysis Using the UPPS-P Model of Impulsivity and Reward Sensitivity. Drug Alcohol Depend. 2018 Apr 1;185:149–167. https://doi.org/10.1016/j.drugalcdep.2018.01.003.

424. López-Torrecillas, F., Perales, J.C., Nieto-Ruiz, A., Verdejo-García, A. Temperament and Impulsivity Predictors of Smoking Cessation Outcomes. PLoS ONE. 2014;9(12):e112440. https://doi.org/10.1371/journal.pone.0112440.

425. Benowitz, N.L. Nicotine Addiction. N Engl J Med. 2010 Jun 17;362(24):2295–2303. https://doi.org/10.1056/NEJMra0809890.

2 WHO IS (STILL) SMOKING? **141**

426. Pierce, J.P., Gilpin, E.A. News Media Coverage of Smoking and Health is Associated with Changes in Population Rates of Smoking Cessation But Not Initiation. Tob Control. 2001;10:145–153.

427. Akiyama, O., Nakamura, M., Tabuchi, T. [Awareness of Harm to others from Secondhand Smoke and Smokers' Interest in Smoking Cessation]. Nihon Koshu Eisei Zasshi. 2018;65(11):655–665. Japanese. https://doi.org/10.11236/jph.65.11_655.

428. Petroulia, I., Vardavas, C., Filippidis, F., et al. The Association between the Awareness of the Effects of Smoking/Secondhand Smoke and the Desire to Quit. Tob Induc Dis. 2018;16(1):710. https://doi.org/10.18332/tid/84622.

429. Viscusi, W.K. (1992). *Smoking: Making the Risky Decision*. Oxford University Press.

430. Krosnick, J.A., Malhotra, N., Mo, C.H., Bruera, E.F., Chang, L, et al. Correction: Perceptions of Health Risks of Cigarette Smoking: A New Measure Reveals Widespread Misunderstanding. PLoS ONE. 2019;14(2):e0212705. https://doi.org/10.1371/journal.pone.0212705.

431. Viscusi, W.K. Do Smokers Underestimate Risks? J Polit Econ. 1990;98(6):1253–1269. http://www.jstor.org/stable/2937757.

432. Martins, R.S., Junaid, M.U., Khan, M.S., et al. Factors Motivating Smoking Cessation: A Cross-sectional Study in a Lower-middle-income Country. BMC Public Health. 2021;21:1419. https://doi.org/10.1186/s12889-021-114 77-2; See also Gallus, S., Muttarak, R., Franchi, M., Pacifici, R., Colombo, P., Boffetta, P., Leon, M.E., La, Vecchia, C. Why Do Smokers Quit? Eur J Cancer Prev. 2013.https://doi.org/10.1097/CEJ.0b013e3283552da8.

433. Chaiton, M., Diemert, L., Cohen, J.E., Bondy, S.J., Selby, P., Philipneri, A., Schwartz, R. Estimating the Number of Quit Attempts it takes to Quit Smoking Successfully in a Longitudinal Cohort of Smokers. BMJ Open. 2016 Jun 9;6(6):e011045. https://doi.org/10.1136/bmjopen-2016-011045.

434. Borland, R., Partos, T.R., Yong, H.H., et al. How much Unsuccessful Quitting Activity is Going on Among adult smokers? Data from the International Tobacco Control Four Country

Cohort Survey. Addiction. 2012;107:673–682. https://doi.org/10.1111/j.1360-0443.2011.03685.x.
435. Centers for Disease Control and Prevention. Smoking Cessation: Fast Facts, accessed 22 July 2022. https://www.cdc.gov/tobacco/data_statistics/fact_sheets/cessation/smoking-cessation-fast-facts/index.html.
436. Zhou, X., Nonnemaker, J., Sherrill, B., Gilsenan, A.W., Coste, F., West, R. Attempts to Quit Smoking and Relapse: Factors Associated with Success or Failure from the Attempt Cohort Study. Addictive Behavior. 2009. https://doi.org/10.1016/j.addbeh.2008.11.013; Vangeli E, Stapleton J, Smit ES, Borland R, West R. Predictors of Attempts to Stop Smoking and their Success in Adult General Population Samples: A Systematic Review. Addiction. 2011;106:2110–2121. https://doi.org/10.1111/j.1360-0443.2011.03565.x.
437. Hartmann-Boyce, J., Hong, B., Livingstone-Banks, J., Wheat, H., Fanshawe, T.R. Additional Behavioural Support as an Adjunct to Pharmacotherapy for Smoking Cessation. Cochrane Database Syst Rev. 2019;(6). https://doi.org/10.1002/14651858.CD009670.pub4; See also Stitzer, M.L. Combined Behavioral and Pharmacological Treatments for Smoking Cessation. Nicotine Tobacco Res. 1999. https://doi.org/10.1080/14622299050012041.
438. Els, C., van Wijk, L.L., Landais, J.H. Understanding the Multitude of Barriers that Prevent Smokers in Lower Socioeconomic groups from Accessing Smoking Cessation Support: A Literature Review. Prev Med. 2019:123:143–151. ISSN 0091–7435. https://doi.org/10.1016/j.ypmed.2019.03.029.
439. Levesque, J.F., Harris, M.F., Russell, G. Patient-centred Access to Health Care: Conceptualising Access at the Interface of Health Systems and Populations. Int J Equity Health. 2013;12:18. https://doi.org/10.1186/1475-9276-12-18.
440. Morphett, K., Partridge, B., Gartner, C., Carter, A., Hall, W. Why Don't Smokers Want Help to Quit? A Qualitative Study of Smokers' Attitudes towards Assisted vs. Unassisted Quitting. Int J Environ Res Public Health. 2015 Jun 10;12(6):6591–6607. https://doi.org/10.3390/ijerph120606591.
441. Raupach, T., Brown, J., Herbec, A., Brose, L., West, R. A Systematic Review of Studies Assessing the Association between

Adherence to Smoking Cessation Medication and Treatment Success. Addiction. 2014 Jan;109(1):35–43. https://doi.org/10.1111/add.12319. See also Pound, C.M., Zhang, J.Z., Kodua, A.T., et al. Smoking Cessation in Individuals Who Use Vaping as Compared with Traditional Nicotine Replacement Therapies: A Systematic Review and Meta-analysis. BMJ Open. 2021;11:e044222. https://doi.org/10.1136/bmjopen-2020-044222.

442. Mersha, A.G., Gould, G.S., Bovill, M., Eftekhari, P. Barriers and Facilitators of Adherence to Nicotine Replacement Therapy: A Systematic Review and Analysis Using the Capability, Opportunity, Motivation, and Behaviour (COM-B) Model. Int J Environ Res Public Health. 2020. https://doi.org/10.3390/ijerph172 38895.

443. U.S. Food and Drug Administration. Distribution of Full-Time Equivalent, 2021. https://www.fda.gov/about-fda/fda-basics/how-many-people-are-employed-fda-and-what-areas-do-they-work.

444. Lynch, S. FDA Criminal Office Draws Fire from Agents and Doctors over Drug Import Crackdown. Reuters, 2016. https://www.reuters.com/investigates/special-report/usa-fda-cases/.

445. Malone, R.E., Proctor, R.N. Prohibition no, Abolition Yes! Rethinking How We talk About Ending the Cigarette Epidemic. Tob Control. 2022;31:376–381.

446. Paraje, G., Stoklosa, M., Blecher, E. Illicit Trade in Tobacco Products: Recent Trends and Coming Challenges. Tob Control. 2022 Mar;31(2):257–262. https://doi.org/10.1136/tobaccocontrol-2021-056557.

447. Goodchild, M., Paul, J., Iglesias, R., Bouw, A., Perucic, A.M. Potential Impact of Eliminating Illicit Trade in Cigarettes: A Demand-side Perspective. Tob Control. 2022;31(1):57–64.

448. CDC. Preventing and Reducing Illicit Tobacco Trade in the United States, National Center for Chronic Disease Prevention and Health Promotion, 2015. www.cdc.gov/tobacco/stateandc ommunity/pdfs/illicit-trade-report-508.pdf.

449. He, Y., von Lampe, K., Wood, L., Kurti, M. Investigation of Lead and Cadmium in Counterfeit Cigarettes Seized in the United States. Food Chem Toxicol. 2015;81:40–45. https://doi.org/10.1016/j.fct.2015.04.006.

450. Lisboa, T.P., Mimura, A.M.S., da Silva, J.C.J., de Sousa, R.A. Chromium Levels in Tobacco, Filter and Ash of Illicit Brands Cigarettes Marketed in Brazil. J Anal Toxicol. 2020;44(5):514–520. https://doi.org/10.1093/jat/bkz106.

451. Aitken, C.K., Fry, T.R., Farrell, L., Pellegrini, B. Smokers of Illicit Tobacco Report Significantly Worse Health than Other Smokers. Nicotine Tob Res. 2009 Aug;11(8):996–1001. https://doi.org/10.1093/ntr/ntp102. Epub 2009 Jun 18.

452. Remeikienė, R., Gasparėnienė, L., Yorulmaz, Ö., Gagytė, G., Menet, G. Is Money Laundering the Main Funding Source for Cigarette Smuggling in (non) European Countries? Bus: Theory Pract. 2022;23(1):198–207.

453. U.S. Bureau of Alcohol, Tobacco, Firearms, and Explosives (ATF). (2018, May). Fact Sheet - Tobacco Enforcement. https://www.atf.gov/resource-center/fact-sheet/fact-sheet-tobacco-enforcement.

454. U.S. Department of State. The Global Illicit Trade in Tobacco: A Threat to National Security. United States Department of State, 2015. https://2009-2017.state.gov/documents/organization/250513.pdf.

455. Sanderson, T.M. Transnational Terror and Organized Crime: Blurring the Lines. SAIS Rev Int Aff. 2004;24(1):49–61.

456. Shelley, L.I., Melzer, S.A. The Nexus of Organized Crime and Terrorism: Two Case Studies in Cigarette Smuggling. Int J Comp Appl Crim Justice. 2008;32(1):43–63.

457. Kulick, J., Prieger, J., Kleiman, M.A. Unintended Consequences of Cigarette Prohibition, Regulation, and Taxation. Int J Comp Appl Crim Justice. 2016;46:69–85.

458. Werb, D., Rowell, G., Guyatt, G, Kerr, T., Montaner, J., Wood, E. Effect of Drug Law Enforcement on Drug Market Violence: A Systematic Review. Int J Drug Policy. 2011;22(2):87–94.

459. Prieger, J.E., Kulick, J. Unintended Consequences of Enforcement in Illicit Markets. Econ Lett. 2014;125(2):295–297.

460. Prieger, J.E., Kulick, J. Violence in Illicit Markets: Unintended Consequences and the Search for Paradoxical Effects of Enforcement. BE J Econ Anal Policy. 2015;15(3):1263–1295.

461. Franklin, N. (2021, November 1). Can Higher Tobacco Taxes Help Pay for the Reconciliation Bill?– Law Enforcement Action

Partnership, Reason Foundation Panel Discussion [video transcript]. Reason Foundation. https://reason.org/commentary/watch-panel-discussion-can-higher-tobacco-taxes-help-pay-for-the-reconciliation-bill.

462. Bayer, R., Stuber, J. Tobacco Control, Stigma, and Public Health: Rethinking the Relations. Am J Public Health. 2006 Jan;96(1):47–50. https://doi.org/10.2105/AJPH.2005.071886.

463. Bell, K. Tobacco Control, Harm Reduction and the Problem of Pleasure. Drugs and Alcohol Today. 2013;13(2):111–118. https://doi.org/10.1108/DAT-03-2013-0013.

464. Volkow, N.D. Stigma and the toll of addiction. N Engl J Med. 2020;382(14):1289–1290.

465. Oshio, T., Nakamura, R. Trends and Determinants of Cigarette Tax Increases in Japan: The Role of Revenue Targeting. Int J Environ Res Public Health. 2022 Apr 18;19(8):4892. https://doi.org/10.3390/ijerph19084892.

466. Callard, C. Follow the Money: How the Billions of Dollars that Flow from Smokers in Poor Nations to Companies in Rich Nations Greatly Exceed Funding for Global Tobacco Control and What Might Be Done About It. Tob Control. 2010 Aug;19(4):285–290. https://doi.org/10.1136/tc.2009.035071.

467. ASH. (2022). U.S. Tobacco Lobbyist and Lobbying Firm Registration Tracker. ASH.

468. European Commission. (2011). Report on the public consultation on the possible revision of the Tobacco Products Directive (2001/37/EC) Brussels: Health and Consumers Directorate-General—Directorate D—Health systems and products D4—Substances of Human Origin and Tobacco Control. Jul, Report No.

European Commission. (2010). Health and Concumers Directorate-General. In: Assesment DC—PHaR, editor. Posible revision of the Tobacco Products Directive 2001/37/EC Public consultation document. Brussels: European Commission.

469. Hiilamo, H., Glantz, S.A. Old Wine in New Bottles: Tobacco Industry's Submission to European Commission Tobacco Product Directive Public Consultation. Health Policy. 2015

Jan;119(1):57–65. https://doi.org/10.1016/j.healthpol.2014.11.002.

CHAPTER 3

E-cigarettes: The Technology, the Market, and the Practice of Vaping

1 ALTERNATIVE NICOTINE

Anyone who would ponder the [tobacco] endgame must acknowledge that the continuum of risk exists and pursue strategies that are designed to drive consumers from the most deadly and dangerous to the least harmful forms of nicotine delivery.

Mitch Zeller, director of the Center for Tobacco Products (March 2013 to April 2022)[1]

1.1 Nicotine ≠ Tobacco

In the public's consciousness, nicotine is often synonymous with tobacco. Since nicotine has historically been derived from tobacco and, until the 1980s, nicotine was not available in non-tobacco products, the two were considered interchangeable. But nicotine is not tobacco, nor is it directly responsible for tobacco-related disease and mortality. Nicotine is addictive, and its presence in combustible tobacco products keeps people using cigarettes, which kill half of users prematurely. However, it is the combustion of tobacco, not nicotine, that produces the tars, carcinogens, and toxicants that lead to the cancers and cardiovascular and lung diseases that afflict smokers. Still, almost 50 years after Michael Russell stated, "People smoke for the nicotine, but they die from the tar,"[2] nicotine continues to be inextricably associated with tobacco and smoking harms

© The Author(s), under exclusive license to Springer Nature Switzerland AG 2024
S. C. Hampsher-Monk et al., *Tobacco Regulation, Economics, and Public Health, Volume I*, https://doi.org/10.1007/978-3-031-41312-4_3

147

148 S. C. HAMPSHER-MONK ET AL.

in the public eye. A nationally representative study of American adults in 2017 reported that approximately 75% of adults were either unsure of the relationship between nicotine and cancer or incorrectly believed that nicotine causes cancer.[3] That misunderstanding persists even among trained medical professionals. In 2020, 80% of physicians from specialties including family medicine, internal medicine, obstetrics and gynecology, cardiology, pulmonary & critical care, and hematology & oncology believed, incorrectly, that nicotine directly causes cancer.[4] Americans are not peculiar in this regard: Widespread misperceptions about the harms of nicotine have also been reported elsewhere,[5] including in Greece, India, Japan, Norway, and South Africa.[6] In England, misperceptions surrounding nicotine have deteriorated in recent years: Between 2014 and 2019 the proportion of the Britons who correctly believed e-cigarettes were less harmful than cigarettes declined from 45 to 34%.[7]

The persistence of the misunderstanding about nicotine is especially perplexing given the widespread acceptance of nicotine replacement therapies (NRTs). Patches, gums, lozenges, sprays, and inhalators, widely available since the 1980s, are broadly approved by national regulators and deemed "essential medicines" by the WHO.[8] There is robust evidence confirming NRT's efficacy as cessation aids.[9] Adverse reactions tend to be relatively rare, and minor at that.[10] Once decoupled from combustion, nicotine poses little risk to health and continued use can play an important role in helping people transition away from dangerous combustible tobacco products. However, misunderstandings about the safety and efficacy of NRTs impede uptake.[11] Further, for those who do not consider themselves to be physiologically addicted, medical NRTs may seem inappropriate.[12] As commercial alternatives, non-combustible nicotine products may also help nicotine-dependent smokers who are unable or unwilling to quit with other means to avoid known smoking-related harms without facing what is for many an impassible barrier: forgoing nicotine. In some countries, these products are proving to be more popular cessation aids than conventional NRTs. According to Public Health England (PHE) in 2020, 27.2% of quitting attempts used nicotine vaping products, while 18.2% used NRTs.[13] Similar preferences have been reported in the U.S.[14]

1.2 What Are Alternative Nicotine Products?

Just as there are many different types of combustible tobacco products (including cigarettes, roll-your-own tobacco, cigars, pipes, hookah, and cigarillos), alternative nicotine products are a heterogenous category, including not only e-cigarettes of various descriptions but also Heated Tobacco Products, oral tobacco, and modern oral nicotine products. The products in this category share some similarities: Alternative nicotine products are all combustion-free, thus detached from the key driver of smoking harms. However, the safety profile of each product varies, both in relation to combustible tobacco and other combustion-free alternatives,[15] and none is without risk. Each contains nicotine and therefore each product in this category is addictive—though, again, to differing extents.[16] However, the products in this category vary in almost every other respect, including form, appeal, rates of use, regulatory status, safety, and efficacy for smoking cessation, making further differentiation necessary.

Within the larger category of non-combustible alternative nicotine products, there are four sub-groups: Smokeless tobacco, Heated Tobacco, modern oral nicotine products, and e-cigarettes.

Smokeless tobacco refers to tobacco (or tobacco-derived) products that are chewed, sucked, or sniffed rather than smoked. In such products, nicotine is absorbed through the mouth or nose. Smokeless tobacco comes in several forms: Chewing tobacco—"chew," "spitting tobacco," or "spit"—includes loose, braided (twists) and compressed (plugs) tobacco leaves, which are inserted into the gap between the cheek and gum. Snus (or "dip"), is a particular kind of moist oral tobacco originating in Sweden that is pasteurized to kill harmful bacteria. Snus is finely ground tobacco, available in either dry or moist forms, contained in pouches or sold loose. A pouch or a pinch of snus is placed between the cheek and gum, or inside the inner lip below the front teeth. Both chewing tobacco and snus allow flavorings (if present) to leach out into the saliva, and nicotine is absorbed into the blood through the mucosa lining the inside of the mouth. Dissolvable products represent a final sub-type of smokeless tobacco, whereby powdered tobacco is formed into tablets, sticks, or strips that are either sucked or chewed until they dissolve.

Heated tobacco products (HTPs), also referred to as Heat-not-burn (HNB) devices, heat tobacco without burning it, creating an aerosol containing bio-available nicotine that is inhaled through a mouthpiece. Tobacco's combustion point is around 750°C. HTPs heat tobacco sticks resembling short cigarettes to a lower temperature, typically around 350°C—hot enough to aerosolize nicotine but far lower than the temperatures required for combustion (the actual temperature varies widely between models). The tobacco sticks consist of dried rolled tobacco, humectants binding agents, and flavorings contained in an acetate tube connected to a polymer film filter. The heat source in modern HTPs, such as IQOS, glo, and Pax, is an electric battery. Earlier models such as Eclipse used a carbon tip wrapped in a fiberglass heat barrier, allowing the tobacco to be heated without being ignited. Modern devices feature a rechargeable battery powering a heating element and a mouthpiece. The products may include a shut-off that activates after a period of use or after a designated number of puffs.

Like HTPs, e-cigarettes (also referred to as "electronic nicotine delivery systems" or "ENDS", "nicotine vaping products" or "NVPs" "electronic cigarettes"; "vape pens"; or simply "vapes") are electronic devices. However, instead of heating tobacco, e-cigarettes aerosolize an e-liquid, which typically contains nicotine as well as flavorings, suspended in a humectant such as propylene glycol (PG) or vegetable glycerin (VG). The e-liquid is absorbed from a chamber by a wick, aerosolized and inhaled by the user through a mouthpiece. Like HTPs, and unlike combustible tobacco products, e-cigarettes do not burn tobacco and so do not produce smoke. While the use of both HTPs and e-cigarettes may be described colloquially as "vaping," e-cigarettes are a distinct category of nicotine product.

The design and appearance of e-cigarettes varies widely between models. However, e-cigarettes share common components: Batteries (typically rechargeable unless the device is disposable) produce power to activates a heating element. Rechargeable e-cigarettes use a charging port, typically compatible with a USB micro cable, to allow the user to connect the device to an external power source. A wick, usually cotton, rayon, or silica, is used to absorb e-liquid and transfer it to the heating coil.[17] That element is made of a resistant material such as copper, which heats up when electricity is passed through it. The e-liquid is vaporized upon contact with the coil, much as water turns to steam when coming into contact with a hot pan,[18] producing aerosol that is then inhaled by the user. The atomizer is a single unit that contains both the wick and the coil. Some designs allow the user to alter the volume of aerosol

3 E-CIGARETTES: THE TECHNOLOGY, THE MARKET ... 151

produced either by utilizing a larger wick or by changing the power or resistance in the coil, affecting the temperature of the coil. A chamber (either a refillable tank, interchangeable pod, or, in the case of disposables, a fixed closed reservoir), is used to store e-liquid. E-cigarettes that allow the user to refill the tank have a fill port—an opening padded with silicone. Some pod-based systems have a fill port on the pods themselves, allowing for pods to be reused a number of times. Refillable pods may also contain the heating element within the pod. Even refillable pods need to be replaced periodically as oxidation of the coil occurs over time, affecting the aerosolization process. Some, though not all, e-cigarettes have buttons to turn the device off or on, increase the power and resistance, or check the battery life. An airflow control allows the user to change the amount of air moving through the atomizer, which affects the production of aerosol. This allows the user to manually titrate their intake of aerosol. Titration may also be achieved by inhaling more vigorously or more frequently.

1.3   A Lexicon of Alternative Nicotine

Collectively, "alternative nicotine products" refer to any tobacco or nicotine product that does not use combustion as a mechanism for nicotine delivery. This mix of products has other names, including Non-combustible alternatives (NCAs), Safer Nicotine Products (SNPs), Reduced Risk Products (RRPs), Reduced Harm Products (RHPs), Modified Risk Tobacco Products (MRTPs), or Alternative Nicotine Delivery Systems (ANDS). Traditionally, medicalized NRTs are not included in this category, though that distinction is somewhat semantic since it depends on the decisions of a given regulator rather than any intrinsic characteristics of a product or the motivations of the user. The U.K.'s Medicines and Healthcare Products Regulatory Agency (MHRA) has issued requests for proposals from manufacturers for an e-cigarette to be regulated as a medical device.[19] The medical pathway is also technically possible in many other countries, though the considerable barriers to medical authorization may prevent manufacturers seeking such authorizations. As of 2023, there are no medically approved e-cigarettes anywhere in the world. However, if a regulator such as the MHRA does issue such an approval then e-cigarettes, or at least one example of an e-cigarette, would qualify as an NRT—at least in that specific context.

152   S. C. HAMPSHER-MONK ET AL.

By any inclusion criteria, alternative nicotine products are a heterogeneous group. While the category as a whole may be useful to differentiate these products from combustible tobacco, the important differences between the various alternative nicotine products make further differentiation imperative. While e-cigarettes and HTPs are sometimes aggregated through the use of terms like "vaping," that term may also describe inhaling aerosolized cannabis products, the consequences of which, both short term and long term, are different from the use of nicotine e-cigarettes.[20] Differentiating between HTPs and e-cigarettes is necessary because each product may be treated differently at the regulatory level, and while both products are likely to be far safer than combustible tobacco, they appear to have different risk profiles.[21] Moreover, available evidence for the safety and efficacy of each product for the purposes of smoking cessation also differs. While there is increasingly strong evidence that e-cigarettes support smoking cessation, the evidence on whether HTPs do so is less robust.[22]

The literature contains frequent references to "Electronic Nicotine Delivery Systems (ENDS)"—a term favored by the WHO. "ENDS" excludes HTPs such as IQOS, Ploom, and Glo, and refers only to e-cigarette devices such as Juul, Vuse, and Puff bar as well as e-pipes and e-cigars. However since, semantically at least, HTPs are also electronic systems that deliver nicotine, the distinction may be somewhat confusing for the casual observer. "ENDS" also excludes vaping devices that do not contain nicotine, which are sometimes referred to, again somewhat confusingly, as Electronic Non-Nicotine Delivery Systems (EN&NDS or ENNDS). Consumers generally use terms like "e-cigarettes" or "vapes" in lieu of "ENDS." This book uses the term "e-cigarettes" to describe nicotine aerosolizers. If an e-cigarette does not contain nicotine, this is specified as "non-nicotine e-cigarette." The term "HTP" is used to describe devices for heating tobacco without combustion.

Alternative nicotine products may be differentiated on the basis of whether they contain tobacco. Smokeless Tobacco and Heated Tobacco Products do, as the names suggest. Conversely, many modern oral nicotine products and e-cigarettes are often described as "tobacco-free." Problematically, however, many ostensibly tobacco-free alternative nicotine products use tobacco-derived nicotine, extracted from the tobacco plant and crystalized into nicotine salts, leaving their status as "tobacco-free" open to interpretation. On the other hand, manufacturers have begun to utilize lab-synthesized nicotine, producing nicotine that is etiologically free from tobacco. The precise methods for synthesizing nicotine are proprietary, but several chemical reactions could convert ethyl nicotinate, an ester of nicotinic acid also known as niacin or vitamin B3, into nicotine.[23] Given that it would be incorrect to describe NRTs as "tobacco products," it may seem inconsistent to describe e-cigarettes in this manner, especially if the nicotine contained in these products is not even derived from tobacco.

Practically, however, regulators may overlook this distinction, treating all commercial nicotine products as "tobacco" regardless of origin. In 2022, for example, the U.S. FDA extended its authority to regulate synthetic nicotine products eliminating a loophole that had exempted synthetic nicotine e-cigarettes from its oversight.[24] In terms of the risk potential, there is no evidence to suggest that synthetic nicotine is less addicting than tobacco-derived nicotine. Though synthetic nicotine is free from the tobacco-specific nitrosamines (TSNAs) in naturally occurring nicotine and some tobacco-derived nicotine,[25] research investigating any relative benefits of synthetic nicotine over tobacco-derived nicotine is in its infancy. Secondly, the presence of tobacco in a product is a poor measure of the harms associated with that product's use. It has been suggested that all tobacco products are risky,[26] but that overlooks that risks are relative and some tobacco products are more risky than others. Kozlowski and Sweanor argue that the failure to disclose this key health-relevant information effectively blindfolds current and potential consumers, impairing their ability to make informed decisions.[27] Further, there is likely to be a wide variation between any two products even within a single category. Taking e-cigarettes as an example, differences in nicotine strength and formulation; chemical constituents in e-liquids, flavorings, temperature of the heating elements, and volume of aerosol produced, etc., likely all affect toxicity and addiction potential,[28] making it difficult to make sweeping comparisons about the relative safety of two products, much less two groups of products, purely on the basis of whether one uses tobacco, or nicotine derived from tobacco.

1.4   What's in a Name?

Different agencies, manufacturers, researchers, and consumers deploy different terms to describe these products and their use. In particular, the difference between the lexicon of public health science and the colloquial terms used to describe nicotine product use can inhibit the precision with which researchers can characterize consumption patterns and their consequences for health. Consider for example that U.S. physicians and medical exams conducted for life insurance companies might inquire about a person's smoking status, but typically do not enquire about the use of smokeless tobacco or alternative nicotine products. Population and cohort studies might inquire about one's status as a "tobacco user," but respondents using e-cigarettes may not consider themselves to be tobacco users, in which case this categorization may fail to identify any risks associated with exclusive e-cigarette use. It would also fail to distinguish between users of smokeless tobacco, heated tobacco, and combustible tobacco. For example, some forms of smokeless tobacco, especially gutkha, khaini, and zarda, the use of which are prevalent in India, Pakistan, and the countries of South East Asia, have been linked to a condition known as "fish mouth" resulting from submucosal fibrosis and oral cancers caused by the slaked lime, nitrosamines, and other chemical additives in oral tobacco products.[29,30,31] The literature generally agrees that nicotine products exist on a continuum of risk,[1] with combustible tobacco products at the high end, and NRTs at the low end. Non-combustible nicotine products are located between these extremes, being somewhat riskier than NRTs and somewhat less risky than combustibles. How much less risky e-cigarettes are in relation to combustible tobacco is hotly contested. It has been argued that the degree to which combustibles are more dangerous is sufficient to describe the relative risk not as a continuum but as a cliff.[32] On the other hand, while most commentators acknowledge that e-cigarettes are safer than smoking, many emphasize the residual risks and suggest that they should not be considered as an alternative. The American Lung Foundation, for example, maintains that "switching to e-cigarettes does not mean quitting."[33] Taking the opposite approach, the U.K. government specifically encourages smokers to "Swap to Stop," offering free e-cigarettes to many smokers for this purpose.[34]

Regardless of the appropriate schema, characterizing a product's risk with sufficient accuracy presents a significant challenge because both the relative and absolute risk profiles are unsettled (as discussed in Volume II, Chapter 1). Further, the risks posed reflect consumption patterns and device characteristics and so vary between users. Efforts to resolve these "knowledge gaps" via consumer surveys may be complicated by ambiguities in the lexicon. For example, surveys could ask respondents to identify not only as smokers/non-smokers but as users of any nicotine product.

But that would fail to differentiate ex-smokers using NRTs to remain abstinent from current consumers from never-smokers using e-cigarettes. "Do you smoke?" begs the question "Smoke what?". Should those who smoke cannabis but do not smoke tobacco answer in the affirmative? "Do you smoke tobacco?" is more specific, but risks aggregating oral tobacco, heated tobacco, and e-cigarette users with those not using any nicotine or tobacco product, all of whom might answer truthfully in the negative.

In recent years, researchers have made efforts to adapt existing surveys to gain greater insights into consumption patterns in the population, and to assess the health consequences thereof. However, even within ostensibly narrow categories such as "nicotine e-cigarettes," differences in the brand, liquid composition, method of vaping, battery-power, and device design obscures generalizable risk categorization.[35] More challenging still, to accurately determine the health consequences of nicotine product use, it is also important to assess the duration, frequency, and intensity of use,[36] all of which vary between users and across time. The tendency for consumers to use multiple products simultaneously adds yet another level of complexity. Ideally, surveys would account for poly-use, but framed as a binary option, "poly-use" masks a wide range of possible combinations. A consumer using one product, say combustible cigarettes, once or twice per month and another, nicotine e-cigarettes, multiple times a day, may expect very different health outcomes than a consumer using both products interchangeably on a daily basis. The almost limitless variation in consumption modalities means it can be extremely difficult to establish "normal" or "typical" use. This obscures researchers' ability to accurately attribute health outcomes to consumption in the population, and to ensure that clinical investigations reflect real-world use.

2 The Technology of E-cigarettes

2.1 Precursors to Modern E-cigarettes

The notion that nicotine could be decoupled from combustion is not new. In the twentieth century, the emerging evidence on the dangers of tobacco smoking prompted a series of attempts to design a product that would allow the user to inhale nicotine without inhaling smoke. The first such documented device was a patent for an "electronic drug vaporizer" filed by Joseph Robinson in 1927.[37] The device was never commercialized, and it is not known if a prototype was ever produced. Another patent[38] filed in 1963 by Herbert Gilbert for a "smokeless non-tobacco cigarette" also failed to be commercialized, although Gilbert did at least produce a prototype. In 1979, NASA scientist Phil Ray and his physician Dr. Norman Jacobson created a device which allowed the user to inhale nicotine through a plastic tube containing filter paper soaked in nicotine. The device involved no combustion and, with the assistance of American Tobacco Products Inc., the pair brought the "smokeless" cigarette to the U.S. market under the tradename "Favor." It was not a commercial success. The Favor's nicotine was unstable, quickly decomposing into cotinine. Moreover, the FDA deemed that the Favor was a "new drug" and ruled that it could not be sold without their approval.[39] The one enduring legacy of the Favor is that its designers are accredited with coining the term "vaping." Technically, however, in its application to e-cigarettes, "vaping" is a misnomer. E-cigarettes do not produce "vapor," but aerosol: a suspension of particles in a gas.

In 1988, RJ Reynold's "Premier" became the first heated tobacco product to be commercially marketed[40] as a "safer alternative to cigarettes." Resembling conventional cigarettes, the Premier used a combustible carbon tip to heat processed tobacco allowing the user to inhale nicotine aerosol. The Premier proved deeply unpopular with test markets, with the typical subject being particularly unhappy with the taste, smell, and user experience,[41] and it was pulled from production less than one year after its launch at a loss valued at US$800 million.[42] However, in the 1990s, Reynolds continued to develop its HTP technology, resulting in the release of the Eclipse[43] in 1996. Philip Morris introduced the "Accord" device in 1998, marketed with reference to its perceived benefits such as reduced second-hand smoke, odor, and ash. Like the Premier before it, the Accord was discontinued in 1996[44] due to poor sales. Since the 2010s a new generation of HTP products have been launched: JTI launched Ploom in 2013; PMI launched iQOS in Italy and Japan in 2014; and BAT launched Glo in 2015. Examples of other brands include Lil (launched by Korea Tobacco in 2017), Mok (launched in 2018 by China Tobacco), Revo (launched in 2014 by BAT), and Pulze (launched in 2019 by Imperial Tobacco). By 2019, all of the major tobacco companies had either acquired HTP brands, or developed them in-house. The development of these products is integral to the development of e-cigarettes since both HTPs and e-cigarettes are born out of a desire to decouple smoking-related harms from the combustion of tobacco. However, these products are technologically different from e-cigarettes, for the reasons discussed earlier.

2.2 The Evolution of the Modern E-cigarette

Early e-cigarettes resembled conventional cigarettes—an approximation which appears to have been intended to aid their acceptability as a substitute for combustible cigarettes. These "cig-a-likes," even incorporated an orange "filter" and a red LED that activated upon inhalation to create a passing resemblance to the glowing ember of a lit cigarette. First-generation devices generally had fixed low-voltage batteries, and typically contained separate atomizing units, batteries, and tanks. Later cig-a-likes combined the atomizer and tank into a two-piece device with a separate battery, or even combined all three into a single disposable device.[45]

"Clearomizers" represent a second generation of e-cigarettes, typically utilizing removable atomizers with larger e-liquid tanks than cig-a-likes which, unlike many earlier models were often refillable. These products also began to utilize larger variable voltage batteries. The effect of these adaptations was to increase convenience and decrease the relative expense associated with replacing hardware. Second-generation devices usually retained the cylindrical form but were larger than earlier cig-a-likes. The design moved away from an attempt to mimic the appearance of conventional cigarettes, which may be indicative of the distinction that e-cigarette users were increasingly eager to make between vaping and smoking.

Third-generation devices, often referred to as "mods," allowed consumers to further vary the voltage and wattage produced by the battery. The use of interchangeable parts, modifiable atomizers, larger batteries, and refillable tanks provided functionality which allowed the consumer to modify their experience, for example, varying the amount of aerosol produced by changing the power deployed by their device or the size of the wick. These modifications gave these devices their name; Mods, or "box mods," and they became popular with "cloud chasers"— users eager to produce large volumes of aerosol more akin to a waterpipe than a cigarette. This, again, was indicative of the emerging and distinctive vaping sub-culture.

Since around 2015, a fourth generation of e-cigarettes has emerged, deploying disposable (and sometimes refillable) pods containing nicotine

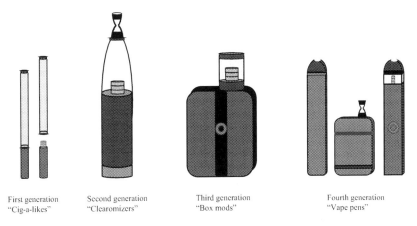

| First generation | Second generation | Third generation | Fourth generation |
| "Cig-a-likes" | "Clearomizers" | "Box mods" | "Vape pens" |

Fig. 1 The evolution of the e-cigarette (*Source* Authors' elaborations)

e-liquid that are inserted into a small device containing a fixed atomizer and battery in a housing unit often resembling a USB flash drive. Juul, introduced by Pax Labs in 2015, became the best-known example of the now ubiquitous USB-style vape pen. The popularity of Juul's products was such that, in many circles in the late 2010s "vaping" became known as "Juuling." Following Juul's commercial success many other producers sought to mimic Juul's design, the legacy of which are the many, often flavored, disposable products which are rapidly becoming the most popular market segment in North America and the U.K.

Figure 1 depicts generic examples of each of the four generations of e-cigarettes. Note that the physical resemblance to combustible e-cigarettes is absent in the second-, third-, and fourth-generation products. Fourth-generation products include both rechargeable devices and disposables. Images are not to scale.

3 THE MARKET FOR E-CIGARETTES

3.1 First Movers; 2003–2012

Hon Lik is credited with the invention of the e-cigarette in 2003. Lik, a recalcitrant smoker, created the device after his heavily smoking father died from lung cancer. Lik's employer, Golden Dragon Holdings, developed Lik's innovation under the name Ruyan, meaning "*like smoke*," introducing the product to Chinese markets in 2004. The subsequently rebranded firm, Dragonite International Ltd., was the world's first e-cigarette company, developing and producing a line of rechargeable cartridge-based electronic cigarettes, e-pipes, and e-cigars for the Chinese market.

By April 2006, e-cigarettes were being introduced to Europe and, according to U.S. Customs and Border Protection, they first entered the U.S. market in August of that year.[46] Sensing commercial opportunity, U.S. producers began to develop their own models. Between 2006 and 2010, a flurry of U.S. companies entered the e-cigarette market, with Green Smoke (2006), NJOY (2007) Safe Cig (2007), White Cloud Electronic Cigarettes (2008), Smoke Anywhere (2008), Blu e-Cigs (2009), Madvapes (2009), VMR (2009), Logic Technology Development (2010), and International Vapor Group (IVG) (2010) among the first movers.

Elsewhere, the market for e-cigarettes was also attracting new companies. Nicolite (2007), Gamucci (2007), Ten Motives Ltd (2008), CN Creative (2008), and Skycig (2011) were among the first entrants to the U.K. market. Typically, however, manufacturing has been concentrated in China.[47] Responding to international demand, Chinese companies, mostly based in Shenzhen province, began producing for the international wholesale market, but subsequently created devices for domestic and international markets under their own brand names, too. Some of the best-known Chinese brands include Smoore Technology Limited (2006), Joyetech, (2007), KangerTech (2007), and Innokin Technology (2011).[48]

Appendix 4.5 to the 2016 Surgeon General's Report[49] describes the changing market share of e-cigarette brands in the U.S. between 2010 and 2014. During this time, the number of e-cigarette brands with significant market share increased from two to six, though by the end of this period there were hundreds of available brands.[50] At the start of 2010, the market was highly concentrated, with Gamucci, accounting for approximately 90% of the Nielsen-tracked sales. However, NJOY quickly grew its market share, becoming the market leader with over 60% market share by the end of 2010. Throughout 2011, 21st Century Smoke and blu won significant market share from NJOY, and by 2012, Mistic, NJOY, blu, and 21st Century Smoke shared approximately 80% of the U.S. market. Blu and, to a lesser extent, Logic increased market share throughout the latter part of 2012 and 2013; however in 2014, both brands lost out to

160 S. C. HAMPSHER-MONK ET AL.

newcomer VUSE. Having diversified through 2010 and 2011, Lorillard's acquisition of blu in April 2012 prefaced a return to market concentration. By the end of 2014, blu, Logic, MarkTen, and Vuse accounted for more than 85% of total market share. In these four years, market leadership changed from Gamucci to NJOY, to 21st Century Smoke, to Mistic, back to NJOY, to blu, and finally to VUSE at the end of 2014.[51]

3.2 Enter: Transnational Tobacco Companies; 2012–Present

By one estimate, in 2014 there were already 466 e-cigarette brands, with an additional 10 brands coming to market each month.[52] While many independent e-cigarette firms grew quickly, profiting from the rising popularity of e-cigarettes, manufacturers continued to be dwarfed by the tobacco-producing giants. However, e-cigarette-producers had something that the tobacco firms did not: a growing market. In markets such as the U.S., tobacco sales had been declining for several years.[53] Sensing the commercial opportunity, and facing disruption to their traditional business model, transnational tobacco companies (TTCs) increasingly sought to acquire independent producers and develop their own e-cigarette brands through in-house R&D. Lorillard acquired Blu E-cigs in April 2012—the first acquisition of an e-cigarette company by a tobacco company in the U.S. Lorillard subsequently also purchased Skycig in October 2013 in a deal worth $60 million, giving Lorillard a presence in the British and Irish e-cigarette markets. Skycig was then rebranded as Blu. Reynolds acquired Lorillard in July 2014 for $27.4 billion, and Blu was subsequently sold to Imperial Brands (formerly Imperial Tobacco) along with the Kool, Winston, and Salem cigarette brands for $7.1 billion. Following the sale, Blu became Imperial's flagship brand, offering disposable and rechargeable products in a range of flavors, as well as a tank system called the blu-PLUS.

In December 2012 British American Tobacco (BAT) acquired CN Creative, a U.K.-based e-cigarette company known for developing the Intellicig brand, marking the first acquisition of a British e-cigarette firm by a transnational tobacco company. Under BAT's ownership, CN Creative was subsequently merged into Nicoventures. BAT launched Vype in the U.K. in August 2013, offering both disposable and rechargeable devices. BAT's also developed Voke (originally Oxette), a commercialized nicotine inhaler, and eVoke (called nicadex under Creative)—the only known example of a medically licensed e-cigarette. But neither Voke nor eVoke were ever commercialized. Having formed a "strategic partnership" with Reynolds American Inc (RAI) in 2014, BAT acquired Reynolds outright in 2017, along with its popular Vuse e-cigarette brand, into which Vype was consolidated in 2020.

Imperial Tobacco Group acquired Dragonite (formerly Ruyan) in August 2013 for $75 million. Imperial also struck a deal with U.K. pharmacy *Boots* in February 2014 to sell Puritane—a cig-a-like disposable. In February 2015, Imperial released Jai—a rechargeable cig-a-like in French and Italian markets, then acquired Blu in June of the same year.

Altria, operating in the e-cigarette market under the name NuMark, launched its own rechargable cig-a-like in 2013, the MarkTen. The MarkTen was manufactured in China, with e-liquids under the same brand produced by an affiliate in the U.S. NuMark also acquired the Green Smoke brand in April 2014 for $110 million. Both MarkTen and Green Smoke were discontinued in December 2018 when Altria acquired a 35% stake in Juul Labs for $12.8 billion.

Reynolds American Inc (RAI) established itself as a vertically integrated e-vapor company with the launch of a subsidiary; Reynolds Vapor Company in 2012, launching Vuse a cartridge-based e-cigarette with pods coming in a variety of flavors in 2013. Reynolds promoted Vuse with direct mail and TV advertising. Vuse quickly became a leading e-cigarette company dominating the U.S. market in 2015–2017, before losing market share to Juul.[54] In recent years, following intense media and regulatory pressure as well as legal challenges, Juul has lost market share to Vuse.[55] Juul's peak market share, 47% of the e-vapor market in the U.S. (by revenue), occurred in 2019.[56]

Under a strategic agreement with Altria in December 2013, Philip Morris International (PMI) agreed to commercialize Altria's e-cigarette products (including the MarkTen) outside of the U.S. PMI then acquired U.K. e-cigarette company "Nicocigs" from its owner Nicolite in June 2014. At that time, Nicolite offered cig-a-like starter-kits, disposables, and refills and the acquisition of Nicocig brand has been seen as an attempt to gain entry to the U.K. market.[57] PMI went on to develop its own brand of e-cigarette, iQOS Mesh for the U.K. market, introducing it in 2018, but it was subsequently withdrawn and rebranded as Veev in 2020.

Finally, Japan Tobacco International (JTI), acquired E-lites from Zandera in June 2014 for an undisclosed sum, and acquired Logic in the following year, which according to a Wall Street Journal article had achieved a 20% share of the U.S. convenience store market for e-cigarettes.[58] E-lites was rebranded as Logic in 2016 and the brand has since included both closed and open tank systems.

By 2018, the big tobacco giants—BAT, Imperial, JTI, and PMI—had each developed or acquired flagship e-cigarette brands. But it was another brand that revolutionized the e-cigarette market. Adam Bowen and James Monsees founded Juul Labs in May 2015. Their product, JUUL, a fourth-generation rechargeable e-cigarette utilized disposable pod-based technology. Resembling a USB Flash drive, Juul devices are recharged by docking them with a magnetic USB port. Disposable pods, containing nicotine salt (59 mg/ml in the U.S.) were, initially at least, much stronger than many of the formulations offered by competitors. Originally, Juul pods came in eight flavors: Classic tobacco, Virginia tobacco, Cucumber, Crème Brulé, Mango, Cool Mint, Menthol, and Fruit Medley.

Juul quickly rose to become the most popular e-cigarette in the U.S. by 2018.[59] Between 2016 and 2017 Juul's revenue climbed from US$60 to $245 million[60] and for calendar 2018 it topped $1 billion.[61] That year, Juul was valued at more than $16 billion, beating Facebook to become the fastest start-up in U.S. history to reach a valuation exceeding $10 billion.[62] In October 2018, Nielsen data reported that Juul accounted for over 70% of the U.S. market covered by its participating retail merchants; data from Eurmonitor shows that Juul's market share was 36.5% in 2018 and 47.0% the year after.[63,64] Two months later Altria purchased a 35% stake in Juul for $12.8 billion. For Altria, the acquisition may have been motivated by a desire to protect its own stock price which had been declining since July 2017.[65] Disappointing sales of Altria's e-cigarette brand, the Mark Ten, may also have prompted the move.[66] In the public eye, the sale muddied what remained of the distinction between the e-cigarette industry and big tobacco.[67] Still, for Juul, the advantages were clear: in addition to financing growth, the acquisition allowed Juul access to Altria's extensive distribution channels in the U.S.[65] In 2018 and 2019, Juul introduced its products to Israel, the U.K., Canada, Russia, South Korea, Ireland, Germany, and the Ukraine. The acquisition also gave Juul access to Altria's experience in regulatory compliance—the lack of which was beginning to show.

In her 2021 book, *Big Vape: The Incendiary Rise of Juul*,[68] Jamie Ducharme provides an in-depth historical account of the development of Juul, and how it came to dominate the U.S. market, detailing some of the mistakes that resulted in the company losing favor with the regulator.

First and foremost, Juul was criticized for its marketing practices. Juul is not unusual among e-cigarette manufacturers in spending significant sums on marketing. However, Juul relied on social media to an unusual extent. This form of relatively inexpensive advertising has been found to be highly conducive to sales.[69] However, social media platforms are heavily used by young people and minors. Moreover, Juul's critics suggest that the company specifically targeted youth, using young-looking models, images designed to appeal to young audiences, and alluring themes such as sexuality and freedom that have nothing to do with switching away from smoking.[70] Juul has also faced criticism for using celebrity endorsements from influencers who have large followings among underage social media users.[71] Damningly, Juul also advertised their products on websites targeted to school-aged children such as coolmathgames.com and socialstudiesforkids.com and child-oriented media outlets including Nickelodeon, Nick Jr., The Cartoon Network, and Seventeen Magazine.[72]

Juul has also attracted criticism for the nicotine potency of its e-liquids. Whereas other competitors were still using free-base nicotine, Juul's products combined tobacco-derived nicotine with an acid. The resulting "nicotine salt" is less irritating than free-base nicotine, making it easier to inhale more frequently and more deeply.[73] Relative to free-base nicotine, salt nicotine has been demonstrated to have greater appeal and improve the sensory experience of vaping, particularly among never-smokers.[74] Nicotine salts may be more readily absorbed than free-base nicotine.[75] And Juul pods contained more than double the amount of nicotine found in many other brands at the time[76] -5% nicotine by volume vs. 2% in contemporaneous products. By using greater quantities of nicotine, and in this specific format, it is argued that the use of Juul and similar products would be more addictive than other e-cigarettes.[77] Competitors proved eager to emulate Juul's success and incorporated nicotine salt formulations in their own devices. Robert Jackler, professor of neurosurgery at Stanford University School of Medicine, has characterized the shift toward higher potency nicotine e-cigarettes as an "arms race."[78] Today many of the e-liquid formulas sold in the U.S. as pods, disposables, and e-liquids contain 5% nicotine by weight: more than double the amount sold in the EU, U.K., and Canada, where nicotine limits are capped to 20 mg/ml. Juul argues that it was trying to make a product that appealed to smokers, but it is undeniable that the product also appealed to large numbers of underage consumers, many of whom had no history of smoking.[79]

In April 2018, in an attempt to understand the high rates of youth use of Juul products, the FDA demanded Juul turn over documents detailing the company's design and marketing considerations, product safety research and information on whether certain product features appeal to specific age groups.[80] Juul complied and voiced support for raising the federal minimum legal sale age from 18 to 21.[81] The company also announced that, in addition to working with the FDA, they would spend $30 million to prevent youth access.[82] But in September of that year, the FDA sent warning letters to Juul, along with the other four largest U.S. e-cigarette brands (Vuse, MarkTen, blu, and Logic) demanding that the firms outline their plans to address youth vaping, under threat of their products being removed from the market.[83] Again, Juul announced that it would comply.[84] A Juul spokesperson cited the company's existing program to identify retailers that do not enforce age restrictions and stating that the company had requested the removal of more than five thousand posts violating the age restrictions from websites including Instagram, Facebook, and Amazon.[85] The FDA was unconvinced; Commissioner Scott Gottlieb argued that the failure of Juul's efforts was evident in the current statistics on prevalence of youth use.[85] In an unannounced inspection of Juul's San Francisco headquarters in September 2018, the FDA seized thousands of pages of documents detailing Juul Lab's business practices, marketing, online age verification protocols, and youth prevention efforts.[84] Then, on June 13, 2019, Chairman Raja Krishnamoorthi of the congressional Subcommittee on Economic and Consumer Policy launched an investigation into the youth e-cigarette epidemic and whether JUUL had actively marketed its product to children.[86] Testimony heard by the subcommittee found that Juul had violated FDA restrictions by making unapproved claims regarding their products' safety and utility as a cessation aid,[86] reportedly going as far as to tell school children that their products were "totally safe."

Later that year, as part of a settlement with the Center for Environmental Health,[87] Juul agreed that it would:

- Not promote products in any media format where more than 15% of the audience was under 21 years of age.
- Stop using social media platforms for marketing purposes (unless age-gated).

- Not sponsor sporting events or concerts where under 21s would be present.
- Never pay for or attend educational or youth-oriented events.
- Revise warning labels to replace the phrase "adults only" and "not for use by minors," which might entice engagements by rebellious youth, with the phrase "the sale of tobacco products to minors is prohibited by law."
- And establish purchasing limits for online and brick-and-mortar stores, and continue its secret shopper program to prevent sales of Juul products to minors.

On June 23, 2022, the FDA issued Juul a Marketing Denial Orders (MDO) banning any further marketing or sale of the products effective immediately.[88] The FDA's rejection would have deprived Juul of its largest market, in addition to the bans its products faced in Israel[89] and in other markets such as India, Japan, and Australia where e-cigarettes are prohibited on a de facto or de jure basis. However, the U.S. Court of Appeals blocked the order on June 24th, leaving Juul's products available on the U.S. market at least temporarily.[90] The FDA reopened Juul's premarket tobacco product authorization (PMTA) application. At the time of writing it is unclear whether Juul will be permitted to continue selling its products in the U.S.

Almost 6,000 lawsuits filed against Juul in the U.S. have been combined in multidistrict litigation (MDL), MDL-2913. These cases include class action lawsuits and individual personal injury cases filed in four states. In December 2022, Juul agreed to settle thousands of these cases in the MDL, for an undisclosed amount, rumored to be US$1.2 billion.[91] Additionally, several states have sued Juul Labs Inc. for their role in the "youth vaping epidemic." In June 2021, Juul settled with North Carolina, agreeing to pay $40 million to the state.[92] Furthermore, in September 2022, Juul agreed to pay $438.5 million to settle a two-year-long investigation into the company's marketing and sales practices, led by several other U.S. states and territories.[93] In 2023, Juul settled a class action lawsuit in California over Juul's deceptive marketing practices and settled with the city of Chicago on claims that it has deceptively marketed products and sold to underage consumers.[94]

In response to regulatory scrutiny and legal actions, Altria consistently wrote down its investment in Juul, cutting its initial valuation from US$16 billion to just $450 million by July 2022.[95] The losses adversely affected Altria's share price, prompting an investor class action lawsuit against the company,[96] alleging that it failed in its responsibility to conduct due diligence prior to investing in Juul and misled investors about risks associated with the Juul investment. The case concluded in December 2021 with a $90 million settlement agreement.[97] In September 2022, Altria disclosed to the U.S. Securities Exchange Commission its intention to terminate its non-compete agreement with Juul.[98] That removed a legal barrier preventing Altria from acquiring one or more of Juul's competitors and developing its own product range. Altria announced in March 2023, that it would buy NJOY for at least $2.75 million. By that time, NJOY had gained PMTAs for six products.[99] At the same time, Altria exchanged its ownership stake in Juul, valued at just $250 million at the end of 2022, for intellectual property related to Juul's Heated Tobacco technology.[100] Public criticism, regulatory scrutiny, and litigation have eroded Juul's market share, with consumer demand shifting toward other products including Juul's competitor, Vuse. By March 2023, Vuse was more than 16 percentage points ahead in the U.S. Market (42.2% vs. 26.1%). Meanwhile, former heavyweights, NJOY and Blu had less than 2.7% and 1.4% respectively.[101]

3.3 Global Market Trends

The global e-cigarette market has experienced robust year-on-year growth in recent years. *Euromonitor* report that the global e-cigarette market doubled in size two times between 2013 and 2019.[102] By 2021 the global market for e-cigarettes was estimated to be worth more than US$20 billion.[103,104] The U.S. has consistently represented the largest national e-cigarette market, more than tripling in size from $2.6 billion in 2014 to $9.6 billion in 2019. In the Western European region the market grew from $2.3 billion to $5.5 billion during the same period, though growth has since slowed. The U.K. represents the largest European market, valued at over $2.9 billion in 2019. Elsewhere in Europe, Hungary, the Czech Republic, and Poland also saw robust growth from 2015 on, and Ukraine doubled in size between 2018 and 2019, reaching a value of $150 million. Growth has also been strong in the Asia-Pacific region, growing from less than $1.2 billion in 2014 to $2.2 billion in 2019. The market in Latin America continues to be significantly smaller than other regions, not least due to regulatory conditions. Still, between 2014 and 2019 the regional market almost tripled in size to $62.5 million, with

Colombia, Chile, and the Dominican Republic exhibiting the strongest growth. In no small part due to the stance of regulators, the markets for e-cigarettes in Australia and the Middle East remained small, with more muted growth.

Forecasting the size of the global e-cigarette market is fraught because it depends on a number of unpredictable variables including future policy decisions, economic growth, changes in disposable income, and evolving knowledge, beliefs, and attitudes among consumers and potential consumers. Notwithstanding, there seems to be a consensus that the market will continue to exhibit robust growth through the 2020s, although the estimates for projected growth offered by market research organizations vary widely. At the high end, Allied Market Research projects a compound annual growth rate (CAGR) of 16.8% between 2022 and 2031, resulting in a global market size of US$94 billion by 2031.[105] A more conservative estimate, offered by IMARC consulting group, projects a CAGR of 4.4% between 2023 and 2028, resulting in a global market valued at $31.9 billion at the end of that time horizon.[106]

The market share of independent e-cigarette companies has consistently declined, from 82.0% in 2014 to 56.2% in 2019, meaning that independent e-cigarette companies lost more the 5% per year to TTCs and their affiliates.[107] This market concentration has been driven by at least two factors: First, as discussed, TTCs have increasingly invested in e-cigarettes by acquiring formerly independent brands. Second, the adoption of increasingly robust regulations, and in some cases international tariffs, have made it more difficult for smaller independent firms to operate. VMR ceased trading in 2018, citing the combination of regulatory compliance costs associated with the PMTA application process and import tariffs implemented by the Trump administration, which increased production costs by up to 50%.[108]

3.4   U.S. E-cigarette Market Trends

The U.S. is the largest national market for e-cigarettes, representing, by some estimates, almost half of all global sales.[109] As is evident globally, the U.S. e-cigarette market has seen robust growth in recent years. The FTC's reports on e-cigarettes provide data indicating the pace of growth (Fig. 2).

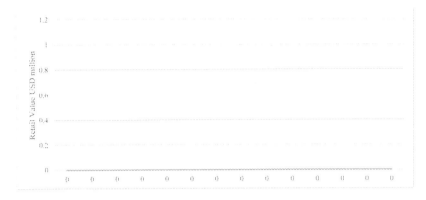

Fig. 2 U.S. e-cigarette sales, 2008–2021 (*Note* The U.S. e-cigarette market has experienced robust growth throughout the time series, with the exception of the year-on-year decline in 2019–2020 coinciding with the COVID-19 pandemic which has been reported to have adversely affected in-person sales.[110] *Source* Euromonitor[111])

The scale of the U.S. market and the geopolitical influence of the U.S. government on the world stage had an important influence on e-cigarette regulation beyond the U.S. border. As such, the trends in the U.S. market over the past decade can exemplify developments in the broader international market.

3.4.1 Disposables

Between 2010 and 2013, U.S. sales of disposable e-cigarettes increased in value to about US$100 million in Q2 2013. In terms of unit sales, less than 100,000 disposables were purchased nationwide in 2010. In the first quarter of 2014 alone, there were almost 11 million sold. Price declines driven by the improvements in technology and economies of scale, along with industry promotions, may have driven the increase: The average price of a disposable e-cigarette sold in the U.S. declined from $17 in 2010 to $9 in 2014.[112] However, the quarterly volume of disposable e-cigarettes subsequently declined from 11 million to approximately three million over the course of 2014, as demand shifted toward tank-based and modifiable devices. That shift corresponds with the decline in price of rechargeable devices from an average of $37 in 2010 to just $12 by the end of 2014. These price declines meant that modular devices represented an increasingly economical means of consuming nicotine. Subsequently, the introduction of pod-based systems like Juul and Vuse saw similarly dramatic increases from $260 million in 2015 to $1.97 billion in 2018.[113] By May 2023, past-year sales were $3.94 billion in the U.S. for these two brands, which held about 55% market share by revenue and about 75% share by units sold.[114]

Since 2018 consumer preferences appear to have shifted back to disposables. Data published by the CDC foundation[111] reports that between 2018 and 2021 unit sales of e-cigarettes in the U.S. increase from 178.2 to 326.6 million units, of which the portion of disposables increased from 13.2% in 2018 to 45.9% in 2021.[115] The data accompanying the FTC's second report on e-cigarettes also demonstrate that the average nicotine concentration of disposables sold in the U.S. has increased from just over 25 mg/ml in 2015 to almost 41 mg/ml in 2020.[116] Modern disposable e-cigarettes, many resembling Juul's USB-stick-like form and proportions, have proven especially popular among young e-cigarette users in the U.S., thanks in part to an exemption from FDA's 2020 ban on characterizing flavors in pod-based systems. Having responded to pressure from the FDA, Juul discontinued sales of its flavored products in 2019.[117] But between 2019 and 2020, while overall use of e-cigarettes among middle- and high-school students declined by 1.8 million users, the use of disposables increased from 3% of middle school e-cigarette users in 2019 to 15.2% in 2020, and from 2.4% of high-school e-cigarette users to 26.5% during the same period.[118] Sales data also report a general increase in the demand for disposables.[119] According to the NYTS, while less than 7% of past-month current smokers reported using Juul as their usual brand, almost 27% now report a preference for PuffBar, a brand of flavored disposables.[120]

The FDA's Center for Tobacco Products sent warning letters to Cool Clouds (doing business as PuffBar) in February 2020, along with nine other companies, signaling that their products could be removed from the market for not having achieved the necessary premarket authorization. The FDA also called out other companies[121] for illegally marketing disposable cigarettes and targeting youth with flavors designed to appeal to minors including Twinkies, Cherry Coke, and Cinnamon Toast Crunch cereal. In response PuffBar attempted to circumvent the FDA's scrutiny by switching to synesthetic nicotine. However, in March 2022 U.S. lawmakers extended the FDA's authority to include synthetic nicotine,[122] requiring that all nicotine products, regardless of origin, comply with the existing regulations, including the requirement to submit a PMTA (discussed shortly).

The rise in popularity of disposables is also evident in Canada and the U.K., albeit to a slightly lesser extent. Hammond and colleagues[123] examine young (16–19 year olds) past-month e-cigarette users, before (2017, 2018, 2019), during (February 2020), and after (August 2020) implementation of U.S. flavor restrictions. They report that the use of disposable e-cigarettes increased to the greatest extent among U.S. respondents (13.2% to 36.8%), though a similar demand shift was observed in Canada (7.7% to 14.2%) and England (10.8% to 16.4%). In the U.K., ASH reports[124] that an uptick in the proportion of 11 to 17 year olds admitting to current e-cigarette use (7% in 2022 Vs. 3.3% in 2021) coincides with a large increase in the proportion of young e-cigarette users using disposables, increasing from 7.7% in 2021 to 52% in 2022. The concurrent rise in the popularity of disposable e-cigarettes outside of the U.S. may suggest that the other factors besides the FDA's regulatory strategy were operative. On the other hand, given the size of the U.S. market, if the FDA's regulatory strategy were sufficient to stimulate demand for e-cigarettes in the U.S. market, this might be expected to influence the international supply chain with spill-over effects in other markets.

3.4.2 Demand for Flavors

The demand for flavored e-cigarettes has been a consistent feature of the e-cigarette market. Some of the first-mover brands did not initially sell non-tobacco-flavored products; however, by 2015 most producers were offering some varieties of flavor.[125] The FTC reported a dramatic increase in sales of flavored products between 2015 and 2018: Sales of fruit-flavored e-cigarettes had already tripled between 2012 and 2013 from $4.9 million to $16.7 million.[112] Fruit-flavored pods represented 4.7% of cartridges sold in 2015, but by 2018 that figure was 29.7%. Candy and dessert-flavored pods and flavored disposables also saw significant increases, which the FTC said raised "serious concerns that such products might have maintained or increased youth use of e-cigarette products."[113] The FTC data demonstrates robust compliance with the flavor ban in pod systems: such products represented less than 1% of pod sales in 2020. However, demand for flavors remains high. In 2020, "other flavors"— not tobacco mint or menthol—represented more than 80% of e-liquids sold. Data from the CDC Foundation[126] show the rapid decline in sales

3   E-CIGARETTES: THE TECHNOLOGY, THE MARKET ...   171

of non-tobacco-mint-menthol flavored cartridges at the end of 2019 and the start of 2020 is offset by a growth in other flavors of disposables through April 2022. Unit sales of other flavors outpaced those of tobacco and mint/menthol flavors by the end of this period.

3.4.3   Marketing and Promotion

Like the traditional tobacco industry, e-cigarette producers have used a range of marketing channels and strategies to advertise and promote their products, including television. The latter option was, in the U.S., illegal for combustible tobacco products after 1971. Other marketing activity involves product placement, advertising in print media, point-of-sale advertising, e-commerce, and social media advertising.[127] E-cigarette brands have sponsored music festivals and sporting events. In 2011, Blu sponsored NASCAR, and e-cigarette advertisements at the NFL Super Bowl in 2012 reached an estimated 100 million people.[128] Juul even sponsored political party conferences, including the California Democratic Party convention in 2019 and the U.K.'s Conservative Party Conference. Cigarette manufactures have been banned from such activities since the Master Settlement Agreement in 1998.

Advertising and marketing have driven demand for e-cigarettes, raising concerns, particularly since the tactics and themes deployed by early e-cigarette advertisements often resembled those used by the tobacco industry.[129] These themes include personal liberty, rebellion, sexuality, and glamor.[130] The FTC reported that e-cigarette companies' spending on advertising and promotion ballooned from under US$200 million in 2015 to over $1 billion in 2019.[131] E-cigarette companies spent more than $90 million on TV advertising in 2019 and more than $50 million on radio advertising. Some companies evaded the FDA's ban on free samples by offering products discounted to $1.[132] Expenditures on price discounts increased 16-fold from just over $11 million in 2015 to more than $180 million in 2019, and expenditures on promotional allowances paid to wholesalers and retailers increased from almost $50 million in 2015 to almost $180 million over the same period.[133] Critics were further alarmed by the use of health and cessation-related claims, which were considered unsubstantiated. Social media represented another important marketing channel for e-cigarettes via promotions on Twitter, Facebook, YouTube, and Instagram, prompting fears that raising public awareness of e-cigarettes would drive uptake by non-smokers, especially youth and young adults, grounded in evidence that exposure to tobacco advertising has a dose-dependent relationship with cigarette smoking.[134] Some use of these marketing channels has been found to have targeted minors specifically.[135,136]

3.4.4 Brick-and-Mortar E-cigarette Retailers

Early U.S. e-cigarette sales were concentrated in e-commerce stores and kiosks in shopping malls, but by the mid-2010s e-cigarettes were also being sold in gas stations, convenience stores, tobacconists, pharmacies, "big box" retail chains, and brick-and-mortar vape shops specializing in e-cigarette products.[47] In 2013, the California Department of Public Health reported that e-cigarettes were available in more than half of the outlets where tobacco was sold.[137] The brick-and-mortar vape store sector has grown significantly in the U.S. market.[138] Estimates vary, but according to the American Vaping Association, by 2014 there were 15,000 such stores nationwide.[139] Vape shops typically offered refillable devices, tank systems, and e-liquids. Levy et al.[140] estimate that in 2017, vape stores represented more than 40% of sales of open systems. Some also offer disposables and traditional tobacco products, too. Many states do not require vape shops to obtain a tobacco retailer license if they do not sell combustible tobacco. Vape shops have traditionally been an under-studied sales channel.[141] A 2015 study reported that some vape shops may be using free samples, loyalty programs, sponsored events, direct mail, advertising through social media, and price promotions to adver-tise their products, particularly among target groups including college students.[142] By 2015, brick-and-mortar stores surpassed e-commerce as the dominant sales channel for e-cigarettes.[112] By one estimate, in the same year, two-thirds of U.S. colleges had at least one vape shop within a three-mile radius of the campus.[143]

3.4.5 E-commerce

By 2015, online sales accounted for approximately 30% of e-cigarette sales volume.[144] E-commerce continues to be a significant market segment,[145] not least since many brick-and-mortar retailers turned to e-commerce in response to COVID-19 era restrictions,[146] which prompted many retailers to close or limit in-person sales.[147] E-cigarettes are sold online by websites owned by manufacturers (including brands developed or acquired by the tobacco industry, and by independent e-cigarette producers). E-cigarettes have also been widely promoted on social media platforms such as YouTube, Twitter, Instagram, and Facebook, many of which do not require age verification.[112] The industry has also extensively sponsored online banner and video advertising on websites including music and entertainment websites targeted to youth.[148] One study identified more than 3,000 websites selling e-cigarettes in 2014. A content analysis performed on the 281 most popular websites, judged by web traffic, found that most (71.9%) were based in the U.S., though 16.7% were sited in the U.K. and a further 5.3% in China. E-cigarette starter-kits were the most common products (sold on 92.5% of sites) followed by disposables (55.2%). Most websites sold flavored e-cigarette products, with fruit being the most popular (79.4%), followed by candy (75.2%), coffee (68.0%), and alcohol (45.6%). Some sort of health warning was featured on 71.5% of the websites, but 69.4% also claimed health advantages for e-cigarettes over other tobacco products, and 32.7% claimed e-cigarettes helped people to quit smoking conventional cigarettes.[149] Legally, e-commerce sites should verify the ages of customers, but it appears that many e-commerce sites do not routinely check IDs, making internet sales an important driver of youth access. A 2015 study[150] found that 14- to 17-year-old consumers were able to purchase e-cigarettes from 75 of 80 sites that were able to process online payment. Five vendors claimed that a third-party shipping company would verify age at delivery, but none actually did.

3.4.6 Nicotine Potency

Another trend noted with concern by the FTC was that the nicotine strength of disposables appears to have increased from an average of 25 mg/ml in 2015 to 39.5 mg/ml in 2018.[151] Pod-based systems were often even stronger, with popular brands ranging from 51 to 61 mg/ml. CDC Principal Deputy Director Dr. Anne Schuchat told a congressional committee that salt nicotine could have a potentially more harmful effect on the developing brains of adolescents.[152] Given that nicotine is addictive, higher nicotine content could plausibly accelerate the transition from experimental use into subsequent addiction, leading to greater consumption in the long term. However, it is not clear how more-potent nicotine effects health outcomes in the population . If e-liquids do contain harmful chemicals, then higher nicotine content might be preferable from a safety perspective, if higher potencies could satisfy nicotine dependence while exposing the consumer to a smaller volume of aerosol.[153] On the other hand, from an abuse liability perspective, higher nicotine content might

174   S. C. HAMPSHER-MONK ET AL.

accelerate or perpetuate nicotine dependence. Moreover, higher potencies may increase risks of accidental exposure and ingestion. Following such concerns, the EU, U.K., and Canada are among those who have capped the nicotine content of e-cigarettes to 20 mg/ml. The consumer responses to these regulations and their potential impacts on public health will be discussed further in Volume III, Chapter 1.

3.4.7   Pre-market Tobacco Applications

As of August 8, 2016, the FDA considered all vaping products to be tobacco products, requiring all manufacturers to obtain a pre-market tobacco product authorization (PMTA)—the mechanism by which the FDA approves or denies companies permission to market new tobacco products. According to the agency, PMTA applications must provide evidence that the product is "appropriate for the protection of public health." In order to reach such a decision and to authorize marketing, FDA considers, among other things:

- Risks and benefits to the population as a whole, including people who would use the proposed new tobacco product as well as non-users;
- Whether people who currently use any tobacco product would be more or less likely to stop using such products if the proposed new tobacco product were available
- Whether people who currently do not use any tobacco products would be more or less likely to begin using tobacco products if the new product were available; and
- The methods, facilities, and controls used to manufacture, process, and package the new tobacco product.

FDA-issued guidance demonstrates the exhaustive requirements necessary to gain approval.[154] Applicants must provide extensive toxicological and epidemiological data on the likely consequences of product use under a range of scenarios (intended and otherwise). Unsurprisingly, and perhaps by design, this is an extremely onerous task, especially for small and medium-sized businesses. The FDA projects that the cost of an individual PMTA could be up to US$400,000, though others estimate that the costs could reach several million dollars.[155] And businesses must submit a new PMTA for each product, and resubmit every time they change a product, al-be-it with some degree of replication.

The final deadline by which companies could submit PMTAs passed on May 14, 2022. Applicants who had submitted prior to this date could keep their products on the market while awaiting a decision from the FDA, but after this date, any product for which a PMTA had not been submitted faced removal from the market. The FDA received applications from more than 500 companies for more than 6.5 million e-cigarette and vapor products.[156] In a move resembling a Denial of Service (DOS) attack, a single company—JD Nova submitted PMTAs for 4.5 million products, including many for products that were not actually on the market, and with only subtle differences in ingredients. The FDA rejected these in a single judgment in August 2021 on the basis that the company had failed to provide an Environmental Impact Assessment (EA) in any of their applications,[156] issuing a Refuse To File (RFT) letter. Note, however, that unlike the Marketing Denial Order (MDO), the RTF allowed companies to resubmit at a later date, albeit having first removed their products from the market. Nevertheless, MDOs were quick to follow; the first coming for roughly 55,000 flavored e-cigarette products produced by Great American Vapes, Vapor Salon, and JD Nova (again).

By September 2022 the FDA had rejected PMTAs for more than 7.7 million products. Many of these rejections used a standard referred to as the "Fatal flaw." An FDA memorandum dated July 9, 2021 describes plans to apply the Fatal Flaw Review to non-tobacco-flavored EJDS products' PMTAs not in Phase III (review) at that time.[157] This standard would mean that any applications in Phase II that did not include longitudinal cohort studies or Randomized Controlled Trials (RCTs) would be issued an MDO, without any of the other merits of an application being considered. Feeling that the FDA had moved the goalposts by offering new guidance mid-process and that the rejection of their applications qualifies as "arbitrary and capricious," several applicants including Triton,[158] and Gripum[159] suedthe FDA, leading to temporary court-ordered stays of the MDOs. But, in these cases, the courts upheld the FDA's MDO. The Supreme Court in 2021 upheld a decision of the 6th circuit court,[160] resulting in an MDO issued to Breeze Smoke, LLC withstanding. Other plaintiffs, however, have been more successful: Fumizer and Turning Point Brands had their MDOs rescinded by the FDA following legal action by the applicants, allowing the companies to keep marketing their products while the agency reexamines the submissions. In August 2022, an appeals court sided with petitioners Bidi Vapor LLC, Diamond Vapor LLC, Johnny Cooper LLC, Vapor Unlimited LLC, Union Street Brands, and Pop Vapor Co. LLC, finding that the FDA's MDOs issued to these companies were arbitrary and capricious.[161] In 2023, another court ordered[162] a full stay on the MDO issued to R.J. Reynolds Vapor Company for a PMTA application for a menthol-flavored VISE e-cigarettes. The court argued that the FDA had failed to consider alternatives to denial and violated the principles of fair notice and consideration. Additionally, the court argued that the FDA had not adequately addressed the evidence proffered by the plaintiff that their product would result in substantial health benefits as a result of substitution from combustible cigarettes to this product. In particular, the court admonished the agency for applying an unannounced standard by which all applications for flavored e-cigarettes would be rejected. The agency had not provided any public notice or request for comment prior to applying this standard in violation of its legal obligations. The plaintiff was also found to have satisfied the evidentiary burden of proving irreparable harm were the stay to be denied. This case, and others, continue. Moreover, further litigation is likely. The divided circuit court rulings make it more likely that the Supreme Court will take up similar cases in the future.

To date, the only authorizations granted by the FDA have been issued to R.J. Reynolds Vapor Co., NJOY, and Logic. However, decisions are still pending on thousands of other products. The FDA stated first that it would finalize the review of the remaining PMTA applications by June 30, 2023, but subsequently pushed its deadline back a year. While the FDA works its way through thousands of applications from hundreds of companies, the products of companies who submitted PMTA ahead of the deadline remain available, pending FDA ruling. How many of these will be authorized once the FDA has worked through the backlog of applications, much less once the FDA's decisions have been litigated, remains to be seen. How effectively the MDOs can be enforced is another question.

4   The Practice of Vaping

Estimates for the current global prevalence of e-cigarette use are surprisingly rare. A recent study found that only 49 countries had nationally representative surveys on e-cigarette use.[163] Examples of such surveys include the General Lifestyle Survey and the Action on Smoking and

Health surveys in the U.K.; the National Youth Tobacco Survey (NYTS), Monitoring the Future (MTF), and Youth Risk Behavioral Surveillance (YRBS) and National Adult Tobacco Survey in the U.S.; the National Drug Strategy Household Survey (Australia); Healthy Ireland Survey, Malaysia's National E-Cigarette Survey; and the Canadian Tobacco and Nicotine Survey. Such surveys provide data on the rates of e-cigarette use within a national population and, to some extent, subpopulations which can help develop insights regarding the public health benefit or harm caused by e-cigarette uptake. Notably, however, comparison among these surveys is fraught. Variations in the definitions of vaping, timeline and frequency of survey implementation, and methodologies used impede researchers' ability to determine how many people are using e-cigarettes at an international or global level. The most recent round of the Global Adult Tobacco Survey (2018) includes questions about e-cigarettes for only six countries. The WHO STEPs data collection system has also been updated to include questions on cigarettes but these are optional. Sporadic and piecemeal data collection makes for an incomplete picture of e-cigarette use.

In some cases, the available data afford only a limited insight into prevalence even within the national context. Much of the literature on consumption comes from web-based convenience samples, which are unlikely to be representative of the broader population. Surveys that are not validated with cotinine testing are open to reporting biases which could misstate rates of use. Sales data may also provide information on the market for e-cigarettes within a given context, but the relationship between sales and prevalence is often unclear.[164] The point-of-sale (POS) scanner data collected by Nielsen, for example, captures only a fraction of total sales and does not track internet sales or sales from boutique vendors, meaning that the best available data may not be representative of the broader market. More obviously, illicit sales also go untracked.

4.1 Measuring E-cigarette Consumption

The literature tends to differentiate between categories of consumers on the basis of frequency of use. Common categories include those who have never used e-cigarettes; those who have ever used e-cigarettes (even once); those who have used e-cigarettes recently (for example in the past month or past week), those who use e-cigarettes frequently (for example using e-cigarettes on 20 or more days per month, or on a near-daily basis) and those who use e-cigarettes everyday. However, the agencies reporting these data often use different metrics, making cross-comparison difficult. Moreover, many of the metrics adopted fail to provide sufficient resolution: A failure to differentiate between, for example, past-month, frequent or daily use may radically overstate the use of e-cigarettes in a population. "Ever-use" fails to distinguish among users who tried e-cigarettes only once, former users who used e-cigarettes for a time to successfully quit smoking, and current frequent users who never smoked in the first place. "Past-month" use aggregates those who tried e-cigarettes once three weeks ago, didn't like them, and will not use them again with those who use them everyday and have done so for an extended period of time. Even "current use," describing use between 1 and 20 days per month, covers a wide range of consumption patterns and masks more detailed introspection into trajectories of use at the population level. Consider that someone who uses e-cigarettes on one day in January but increases use throughout the year to the point that they use e-cigarettes most weekdays in December would be described as a current user throughout this timeframe. Nonetheless it is important to characterize e-cigarette use in the population with as much specificity as possible. Given the infinite variations in consumer behavior some form of aggregation is necessary. While fraught, these categories are an improvement on a single binary alternative, though there is certainly room for improvement.

4.2 Estimating the Prevalence of E-cigarette Use

To fill the knowledge gap regarding the global prevalence of e-cigarette use, Jerzynski & Stimson[165] imputed data for missing countries by assuming similarity between countries in the same region with similar economic conditions. This assumption, as the authors noted in a previous version of the same study,[166] is a big one: e-cigarette use is related to "a wide range of social phenomena, for example, religious customs and rituals, historical events, and cultural, economic, and political conditions." A failure to understand the context-specific interactions between these phenomena may undermine the veracity of predictions regarding one context informed by data gathered in another. Still, the methodology provides an approximate figure for the global prevalence of vaping in 2021 of 82 million, up from an estimated 58 million in 2018.

The authors note that e-cigarette use skews heavily toward the wealthier nations of North America and Europe. In 2018, it was estimated that 2.1 million e-cigarette users lived in low-income countries, 7.8 million in lower-middle-income countries, 19 million in upper-middle-income countries, and 29.3 million in high-income countries. The 2021 estimates also show that the largest concentrations of e-cigarette users are found in European and Eastern Mediterranean nations, in which the mean prevalence of e-cigarette use among adults is 2.3%. There are an estimated 20.1 million e-cigarette users in Europe, 16.8 million in the Americas, and 16 million in the Western Pacific region. South East Asia, despite a relatively low prevalence (0.7%), has a relatively high population of e-cigarette users (14.4% of the world's total) due to the population sizes in the region. Conversely, despite its high prevalence of e-cigarette users, the Eastern Mediterranean has only 9.2 million e-cigarette users. Africa is home to both the lowest mean prevalence of e-cigarette users (1.0%) and the smallest number of e-cigarette users of any WHO region (5.6 million).

Unsurprisingly, the authors also found that, in 2018,[167] e-cigarette use is heavily concentrated in nations where it is permitted by regulation. Almost two-thirds of the world's e-cigarette users (66.4%) are found in such countries, whereas 17.2% reside in countries with no specific laws. However, interestingly, an estimated 16.4% of global e-cigarette users (9.5 million people) live in countries where e-cigarettes are banned; underscoring that prohibitions rarely, if ever, eliminate the demand for temptation goods.

According to Jerzynski & Stimson[168] the largest market for e-cigarettes is North America, with the U.S. making up the overwhelming majority (estimated at US$10.3 billion in 2021). Canada's market, by contrast, is $1.4 billion, though given the nation's relative population sizes the two markets are comparable. The Western European market, including the sizeable British market, is the next largest region, estimated to be worth $6.6 billion in 2021, followed by the markets of the Asia–Pacific region ($4.4 billion), and Eastern Europe ($1.6 billion). The smallest e-cigarette markets by region are to be found in the Middle East and Africa ($490 million), Latin America ($122 million), and Australasia ($118 million). A look at the nationally representative prevalence data from some of the largest e-cigarette markets provides more detail.

According to data published by the Centers for Disease Control (CDC), in 2020, 3.7% of U.S. adults (9.1 million) currently used e-cigarettes.[169] In contrast, 12.5% (37.5 million) smoked cigarettes. In addition, reporting on data from the National Youth Tobacco Survey for 2022, the CDC reports 14.1% of high-school students and 3.3% of middle school students reported using e-cigarettes in the past 30 days. It should be noted that "past-month use" includes one-off experimental use. Approximately 45% of high-school-aged e-cigarette users vaped on more than 20 days per month and approximately one in five middle-school-aged consumers did so. Even so, that means more than one million U.S. school children are frequent e-cigarette users.[170] The National Survey on Drug Use and Health (NSDUH) publishes data on e-cigarette use and smoking by age range. As depicted in the Fig. 3, e-cigarette use now surpasses smoking in the 12–15 age range, though it is much less common among older adults.

Action on Smoking and Health (ASH) U.K. reports that in 2022 8.3% of adults (4.3 million people) in Great Britain were current e-cigarette users, 57% of which were former smokers and 35% of which were current smokers, with 8.1% identifying as never-smokers.[171] In addition, ASH

Fig. 3 Prevalence of current smoking and e-cigarette use in the U.S. by age (2021) (*Note* Past-30-day e-cigarette use is now more common than past-30-day smoking among under 25 s in the U.S. Note however that this includes experimental use of either product. Among adults aged 26+ smoking remains much more common than e-cigarette use. *Source* 2021 National Survey on Drug Use and Health)

reports that, in 2022, 7.0% of 11–17 year olds were current e-cigarette users, up from 4.1% in 2020, though only 3.1% of 11–17 year olds used e-cigarettes on a regular basis (more than once a week).[172] The Office of National Statistics publishes data on smoking and e-cigarette use by gender and age. Figure 4 depicts the ONS statistics on smoking and e-cigarette use by different age groups. Note that e-cigarette use is most common in the youngest age group and declines with age. Comparatively, smoking rates peak later.

In Canada, the 2021 Canadian Tobacco and Nicotine Survey (CTNS) reports that 5% of Canadians reported using e-cigarettes in the past 30 days. Past-month e-cigarette use is concentrated among teenagers and young adults: 13% of youth (aged 15 to 19) and 17% of young adults (aged 20 to 24) reported past-month vaping, compared with 4% of adults aged 25 or older[173] (Fig. 5).

New Zealand's Health Survey reports that 6.2% of adults were daily e-cigarette users in 2020/21, up from 0.9% in 2015/16. That, again,

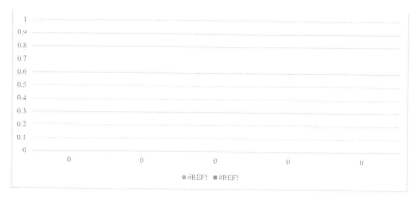

Fig. 4 Prevalence of current smoking and e-cigarette use in Great Britain by age (2021) (*Note* In the U.K., unlike in the U.S. (see previous figure), current e-cigarette use remains less prevalent than current smoking in all age groups. Note also that the prevalence of current e-cigarette use declines with each age group, whereas the prevalence of current smoking is higher for the 25–34, 35–49, and 50–59 age groups relative to the 16–24 age group. Both current e-cigarette use and smoking are least prevalent among those aged 60 and older. *Source* U.K. Office of National Statistics)

Fig. 5 Prevalence of current smoking and e-cigarette use in Canada by age (2021) (*Note* In Canada, current e-cigarette use is more prevalent than current smoking in the 15–19 and 20–24 age groups, and is less prevalent among adults aged 25+. The prevalence of current smoking in Canada increases with each age group, with the highest prevalence found among adults aged 25+. *Source* Canadian Tobacco and Nicotine Survey 2021)

appears to be concentrated among young people aged 18–24 (15.3%) and those of Māori descent (12.5%).[174]

A 2017 European Commission Special Eurobarometer report[175] found that, in that year, the prevalence of current e-cigarette use across 28 member states was 2%, and daily use was 1%. E-cigarette use was concentrated among those with a smoking history, males, 15–39 year olds, and respondents indicating measures of lower socioeconomic status (manual workers, unemployed, etc.).

A 2022 study published in *The Lancet* provided recent prevalence estimates for the current use of e-cigarettes in 14 countries based on data from the Global Adult Tobacco Survey (GATS) collected between Jan 1, 2015, and Dec 31, 2018. Prevalence estimates were provided for Bangladesh, China, Costa Rica, Ethiopia, India, Mexico, Philippines, Romania, Russia, Senegal, Turkey, Ukraine, and Uruguay. Russia and Romania were found to have the highest rates of current adult e-cigarette use at 3.5 and 3.4% respectively. Ethiopia and Senegal had the lowest rates at 0.1% each.[176]

In China in 2018, approximately 0.9% of those over 15 were current e-cigarette users. Use was concentrated among males, the 15–24 age range, college-educated, and urban residents. More than 9 out of 10 Chinese e-cigarette users were also current smokers.[177]

In South Africa, 1.09 million South African adults aged 16 and older (2.7%) used e-cigarettes on "at least some days" during 2018.[178]

That so many people around the world now use e-cigarettes is noteworthy, considering the relatively short period of time during which vaping products have been available, and especially given that so many countries either do not provide support or express opposition toward vaping. The available statistics are also striking considering the strict demand-reduction strategies enacted in many countries where e-cigarettes are regulated. However, the global number of e-cigarette users is still only a small proportion of the overall smoking population (approximately 1.1 billion worldwide).[179]

4.3   Who Vapes?

Just as the prevalence of e-cigarette use varies widely between national populations, different groups within those populations exhibit different rates of e-cigarette use. Efforts to further disaggregate vaping-prevalence data suggest important disparities in rates of use between different social groups. Rates of use have been found to vary according to age, smoking status, socioeconomic status, education, ethnicity, and sexual orientation.

4.3.1   Current Smokers vs. Ex-smokers vs. Non-smokers

While consumption patterns vary over time, vaping has consistently, and across multiple different national contexts, been concentrated among former smokers and current smokers. In the U.K., for example, ASH reports that in 2022, 57% of adult e-cigarette users in Great Britain were former smokers, while 35% are current smokers.[180] Since 2013, the proportion of adult e-cigarette users who is a current smoker declined from 67%, a reduction of more than 47%. Over the same period, the proportion of British e-cigarette users who are ex-smokers has more than doubled from 28 to 57%. Meanwhile, never-smokers represent fewer than one in ten British e-cigarette users. Further, each year since 2017 the portion of ex-smoking e-cigarette users who is long-term (1–3 years) abstinent from cigarettes has increased. Among ex-smokers, 20% used e-cigarettes in their most recent quitting attempt. Additionally, ASH reports that there are 2.4 million British adult ex-smokers who continue to vape, and 2.9 million ex-smokers who no longer vape either. Taken together, these data strongly suggest that e-cigarettes are helping large numbers of British smokers cease using and stay abstinent from cigarettes, many of whom then quit e-cigarettes, too (Fig. 6).

Elsewhere, e-cigarette use also appears to be concentrated among current and former smokers. A 2020 narrative review of 22 studies of EU nations reported that the rates of ever-e-cigarette use were highest among current smokers (20.4% to 83.1%) followed by ex-smokers (7% to 15%). Use of e-cigarettes was universally rarest among non-smokers, with prevalence ranging from 2.3% to 5.6% for ever-use.[182]

Similarly in the U.S., CDC data for 2021[183] report that, among adult (18+) current e-cigarette users[184] 29.4% were current cigarette smokers, 40.3% were former cigarette smokers, and 30.3% had never been cigarette

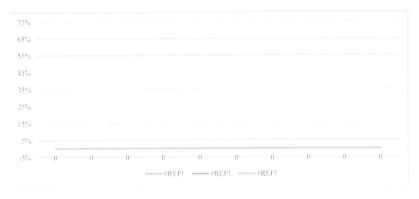

Fig. 6 Smoking status among current adult e-cigarette users (past-30-day use) in Great Britain, 2013–2022 (*Note* In the U.K. never-smokers continue to represent only a small fraction of adult past-30-day e-cigarette users. As a portion of current e-cigarette users, ex-smokers overtook current smokers in 2017. Between 2021 and 2022 ex-smokers as a portion of current e-cigarette users declined, and the portion of current smokers and never-smokers increased. It is not clear whether the increase in current smokers was driven by former ex-smokers relapsing to dual use, or whether smokers who had previously not used e-cigarettes were beginning to do so. It is also not clear from these data whether the decline in the relative prevalence of ex-smokers was driven by some members of that group ceasing to use e-cigarettes, too. Understanding these transitions is important to evaluate the utility of e-cigarettes for the purposes of determining the products' utility as a cessation intervention. *Source* Action on Smoking and Health U.K. [2022][181])

smokers. However, among e-cigarette users aged 18–24 years, 16.3% were current smokers, 22.3% were former smokers, and 61.4% had never been cigarette smokers. That age disparity in the breakdown of e-cigarette users with and without a smoking history is also evident in Canada. Health Canada reports[185] that 5% of Canadians (15+) reported having used e-cigarettes in the past month in 2020. Of these, 37% were current smokers, 33% were former smokers, and 30% reported never having smoked. However, whereas among Canadians 25+ 94% of past-month e-cigarette users had a history of smoking, those with no history of smoking made up 74% of past-month e-cigarette users aged 15–19 and 54% of those aged 20–25. Considering the absolute numbers, there were 711,000 e-cigarette users in Canada aged 15 to 19 in 2020, 1.0 million aged 20–25 and 3.4 million aged 25+. As a result, there were 526,140 non-smoking vapers ages 15–19, 540,000 aged 20–25, and 204,000 aged 25+. Conversely there were 184,860 15–19-year-old e-cigarette users with a history of smoking, 460,000 aged 20–25, and 3,196,000 aged 25+. It should be noted that past-month use includes one-off experimental use.

4.3.2 Age

As is evident in the Canadian statistics discussed above, e-cigarette use appears to be concentrated among late-teen adolescents and young adults. Prevalence statistics report usage increasing with age through school years, peaking in early adulthood, and declining among older adults. Similar findings have also been reported in populations in the U.S.[186,187] U.K.[188,189] Australia,[190] Italy,[191] Poland,[192] the EU[193] and South Korea.[194] One study of 14 countries[176] also reported that current e-cigarette use was higher among young adults aged 15–24 years than those 25 years and older in countries including China, Costa Rica, Mexico, Russia, Senegal, Ukraine, and Uruguay. Elsewhere, notably in Bangladesh, Philippines, Romania, Turkey, and Vietnam, 25 to 44 year olds exhibited the highest rates of e-cigarette use, but in no country was e-cigarette use concentrated in the oldest age group; those over 45. The authors suggest that awareness, perceptions that e-cigarettes were less harmful or addictive than cigarettes, and industry marketing may contribute to greater use among younger people[195] (Fig. 7).

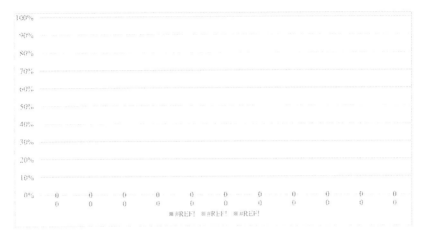

Fig. 7 Past-30-day e-cigarette and smoking status of U.S. middle- and high-school students (*Note* Among U.S. middle- and high-school students, the prevalence of current smoking has declined as e-cigarette use has increased. After 2014 exclusive e-cigarette use and dual use were each, separately, more common than smoking, and after 2017 exclusive e-cigarette use was far more prevalent than smoking and dual use combined. The decline in smoking rates [including dual use] has been particularly marked since 2018. Interestingly, e-cigarette use has also declined since 2019, too. Methodological changes in the NYTS limit the degree to which the data can be compared across years [for example the 2022 data does not differentiate between exclusive smokers and dual users]. *Source* National Youth Tobacco Surveys, 2012–2022)

4.3.3 Gender

As is true for tobacco use, e-cigarette use is more prevalent among males than females.[196] The 14-country study reported that the prevalence of e-cigarette use was higher for men than women in all surveyed countries.[176] Similar findings have been also reported in Indonesia, Malaysia, Qatar, Greece,[197] the U.S.,[186,187,198] Poland,[192] and South Korea.[194]

That finding also appears to be generally true of young e-cigarette users.[199] Using the Global Youth Tobacco Survey data from 2014 to 2019, Sreermardeffy et al.[200] report the differences in e-cigarette use among 13 to 15 year olds in 75 countries and territories. In almost all cases, ever e-cigarette use and current e-cigarette use was more prevalent among boys than girls. In Indonesia and Qatar, e-cigarette use among boys was almost seven times as frequent as among girls. However, while the gender disparities in e-cigarette use generally match those of cigarette use, the magnitude of the gender disparity in smoking tends to be larger than that for "current e-cigarette use." The authors do, however, observe that in several countries the gender disparity in e-cigarette use is either larger or smaller than that of cigarettes in the same context. Interestingly, in Uruguay, Antigua and Barbuda, and Argentina, where more boys vape use e-cigarettes than girls, more girls smoke than boys.

The regionally varying magnitude of the gender disparity in e-cigarette use may be explained, at least in part, by varying degrees of gender equality between nations. Many of the countries with high rates of gender equality appear to have especially small gender disparities in e-cigarette use. Finland, New Zealand, and Germany all fall in the top ten countries with the highest gender equality according to the World Economic Forum (2nd, 4th, and 10th respectively).[201] In Finland, in 2020, 2% of male adults and <1% of female adults are daily users of e-cigarettes, with similar levels among youth[202]; in New Zealand, in 2016, 1.2% of adults use e-cigarettes daily compared to 0.8% of adult females[203]; and in Germany, the current prevalence vaping was 2.6% for men and 1.3% for women in 2016/17.[204] Of the countries reported on by Pan et al.,[176] the country with the highest gender equality ranking (Costa Rica) also has the lowest relative disparity, and China, which had the highest gender disparity (male current e-cigarette use was 16 times that of females), also had among the lowest WEF equality scores (ranking 102nd). However, Mexico and the Philippines have relatively high equality scores (ranking 31st and 19th respectively) and relatively high gender disparities in e-cigarette use. Relative to those countries, India and Turkey had lower gender disparities despite a significantly lower WEF equality ranking (135th and 124th respectively). So while prevailing gender equality may be a factor, that alone would not seem to explain the prevailing gender disparities in e-cigarette use. Pan et al.[176] conclude that the underlying reasons for the gender differences in e-cigarette use are unclear and require further research.

There is some evidence for gender differences in reasons for e-cigarette use. Yimsaard and colleagues report that, compared with men, women in Australia, Canada, England, and the U.S. are more likely to report e-cigarette use because it is "less harmful to others" (OR: 1.64) but less likely to do so because e-cigarettes are "Less harmful than cigarettes"

(OR: 0.85). Women were more likely to report "acceptability," "enjoyment," and "affordability" as reasons for e-cigarette use (ORs 1.10, 1.18, and 1.11 respectively).[205]

4.3.4 Class and Socioeconomic Status

Lower income and/or socioeconomic status has been associated with increased odds of smoking in many countries in the final stages of the tobacco epidemic. However, the literature contains mixed reports on whether e-cigarette use is similarly concentrated among higher or lower socioeconomic groups. Pan et al.[176] report e-cigarette use to be concentrated among adults with higher individual wealth index in all of the countries surveyed. A previous analysis of GATS data also reported a higher prevalence of current e-cigarette use among wealthier adults in Indonesia and Greece.[197] Adkisonet al.[190] reported in 2013 that the use of e-cigarettes was more prevalent among higher income groups in the U.S., U.K., Australia, and Canada. Kock et al. similarly report that among past-year adult smokers in the U.K., lower SES groups had lower overall odds of e-cigarette use compared with the highest SES group, though the differences in e-cigarette use reduced over time.[206] Similarly for the general population of current smokers, Brown et al. report that e-cigarette use was associated with higher socioeconomic status in Great Britain.[207] Similar findings have been reported in the U.S., too.[208,209]

Others, however, have reported the opposite association. Green et al.[210] report that both adults and youth from disadvantaged socioeconomic groups in the U.K. have a higher likelihood of using e-cigarettes, largely because smoking is already concentrated in these groups. Similarly, Kock et al. (2020) report that a lower socioeconomic position is associated with higher odds of e-cigarette use.[211] Similarly, among U.S. adult workers, a higher prevalence of current e-cigarette use is found among those of lower family income.[212]

The absence of clear patterns in such studies has been noted by Hartwell et al. 2017[196] and Lucherini et al.,[213] who also highlight the heterogeneity in the socioeconomic spread of e-cigarette use across 11 countries. According to the authors, if there is a noticeable socioeconomic gradient in e-cigarette use, it is possible that this trend may become less pronounced over time. That fits with the literature on the diffusion of innovation popularized by Everette Rogers,[214] which suggests that innovations are taken up more rapidly by higher SES groups. To the extent that e-cigarettes replace smoking, the more rapid uptake of e-cigarettes among higher SES groups could protract smoking-related health disparities between socioeconomic groups by concentrating the benefits of cessation, initially at least, among wealthier communities. However, even if e-cigarette use were uniform across SES groups, that would not necessarily suggest that the balance of risks and benefits were similarly uniform. Differences in rates of e-cigarette use by non-smokers, different rates of dual use, different frequencies of e-cigarette-supported cessation, and different durations of use subsequent to smoking cessation could all vary between SES groups, influencing the balance of risks and benefits. More research is needed on this topic to investigate the balance of these apparently contradictory associations, and explore ways in which the benefits could be maximized without exacerbating inequalities experienced by vulnerable groups.[210]

4.3.5 Race and Ethnicity

Another potential disparity in e-cigarette use relates to race and ethnicity. In multicultural societies (notably the U.S.), several studies have reported greater use of e-cigarettes among majority White communities, relative to racial and ethnic minorities: Four of the five high and medium-quality studies reporting ever-use reviewed by Hartwell et al.[215] reported a positive association with White ethnicity. Among U.S. adults (18–49) current and former smokers, Richardson et al.[187] reported that compared with non-Hispanic Whites, non-Hispanic Black and Hispanic survey respondents both had significantly lower odds of reporting ENDS use (0.48 and 0.23 respectively). Lippert et al.[191] report similar findings among U.S. adolescents: compared to non-Hispanic White adolescents, lifetime e-cigarette use was lower for non-Hispanic Black youth (0.37), and Mexican–American youth (0.56). Evidence proffered by Giovenco et al.[216] suggest that this pattern holds for current use, too, (defined as use of an e-cigarette at least once in the past 30 days) and established use (defined as use of an e-cigarette at least once in the past 30 days and more than 50 times in their lifetime): Compared with others, the adjusted odds ratio for established e-cigarette use among non-Hispanic White respondents was 2.56.

More recent reports suggest that the racial disparity in e-cigarette use in the U.S. has persisted. Using Monitoring the Future data 2017–2020, Usidame et al.[217] report that among U.S. 8th, 10th, and 12th graders,

190   S. C. HAMPSHER-MONK ET AL.

White students were generally more likely to use e-cigarettes, either exclusively or with otherwise, than non-Hispanic Black students, Hispanic students, or non-Hispanic students of other ethnicities. The reduced odds of e-cigarette use among minority U.S. high-school students may protect these groups from any future harms resulting from e-cigarette use. But to the extent that substitution to e-cigarettes helps reduce smoking-related harms among adults, less frequent use among adults from these communities may contribute to smoking-related disparities. Using data from the Population Assessment in Tobacco and Health study (waves 1 and 2), Harlow et al.[218] report that non-Hispanic Black and Hispanic cigarette smokers were significantly less likely than non-Hispanic White cigarette smokers to begin using e-cigarettes in any way (OR 0.55 and 0.56 respectively). Compared with White cigarette smokers, Black and Hispanic cigarette smokers were also much less likely to transition to exclusive e-cigarette use, i.e., quit with e-cigarettes (OR 0.26 and 0.26 respectively). Dual use was also less common among Black and Hispanic cigarette smokers (OR 0.56 and 0.62 respectively), though it was more common among non-Hispanic Other smokers (OR 1.09). However, while Black cigarette smokers were less likely than White cigarette smokers to quit cigarettes without having used e-cigarettes (OR 0.66), Hispanic cigarette smokers and those of other backgrounds were more likely than Whites to quit cigarettes regardless of e-cigarette use (OR 1.42 and 1.61 respectively).

To further explore these nuances, Harlow et al. examine the tobacco- and e-cigarette-related attitudes and beliefs across different race/ethnicities. The authors' adjusted analysis found that both Hispanic and non-Hispanic Black smokers were more likely to believe that e-cigarettes were more harmful than combustible cigarettes; fewer Hispanic users reported using e-cigarettes because they may be less harmful than cigarettes and because they are more acceptable to non-tobacco users; and Black e-cigarette users and users of other races were more likely to use e-cigarettes because of appealing advertising, and for socializing reasons. All participants who became e-cigarette users were equally likely to report using e-cigarettes because they help them quit smoking, regardless of SES or race/ethnicity. These data emphasize that while e-cigarette use is associated with smoking cessation in some groups, e-cigarettes are not a panacea; some use them and do not quit, and many do not use them and quit anyway. However, misperceptions of e-cigarette risks (including the belief that e-cigarettes are more harmful than cigarettes) impede the uptake of e-cigarettes. In groups with lower rates of cessation (Black U.S. adults, in this case) misinformation about e-cigarette risks could be perpetuating smoking and related risks, and contributing to health-related disparities between these groups, and others in which quitting is more likely.

The concentration of e-cigarette use among White-majority groups has been reported in other countries, too: In New Zealand, Oakley et al.[203] report that, compared with European New Zealanders, those of Pacific Islander descent had double the adjusted risk ratio of "current use" (2.0) (though only a slightly higher risk of daily use [1.1]), and those of Asian descent had an elevated risk of daily use (1.9) but not current use (1.0). Māori New Zealanders are more likely than others to try e-cigarettes, but after adjusting for other factors (primarily smoking status) they were not significantly more likely to use e-cigarettes currently, or daily. Since smoking rates are higher among Māori communities, it has been suggested that e-cigarettes could help Māori smokers quit and thereby reduce disparities in smoking prevalence. However, the authors that whether targeted promotion of e-cigarettes for the purposes of smoking cessation would reduce the extant disparities in New Zealand remains to be seen.

In the U.K., Beard et al.[219] report that, between 2013 and 2019, White ethnic Britons were more likely to use e-cigarettes to cut down on smoking or support temporary abstinence (18.3%) than mixed-race respondents (17.2%), or those with Asian (14.7%), Black (15.5%), or Arab/other heritage (10.6%). In Canada, there is evidence that e-cigarette use is concentrated among First Nations communities: 37.7% of indigenous youth reported past-month e-cigarette use in 2019, compared with 22% of non-indigenous youth.[220] E-cigarette use appears to be more common among Canadian-born youth, relative to immigrants. In 2019, more than one in four Canadian-born youth aged 15–17 reported past-month e-cigarette use, compared to one in ten foreign-born Canadians of the same age.[220] Similar findings have been reported among immigrants to the U.S.[221]

4.3.6 Education

As with smoking, educational attainment may interact with e-cigarette use. Hartwell et al.[222] report a general pattern in the "higher quality" literature whereby e-cigarette use (particularly "ever-use") is positively associated with educational attainment. Adkison et al.[223] report this finding in Canada, Australia, the U.S., and England. Similarly, Harlow et al. report that among U.S. adult current smokers, those without any college education are less likely to use e-cigarettes in any capacity, and less likely to quit smoking (with or without transitioning to e-cigarettes) relative to those with at least some college education. In the 14 countries surveyed by Pan et al., e-cigarette use was concentrated in those with secondary education or higher in most of the countries studied, including China, India, Mexico, Philippines, Russia, and Turkey, with Vietnam as the exception.

Other studies, however, have reported that e-cigarette use is concentrated in less educated groups.[186,224,225] Rotermann and Gilmour[220] report that, in Canada, lower academic scoring remained significantly associated with vaping in the multivariable analysis among older adolescents. A reduced prevalence of vaping has also been reported among youth attending more academically focused programs in Germany[226] and adolescents reporting above-average academic performance in Ireland.[227]

On the other hand, several studies have reported no significant association between e-cigarette use and educational attainment exists.[190,216,228,229] Once again, there may be important nuances to consider. Usidame et al.[217] report that, among U.S. adolescents, while higher parental education is associated with lower exclusive combustible use or multiple nicotine/tobacco product use, it is associated with *higher* exclusive e-cigarette use. This finding has been reported elsewhere, too.[230,231,232,233] Regan et al. (2013) reported that U.S. adults with less than a high-school education were more likely to use e-cigarettes although the same group was also less likely to be aware of e-cigarettes.[234] Pan et al.[176] explain the apparent bifurcation: Greater awareness may be associated with higher education, but awareness could work in two dimensions: decreasing use among those who perceived e-cigarette-related risks, and increasing it among those who perceived health-related or other advantages, especially over smoking. Thus, the associations between e-cigarette usage and education should be expected to vary. Once again, further research is required.

4.3.7 Mental Health

Smoking rates have been associated with poorer physical and mental health. Substitutions to e-cigarettes may reduce some of the physical and mental health consequences of smoking. Accordingly, Pearson et al.[235] report that among U.S. adult smokers, ever-use of e-cigarettes was associated with better self-reported health status. On the other hand, perhaps because e-cigarette use is concentrated among those with a history of smoking, in the general population, e-cigarette use has also been positively associated with poorer physical and mental health. For example, Hayes et al.[236] report that current e-cigarette use was positively associated with medical illnesses, greater depressed mood, and greater alcohol use. Becker et al.[237] surveyed the literature on e-cigarette use and mental health comorbidities among adolescents and young adults, categorizing mental health disorders into three groups: internalizing disorders (including depression, anxiety, suicidality, eating disorders, and post-traumatic stress disorder), externalizing disorders (attention-deficit/hyperactivity disorder and conduct disorder), and transdiagnostic concepts (impulsivity and perceived stress). The reports identified by the authors are of mixed quality and provide evidence both for and against the association between e-cigarette use and mental health disorders in the target age group (12–26). The authors of the study suggest that e-cigarette use is linked to various internalizing problems such as depression, suicidal tendencies, disordered eating, and externalizing problems such as ADHD, conduct disorder, impulsivity, and perceived stress. However, the authors note that some of these issues have also been associated with cigarette use, and they acknowledge that many studies indicate weaker associations with e-cigarette use compared to cigarette use. As the authors emphasize, the directionality of the association also remains uncertain, i.e., it is unclear whether the use of e-cigarettes leads to poorer mental health, or whether those with pre-existing mental health disorders, or even a predisposition toward them, are more likely than others to take up vaping.

4.3.8 Sexual Orientation

Emerging evidence suggests that e-cigarette use may be concentrated among lesbian, gay, bisexual, transgender, and queer (LGBTQ+) groups. Reporting on U.S. adults in 2014, Agaku et al.[224] report that those identifying as lesbian, gay, and bisexual were more likely to report current e-cigarette use relative to those identifying as heterosexual or not reporting sexual orientation. Kcomt et al.[238] also report that smoking, dual use, and exclusive e-cigarette use were all more common among

194 S. C. HAMPSHER-MONK ET AL.

visually nonconforming individuals. The authors note that the experience of discrimination including unequal treatment, verbal harassment, or physical assault contributes to these disparities. "Transgender people who experienced all 3 types of discrimination had two times greater odds of current cigarette smoking and dual use than those who had not experienced discrimination."

4.3.9 Peer Influence and Social Environment

As with other forms of substance use, e-cigarette use has been linked with peer influence and social environment. Writing for Statistics Canada, Rotermann and Gilmour[220] report that adolescents who had wider social circles, admitted to truancy, consumed alcohol, and had lower educational motivation were twice as likely to use e-cigarettes as compared to their peers whose friends did not exhibit these behaviors. The authors also report that higher sociability (indicating a greater sense of closeness and belonging with others) had lower odds of vaping, corroborating Enns and Orpana's observation that higher relatedness was associated with lower odds of substance use among adolescents.[239]

4.4 Why Do People Vape?

People use e-cigarettes for a variety of different reasons.[240] Some use them to facilitate cigarette smoking cessation, to maintain abstinence having quit, or to reduce the amount they smoke. Such goals may be motivated by concern for one's own health or that of others, or for non health reasons such as avoiding the cost of smoking, the stigma of being identified as a smoker, or the inconvenience of complying with smoke-free laws. For others, curiosity, positive sensory experience and the appeal of flavors may motivate use. Peer pressure may also be a factor. Others may simply enjoy vaping. This section reviews quantitative and qualitative analyses of state motivations for vaping.

4.4.1 Quantitative Data

Several attempts have been made to categorize e-cigarette users according to their motivations for use. For example, Harlow et al. identified four distinct subgroups of e-cigarette users: "vaping enthusiasts" (54%); those vaping for "convenience and social acceptability" (20%); those vaping for "quitting smoking and harm reduction" (16%); and "experimenters" (10%).[241] Alternatively, Evans-Polce et al. identify three sub-groups: those who substitute e-cigarette use for smoking, those who use e-cigarettes for recreation, and experimenters.[242] Armin et al. differentiate between those who take up e-cigarettes for social reasons (including peer influence and social pressures), health reasons (reduced risk from smoking), and other personal reasons, such as cost.[243]

Arguably, one problem with this kind of categorization is that the groups are not necessarily distinct: a "vaping enthusiast" may be enthusiastic about e-cigarettes because they believe that e-cigarettes are less harmful than smoking, and a smoker motivated to use e-cigarettes by concerns about their health may also be motivated by the convenience and social acceptability vaping. Consumers' motivations around use may also change over time. For example, a smoker may be curious about e-cigarettes initially, and then find that e-cigarette use supports a reduction in smoking or even smoking cessation. That some e-cigarette users switch unintentionally[244] is an important component of their utility as a public health intervention, and highlights that consumers initial motivations may not be predictive of health-relevant behavior change.

In fact, consumers' motivations may be neither necessary nor sufficient for e-cigarettes to be useful for quitting smoking. E-cigarette use may be motivated by a smoker's desire to protect their health and the belief that e-cigarettes are safer than cigarettes, but that belief does not protect against any resulting harms in the event that the belief turns out to be wrong. Conversely, the literature often frames e-cigarette use that is motivated by non-health-related factors as being more harmful than use that is motivated by, for example, a desire to quit smoking. E-cigarette use may be harmful to some degree, but consumers' motivations do not necessarily make it so. E-cigarette use that displaces smoking with a genuinely safer alternative would confer upon the consumer a health benefit regardless whether the consumer's primary motivations were related to health. Of course smokers who have motivations for e-cigarette use other than quitting or reducing smoking may be less likely to quit, but again it is the "not quitting" rather than the motivation that causes the harm (i.e., the forgone benefit). Still, as Harlow et al. note, changing those motivations toward using e-cigarettes as a complete substitute could be a productive strategy.[245] Thus, the study of consumer motivations is important.

Nonetheless, health concerns regarding smoking are often a primary motivation for e-cigarette use. Numerous sources report that e-cigarette use is often motivated by a desire to quit smoking.[246,247,248] In a

196   S. C. HAMPSHER-MONK ET AL.

cross-sectional survey of adult e-cigarette users in Australia, Canada, England, and the U.S., the desire to reduce smoking and the belief that e-cigarettes are less harmful to others were among the most common reasons for vaping endorsed current smokers. Only 14.2% of current smokers reported vaping exclusively for reasons other than to reduce or quit smoking. In this study more than 9 out of 10 former smokers also endorsed the motivations that e-cigarettes are less harmful than smoking and that e-cigarettes facilitated continued abstinence from smoking (selections were not exclusive).[249] Similarly in the U.K., Action on Smoking Health (ASH U.K.) reports that the desire to quit and remain abstinent from smoking are important factors motivating e-cigarette use among adult e-cigarette users.[250] That has also been reported in the United Arab Emirates, where more than seven in ten smokers report using e-cigarettes to support smoking cessation.[251]

Those who have not yet fully quit smoking may still be motivated by a desire to avoid smoking-related harms. In the ASH data, compared with ex-smokers, relatively fewer dual users use e-cigarettes to support cessation (though 15% still do so). In this group the most-cited motivation was "to help reduce the amount of tobacco I smoke" (17%). Hummel et al. (2015) also found that among Dutch e-cigarette users, the most commonly cited reasons for use were "to make it easier to cut down on the number of cigarettes smoked" (79%) and "they may be not as bad for your health [as conventional cigarettes]" (77%).[252] A survey of adult students in Saudi Arabia also reported that the most common reason for using e-cigarettes, cited by 89% of respondents with no intention of quitting smoking, was to reduce tobacco consumption. 88.4% were motivated by E-cigarette being less toxic than tobacco and 62% were motivated by the fact that e-cigarettes meant they could avoid having to go outside to smoke (which may not be entirely unrelated to health given that summertime temperatures in Saudi Arabia can top 50°C (122°F).[253]

In addition to concerns for their own health, many smokers may be rightly concerned that their smoking exposes their friends and family to the harmful toxins and carcinogens present in passive and side-stream smoke. Gravely et al. report that, among current smokers, 77.4% of those using e-cigarettes daily and 70.8% of those e-cigarettes weekly endorsed vaping on the basis that it is less harmful than smoking to others.[249] Harlow et al.[254] also find concern for others to be a strong motivating factor for a subset of adult e-cigarette users. Rather than to quit smoking, this subset primarily uses e-cigarettes for convenience, i.e., to comply with smoke-free laws, and because they perceive e-cigarettes to be more acceptable to non-tobacco users. Adult users classified in this group had low probability of being motivated by quitting, but a high probability of being motivated by the belief that e-cigarettes are less harmful to bystanders than cigarettes. Gravely et al. report that 72% of current smokers and 65% of ex-smokers using e-cigarettes daily endorsed "vaping is more acceptable than smoking" as a primary factor motivating use.[249] In the Dutch study, 57.4% of respondents endorsed the fact that e-cigarettes allow them to consume nicotine in contexts where smoking is undesirable or impractical as a motivation for use,[252] as did 60.5% of ex-smokers and 67.2% of dual users in the four-country study.[249] Relatedly, the lack of offensive odors and the ability to use the product discreetly are factors motivating e-cigarette use.[255] Among current and former smokers, e-cigarette use is also motivated by a desire to avoid the undesirable characteristics of smoking, such as ash, smell, and litter.[256]

Economic factors are also important for many e-cigarette users with a history of tobacco use. Combustible tobacco is often heavily taxed, and in jurisdictions where e-cigarettes are untaxed, or taxed less severely, vaping may be a significantly cheaper way of consuming nicotine.[257] Over three-fifths of e-cigarette users endorsed vaping as a cost-saving alternative to smoking,[252] and ASH U.K. reports that 16% of smokers and 12% of ex-smokers were motivated by the fact that e-cigarettes allowed them to "save money relative to smoking tobacco."[258] Gravely et al. report that cost saving motivated e-cigarette use among 74.1% of current smokers using e-cigarettes daily and 90.5% of ex-smokers using e-cigarettes daily.[249]

Of course, not all e-cigarette users have a history of smoking, and for never-smokers other factors dominate their motivations for use. Among adolescents, the literature cites a variety of different reasons for e-cigarette use; use among familial or peer groups, flavors, and the belief that e-cigarettes are less harmful than alternatives.[259] Curiosity,[260] experimentation,[261] and enjoyment[262] are also cited as primary motivations for e-cigarette use in this age group. Compared with older users, relatively fewer adolescents (<10%) endorse smoking cessation as a primary motivating factor.[263,264] Accordingly, ASH U.K. reports that, among youth 11–17 in 2022, curiosity is the main reason for use among 65.4% of never-smokers[265] and even among older adult never-smokers, curiosity is among the primary motivators (endorsed by 26%).[266] Lindper et al.[267] also cite curiosity as the primary factor motivating e-cigarette use among U.S.

198   S. C. HAMPSHER-MONK ET AL.

school children 42.1% of whom endorse this reason. But there are other reasons, too, presented here in order of importance: A friend used them (35.4%); ability to perform tricks (24.5%); flavors (19.5%); the ability to use discreetly (16.8%); the belief that they are less harmful relative to cigarettes (13.5%); a family member used them (9.0%); tobacco use cessation (6.9%); access relative to cigarettes (4.8%); cost relative to cigarettes (3.1%); and behavioral modeling in media (2.8%).

Motivations behind youths' use of e-cigarettes are further complicated, but self-administred surveys and self-reporting shed some light on the subject. In the U.S., the National Youth Tobacco Survey (NYTS) asked middle (grades 6–8) and high-school (grades 9–12) students who reported ever using e-cigarettes to rank the reasons as to why they tried it. Curiosity is the most important factor motivating e-cigarette use among middle and high-school students in 2019. Familial or peer-group modeling, flavors, and the ability to perform "tricks" are motivating factors for 22% of respondents. In this age group, access, product placement, cost, and smoking cessation were among the least important factors motivating e-cigarette use. Respondents were able to select multiple options (Fig. 8).

Given the attention that flavors have received, mooted as a driver of vaping,[269,270,271] it may be surprising that flavors do not rank more highly as a factor motivating e-cigarette use. Note that for Lindpere et al.[272] the ability to perform tricks is more widely endorsed. ASH U.K. reports that, of the 11% of 11 to 17 year olds who had ever tried vaping, only around one in five said they did so because of the flavors.[273]

Other factors motivating e-cigarette use among youth include appetite control and weight loss[274,275] and influence of family and friends.[276,277,278] An analysis of National Youth Tobacco Survey data for 2021 also found that the most commonly cited reason for initiating e-cigarette use among school students was not flavors, but "a friend used them" (57.8%), and the most commonly cited reason for current use was "I am feeling anxious, stressed, or depressed" (43.4%).[279] A school-based survey of 10th and 12th grade students in California recently reported that relaxation and coping with stress and/or anxiety was the most important reason for youth e-cigarette use.[280] As e-cigarette use rises, social factors may reinforce vaping among adolescents. E-cigarette use by peers, increased e-cigarette exposure and prevalence in college have all been reported as contributing to e-cigarette use among young people.[270] Industry innovations, including both disposables and pod-type design in

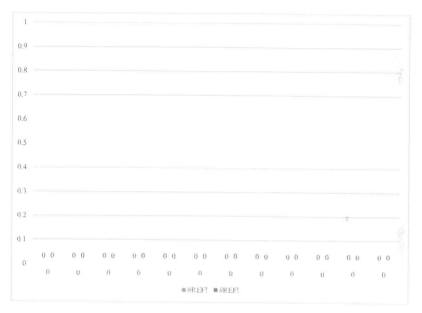

Fig. 8 Reasons for e-cigarette and tobacco use among middle- and high-school students who reported ever using e-cigarettes, 2019 (*Source* U.S. CDC National Tobacco Youth Survey, 2019[268])

4th-generation products may also prompt interest in e-cigarettes, with the design, convenience, and discretion making vaping appealing.[270]

As is now apparent, consumer motivations vary according to smoking status and the duration or frequency of e-cigarette use. Gravely et al. explain[281]: e-cigarette users with a history of smoking cite multiple reasons for using e-cigarettes, but those whose use was more frequent (daily) reported a greater number of motivations. That accords with the idea that less than daily use is experimental "and/or situationally cued" and not primarily motivated for reasons that relate to smoking.[282] Smokers who have positive experiences with e-cigarettes will likely continue using them; initial motivations relating to smoking cessation or reduction may evolve over time with consumers finding additional reasons to continue use. Accordingly Hairi et al. report that, in Malaysia, daily e-cigarette users frequently reported that they vaped "to reduce the number of cigarettes smoked" (91.3%), while those who vaped less frequently

200 S. C. HAMPSHER-MONK ET AL.

were more motivated by the "pleasant taste" (weekly, 89.4%; monthly, 87.5%).[283]

Finally, many consumers simply report e-cigarette use as enjoyable. "Enjoyment" was the most-cited factor motivating e-cigarette use among ex-smokers (94.8%), and the second most-cited factor among current smokers (83.6%).[249]

Evidently, there are numerous different and overlapping motivations for e-cigarette use. For those with a history of smoking, vaping provides an opportunity to avoid smoking-related harms, financial costs, and social stigma associated with smoking. But such advantages and, no less, consumer's ability to perceive them, depends largely on the regulatory environment as well as the prevailing public attitudes toward e-cigarettes including consumer knowledge and beliefs, all of which respond to regulation and media reporting on vaping. The contextual differences that contribute to behaviors around e-cigarette use also operate at the subnational and local levels. Ultimately, motivations for e-cigarette use may be unique to each individual consumer.

4.4.2 Qualitative Data

Consumer testimony also provides illustrative insights into the motivations behind consumption. In early surveys of former smokers who had switched to e-cigarettes, the throat hit and vapor cloud from e-cigarettes were often reported as being subjectively important: "That feeling when it …hits your throat and you inhale it, that's… a big deal for us all."[284] The ability of consumers to swap e-cigarettes into their usual smoking routine was also appealing: "… my fixation with… vaping, is very similar [to smoking]. …I like to vape while I'm in the car, I like to vape after I have a meal, or when I have a coffee, or when I'm drinking, and so on.…" The convenience of e-cigarettes also seems to contribute to the appeal of e-cigarettes: "I could just puff on it at home, and I could keep… a constant head high if I just keep puffing it. Whereas cigarettes it's like after you finish it it's over"; "e-cigarettes I like because when I'm stressed out it takes the edge off"; "I might just want one little hit of nicotine, so I'll take a couple puffs and put it back in my pocket."[285]

More recent focus groups have corroborated the survey evidence discussed previously that smokers are initially interested in e-cigarettes because of smoking cessation beliefs. "My purpose for trying them was …I thought it would curb me from smoking cigarettes."[286] Convenience and social acceptability are also important to smokers: "Not having to go

3 E-CIGARETTES: THE TECHNOLOGY, THE MARKET ...   201

outside in the rain to vape"[287]; "my clothes and hair not smelling like an ashtray"; "not having to find a lighter"[287] and "... I'm not smelling, and reeking of cigarettes."[286]

Some smokers respond positively to the variety of flavors available in e-cigarettes: "I like the options. I like to have different flavors... As opposed to cigarettes, you've just got cigarettes,"[286] while others find that "It didn't have any flavor in it, for me... with cigarettes, you can kind of taste the tobacco."[286] A common theme among smokers who have tried and rejected e-cigarettes is that vaping is unable to satisfy their nicotine craving: "When you vape, you don't feel that sensation quite like you do when you smoke a cigarette in the morning."[286]

Perceptions of risk deter some smokers from taking up e-cigarette use: "I knew that smoking would damage my lungs, and my fear was that the vaping would damage it even more."[286] Some want proof that e-cigarettes are safer than cigarettes: "I would want to see the data and know it's safer than smoking a regular cigarette before I tried it;"[286] "Normal smoking has been around for so long. You know where you are with normal traditional smoking." [287]

E-cigarette users frequently report that their first use of an e-cigarette occurred when they were with friends who were vaping: "I was curious to be honest because I'd seen other people with them."[288] They might also be tempted because e-cigarettes are perceived as less risky than smoking: "The fact that it's slightly healthier gives you a lot of motivation to do it instead of smoking."[288]

For those who continue to vape, the variety of flavors, the perceived element of fun and lack of offensive smell are features that appeal: "Because when you're vaping it smells nice... I just like the flavor and liked playing with the smoke"; "Like I've never had a desire to do it, it's just if it's there and I can do cool things with it... I just like blowing circles with the smoke and trying like tricks."[288]

Among adolescents, as well as the appeal of flavors and discreetness, e-cigarettes may be used to relieve boredom: "...it's just something to do, because it's in moments where we're just really bored or there's nothing else to do around there" and "I'd just keep it [e-cigarette] with me in my pocket and when I felt like having a taste of something ... I'd just take a hit ... when you smell like blue raspberry and green apple, no one is going to question why you smell like that"; and "... it's really cool to see that much smoke come out of your mouth and I enjoy the flavor, honestly."[289]

202   S. C. HAMPSHER-MONK ET AL.

For U.S. college students, a population with an increasing prevalence of vaping, e-cigarettes are seen as cool, while traditional cigarettes are dated: "like your parents or like grandparents smoked cigarettes" and "when I think of cigarettes, I would think of the Marlboro man and [think that is] kind of old."[290] E-cigarette users may also viewed as more refined and classier than traditional smokers.[290]

4.5   Why Don't More Smokers Switch to E-cigarettes?

Satisfactory nicotine delivery is critical to the acceptability of e-cigarettes. Nicotine withdrawal makes abstaining from smoking difficult. Many e-cigarettes offer a better approximation of the pharmacokinetic properties of smoking relative to NRTs. However, smokers' cravings are enhanced by a variety of cues.[291] Quitters report missing the act of smoking, including puffing, inhaling and exhaling smoke, taste, aroma, and respiratory tract sensations.[292] Some studies have found that sensory components are important in terms of satiating the desire to smoke, alleviate cravings, and suggest that e-cigarettes might help smokers to quit when other cessation methods have not worked.[293] After developing the hand-to-mouth habit associated with smoking, vaping avoids the need for ex-smokers to develop a new way of acting, which some studies suggest can contribute to reductions in cravings.[294]

Still, that e-cigarettes supportsmoking cessation in some does not suggest that e-cigarettes will be effective for all smokers, nor that all e-cigarettes will be equally effective. In an ASH survey of adults, dissatisfaction regarding the nicotine delivery was among the most common reasons for smokers to reject e-cigarettes, reported in 14% of cartridge users and 13% of tank users). Ease of use was also cited as an impediment in 11% of each group and price was important for 10% of cartridge users and 12% of tank users.[295] Likewise, in a cross-sectional study of 2,722 smokers and ex-smokers who had vaped, 78% of current smokers discontinued vaping because it was not satisfying, 63% because it did not assuage cravings, and 52% because it was not helpful for quitting smoking. Among ex-smokers, popular reasons for giving up vaping were that they were not satisfying (50%) and safety concerns (44%). Compared to smokers who had stopped vaping, ex-smokers were more likely to have stopped using e-cigarettes due to addiction concerns (AOR = 2.86, 95% CI = 1.59–5.15, $p < 0.001$) and less likely to have stopped because of a lack of product satisfaction (AOR = 0.28, 95% CI = 0.18–0.44, $p < 0.001$).[296]

Wadsworth et al.[297] found that the ease of using simple first-generation e-cigarettes was appealing for first-time vapers due to confidence in the nicotine dose, the lack of necessary maintenance, and product availability, but also that they were often found to be unsatisfactory. Later-generation modifiable devices were considered "bulky" or "scary."[297] Some smokers who tried e-cigarettes have reported stopping vaping because their product did not provide a sufficiently close approximation of smoking or did not have a satisfying taste.[298]

The tendency for some portion of e-cigarette users to continue using combustible tobacco may be a specific consequence of unsatisfactory product design. The low nicotine delivery of early-generation products may have offered a less satisfying user experience for nicotine accustomed smokers, relative to modern devices.[299] The latest generation of e-cigarettes (so-called pod or pod-mod systems) may resolve some of these shortcomings by combining intuitive user experience with sufficient power to deliver high aerosol mass and meet users' nicotine delivery preferences while allowing the consumer the flexibility to choose between flavor by refilling with different e-liquids or simply by using a new disposable. Given such innovations, assessments of older products may be redundant and new assessments of modern products are needed to determine the extent to which today's products support smoking cessation. In studies among smokers attempting to quit smoking using later-generation e-cigarettes, frequency of vaping has been positively associated with quit durations of 2–6 years.[300,301] A large 1-year study in the U.K. showed that the smoking abstinence rate among people who switched to later-generation e-cigarettes was roughly double that among those who switched completely to NRT.[302]

The subjective acceptability of e-cigarettes for smokers has important implications for their efficacy as cessation aids. Not surprisingly, those who use e-cigarettes more frequently (finding them to be sufficiently acceptable) exhibit a greater likelihood of smoking cessation compared with infrequent users. Biener et al.[303] explain, frequent use, especially for an extended period of time, is suggestive of the user committing to e-cigarettes. Thus, it is among frequent users that the many-multiples odds of successful smoking cessation are observed. Conversely, intermittent use reflects experimentation or temporary situationally cued substitution. That is not significantly associated with increased smoking cessation. The finding regarding the importance of e-cigarette-use frequency on smoking cessation outcomes underscores the need for more focus on detailed

204   S. C. HAMPSHER-MONK ET AL.

measures of patterns of e-cigarette use, which has been called for by other researchers.[216]

4.6   What Does Vaping Feel Like, Compared with Smoking?

Inhaling the aerosol of nicotine e-cigarettes produces dopamine. In nicotine-dependent users, the consumption of nicotine may reduce stress and anxiety; both of these are symptoms of nicotine withdrawal. Smokers may use nicotine to regulate their mood and improve their concentration.[304] Accordingly, e-cigarette users have been reported to vape for relaxation and to cope with stress and anxiety.[280] At the point of vaping initiation, users report positive subjective effects including "feeling relaxed" and "feeling a pleasurable rush or buzz," whereas smokers may additionally report "dizziness" on smoking their first cigarette.[305,306] Emotionally pleasurable connections with e-cigarette use have been reported,[307] and there is some evidence that the perceived psychological benefits of e-cigarette use are greater among those with higher impulsivity.[276]

Among smokers abstaining from cigarettes, e-cigarettes can reduce nicotine withdrawal symptoms and lessen the urge to smoke, but there is some evidence that e-cigarette use is less rewarding to an accustomed smoker and reduces craving to a lesser degree than cigarettes.[308,309] However, unlike traditional cigarettes, which burn out, most e-cigarettes have no built-in mechanism by which the user can track their consumption. Moreover, the (sometimes) greater social acceptability of e-cigarettes may remove an impediment to nicotine consumption that is operative among cigarette smokers.[310] Distraction techniques (e.g., hobby, gaming, and mindfulness exercises) and a positive mindset may help facilitate quitting e-cigarette use.[311]

The acute physiological effects of vaping nicotine include increased blood pressure and heart rate,[312] the perception of which contributes to the so-called nicotine rush, which may be pleasurable for some people. In addition, e-cigarette use increases, in the short term,[313] airway resistance and inflammation,[312] and causes negative changes in vascular endothelial function.[314] These physiological effects are often similar to—but may be less than—those of tobacco smoke inhalation.[312] Volume II, Chapter 1 discusses the health consequences of e-cigarette use in more detail.

The subjective experience of e-cigarette use is also informed by the manner in which the devices are used. Mouth to Lung (MTL) vaping involves inhaling aerosol first into the mouth, and then into the lungs; much as smokers inhale from a cigarette, mixing the smoke in the mouth and throat with air. MTL e-cigarette users tend to use devices that deliver a smaller volume of aerosol, often offset with a higher nicotine content e-liquid. Direct-Lung (DL) vaping involves inhaling through the device and inhaling, as the name suggests, directly into the lungs, without titrating the aerosol with air. DTL vaping typically involves lower-powered atomizers (sub-ohm) which use a lower nicotine content liquid. The aerosol consumed feels wetter and warmer than MTL vaping. Some devices offer "restricted direct-to-lung vaping," offering thicker vapor than mouth-to-lung vaping, but with a more restrictive draw than a sub-ohm device. Drawing more heavily, more frequently, for a longer duration and inhaling directly into the lungs increases the uptake of nicotine. The method of use may vary widely from user to user, and according to the specifications of the device used and the consumer's experience with e-cigarettes and combustible tobacco products.

4.7   How Is Vaping Perceived?

4.7.1   The World Health Organization

The WHO plays a vital role in informing public (and private) thinking on e-cigarettes. The WHO has been vocally skeptical about e-cigarettes' potential to reduce smoking-related harms. Dr. Tedros Adhanom Ghebreyesus, WHO Director-General, has argued, "Electronic nicotine delivery systems are harmful and must be better regulated. Whether or not they are banned, governments should adopt appropriate policies to protect their populations from the harms of electronic nicotine delivery systems, and to prevent their uptake by children, adolescents, and other vulnerable groups."[315] While this statement does not explicitly equate the alleged harms of e-cigarette use with those of smoking, the emphasis on e-cigarettes risk remains. But what exactly is meant by "harmful" and what evidence is there for this claim? The WHO's guidance on e-cigarettes fails to report that, on the basis of the available evidence, e-cigarettes are substantially less risky than combustible tobacco: "Both tobacco products and ENDS pose health risks. The safest approach is not to use either." While technically true, this equivalency ignores the fact that people do use these products, and some tobacco products (cigarettes) are more dangerous than others. WHO publications continue to reject the evidence that e-cigarettes help smokers quit, "To date, evidence on the use of ENDS as a cessation aid is inconclusive."[315]

The WHO's stance on e-cigarettes has come under increasing scrutiny from public health scholars and officials. Dr Jamie Hartmann-Boyce, Senior Research Fellow in Health Behaviors at Oxford University, has expressed alarm that the WHO's guidance misinforms the public, and smokers in particular and may alarm those who have switched to e-cigarettes and those who may yet do so: "...it's incredibly important public health messaging is clear –Evidence shows e-cigarettes with nicotine can help people quit smoking and that they are considerably less harmful than smoking. The ... WHO should not discourage people who smoke from switching ...."[316]

Professor John Britton, Emeritus Professor of Epidemiology at the University of Nottingham, and special advisor to the Royal College of Physicians on Tobacco put it more bluntly: "sadly, the WHO still doesn't understand the fundamental difference between addiction to tobacco smoking, which kills millions of people every year, and addiction to nicotine, which doesn't. The WHO is also evidently still content with the hypocrisy of adopting a position which recommends the use of medicinal nicotine products to treat addiction to smoking, but advocates prohibition of consumer nicotine products which do the same thing, but better."[317]

4.7.2 National Regulators and Public Health Agencies

The attitudes of national regulators and public health agencies toward e-cigarettes and vaping range from extreme skepticism to cautious optimism. This diversity of perspectives contributes to radically different regulatory environments for e-cigarettes around the world. While some regulators take the approach of banning and even criminalizing use of e-cigarettes, others actively encourage smokers to substitute to these products, using regulation to provide additional incentives. Most regulatory approaches fall somewhere in the middle, applying some, if not all of the restrictions that are applied to combustible cigarettes. A detailed discussion of the different regulatory approaches to e-cigarettes is presented in Volume III, Chapter 1.

In over 30 countries, including Argentina, Brazil, Mexico, India, Thailand, and Uganda e-cigarettes are banned. Not one of these countries bans combustible cigarettes.[318] In Brazil, for example, the import, advertising, and sale of electronic cigarettes has been banned since 2009. On July 6, 2022, Brazil's National Health Surveillance Agency unanimously voted to extend the nation's ban on e-cigarettes[319] arguing that e-cigarettes are not useful smoking cessation aids. The ban further argued that the presence of nicotine in e-cigarettes causes dependence and health risks; reducing the emission of certain substances does not mean reducing risk or harm to health; there is a lack of medium- and long-term studies on the health impacts of e-cigarettes; e-cigarette use among young people leads to subsequent smoking; and the variations in products makes it impossible to predict risks.[320]

The Indian government banned the production, manufacture, import, export, transport, sale, distribution, storage and advertisement) of all ENDS from September 2019, following the recommendation of the Indian Council of Medical Research.[321] The ban was intended to "protect [the] population, especially the youth and children, from the risk of addiction through E-cigarettes."[322] The rationale for the decision drew heavily on WHO guidance and rejected the claim that ENDS were safer alternatives for conventional cigarettes. The rationale provided by the government also voiced concerns that ENDS "may act as [a] gateway to addiction and subsequent use of conventional tobacco products" and claimed that "e-cigarettes efficacy and safety as a quitting aid has not yet been established."

Other countries, while technically stopping short of prohibitions, severely restrict consumers' access to these products. Australians need a prescription to legally access nicotine-containing e-cigarette products for any purpose. An initial lack of physicians willing to issue such prescriptions means that access to e-cigarettes is severely restricted in Australia, while combustible cigarettes remain widely available.[323] Australia's Department of Health emphatically states,

Even though scientists are still learning about e-cigarettes, they do not consider them safe... Hazardous substances have been found in e-cigarette liquids and ...aerosol. ... many scientists are concerned that using e-cigarettes could increase the risk of lung disease, heart disease and cancer...Currently, there is insufficient evidence to promote the use of e-cigarettes for smoking cessation.[324]

A similar de facto ban exists in Japan, where nicotine e-cigarettes are classified as "medicinal products" and therefore regulated under the laws governing pharmaceuticals. Japan's Ministry of Health, Labor and Welfare—the authority responsible for the sale, advertisement, manufacture, importation, and distribution of medicinal products—has not approved any e-cigarettes for such purposes. Despite this, e-cigarette devices are legally sold in Japan and consumers may import up to a one-month supply of nicotine e-liquid or pre-filled e-cigarettes for private use. In Jamaica, nicotine e-cigarettes are also classified as medicinal products under the Food and Drugs Act, which prohibits the sale, distribution, importation, or manufacture of a product that is not registered with the Ministry of Health. As in Japan, no approval has been granted for nicotine e-cigarettes to date.

In other countries, where e-cigarettes are permitted, they are regulated more stringently than combustibles. In 2009, the South African Pharmacy Council resolved not to endorse the sale of e-cigarettes, deferring to the Medicines Control Council (MCC) to determine whether the sale of electronic cigarettes would be regulated under medicine control.[325] The Medicines Control Council classified nicotine e-cigarettes as a "scheduled drug" under the Medicines and Related Substances Act, meaning that e-cigarettes may technically only be legally sold at pharmacies and purchased with a prescription. Meanwhile combustible tobacco is ubiquitously available.

Since 2022, Israel has taxed e-cigarettes using both a 270% wholesale tax (ad valorem) and 8.16 NIS (about $2.36) specific excise per milliliter tax on e-liquid. For disposables, the tax is 360% of the wholesale price, and cannot be less than NIS 32.72 per unit. This tax structure makes e-cigarette use more expensive on a cost/unit of nicotine basis than smoking. In Israel, a popular pack of cigarettes costs 30 NIS[326] or US$8.25. Estimates for the nicotine content of cigarettes vary and only a fraction of the nicotine in cigarettes is inhaled, but a reasonable estimate[327] might be that between 1 and 2 mg per cigarette (20 mg to 40 mg/pack) is inhaled by the consumer. Splitting the difference, we can estimate the cost to inhale nicotine from this pack is $0.275/mg. Rather than taking a real-world product as a comparator, assume a disposable with 2 ml of 20 mg/ml Nicotine salt e-liquid (40 mg nicotine in total) were sold in Israel for the minimum price permitted by law: 65.44 NIS, about $17.96. Unlike cigarettes, for which the majority of the nicotine content is lost to combustion, most (not all) of the nicotine content of e-liquid is inhaled by the user, but for this exercise, assume that 100% of the e-cigarette's nicotine is delivered. That puts the price of e-cigarette nicotine at $0.45/mg nicotine inhaled; about 60% more than cigarettes on a unit of nicotine basis.

Other nations, while making e-cigarette available, treat them comparably to conventional cigarettes. In January 2015, South Korea's Ministry of Health and Welfare (MOHW) issued a press release stating "E-cigarette is Cigarette, not Smoking Cessation Aid!".[328] The MOHW argued that e-cigarettes need to be treated as conventional cigarettes since e-cigarettes contain nicotine, expose the user to harmful chemicals, and "may serve as a gateway to nicotine addiction and ultimately smoking."

Elsewhere, rather than emphasizing risks, regulators' pronouncements and decisions regarding e-cigarettes have used the available evidence for their relative safety (see Chapter 3) and efficacy as a cessation aid (see Volume II, Chapter 1) to encourage smokers who are unable or unwilling to quit smoking to use e-cigarettes to avoid smoking-related harms. The countries that best exemplify this "risk-proportionate" approach include the U.K. and New Zealand.

The much-cited *E-cigarette Evidence Reviews* by Public Health England (PHE) (2014–2021) have been informative in the development of risk-proportionate e-cigarette policy. The authors of the original report concluded that "While vaping may not be 100% safe, most of the chemicals causing smoking-related disease are absent and the chemicals that are present pose limited danger... EC [e-cigarettes] are around 95% safer than smoking."[329] The reports also highlight that, then to date, biomarkers of exposure are consistent with significant reductions in harmful effects and "vaping is positively associated with quitting smoking successfully." The conclusion that e-cigarettes are significantly safer than cigarettes, and the switching is likely to reduce harm has also been drawn by the House of Commons, Science & Technology Committee,[330] the Committee on Toxicity of Chemicals in Food, Consumer Products and the Environment (COT),[331] and in a joint statement by PHE and Action on Smoking and Health, Association of Directors of Public Health, British Lung Foundation, Cancer Research U.K., Faculty of Public Health, Fresh North East, Healthier Futures, Public Health Action, Royal College of Physicians, Royal Society for Public Health U.K., Centre for Tobacco and Alcohol Studies U.K. and Health Forum.[332]

In July 2017, the Tobacco Control Plan for England stated:

> The evidence is increasingly clear that e-cigarettes are significantly less harmful to health than smoking tobacco. The government will seek to support consumers in stopping smoking and adopting the use of less harmful nicotine products. [...] We welcome innovation that will reduce the harms caused by smoking and will evaluate whether products such as novel tobacco products have a role to play in reducing the risk of harm to smokers.

In pursuit of the government's goal of reducing smoking prevalence to 5% or lower in any group, the government has stated a commitment to "Help people to quit smoking by permitting innovative technologies that minimize the risk of harm" and "Maximize the availability of safer alternatives to smoking." NHS guidance on smoking cessation encourages active smokers to try e-cigarettes to quit.[333] This message has also been included in the Government's annual stop-smoking campaign "Stoptober."[334] In 2023 the government announced its "swap to stop" campaign which, among other things, would provide one in five smokers in the U.K. with a free e-cigarette starter-kit to encourage substitutions that lead to smoking cessation.[335]

Since 2018, New Zealand's Ministry of Health has also acknowledged the role that e-cigarettes could play in achieving New Zealand's smoke-free target of 5% smoking incidence by 2025, and like the U.K., New Zealand's Ministry of Health has issued the following statement: "Vaping products are a less harmful way of delivering nicotine than conventional tobacco cigarettes. ... vaping products cannot be regarded as being harmless: they still produce a range of toxicants, including some known carcinogens, in the vapour that users inhale, but at much lower levels than those found in cigarette smoke and at levels unlikely to cause harm...Emerging research suggests that people can use vaping products to help them transition from smoking cigarettes. Combining behavioural support with stop-smoking medication gives a person the best chance of quitting smoking. Using behavioural support with vaping products is likely to have a similar result."[336] The Ministry calls on stop-smoking services to "be vaping friendly towards clients who choose to use a vaping product in their quit smoking attempt; provide accurate information to people about the benefits and risks of vaping so that people can make an informed decision; provide accurate advice about where people can obtain a vaping product and get advice on using and maintaining the product; and help people who wish to transition off vaping once confident that they will not relapse to smoking cigarettes."[337] New Zealand has also exempted ENDS from some of the packaging restrictions and warning label requirements applied to combustible tobacco from 2020, and from some of the restrictions on combustibles proposed in the 2021 Smokefree Action Plan,[338] which included reducing the number of retail outlets, lowering nicotine content of cigarettes and introducing a sliding minimum legal sale age limit that would mean that those born after 2008 would never reach the age at which they could legally purchase combustible tobacco.

Other countries have also adopted risk proportionality at the regulatory level. For example, in 2019 the Czech Government's National Strategy for Prevention and Harm Reduction with regard to Addictive Behaviors 2019–2027 requires that the Ministry of Finance "Regularly increase excise duty on tobacco products *while respecting the differentiation according to the degree of harmfulness of each product for the society.*" Also in 2019, Greek legislation (Law 4715/2020) enshrined some elements of Tobacco Harm Reduction by affording Greek citizens the right to access accurate information about non-combusted tobacco products and reduced-risk messages subject to regulatory overview.

U.S. regulators' concerns with e-cigarettes, and U.S. experiences including the "epidemic in youth vaping" and the so-called EVALI crisis are often cited by other countries in support of e-cigarette restrictions, some of which surpass those of the U.S. in stringency. However, the U.S. has acknowledged the role that alternative nicotine products have in supporting smoking cessation. Announcing a new Strategic Plan in July 2017, FDA Commissioner Scott Gottlieb implicitly referenced risk-proportinate regulation, stating that the FDA would increase restrictions on cigarettes by limiting the nicotine content of combustibles while allowing greater flexibility for non-combustible alternatives. "Envisioning a world where cigarettes would no longer create or sustain addiction, and where adults who still need or want nicotine could get it from alternative and less harmful sources, needs to be the cornerstone of our efforts – and we believe it's vital that we pursue this common ground."[339] The subsequently released 2018 Strategic Policy Roadmap reiterated that combustion, not nicotine, is responsible for smoking-related morbidity and mortality:

212   S. C. HAMPSHER-MONK ET AL.

With appropriate product regulation, new technology, and product innovation – including new medicinal nicotine products and electronic nicotine delivery systems (ENDS) – could present an opportunity for more smokers to quit combustible tobacco and stay quit... In a properly regulated market, these products would be available for adults who want to enjoy satisfying levels of nicotine through routes that may not pose all of the same risks as combusting tobacco. We will also take new steps to make sure these products are not available to kids.

Whether the FDA's rules achieve this balance is another question, but the FDA has at least granted PMTAs to some e-cigarette companies for specific products, including R.J. Reynolds Vapor Company for Vuse Solo (October 2021), Vuse Vibe and Vuse Ciro (May 2022); Logic, LLC for Logic Vapeleaf, Logic Pro, Logic Power (March 2022); and NJOY LLC for NJOY Ace (April 2022), and NJOY Daily (June 2022). Such approvals acknowledge that at least some such products "could benefit addicted adult smokers who switch to these products—either completely or with a significant reduction in cigarette consumption—by reducing their exposure to harmful chemicals...."[340] Such moves echoed the measured conclusion of the 2018 report by the National Academy of Science, Medicine and Engineering (NASEM): "*For these populations who continue to expose themselves and others to harm from combustible tobacco use, it is appropriate to consider strategies that minimize or reduce but not eliminate harm from smoking... if e-cigarettes confer lower health risks compared with combustible tobacco cigarettes, encouraging use of this reduced risk product rather than encouraging abstinence only could have public health benefits.*"[341]

Health Canada,[342] New Zealand's Ministryof Health,[343] and the Dutch National Institute for Public Health and the Environment (RIVM)[344] have also publicly acknowledged the scientific consensus that, while not completely safe, e-cigarettes are substantially less risky than conventional cigarettes and that complete substitution could serve public health. The question for these, and other regulators, is how best to manage the tradeoffs between preventing possible risks and securing evident benefits. That work begins with an accurate assessment of the harms of e-cigarette use. Volume II, Chapter 1 explores the available evidence.

Notes

1. Zeller, M. Reflections on the "Endgame" for Tobacco Control. Tob Control. 2013;22:i40–i41.
2. Russell, M. Low-Tar Medium-Nicotine Cigarettes: A New Approach to Safer Smoking. BMJ. 1976;1:1430–1433.
3. O'Brien, E.K., Nguyen, A.B., Persoskie, A., Hoffman, A.C. U.S. Adults' Addiction and Harm Beliefs About Nicotine and Low Nicotine Cigarettes. Prev Med. 2017;96:94–100. https://doi.org/10.1016/j.ypmed.2016.12.048.
4. Steinberg, M.B., Bover Manderski, M.T., Wackowski, O.A. et al. Nicotine Risk Misperception Among US Physicians. J Gen Intern Med. 2021;36:3888–3890. https://doi.org/10.1007/s11606-020-06172-8.
5. Patwardhan, S. Confidence in Nicotine for Tobacco Harm Reduction—Bridging the Policy–Practice Gap. Drug Test Anal. 2022;1–6. https://doi.org/10.1002/dta.3413.
6. Rajkumar, S., Adibah, N., Paskow, M.J., Erkkila, B.E. Perceptions of Nicotine in Current and Former Users of Tobacco and Tobacco Harm Reduction Products from Seven Countries. Drugs and Alcohol Today. 2020;20(3):191–206. https://doi.org/10.1108/DAT-04-2020-0022.
7. McNeill, A., Brose, L., Calder, R., Bauld, L., Robson, D. *Vaping in England: An Evidence Update Including Mental Health and Pregnancy, March 2020: A Report Commissioned by Public Health England*. London: Public Health England; 2020.
8. World Health Organization. World Health Organization Model List of Essential Medicines: 22nd List (2021). World Health Organization. https://apps.who.int/iris/handle/10665/345533. License: CC BY-NC-SA 3.0 IGO.
9. Hartmann-Boyce, J., Chepkin, S.C., Ye, W., Bullen, C., Lancaster, T. Nicotine Replacement Therapy Versus Control for Smoking Cessation. Cochrane Database Syst Rev. 2018 May 31;5(5):CD000146. https://doi.org/10.1002/14651858.CD000146.pub5.
10. Mills, E.J., Wu, P., Lockhart, I., Wilson, K., Ebbert, J.O. Adverse Events Associated with Nicotine Replacement Therapy (NRT) for Smoking Cessation. A Systematic Review and Meta-Analysis of

One Hundred and Twenty Studies Involving 177,390 Individuals. Tob Induc Dis. 2010 Jul 13;8(1):8. https://doi.org/10.1186/1617-9625-8-8.

11. Ferguson, S.G., Gitchell, J.G., Shiffman, S., Sembower, M.A., Rohay, J.M., Allen, J. Providing Accurate Safety Information May Increase a Smoker's Willingness to Use Nicotine Replacement Therapy as Part of a Quit Attempt. Addict Behav. 2011 Jul;36(7):713–716. https://doi.org/10.1016/j.addbeh.2011.02.002.

12. Amos, A., Wiltshire, S., Haw, S., McNeill, A. Ambivalence and Uncertainty: Experiences of and Attitudes Towards Addiction and Smoking Cessation in the Mid-to-Late Teens. Health Educ. Res. 2006;21:181–191. https://doi.org/10.1093/her/cyh054.

13. Public Health England. Vaping Better Than Nicotine Replacement Therapy for Stopping Smoking, Evidence Suggests. Public Health England, 2021, available at: https://www.gov.uk/government/news/vaping-better-than-nicotine-replacement-therapy-for-stopping-smoking-evidence-suggests.

14. Pierce, J.P., Benmarhnia, T., Chen, R., White, M., Abrams, D.B., Ambrose, B.K., Blanco, C., Borek, N., Choi, K., Coleman, B., Compton, W.M., Cummings, K.M., Delnevo, C.D., Elton-Marshall, T., Goniewicz, M.L., Gravely, S., Fong, G.T., Hatsukami, D., Henrie, J., Kasza, K.A., Kealey, S., Kimmel, H.L., Limpert, J., Niaura, R.S., Ramôa, C., Sharma, E., Silveira, M.L., Stanton, C.A., Steinberg, M.B., Taylor, E., Bansal-Travers, M., Trinidad, D.R., Gardner, L.D., Hyland, A., Soneji, S., Messer, K. Role of E-cigarettes and Pharmacotherapy During Attempts to Quit Cigarette Smoking: The PATH Study 2013-16. PLoS One. 2020 Sep 2;15(9):e0237938. https://doi.org/10.1371/journal.pone.0237938.

15. Abrams, D.B., Glasser, A.M., Pearson, J.L., Villanti, A.C., Collins, L.K., Niaura, R.S. Harm Minimization and Tobacco Control: Reframing Societal Views of Nicotine Use to Rapidly Save Lives. Annu Rev Public Health. 2018 Apr 1;39:193–213. https://doi.org/10.1146/annurev-publhealth-040617-013849.

16. Abrams, D.B., Glasser, A.M., Pearson, J.L., Villanti, A.C., Collins, L.K., Niaura, R.S. Harm Minimization and Tobacco Control: Reframing Societal Views of Nicotine Use to Rapidly

Save Lives. Annu Rev Public Health. 2018 Apr 1;39:193–213. https://doi.org/10.1146/annurev-publhealth-040617-013849.

17. A continuous supply of e-liquid through the wick to the coil is important to deliver a consistent supply of aerosol and prevent a "dry hit," in which the wick itself may get hot enough for pyrolysis to occur. Dry hits may expose the user to dangerous chemicals (which are not produced by correct vaping technique) as well as an unpleasant taste and/or sensation.

18. Of course, e-cigarette aerosol is not "water vapor," but an aerosolized form of the e-liquid.

19. Wickware, C. UK Medicines Regulator to Approve E-cigarettes for Medical Use. The Pharmaceutical Journal PJ. October 2021;307(7954). https://doi.org/10.1211/PJ.2021.1.112822.

20. Bhat, T.A., Kalathil, S.G., Goniewicz, M.L., et al. Not All Vaping Is the Same: Differential Pulmonary Effects of Vaping Cannabidiol Versus Nicotine *Thorax* Published Online First: 23 February 2023. https://doi.org/10.1136/thorax-2022-218743.

21. Stephens, W.E. Comparing the Cancer Potencies of Emissions from Vapourised Nicotine Products Including E-cigarettes with Those of Tobacco Smoke. Tob Control. 2018;27:10–17.

22. Tattan-Birch, H., Hartmann-Boyce, J., Kock, L., Simonavicius, E., Brose, L., Jackson, S., Shahab, L., Brown, J. Heated Tobacco Products for Smoking Cessation and Reducing Smoking Prevalence. Cochrane Database of Systematic Reviews. 2022; Issue 1. Art. No.: CD013790. https://doi.org/10.1002/14651858. CD013790.pub2.

23. Huang, K., Ortiz-Marciales, M., De Jesús, M., Stepanenko, V. A New and Efficient Approach to the Synthesis of Nicotine and Anabasine Analogues. J Heterocycl Chem. 2009 Nov 6;46(6):1252–1258. https://doi.org/10.1002/jhet.233.

24. King, B. Perspective: Update on FDA Review and Enforcement of Non-Tobacco Nicotine Products, Director's Office of the FDA's Center for Tobacco Products, FDA, 2022, available at: https://www.fda.gov/tobacco-products/ctp-newsroom/perspe ctive-update-fda-review-and-enforcement-non-tobacco-nicotine-products.

25. Zeller, M.R. Updates from FDA's Center for Tobacco Products. Tobacco and Nicotine Products Regulation and Policy Conference; October 27, 2021; Virtual.
26. WHO. Fact Sheet: Tobacco, World Health Organisation, 2022, available at: https://www.who.int/news-room/fact-sheets/detail/tobacco.
27. Kozlowski, L.T., Sweanor, D. Withholding Differential Risk Information on Legal Consumer Nicotine/Tobacco Products: The Public Health Ethics of Health Information Quarantines. Int J Drug Policy. 2016 Jun;32:17–23. https://doi.org/10.1016/j.drugpo.2016.03.014.
28. Li, Y., Burns, A.E., Tran, L.N., Abellar, K.A., Poindexter, M., Li, X., Madl, A.K., Pinkerton, K.E., Nguyen, T.B. Impact of e-Liquid Composition, Coil Temperature, and Puff Topography on the Aerosol Chemistry of Electronic Cigarettes. Chem Res Toxicol. 2021 Jun 21;34(6):1640–1654. https://doi.org/10.1021/acs.chemrestox.1c00070.
29. Patwardhan, S. Confidence in Nicotine for Tobacco Harm Reduction-Bridging the Policy-Practice gap. Drug Test Anal. 2022;15(10):1205–1210. https://doi.org/10.1002/dta.3413.
30. Zain, R.B., Ikeda, N., Gupta, P.C., Warnakulasuriya, S., van Wyk, C.W., Shrestha, P., Axéll, T. Oral Mucosal Lesions Associated with Betel Quid, Areca Nut and Tobacco Chewing Habits: Consensus from a Workshop Held in Kuala Lumpur, Malaysia, November 25–27, 1996. J Oral Pathol Med. 1999;28(1):1–4. https://doi.org/10.1111/j.1600-0714.1999.tb01985.x.
31. Nair, U., Bartsch, H., Nair, J. Alert for an Epidemic of Oral Cancer Due to Use of the Betel Quid Substitutes Gutkha and Pan Masala: A Review of Agents and Causative Mechanisms. Mutagenesis 2004;19(4):251–262. https://doi.org/10.1093/mutage/geh036.
32. Proctor, C., Patwardhan, S. and Murphy, J. A Model Risk Continuum for Tobacco and Nicotine Products, Food and Drug Law Institute, 2017, available at: https://www.fdli.org/2017/08/spotlight-tobacco-model-risk-continuum-tobacco-nicotine-products/.
33. American Lung Association. American Lung Association Urges Smokers to 'Quit, Don't Switch' to E-Cigarettes, American Lung

34. UK Department of Health and Social Care. Smokers Urged to Swap Cigarettes for Vapes in World First Scheme [Press release]. April 11, 2023. https://www.gov.uk/government/news/smokers-urged-to-swap-cigarettes-for-vapes-in-world-first-scheme.

35. Tegin, G., Mekala, H.M., Sarai, S.K., Lippmann, S. E-cigarette toxicity. South Med J. 2018;111(1):35–38. https://doi.org/10.14423/SMJ.0000000000000749.

36. Biener, L., Hargraves, J.L. A Longitudinal Study of Electronic Cigarette Use Among a Population-Based Sample of Adult Smokers: Association with Smoking Cessation and Motivation to Quit. Nicotine Tob Res. 2015 Feb;17(2):127–33. https://doi.org/10.1093/ntr/ntu200.

37. Robinson, J. U.S. Patent No. 1,775,947—Electronic Vaporizer, U.S. Patent Office, 1930, available at: https://patentimages.storage.googleapis.com/cf/3d/d4/a46751164d1ee0/US1775947.pdf.

38. Gilbert, H. U.S. Patent No. 3,200,819—Smokeless Non-Tobacco Cigarette, U.S. Patent Office, 1965, available at: https://i0.wp.com/pointshistory.com/wp-content/uploads/2015/01/e-cig-patent.png?ssl=1.

39. Regulatory Letter from Daniel L. Michels, Dir., DHHS, Office of Compliance, Ctr. For Drugs & Biologics. (February 9, 1987). http://www.legacy.library.ucsf.edu/documentStore/h/e/b/heb65e00/Sheb65200.pdf.

40. Elias, J., Ling, P.M. Invisible Smoke: Third-Party Endorsement and the Resurrection of Heat-Not-Burn Tobacco Products. Tob Control. 2018;27(suppl 1): s96–s101. https://doi.org/10.1136/tobaccocontrol-2018-054433.

41. Burrough, B., Helyar, J. *Barbarians at the Gate: The Fall of RJR Nabisco.* New York: Harper Business, 2008. pp. 75.

42. Tillinghast, J. *Big Money Thinks Small: Biases, Blind Spots, and Smarter Investing.* Columbia University Press, 15 August 2017. pp. 138.

43. Slade, J., Connolly, G.N., Lymperis, D. Eclipse: Does It Live Up to Its Health Claims? Tob Control. 2002;11:ii64–ii70.

218 S. C. HAMPSHER-MONK ET AL.

44. Ontario Tobacco Research Unit, OTRU Update: Heat-Not-Burn Tobacco products: Claims and Science, November 2016.
45. Williams M., Talbot, P. Design Features in Multiple Generations of Electronic Cigarette Atomizers. Int J Environ Res Public Health. 2019 Aug 14;16(16):2904. https://doi.org/10.3390/ijerph16162904.
46. U.S. Customs and Border Protection website database. August 22, 2006. NY M85579, available at: https://rulings.cbp.gov/search?term=m85579.
47. National Center for Chronic Disease Prevention and Health Promotion (US) Office on Smoking and Health. E-Cigarette Use Among Youth and Young Adults: A Report of the Surgeon General [Internet]. Atlanta (GA): Centers for Disease Control and Prevention (US); 2016. Chapter 1, Introduction, Conclusions, and Historical Background Relative to E-Cigarettes, available at: https://www.ncbi.nlm.nih.gov/books/NBK538684/.
48. Appendix 4.1 of the U.S. Surgeon General's report *E-Cigarette Use Among Youth and Young Adults* provides a comprehensive list of independent, public, and private e-cigarette companies, as well as descriptions of the companies and their products and brands. This source also details some of the major e-liquid, flavor, and battery companies.
49. U.S. Surgeon General (2016). Appendix 4.5 Evolution of Market Share in the E-Cigarette Market, Centers for Disease Control and Prevention, available at: https://www.cdc.gov/tobacco/data_statistics/sgr/e-cigarettes/pdfs/2016_SGR_App_4-5_508.pdf.
50. Zhu, S.H., Sun, J.Y., Bonnevie, E., Cummins, S.E., Gamst, A., Yin, L., Lee, M. Four Hundred and Sixty Brands of E-cigarettes and Counting: Implications for Product Regulation. Tob Control. 2014;23(suppl 3):iii3–iii9.
51. U.S. Surgeon General (2016). Appendix 4.5 Evolution of Market Share in the E-Cigarette Market, Centers for Disease Control and Prevention, available at: https://www.cdc.gov/tobacco/data_statistics/sgr/e-cigarettes/pdfs/2016_SGR_App_4-5_508.pdf.
52. Zhu, S.H., Sun, J.Y., Bonnevie, E., Cummins, S.E., Gamst, A., Yin, L., Lee, M. Four Hundred and Sixty Brands of E-cigarettes and Counting: Implications for Product Regulation. Tob Control. 2014;23:(suppl 3):iii3–iii9.

53. Nkosi, L., Odani, S., Agaku, I.T. 20-Year Trends in Tobacco Sales and Self-Reported Tobacco Use in the United States, 2000–2020. Prev Chronic Dis 2022;19:210435. https://doi.org/10.5888/pcd19.210435.
54. King, B.A., Gammon, D.G., Marynak, K.L., Rogers, T. Electronic Cigarette Sales in the United States, 2013–2017. JAMA. 2018 Oct 2;320(13):1379–1380. https://doi.org/10.1001/jama.2018.10488. PMID: 30285167; PMCID: PMC6233837.
55. Vapor Voice (2023), Juul's Market Share Still Falling, Vuse Continues Growth, Vapor Voice, available at: https://vaporvoice.net/2023/01/12/juuls-market-share-still-falling-vuse-continues-growth/.
56. Datum is from Euromonitor International's Passport database. While many media outlets reported that Juul had around three-quarters of the market in the late 2010s, such claims were based on data from Nielsen's point-of-sale data, which do not cover all sales in the U.S. Euromonitor's data are more complete.
57. Bauld, L., Angus, K., De Andrade, M., Ford, A. *Electronic Cigarette Marketing: Current Research and Policy.* Cancer Research UK, 2016, available at: http://www.cancerresearchuk.org/sites/default/files/electronic_cigarette_marketing_report_final.pdf.
58. Mickle, T. (2015, April 30). Japan Tobacco to Acquire U.S. Electronic Cigarette Company Logic Technology Development. Wall Street Journal. http://www.wsj.com/articles/japan-tobacco-to-acquire-u-s-electronic-cigarette-company-logic-technology-development-1430423065.
59. King, B.A., Gammon, D.G., Marynak, K.L., Rogers, T. Electronic Cigarette Sales in the United States, 2013–2017. JAMA. Oct 2, 2018;320(13):1379–1380. https://doi.org/10.1001/jama.2018.10488. PMC 6233837. PMID 30285167.
60. Primack, D. Scoop: The Numbers Behind Juul's Investor Appeal. Axios, 2018 avaiable at: https://www.axios.com/2018/07/02/numbers-juul-investor-appeal-vaping.
61. Kumar, S.U. Altria Says Juul Sales Skyrocket to $1 Billion in 2018. *Reuters.* 2019, available at: https://www.reuters.com/article/us-altria-group-juul/altria-says-juul-sales-skyrocket-to-1-billion-in-2018-idUSKCN1PP1YJ.
62. Guzman, Z. (2018). Juul Surpasses Facebook as Fastest Startup to Reach Decacorn Status. *Yahoo! Finance,* available

at: https://finance.yahoo.com/news/juul-surpasses-facebook-fastest-startup-reach-decacorn-status-153728892.html.

63. See note above on Juul's market share.

64. Bach, L. JUUL and Youth: Rising E-Cigarette Popularity. *CTFK*, 2021, available at: https://www.tobaccofreekids.org/assets/factsheets/0394.pdf.

65. Levy, D.T., Sweanor, D., Sanchez-Romero, L.M., et al. Altria-Juul Labs Deal: Why Did It Occur and What Does It Mean for the US Nicotine Delivery Product Market. Tob Control. 2020;29:e171–e174. https://doi.org/10.1136/tobaccocontrol-2019-055081.

66. Maloney, J., Mattioli, D. Why Marlboro Maker Bet on Juul, the Vaping Upstart Aiming to Kill Cigarettes. The Wall Street Journal. March 23, 2019.

67. Glenza, J. Is Juul the New Big Tobacco? Wave of Lawsuits Signal Familiar Problems. *The Guardian*, (September 10, 2019).

68. Ducharme, J. Big Vape: The Incendiary Rise of Juul. Hodder & Stoughton, 2023.

69. Huang, J., Duan, Z., Kwok, J., Binns, S., Vera, L.E., Kim, Y., Szczypka, G., Emery, S.L. Vaping Versus Juuling: How the Extraordinary Growth and Marketing of Juul Transformed the US Retail E-cigarette Market. Tob Control. May 2018;28(2):146–151. https://doi.org/10.1136/tobaccocontrol-2018-054382.

70. PBS Newshour (2022). Juul to Pay Nearly $440 Million to Settle Probe into Underage Marketing of Vape Products, Public Broadcasting Service, 2022, available at: https://www.pbs.org/newshour/nation/juul-to-pay-nearly-440m-to-settle-probe-into-underage-marketing-of-vape-products.

71. Nedelman, M., Selig, R., Azad, A. #JUUL: How Social Media Hyped Nicotine for a New Generation, CNN, 2018, available at: https://www.cnn.com/2018/12/17/health/juul-social-media-influencers/index.html.

72. Office of Attorney General Maura Healey. Press Release: AG Healey Sues JUUL for Creating Youth Vaping Epidemic, Reveals New Facts About Campaign Targeting Young People, 2020, available at: https://www.mass.gov/news/ag-healey-sues-juul-for-creating-youth-vaping-epidemic-reveals-new-facts-about-campaign-targeting-young-people.

73. Leventhal, A.M., Madden, D.R., Peraza, N., Schiff, S.J., Lebovitz, L., Whitted, L., Barrington-Trimis, J., Mason, T.B., Anderson, M.K., Tackett, A.P. Effect of Exposure to e-Cigarettes With Salt vs Free-Base Nicotine on the Appeal and Sensory Experience of Vaping: A Randomized Clinical Trial. JAMA Netw Open. Jan 4, 2021;4(1):e2032757. https://doi.org/10.1001/jamanetworkopen.2020.32757.

74. Leventhal, A.M., Madden, D.R., Peraza, N., Schiff, S.J., Lebovitz, L., Whitted, L., Barrington-Trimis, J., Mason, T.B., Anderson, M.K., Tackett, A.P. Effect of Exposure to e-Cigarettes With Salt vs Free-Base Nicotine on the Appeal and Sensory Experience of Vaping: A Randomized Clinical Trial. JAMA Netw Open. 2021;4(1):e2032757. https://doi.org/10.1001/jamanetworkopen.2020.32757.

75. Gholap, V.V., Kosmider, L., Golshahi, L., Halquist, M.S. Nicotine Forms: Why and How Do They Matter in Nicotine Delivery from Electronic Cigarettes? Expert Opinion on Drug Delivery. 2020;17:12, 1727–1736. https://doi.org/10.1080/17425247.2020.1814736.

76. Tolentino, J., Eliscu, A., Messina, C.R., Boykan, R., Goniewicz, M.L. High Exposure to Nicotine Among Adolescents Who Use Juul and Other Vape Pod Systems ('Pods')". Tob Control. Aug 30, 2018;28 (6): Tobaccocontrol–2018–054565. https://doi.org/10.1136/tobaccocontrol-2018-054565.

77. Lee, S.J., Rees, V.W., Yossefy, N., Emmons, K.M., Tan, A.S.L. Youth and Young Adult Use of Pod-Based Electronic Cigarettes From 2015 to 2019: A Systematic Review. JAMA Pediatr. 2020;174(7):714–720. https://doi.org/10.1001/jamapediatrics.2020.0259.

78. Jackler, R.K., Ramamurthi D. Nicotine Arms Race: JUUL and the High-Nicotine Product Market Tob Control. 2019;28:623–628.

79. Ducharme, J. *Big Vape: The Incendiary Rise of Juul*. Hodder & Stoughton, 2023.

80. Gottlieb. S. (April 24, 2018). Statement from FDA Commissioner Scott Gottlieb, M.D., on new enforcement Actions and a Youth Tobacco Prevention Plan to Stop Youth Use of, and Access to, Juul and Other E-cigarettes (Press release). Silver Spring, MD: Food and Drug Administration.

81. Whyte, L.E., Center for Public Integrity and Dianna M. Náñez (2019). Why Big Tobacco and JUUL Are Lobbying to Raise the Smoking Age. USA Today, available at: https://www.usa today.com/story/news/investigations/2019/05/23/why-big-tobacco-and-juul-lobbying-raise-smoking-age/3758443002/.

82. Juul Labs. JUUL Labs Announces Comprehensive Strategy to Combat Underage Use, 2018, available at: https://www.juullabs.com/juul-strategy-to-combat-underage-use/.

83. Gottlieb S. (September 12, 2018). FDA Takes New Steps to Address Epidemic of Youth E-cigarette Use, Including a Historic Action Against More Than 1,300 Retailers and 5 Major Manufacturers for Their Roles Perpetuating Youth Access (Press release). Silver Spring, MD: Food and Drug Administration.

84. Juul Labs. Statement Regarding Recent FDA Request, 2018, available at: https://www.juullabs.com/statement-from-kevin-burns-juul-labs-chief-executive-officer-regarding-recent-fda-req uest/.

85. Kaplan, S., Hoffman, J. FDA. Targets Vaping, Alarmed by Teenage Use The New York Times, 2018, available at: https://www.nytimes.com/2018/09/12/health/juul-fda-vaping-ecigar ettes.html?action=click&module=Top%20Stories&pgtype=Hom epage.

86. Press Release Chairman Krishnamoorthi of the Subcommittee on Economic and Consumer Policy Opens Investigation into JUUL's Role in the Youth E-Cigarette Epidemic, available at: https://krishnamoorthi.house.gov/media/press-releases/cha irman-krishnamoorthi-subcommittee-economic-and-consumer-policy-opens.

87. Kalvadeer, Z. Press Release: CEH Reaches Legally Binding Settlement with JUUL Restricting Its Marketing to Youth, 2019, available at: https://ceh.org/latest/press-releases/ceh-reaches-legally-binding-settlement-with-juul-restricting-its-marketing-to-youth/.

88. FDA. FDA Denies Authorization to Market JUUL Products: Currently Marketed JUUL Products Must Be Removed from the US Market, US Food and Drug Adminsitration, press release, 2022, available at: https://www.fda.gov/news-events/press-ann ouncements/fda-denies-authorization-market-juul-products.

89. Ben-Ozer, T., Levi, S. Israel Bans High-Nicotine Juul E-cigarettes. The Jerusalem Post, 2019, available at: https://www.jpost.com/HEALTH-SCIENCE/Israel-bans-JUUL-electronic-cigarettes-565442.
90. Reuters. (2022, June 24). Federal Appeals Court Puts FDA Ban on Juul E-cigarette Sales on Hold. Reuters. https://www.reuters.com/legal/litigation/juul-appeals-block-fda-ban-e-cigarettes-2022-06-24/.
91. Feeley, J., Nayak, M. Juul Agrees to Pay $1.2 Billion in Youth-Vaping Settlement, Bloomberg News, 2022, available at: https://www.bloomberg.com/news/articles/2022-12-09/juul-to-pay-1-2-billion-in-youth-vaping-settlement#xj4y7vzkg.
92. Drug Watch (n.d.). E-Cigarette Lawsuits, Drug Watch, accessed 20 May 2023, available at: https://www.drugwatch.com/e-cigarettes/lawsuits/.
93. Associated Press. (2022, September 6). Juul to Pay $440 m After Years-Long Investigation into Teen Vaping. The Guardian. https://www.theguardian.com/us-news/2022/sep/06/juul-teen-vaping-settlement-us-states.
94. Drug Watch (n.d.). E-Cigarette Lawsuits, Drug Watch, accessed 20 May 2023, available at: https://www.drugwatch.com/e-cigarettes/lawsuits/.
95. Nouvelage, E. Altria's $13 Billion Juul Investment Has Lost 95% of Its Value. CNBC, 2022, available at https://www.cnbc.com/2022/07/28/altrias-13b-juul-investment-has-lost-95percent-of-its-value.html.
96. *Klein v. Altria Group Inc.* et al., Case No. 3:20-cv-00075. U.S. District Court for the Eastern District of Virginia.
97. Pomerantz Law (n.d.), Pomerantz Achieves $90 Million Class Action Settlement in Altria and JUUL Litigation, Pomerantz LLP, Retrieved May 20, 2023, from https://pomlaw.com/monitor-issues/pomerantz-achieves-90-million-class-action-settlement-in-altria-and-juul-litigation.
98. Seeking Alpha. Altria Group Ends Noncompete Agreement with JUUL Labs, Seeking Alpha, 2022, available at: https://seekingalpha.com/news/3887442-altria-group-ends-noncompete-agreement-with-juul-labs.

99. Center for Tobacco Products (2023). Premarket Tobacco Product Marketing Granted Orders, US Food and Drug Administration, available at: www.fda.gov, https://www.fda.gov/tobacco-products/premarket-tobacco-product-applications/premarket-tobacco-product-marketing-granted-orders.
100. Sophia DM. (2023, March 6). Altria to Revive Vaping Push with $2.8 bln NJOY Bid After Juul Fiasco. Reuters. https://www.reuters.com/markets/deals/altria-buy-startup-njoy-28-bln-latest-e-cigarette-push-after-juul-blow-2023-03-06/.
101. Tobacco Reporter (2023). Vuse Market Share Grows, Tobacco Reporter, available at: https://tobaccoreporter.com/2023/04/06/vuse-market-share-grows-wh))ile-juul-drops/#:~:text=As%20recently%20as%20May%202019,U.S.%20e%2Dcigarette%20market%20share.
102. Euromonitor Global Market Information Database (GMID) Passport Database (2022), UK E-Cigarette Market Value 2005–2019, Euromonitor International.
103. Grand View Research (n.d.). E-cigarette and Vape Market Size, Share & Trends Analysis Report By Product (Modular Devices, Rechargeable), By Distribution Channel (Online, Retail), By Region (APAC, North America), and Segment Forecasts, 2023–2030, Grand View Research, available at: https://www.grandviewresearch.com/industry-analysis/e-cigarette-vaping-market.
104. Mordor Intelligence (n.d.). E-cigarette Market Size & Share Analysis–Growth Trends & Forecasts (2023–2028), Mordor Intelligence, available at: https://www.mordorintelligence.com/industry-reports/global-e-cigarettes-market-industry.
105. Allied Market Research. Electronic Cigarette Market by Product Type (Disposable, Rechargeable, and Modular), Flavor (Tobacco, Botanical, Fruit, Sweet, Beverage, and Others) and Distribution Channel (Specialist E-Cig Shops, Online, Supermarkets, Tobacconist, and Others): Global Opportunity Analysis and Industry Forecast, 2022–2031, Allied Market Research, 2022, available at: https://www.alliedmarketresearch.com/electronic-cigarette-market

106. Impactful Insights (n.d.). E-Cigarette Market: Global Industry Trends, Share, Size, Growth, Opportunity and Forecast 2023–2028, Impactful Insights, avaiallbe at: https://www.imarcgroup.com/e-cigarette-market
107. Euromonitor Global Market Information Database (GMID) Passport Database (2022), UK e-Cigarette Market Value 2005–2019, Euromonitor International.
108. Prosmoke (n.d.). V2 Electronic Cigarettes Closes Its Doors, Prosmoke, Blogpost, available at: https://www.prosmokestore.com/store/blogs/v2-out-of-business-278#:~:text=V2%20(VMR%20Products)%20Electronic%20Cigarettes%20Is%20Closing%20Its%20doors&text=One%20of%20the%20industries%20largest,longer%20be%20in%20the%20industry.
109. Berg, C.J., Melena, A., Wittman, F.D., Robles, T., Henriksen, L. The Reshaping of the E-Cigarette Retail Environment: Its Evolution and Public Health Concerns. Int J Environ Res Public Health. 2022 Jul 12;19(14):8518. https://doi.org/10.3390/ijerph19148518.
110. Berg, C.J., Callanan, R., Johnson, T.O., Schliecher, N.C., Sussman, S., Wagener, T.L., Henriksen, L. Vape Shop and Consumer Activity During COVID-19 Non-essential Business Closures in the USA. Tob Control. 2021;30:e41–e44. https://doi.org/10.1136/tobaccocontrol-2020-056171.
111. Euromonitor Passport. Tobacco in the US, 2022, available at: https://www.euromonitor.com/tobacco-in-the-us/report.
112. National Center for Chronic Disease Prevention and Health Promotion (US) Office on Smoking and Health. E-Cigarette Use Among Youth and Young Adults: A Report of the Surgeon General [Internet]. Atlanta (GA): Centers for Disease Control and Prevention (US); 2016. Chapter 4, Activities of the E-Cigarette Companies, available at: https://www.ncbi.nlm.nih.gov/books/NBK538679/.
113. E-Cigarette Report for 2015–2018. (2022, March 17). Federal Trade Commission. https://www.ftc.gov/reports/e-cigarette-report-2015-2018.
114. Data are for Juul and Vuse Alto, from Circana market data via Bloomberg.
115. Note that these data exclude specialist vape stores and e-commerce sales, which typically favor open systems and e-liquids, meaning that the published data may not accurately represent the whole market.

116. E-Cigarette Report for 2019–2020, Federal Trade Commission. (n.d.). Retrieved May 20, 2023, from https://www.ftc.gov/rep orts/e-cigarette-report-2019-2020.
117. Kaplan, S. (2019, October 17). Juul Suspends Online Sales of Flavored E-Cigarettes. The New York Times, available at: https://www.nytimes.com/2019/10/17/health/vaping-juul-e-cigarettes.html.
118. Wang, T.W., Gentzke, A.S., Neff, L.J., Glidden, E.V., Jamal, A., Park-Lee, E., Ren, C., Cullen, K.A., King, B.A., Hacker, K.A. Disposable E-Cigarette Use among U.S. Youth—An Emerging Public Health Challenge. N Engl J Med. 2021 Apr 22;384(16):1573–1576. https://doi.org/10.1056/NEJMc2 033943. Epub 2021 Mar 16.
119. Ali, F.R.M., Diaz, M.C., Vallone, D., et al. E-cigarette Unit Sales, by Product and Flavor Type—United States, 2014–2020. MMWR Morb Mortal Wkly Rep 2020;69:1313–1318.
120. Park-Lee, E., Ren, C., Sawdey, M.D., Gentzke, A.S., Cornelius, M., Jamal, A., Cullen, K.A. Notes from the Field: E-Cigarette Use Among Middle and High School Students—National Youth Tobacco Survey, United States, 2021. MMWR Morb Mortal Wkly Rep. 2021 Oct 1;70(39):1387–1389. https://doi.org/10. 15585/mmwr.mm7039a4.
121. In addition to Cool Clouds Distribution, Inc., doing business as Puff Bar, FDA sent warning letters to: HQD Tech U.S., LLC; Myle Vape, Inc; E Cigarette Empire LLC; Eleaf U.S.; Ohm City Vapes Inc.; Hina Singh Enterprises, Inc., doing business as Just Eliquids Distro Inc.; Breazy Inc.; Majestic Vapors, LLC and Vape Deal, LLC.
122. FDA (2022), New Law Clarifies FDA Authority to Regulate Synthetic Nicotine, U.S. Food and Drug Administration. Retrieved May 20, 2023, from https://content.govdelivery.com/ accounts/USFDA/bulletins/30f82ff.
123. Hammond, D., Reid, J.L., Burkhalter, R., Bansal-Travers, M., Gravely, S., Hyland, A., Kasza, K., McNeill, A. E-cigarette Flavors, Devices, and Brands Used by Youths Before and After Partial Flavor Restrictions in the United States: Canada, England, and the United States, 2017–2020. Am J Public Health. 2022;112, 1014–1024. https://doi.org/10.2105/AJPH.2022. 306780.

124. Action on Smoking and Health (ASH). Use of e-cigarettes (vapes) among young people in Great Britain. 2022. https://ash.org.uk/resources/view/use-of-e-cigarettes-among-young-people-in-great-britain.
125. Giovenco, D.P., Hammond, D., Corey, C.G., Ambrose, B.K., Delnevo, C.D. E-cigarette Market Trends in Traditional U.S. Retail Channels, 2012–2013. Nicotine & Tobacco Research 2015;17(10):1279–1283.
126. CDC Foundation. National-E-CigaretteSales-DataBrief, CDC Foundation, 2022, available at: https://www.cdcfoundation.org/National-E-CigaretteSales-DataBrief-2022-July22?inline.
127. E-Cigarette Report for 2015–2018 (2022, March 17). Federal Trade Commission. https://www.ftc.gov/reports/e-cigarette-report-2015-2018.
128. Deans, J. Super Bowl 2012 Sets U.S. TV Ratings Record for Third Year Running, 2012; http://www.theguardian.com/media/2012/feb/07/super-bowl-2012-tv-ratings-record.
129. Centers for Disease Control and Prevention. E-cigarette Ads Reach Nearly 7 in 10 Middle and High-School Students, January 5, 2016a; http://www.cdc.gov/media/releases/2016/p0105-e-cigarettes.html.
130. Grana, R.A., Ling PM. "Smoking Revolution": A Content Analysis of Electronic Cigarette Retail Websites. Am J Prev Med. 2014;46(4):395–403.
131. E-Cigarette Report for 2019–2020, Federal Trade Commission. (n.d.). Retrieved May 20, 2023, from https://www.ftc.gov/reports/e-cigarette-report-2019-2020.
132. E-Cigarette Report for 2015–2018 (2022, March 17). Federal Trade Commission. https://www.ftc.gov/reports/e-cigarette-report-2015-2018.
133. E-Cigarette Report for 2019–2020, Federal Trade Commission (n.d.). Retrieved May 20, 2023, from https://www.ftc.gov/reports/e-cigarette-report-2019-2020.
134. U.S. Department of Health and Human Services. Preventing Tobacco Use Among Youth and Young Adults: A Report of the Surgeon General. Atlanta (GA): U.S. Department of Health and Human Services, Centers for Disease Control and Prevention, National Center for Chronic Disease Prevention and Health Promotion, Office on Smoking and Health, 2012.

135. U.S. Congress. Cigarette, E-Cigarette, and Other Tobacco Product Advertisements and Imagery in Magazines with Large Numbers of Teen Readers, 2014; http://democrats.energycommerce.house.gov/sites/default/files/documents/Report-Tobacco-Magazine-Advertising-2014-9-24.pdf.
136. Duke, J.C., Lee, Y.O., Kim, A.E., Watson, K.A., Arnold, K.Y., Nonnemaker, J.M., Porter, L. Exposure to Electronic Cigarette Television Advertisements Among Youth and Young Adults. Pediatrics 2014;134(1):e29–e36.
137. California Department of Public Health, California Tobacco Control Program. Healthy Stores for a Healthy Community, 2014; http://www.healthystoreshealthycommunity.com.
138. Levy, D.T., Lindblom, E.N., Sweanor, D.T., Chaloupka, F., O'Connor, R.J., Shang, C., Palley, T., Fong, G.T., Cummings, K.M., Goniewicz, M.L., Borland, R. An Economic Analysis of the Pre-Deeming US Market for Nicotine Vaping Products. Tob Regul Sci. 2019 Mar;5(2):169–181. https://doi.org/10.18001/trs.5.2.8.
139. Bour, N. How Many Vape Shops Are There in the USA? (online), available at: https://vapenews.com/november-2014/how-many-vape-shops-are-there-in-the-u-s-a/.
140. Levy, D.T., Lindblom, E.N., Sweanor, D.T., Chaloupka, F., O'Connor, R.J., Shang, C., Palley, T., Fong, G.T., Cummings, K.M., Goniewicz, M.L., Borland, R. An Economic Analysis of the Pre-Deeming US Market for Nicotine Vaping Products. Tob Regul Sci. 2019 Mar;5(2):169–181. https://doi.org/10.18001/trs.5.2.8.
141. Lee, Y.O., Kim, A.E. 'Vape Shops' and 'E-cigarette Lounges' Open Across the USA to Promote ENDS. Tob Control. 2015;24(4):410–412.
142. Cheney, M., Gowin, M., Wann, T.F. Marketing Practices of Vapor Store Owners. Am J Public Health. 2015;105(6):e16–e21.
143. Dai, H., Hao, J. Geographic Density and Proximity of Vape Shops to Colleges in the USA. Tob Control. 2017;26:379–385.
144. Wells Fargo Securities. Nielsen: Tobacco "All Channel" Data Cig Pricing Remains Strong; E-Cig $ Sales Growth Re-Accelerates. Equity Research. San Francisco (CA): Wells Fargo Securities, March 31, 2015a.

145. Berg, C.J., Melena, A., Wittman, F.D., Robles, T., Henriksen, L. The Reshaping of the E-Cigarette Retail Environment: Its Evolution and Public Health Concerns. Int J Environ Res Public Health. 2022 Jul 12;19(14):8518. https://doi.org/10.3390/ije rph19148518.
146. Caruana, D. US Vape Stores: The Media Hurt the Vaping Industry More Than COVID-19, available at: https://www.vap ingpost.com/2021/03/05/us-vape-stores-the-media-hurt-the-vaping-industry-more-than-covid-19/.
147. Berg, C.J., Callanan, R., Johnson, T.O., Schliecher, N.C., Sussman, S., Wagener, T.L., Henriksen, L. Vape Shop and Consumer Activity During COVID-19 Non-essential Business Closures in the USA. Tob Control. 2021;30:e41–e44. https://doi.org/10.1136/tobaccocontrol-2020-056171.
148. Richardson, A., Ganz, O., Vallone, D. Tobacco on the Web: Surveillance and Characterisation of Online Tobacco and E-cigarette Advertising. Tob Control. 2015;24(4):341–347.
149. Williams, R.S., Derrick, J., Liebman, A.K., LaFleur, K., Ribisl, K.M. Content Analysis of Age Verification, Purchase and Delivery Methods of Internet E-cigarette Vendors, 2013 and 2014. Tob Control. 2018 May;27(3):287–293. https://doi.org/10.1136/tobaccocontrol-2016-053616.
150. Williams, R.S., Derrick, J., Ribisl, K.M. Electronic Cigarette Sales to Minors via the Internet. JAMA Pediatrics 2015;169(3):e1563.
151. E-Cigarette Report for 2015–2018. (2022, March 17). Federal Trade Commission. https://www.ftc.gov/reports/e-cigarette-report-2015-2018.
152. Shama, A.L., Elijah. (2019, September 24). CDC Warns of Dangers of Nicotine Salts Used by Vaping Giant Juul in E-cigarettes. CNBC. https://www.cnbc.com/2019/09/24/cdc-warns-of-dangers-of-nicotine-salts-used-by-vaping-giant-juul-in-e-cigarettes.html.
153. Dawkins, L., Cox, S., Goniewicz, M., McRobbie, H., Kimber, C., Doig, M., Kośmider, L. 'Real-World' Compensatory Behaviour with Low Nicotine Concentration E-liquid: Subjective Effects and Nicotine, Acrolein and Formaldehyde Exposure. Addiction, 2018. https://doi.org/10.1111/add.14271.
154. U.S. Department of Health and Human Services Food and Drug Administration Center for Tobacco Products (2019). Premarket

230 S. C. HAMPSHER-MONK ET AL.

Tobacco Product Applications for Electronic Nicotine Delivery Systems. Guidance for Industry, available at: https://www.fda.gov/media/127853/download.

155. Caruana, D. (2020). Colorado Smoke-Free Alliance Talks About the Burdensome PMTA—Vaping Post, Retrieved May 20, 2023, from https://www.vapingpost.com/2020/09/11/colorado-smoke-free-alliance-talks-about-the-burdensome-pmta/.

156. FDA. Press Release: FDA Issues Refuse to File (RTF) Letter to JD Nova Group LLC, 2021, available at: https://www.fda.gov/tobacco-products/ctp-newsroom/fda-issues-refuse-file-rtf-letter-jd-nova-group-llc?utm_source=CTPTwitter&utm_medium=social&utm_campaign=ctp-pmta.

157. Supreme Court of the United States. Emergency Application for a Stay of Agency Order Pending the Disposition by The United States Court of Appeals for the Sixth Circuit of a Petition for Review and any Further Proceedings in This Court, Supreme Court of the United States, 2021, available at: https://www.supremecourt.gov/DocketPDF/21/21A176/201205/2021112317081654_01%20-%20Breeze%20Smoke%20-%20Stay%20Application.pdf.

158. United States Court of Appeals for the Fifth Circuit. Petition for Review of an Order of the Food and Drug Administration, United States Court of Appeals for the Fifth Circuit, 2021, available at: https://vaping.org/wp-content/uploads/2021/10/2021-10-14-Admin-Stay-Issued.pdf.

159. United States Court of Appeals For the Seventh Circuit (2022), On Petition for Review of a Final Marketing Denial Order by the U.S. Food and Drug Administration, no. PM0001689, United States Court of Appeals For the Seventh Circuit, available at: http://media.ca7.uscourts.gov/cgi-bin/rssExec.pl?Submit=Display&Path=Y2022/D08-29/C:21-2840:J:Wood:aut:T:fnOp:N:2924287:S:0.

160. United States Court of Appeals for the Sixth Circuit (2021). Application (21A176) for a Stay, Submitted to Justice Kavanaugh., United States Court of Appeals for the Sixth Circuit, available at: https://www.supremecourt.gov/search.aspx?filename=/docket/docketfiles/html/public/21a176.html.

161. Eleventh Circuit Sets Aside FDA Marketing Denial Orders Issued to Bidi Vapor and Others. (n.d.). JD Supra. Retrieved May 20, 2023, from https://www.jdsupra.com/legalnews/eleventh-circuit-sets-aside-fda-8568550/
162. U.S. Fifth Circuit Court of Appeals (2023). R.J. Reynolds v. FDA, No. 23–60128 (5th Cir. 2023), available at: https://law.justia.com/cases/federal/appellate-courts/ca5/23-60128/23-60128-2023-03-23.html.
163. Jerzyński, T., Stimson, G.V., Shapiro, H. et al. Estimation of the Global Number of E-cigarette Users in 2020. Harm Reduct J. 2021;18:109. https://doi.org/10.1186/s12954-021-00556-7.
164. Jerzyński, T., Stimson, G.V. Estimation of the Global Number of Vapers: 82 Million Worldwide in 2021. Drugs, Habits and Social Policy, Vol. ahead-of-print No. ahead-of-print, 2023. https://doi.org/10.1108/DHS-07-2022-0028.
165. Jerzyński, T., Stimson, G.V. Estimation of the Global Number of Vapers: 82 Million Worldwide in 2021. Drugs, Habits and Social Policy, Vol. ahead-of-print No. ahead-of-print. 2023. https://doi.org/10.1108/DHS-07-2022-0028.
166. Jerzyński, T., Stimson, G.V., Shapiro, H. et al. Estimation of the Global Number of E-cigarette Users in 2020. Harm Reduct J. 2021;18:109. https://doi.org/10.1186/s12954-021-00556-7.
167. Jerzyński, T., Stimson, G.V., Shapiro, H. et al. Estimation of the Global Number of E-cigarette Users in 2020. Harm Reduct J. 2021;18:109. https://doi.org/10.1186/s12954-021-00556-7.
168. Jerzyński, T., Stimson, G.V. Estimation of the Global Number of Vapers: 82 Million Worldwide in 2021. Drugs, Habits and Social Policy, Vol. ahead-of-print No. ahead-of-print. 2023. https://doi.org/10.1108/DHS-07-2022-0028.
169. Cornelius, M.E., Loretan, C.G., Wang, T.W., Jamal, A., Homa, D.M. Tobacco Product Use Among Adults—United States, 2020. MMWR Morb Mortal Wkly Rep 2022;71:397–405. https://doi.org/10.15585/mmwr.mm7111a1.
170. Cooper, M., Park-Lee, E., Ren, C., Cornelius, M., Jamal, A., Cullen, K.A. Notes from the Field: E-cigarette Use Among Middle and High School Students—United States, 2022. MMWR Morb Mortal Wkly Rep 2022;71:1283–1285. https://doi.org/10.15585/mmwr.mm7140a3.

171. ASH (2022). Use of E-cigarettes (Vapes) Among Adults in Great Britain, Action on Smoking and Health UK, available at: https://ash.org.uk/uploads/Use-of-e-cigarettes-vapes-among-adults-in-Great-Britain-2022.pdf?v=1661865959.

172. ASH (2022). Use of E-cigarettes (Vapes) Among Young People in Great Britain, Action on Smoking and Health UK, available at: https://ash.org.uk/uploads/Use-of-e-cigarettes-among-young-people-in-Great-Britain-2022.pdf?v=1661866458.

173. Statistics Canada (n.d.). Canadian Tobacco and Nicotine Survey, 2021, Statistics Canada, available at: https://www150.statcan.gc.ca/n1/daily-quotidien/220505/dq220505c-eng.htm.

174. Manatu, H. Annual Update of Key Results 2020/21: New Zealand Health Survey, New Zealand Ministry of Health, 2021, availabe at: https://www.health.govt.nz/publication/annual-update-key-results-2020-21-new-zealand-health-survey.

175. European Commission. Attitudes of Europeans Towards Tobacco and Electronic Cigarettes. Spec Eurobarometer. 2017;458:19–24, available at: https://doi.org/ec.europa.eu/public_opinion/index_en.htm.

176. Pan, L., Morton, J., Mbulo, L., Dean, A., Ahluwalia, I.B. Electronic Cigarette Use Among Adults in 14 Countries: A Cross-Sectional Study. EClinicalMedicine. 2022 Apr 21;47:101401. https://doi.org/10.1016/j.eclinm.2022.101401.

177. Xiao, L., Yin, X., Di, X., et al. Awareness and Prevalence of E-cigarette Use Among Chinese Adults: Policy Implications. Tob Control. 2022;31:498–504.

178. Agaku, I.T., Egbe, C.O., Ayo-Yusuf, O.A. Potential Revenue from Taxing E-cigarettes and Comparison of Annual Costs of Daily E-cigarette Use Versus Daily Cigarette Smoking Among South African Adults. Tob Induc Dis. 2021 Jan 29;19:07. https://doi.org/10.18332/tid/131861.

179. Jerzyński, T., Stimson, G.V., Shapiro, H. et al. Estimation of the Global Number of E-cigarette Users in 2020. Harm Reduct J. 2021;18:109. https://doi.org/10.1186/s12954-021-00556-7.

180. ASH. Use of E-cigarettes (Vapes) Among Adults in Great Britain, Action on Smoking and Health UK, 2022, available at: https://ash.org.uk/uploads/Use-of-e-cigarettes-vapes-among-adults-in-Great-Britain-2022.pdf.

181. ASH. Use of E-cigarettes (Vapes) Among Adults in Great Britain, Action on Smoking and Health UK, 2022, available at: https://ash.org.uk/wp-content/uploads/2021/06/Use-of-e-cigarettes-vapes-among-adults-in-Great-Britain-2021.pdf.
182. Kapan, A., Stefanac, S., Sandner, I., Haider, S., Grabovac, I., Dorner, T.E. Use of Electronic Cigarettes in European Populations: A Narrative Review. Int J Environ Res Public Health. 2020 Mar 17;17(6):1971. https://doi.org/10.3390/ijerph17061971.
183. QuickStats: Percentage Distribution of Cigarette Smoking Status Among Current Adult E-Cigarette Users, by Age Group—National Health Interview Survey, United States, 2021. MMWR Morb Mortal Wkly Rep 2023;72:270. https://doi.org/10.15585/mmwr.mm7210a7.
184. Current e-cigarette users are persons who have ever tried an e-cigarette or other electronic vaping product even once and are now using everyday or some days.
185. Healthc Canada. Canadian Tobacco and Nicotine Survey (CTNS): Summary of Results for 2020, Government of Canada, 2021, available at: https://www.canada.ca/en/health-canada/services/canadian-tobacco-nicotine-survey/2020-summary.html.
186. King, B.A., Patel, R., Nguyen, K.H., et al. Trends in Awareness and Use of Electronic Cigarettes Among U.S Adults, 2010–2013. Nicotine Tob Res. 2015;17:219–27. https://doi.org/10.1093/ntr/ntu191.
187. Richardson, A., Pearson, J., Xiao, H., et al. Prevalence, Harm Perceptions, and Reasons for Using Noncombustible Tobacco Products Among Current and Former Smokers. Am J Public Health. 2014;104:1437–1444. https://doi.org/10.2105/AJPH.2013.301804.
188. NHS. Smoking, Drinking and Drug Use among Young People in England, 2021, National Health Services UK, 2022, available at: https://digital.nhs.uk/data-and-information/publications/statistical/smoking-drinking-and-drug-use-among-young-people-in-england/2021/part-4-electronic-cigarette-use-vaping#:~:text=Current%20e%2Dcigarette%20use%20increased,chart%20%2D%20see%20table%204.3.
189. Adkison, S.E., O'Connor, R.J., Bansal-Travers, M., et al. Electronic Nicotine Delivery Systems: International Tobacco Control

Four-Country Survey. Am J Prev Med. 2013;44:207–215. https://doi.org/10.1016/j.amepre.2012.10.018.

190. Adkison, S.E., O'Connor, R.J., Bansal-Travers, M., et al. Electronic Nicotine Delivery Systems: International Tobacco Control Four-Country Survey. Am J Prev Med. 2013;44:207–215. https://doi.org/10.1016/j.amepre.2012.10.018.

191. Gallus, S., Lugo, A., Pacifici, R., et al. E-cigarette Awareness, Use, and Harm Perception in Italy: A National Representative Survey. Nicotine Tob Res. 2014;16:1541–1518. https://doi.org/10.1093/ntr/ntu124.

192. Goniewicz, M.L., Zielinska-Danch, W. Electronic Cigarette Use Among Teenagers and Young Adults in Poland. Pediatrics. 2012;130:E879–E85. https://doi.org/10.1542/peds.2011-3448.

193. Vardavas, C.I., Filippidis, F.T., Agaku, I.T. Determinants and Prevalence of E-cigarette Use Throughout the European Union: A Secondary Analysis of 26,566 Youth and Adults from 27 Countries. Tob Control. 2015;24:442–448. https://doi.org/10.1136/tobaccocontrol-2013-051394.

194. Lee, S., Grana, R.A., Glantz, S.A. Electronic Cigarette Use Among Korean Adolescents: A Cross-Sectional Study of Market Penetration, Dual Use, and Relationship to Quit Attempts and Former Smoking. J Adolesc Health 2014;54:684–690. https://doi.org/10.1016/j.jadohealth.2013.11.003.

195. Pan, L., Morton, J., Mbulo, L., Dean, A., Ahluwalia, I.B. Electronic Cigarette Use Among Adults in 14 Countries: A Cross-Sectional Study. eClinicalMedicine. 2022;47. https://doi.org/10.1016/j.eclinm.2022.101401.

196. Hartwell, G., Thomas, S., Egan, M., et al. E-cigarettes and Equity: A Systematic Review of Differences in Awareness and Use Between Sociodemographic Groups. Tob Control. 2017;26:e85–e91.

197. Palipudi, K.M., Mbulo, L., Morton, J., et al. Awareness and Current Use of Electronic Cigarettes in Indonesia, Malaysia, Qatar, and Greece: Findings from 2011–2013 Global Adult Tobacco Surveys. Nicotine Tob Res. 2016;18:501–507.

198. Lippert, A.M. Do Adolescent Smokers Use E-cigarettes to Help Them Quit? The Sociodemographic Correlates and Cessation Motivations of U.S. Adolescent E-cigarette Use. Am J Health

Promot. 2015;29:374–379. https://doi.org/10.4278/ajhp.131 120-QUAN-595.

199. Kim, J., Lee, S., Chun, J. An International Systematic Review of Prevalence, Risk, and Protective Factors Associated with Young People's E-Cigarette Use. Int J Environ Res Public Health. 2022;19(18):11570. https://doi.org/10.3390/ijerph 191811570.

200. Sreeramareddy, C.T., Acharya, K., Manoharan, A. Electronic Cigarettes Use and 'Dual Use' Among the Youth in 75 Countries: Estimates from Global Youth Tobacco Surveys (2014–2019). Sci Rep. 2022;12:20967. https://doi.org/10.1038/s41 598-022-25594-4.

201. World Economic Forum (2022). Global Gender Gap Report 2022, World Economic Forum. Retrieved May 20, 2023, from https://www.weforum.org/reports/global-gender-gap-rep ort-2022/in-full/1-benchmarking-gender-gaps-2022/.

202. Finnish Institute for Health and Welfare (n.d.). Tobacco, Finnish Institute for Health and Welfare, available at: https://thl.fi/en/ web/alcohol-tobacco-and-addictions/tobacco.

203. Oakly, A., Edwards, R., Martin, G. Prevalence of E-cigarette Use from a Nationally Representative Sample in New Zealand. Addictive Behaviors. 2019;98:106024, https://doi.org/10.1016/j. addbeh.2019.06.013.

204. Kotz, D., Böckmann M., Kastaun, S. The Use of Tobacco, E-cigarettes, and Methods to Quit Smoking in Germany: A Representative Study Using 6 Waves of Data Over 12 Months (the DEBRA Study). Dtsch Arztebl Int. 2018;115(14):235.

205. Yimsaard, P., McNeill, A., Yong, H.H., Cummings, K.M., Chung-Hall, J., Hawkins, S.S., Quah, A.C.K., Fong, G.T., O'Connor, R.J., Hitchman, S.C. Gender Differences in Reasons for Using Electronic Cigarettes and Product Characteristics: Findings From the 2018 ITC Four Country Smoking and Vaping Survey. Nicotine Tob Res. 2021 Mar 19;23(4):678–686. https://doi.org/10.1093/ntr/ntaa196.

206. Kock, L., Shahab, L., West, R., Brown, J. E-cigarette Use in England 2014–17 as a Function of Socio-economic Profile. Addiction. 2019 Feb;114(2):294–303. https://doi.org/ 10.1111/add.14446.

207. Brown, J., West, R., Beard, E., Michie, S., Shahab, L., McNeill, A. Prevalence and Characteristics of E-cigarette Users in Great Britain: Findings from a General Population Survey of Smokers, Addictive Behaviors. 2014;39(6):1120–1125, https://doi.org/10.1016/j.addbeh.2014.03.009.
208. Friedman, A.S., Horn, S.J. Socioeconomic Disparities in Electronic Cigarette Use and Transitions from Smoking. Nicotine Tob Res. 2019;21(10):1363–1370. https://doi.org/10.1093/ntr/nty120.
209. Harlow, A.F., Stokes, A., Brooks, D.R. Socioeconomic and Racial/Ethnic Differences in E-cigarette Uptake Among Cigarette Smokers: Longitudinal Analysis of the Population Assessment of Tobacco and Health (PATH) Study. Nicotine Tob Res. 2019;21(10):1385–1393. https://doi.org/10.1093/ntr/nty141.
210. Green, M.J., Gray, L., Sweeting, H. et al. Socioeconomic Patterning of Vaping by Smoking Status Among UK Adults and Youth. BMC Public Health. 2020;20:183. https://doi.org/10.1186/s12889-020-8270-3.
211. Kock, L., Brown, J., Shahab, L. Association of Socioeconomic Position with E-cigarette Use Among Individuals Who Quit Smoking in England, 2014 to 2019. JAMA Network Open. 2020;3(6):e204207–e204207. https://doi.org/10.1001/jamanetworkopen.2020.4207; https://jamanetwork.com/journals/jamanetworkopen/fullarticle/2766788.
212. Syamlal, G., Clark, K.A., Blackley, D.J., King, B.A. Prevalence of Electronic Cigarette Use Among Adult Workers—United States, 2017–2018. MMWR Morb Mortal Wkly Rep. 2021;70:297–303.
213. Lucherini, M., Hill, S., Smith, K. Potential for Non-combustible Nicotine Products to Reduce Socioeconomic Inequalities in Smoking: A Systematic Review and Synthesis of Best Available Evidence. BMC Public Health. 2019;19(1):1469. https://doi.org/10.1186/s12889-019-7836-4.
214. Rogers, E. (16 August 2003). *Diffusion of Innovations*, 5th Edition. Simon and Schuster. ISBN 978-0-7432-5823-4.
215. Hartwell, G., Thomas, S., Egan, M., et al. E-cigarettes and Equity: A Systematic Review of Differences in Awareness and Use Between Sociodemographic Groups. Tob Control. 2017;26:e85–e91.

216. Giovenco, D.P., Lewis, M.J., Delnevo, C.D. Factors Associated with E-cigarette Use: A National Population Survey of Current and Former Smokers. Am J Prev Med 2014;47:476–480. https://doi.org/10.1016/j.amepre.2014.04.009.
217. Usidame, B., Hirschtick, J.L., Mattingly, D.T., Patel, A., Patrick, M.E., Fleischer, N.L. Sociodemographic Patterns of Exclusive and Dual Combustible Tobacco and E-Cigarette Use among US Adolescents—A Nationally Representative Study (2017–2020). International Journal of Environmental Research and Public Health. 2022;19(5):2965. https://doi.org/10.3390/ijerph19052965.
218. Harlow, A.F., Stokes, A., Brooks, D.R. Socioeconomic and Racial/Ethnic Differences in E-Cigarette Uptake Among Cigarette Smokers: Longitudinal Analysis of the Population Assessment of Tobacco and Health (PATH) Study. Nicotine Tob Res. Oct 2019;21(10):1385–1393. https://doi.org/10.1093/ntr/nty141.
219. Beard, E., Brown, J., Jackson, S.E., Tattan-Birch, H., Shahab, L. Differences Between Ethnic Groups in Self-Reported Use of E-cigarettes and Nicotine Replacement Therapy for Cutting Down and Temporary Abstinence: A Cross-Sectional Population-Level Survey in England. Addiction. 2021;116:2476–2485. https://doi.org/10.1111/add.15431.
220. Rotermann, M., Gilmour, H. Correlates of Vaping Among Adolescents in Canada, Statistics Canada, 2022, available at: https://www150.statcan.gc.ca/n1/pub/82-003-x/2022007/article/00003-eng.htm.
221. Wang, Y., Wilson, F.A., Larson, J., Chen, L.W. The Use of E-Cigarettes Among U.S. Immigrants: The 2014 National Health Interview Survey. Public Health Reports. 2016;131(4). https://doi.org/10.1177/0033354916662220.
222. Hartwell, G., Thomas, S., Egan, M., et al. E-cigarettes and Equity: A Systematic Review of Differences in Awareness and Use Between Sociodemographic Groups. Tob Control. 2017;26:e85–e91.
223. Adkison, S.E., O'Connor, R.J., Bansal-Travers, M., et al. Electronic Nicotine Delivery Systems: International Tobacco Control Four-Country Survey. Am J Prev Med. 2013;44:207–215. https://doi.org/10.1016/j.amepre.2012.10.018.

224. Agaku, I.T., King, B.A., Husten, C.G., et al. Tobacco Product Use Among Adults—United States, 2012–2013. MMWR Morb Mortal Wkly Rep 2014;63:542–547.
225. Grana, R.A., Popova, L., Ling, P.M. A Longitudinal Analysis of Electronic Cigarette Use and Smoking Cessation. JAMA Intern Med 2014;174:812–813. https://doi.org/10.1001/jamainternmed.2014.187.
226. Hanewinkel, R., Isensee, B. Risk Factors for E-cigarette, Conventional Cigarette, and Dual Use in German Adolescents: A Cohort Study. Preventive Medicine. 2015;74. https://doi.org/10.1016/j.ypmed.2015.03.006.
227. Bowe, A.K., Doyle, F., Stanistreet, D., et al. E-cigarette-Only and Dual Use Among Adolescents in Ireland: Emerging Behaviours with Different Risk Profiles. International Journal of Environmental Research and Public Health. 2021;18(1):332. https://doi.org/10.3390/ijerph18010332.
228. Martinez-Sanchez, J.M., Ballbe, M., Fu, M., et al. Electronic Cigarette Use Among Adult Population: A Cross-Sectional Study in Barcelona, Spain (2013–2014). BMJ Open. 2014;4:e005894. https://doi.org/10.1136/bmjopen-2014-005894.
229. Sherratt, F.C., Robinson, J., Marcus, M., et al. E-cigarette usage within a local stop smoking service. Presentation at: UK National Smoking Cessation Conference; 12–13 June 2014; London, UK. http://www.uknscc.org/uknscc2014_presentation_319.php
230. Cho, B., Hirschtick, J.L., Usidame, B., Meza, R., Mistry, R., Land, S.R., Levy, D.T., Holford, T., Fleischer, N.L. Sociodemographic Patterns of Exclusive, Dual, and Polytobacco Use Among U.S. High School Students: A Comparison of Three Nationally Representative Surveys. J Adolesc Health. 2021;68:750–757. https://doi.org/10.1016/j.jadohealth.2020.11.019.
231. Patel, A., Hirschtick, J.L., Cook, S., Usidame, B., Mistry, R., Levy, D.T., Meza, R., Fleischer, N.L. Sociodemographic Patterns of Exclusive and Dual Use of ENDS and Menthol/Non-menthol Cigarettes Among US Youth (Ages 15–17) Using Two Nationally Representative Surveys (2013–2017). Int J Environ Res Public Health. 2021;18:7781. https://doi.org/10.3390/ijerph18157781.
232. Assari, S., Mistry, R., Caldwell, C.H., Bazargan, M. Protective Effects of Parental Education Against Youth Cigarette Smoking:

Diminished Returns of Blacks and Hispanics. Adolesc Health Med Ther. 2020;11:63–71. https://doi.org/10.2147/AHMT. S238441.

233. Johnston, L.D., Miech, R.A., O'Malley, P.M., Bachman, J.G., Schulenberg, J.E., Patrick, M.E. *Demographic Subgroup Trends among Adolescents in the Use of Various Licit and Illicit Drugs, 1975–2019*; Institute for Social Research, The University of Michigan: Ann Arbor, MI, USA, 2020.

234. Regan, A.K., Promoff, G., Dube, S.R., Arrazola, R. Electronic Nicotine Delivery Systems: Adult Use and Awareness of the 'E-cigarette' in the USA. Tob Control. 2013;22:19–23. https://doi. org/10.1136/tobaccocontrol-2011-050044.

235. Pearson, J.L., Richardson, A., Niaura, R.S., et al. E-cigarette Awareness, Use, and Harm Perceptions in US Adults. Am J Public Health 2012;102:1758–1766. https://doi.org/10.2105/AJPH. 2011.300526.

236. Hayes, R.B., Scheuermann, T.S., Resnicow, K., et al. POS3–160 Smoking and Quitting History Characteristics Among Current Electronic Cigarette Users in a National Multi-ethnic Adult Smoker Sample. SNRT. Proceedings of the 20th annual meeting of the Society for Nicotine and Tobacco Research; 5–8 Feb 2014; Seattle, USA.

237. Becker, T.D., Arnold, M.K., Ro, V., Martin, L., Rice, T.R. Systematic Review of Electronic Cigarette Use (Vaping) and Mental Health Comorbidity Among Adolescents and Young Adults. Nicotine & Tobacco Research. March 2021;23(3):415–425. https://doi.org/10.1093/ntr/ntaa171.

238. Kcomt, L., Evans-Polce, R.J., Veliz, P.T., Boyd, C.J., McCabe, S.E. Use of Cigarettes and E-cigarettes/Vaping Among Transgender People: Results From the 2015 U.S. Transgender Survey. Am J Prev Med. 2020;59(4):538–547, ISSN 0749–3797, https://doi.org/10.1016/j.amepre.2020.03.027.

239. Enns, A., Orpana, H. Autonomy, Competence and Relatedness and Cannabis and Alcohol Use Among Youth in Canada: A Cross-Sectional Analysis. Maladies Health Promotion and Chronic Disease Prevention in Canada. 2020;40(5/6):201–210. https://doi.org/10.24095/hpcdp.40.5/6.09.

240. Kinouani, S., Leflot, C., Vanderkam, P., et al. Motivations for Using Electronic Cigarettes in Young Adults: A Systematic Review. Subst Abus. 2020;41:315–322.

241. Harlow, A.F., Cho, J., Tackett, A.P., McConnell, R.S., Leventhal, A.M., Stokes, A.C., Barrington-Trimis, J.L. Motivations for E-cigarette Use and Associations with Vaping Frequency and Smoking Abstinence Among Adults Who Smoke Cigarettes in the United States. Drug Alcohol Depend. 2022;238:109583. https://doi.org/10.1016/j.drugalcdep.2022.109583.

242. Evans-Polce, R.J., Patrick, M.E., Lanza, S.T., Johnston, L.D., et al. Reasons for Vaping Among U.S. 12th Graders. J Adolesc Health. 2018;62:457–462. https://doi.org/10.1016/j.jadohealth.2017.10.009.

243. Amin, S., Dunn, A.G., Laranjo, L. Why Do People Start or Stop Using E-cigarettes in Australia? A Qualitative Interview-Based Study. Health Promot J Austr. 2021 Oct;32 Suppl 2:358–366. https://doi.org/10.1002/hpja.442.

244. Kasza, K.A., Edwards, K.C., Kimmel, H.L., et al. Association of E-cigarette Use with Discontinuation of Cigarette Smoking Among Adult Smokers Who Were Initially Never Planning to Quit. JAMA Netw Open. 2021;4(12):e2140880. https://doi.org/10.1001/jamanetworkopen.2021.40880.

245. Harlow, A.F., Cho, J., Tackett, A.P., McConnell, R.S., Leventhal, A.M., Stokes, A.C., Barrington-Trimis, J.L. Motivations for E-cigarette Use and Associations with Vaping Frequency and Smoking Abstinence Among Adults Who Smoke Cigarettes in the United States. Drug Alcohol Depend. 2022 Sep 1;238:109583. https://doi.org/10.1016/j.drugalcdep.2022.109583.

246. Pepper, J.K., Brewer, N.T. Electronic Nicotine Delivery System (Electronic Cigarette) Awareness, Use, Reactions and Beliefs: A Systematic Review. Tob Control. 2014;23:375–384. https://doi.org/10.1136/tobaccocontrol-2013-051122.

247. Spears, C.A. Jones, D.M., Weaver, S.R., et al. Motives and Perceptions Regarding Electronic Nicotine Delivery Systems (ENDS) Use Among Adults with Mental Health Conditions. Addict Behav. 2018;80:102–109. https://doi.org/10.1016/j.addbeh.2018.01.014.

248. Tackett, A.P., Lechner, W.V., Meier, E., et al., 2015. Biochemically Verified Smoking Cessation and Vaping Beliefs Among Vape Store Customers. Addiction. 2015;110:868–874. https://doi.org/10.1111/add.12878.

249. Gravely, S., Yong, H.H., Reid, J.L., East, K.A., Gartner, C.E., Levy, D.T., Cummings, K.M., Borland, R., Quah, A.C.K., Bansal-Travers, M., Ouimet, J., Fong, G.T. Do Current Smokers and Ex-Smokers Who Use Nicotine Vaping Products Daily Versus Weekly Differ on Their Reasons for Vaping? Findings from the 2020 ITC Four Country Smoking and Vaping Survey. International Journal of Environmental Research and Public Health. 2022;19(21):14130. https://doi.org/10.3390/ijerph192114130.

250. ASH. Use of E-cigarettes (vapes) Among Adults in Great Britain, Action on Smoking and Health UK, 2022, available at: https://ash.org.uk/uploads/Use-of-e-cigarettes-vapes-among-adults-in-Great-Britain-2022.pdf?v=1661865959.

251. Barakat, M., Jirjees, F., Al-Tammemi, A.B., Al-Qudah, R., Alfoteih, Y., Kharaba, Z., Al-Obaidi, H. The Era of E-cigarettes: A Cross-Sectional Study of Vaping Preferences, Reasons for Use and Withdrawal Symptoms Among Current E-cigarette Users in the United Arab Emirates. J Community Health. 2021;46(5):876–886. https://doi.org/10.1007/s10900-021-00967-4.

252. Hummel, K., Hoving C., Nagelhout, G.E., de Vries, H., van den Putte, B., Candel, M.J.J.M., et al. Prevalence and Reasons for Use of Electronic Cigarettes Among Smokers: Findings from the International Tobacco Control (ITC) Netherlands Survey. Int J Drug Policy. 2015 Jun 1;26(6):601–608. https://doi.org/10.1016/j.drugpo.2014.12.009.

253. Alzalabani, A.A., Eltaher, S.M. Perceptions and Reasons of E-cigarette Use Among Medical Students: An Internet-Based Survey. J Egypt Public Health Assoc. 2020 Dec;95(1):21. https://doi.org/10.1186/s42506-020-00051-0.

254. Harlow, A.F., Cho, J., Tackett, A.P., McConnell, R.S., Leventhal, A.M., Stokes, A.C., Barrington-Trimis, J.L. Motivations for E-cigarette Use and Associations with Vaping Frequency and Smoking Abstinence Among Adults Who Smoke Cigarettes in the

United States. Drug Alcohol Depend. 2022 Sep 1;238:109583. https://doi.org/10.1016/j.drugalcdep.2022.109583.

255. Alqahtani, M.M., Massey, Z.B., Fairman, R.T., Churchill, V., Ashley, D.L., Popova, L. General and Device-Specific Reasons for ENDS use: A Qualitative Study with Adult ENDS Users. Int J Environ Res Public Health. 2022;19(11):6822. https://doi.org/10.3390/ijerph19116822.

256. Pokhrel, P., Herzog, T.A. Reasons for Quitting Cigarette Smoking and Electronic Cigarette Use for Cessation Help. Psychol Addict Behav. 2015;29(1):114–121. https://doi.org/10.1037/adb0000025.

257. The degree to which e-cigarettes are cheaper than conventional cigarettes depends in part on the prices for conventional cigarettes; in turn dictated largely by taxation. The U.K. for example has relatively high tobacco taxes from which e-cigarettes are exempt. Here, a comparison of expenditures between e-cigarette users and smokers suggests that vaping may cost around one-third as much as smoking (see: Jackson SE, Shahab L, Kock L, West R, Brown J. Expenditure on Smoking and Alternative Nicotine Delivery Products: A Population Survey in England. Addiction. 2019 Nov;114(11):2026–2036.), though usage patterns will affect the relative cost saving on an individual basis. The ratio also depends on the type of e-cigarette used. For example, data from Australia, Canada, England, and the U.S. show that disposable e-cigarette costs were similar to, or more expensive than cigarettes in all countries; prefilled cartridges were more expensive than cigarettes in the U.S. and Canada but lower in Australia and England; but e-liquid for refillable devices were substantially lower after paying the upfront cost for the device. Overall, therefore, it was possible to save considerable amounts of money in the long term by switching from smoking to vaping (see: Cheng KW, Shang C, Lee HM, Chaloupka FJ, Fong GT, Borland R, et al. Costs of Vaping: Evidence from ITC Four Country Smoking and Vaping Survey. Tobacco Control. 2021 Jan;30(1):94–97). In Australia, where the cost of cigarettes is among the highest in the world, the Australia Tobacco Harm Reduction Association suggests that vaping could cost roughly AU$9,000 less than smoking per year, as saving of around 90%

(see: ATHRA. Vaping cost ATHRA, available at: https://www.athra.org.au/vaping/vaping-cost/).

258. ASH, Use of E-cigarettes (Vapes) Among Adults in Great Britain, Action on Smoking and Health UK, 2022, available at: https://ash.org.uk/uploads/Use-of-e-cigarettes-vapes-among-adults-in-Great-Britain-2022.pdf?v=1661865959.

259. Tsai, J., Walton, K., Coleman, B.N., et al. Reasons for Electronic Cigarette Use Among Middle and High School Students—National Youth Tobacco Survey, United States, 2016. MMWR Morb Mortal Wkly Rep. 2018;67(6):196–200.

260. Kong, G., Morean, M.E., Cavallo, D.A., Camenga, D.R., Krishnan-Sarin, S. Reasons for Electronic Cigarette Experimentation and Discontinuation Among Adolescents and Young Adults. Nicotine Tob Res. 2015;17(7):847–854. https://doi.org/10.1093/ntr/ntu257.

261. Patrick, M.E., Miech, R.A., Carlier, C., et al. Self-Reported Reasons for Vaping Among 8th, 10th, and 12th Graders in the US: Nationally-Representative Results. Drug Alcohol Depend. 2016;165:275–278. https://doi.org/10.1016/j.drugalcdep.2016.05.017.

262. Saddleson, M.L., Kozlowski, L.T., Giovino, G.A., et al. Enjoyment and Other Reasons for Electronic Cigarette Use: Results from College Students in New York. Addict Behav. 2016;54:33–39. https://doi.org/10.1016/j.addbeh.2015.11.012.

263. Tsai, J., Walton, K., Coleman, B.N., et al. Reasons for Electronic Cigarette Use Among Middle and High School Students—National Youth Tobacco Survey, United States, 2016. MMWR Morb Mortal Wkly Rep. 2018;67(6):196–200. https://doi.org/10.15585/mmwr.mm6706a5.

264. Patrick, M.E., Miech, R.A., Carlier, C., et al. Self-Reported Reasons for Vaping Among 8th, 10th, and 12th Graders in the US: Nationally-Representative Results. Drug Alcohol Depend. 2016;165:275–278. https://doi.org/10.1016/j.drugalcdep.2016.05.017.

265. ASH. Use of E-cigarettes (Vapes) Among Young People in Great Britain, Action on Smoking and Health UK, 2022, available at: https://ash.org.uk/uploads/Use-of-e-cigarettes-among-young-people-in-Great-Britain-2022.pdf?v=1661866458.

266. ASH. Use of E-cigarettes (Vapes) Among Adults in Great Britain, Action on Smoking and Health UK, 2022, available at: https://ash.org.uk/uploads/Use-of-e-cigarettes-vapes-among-adults-in-Great-Britain-2022.pdf?v=1661865959.

267. Lindpere, V., Winickoff, J.P., Khan, A.S., Dong, J., Michaud, T.L., Liu, J., Daisy, Dai, H. Reasons for E-cigarette Use, Vaping Patterns, and Cessation Behaviors Among US Adolescents. Nicotine Tob Res. May 2023;25(5):975–982. https://doi.org/10.1093/ntr/ntac278.

268. Wang, T.W., Gentzke, A.S., Creamer, M.R., et al. Tobacco Product Use and Associated Factors Among Middle and High School Students—United States, 2019. MMWR Surveill Summ 2019;68(No. SS–12):1–22. https://doi.org/10.15585/mmwr.ss6812a1externalicon.

269. Abadi, M.H., Lipperman-Kreda, S., Shamblen, S.R., Thompson, K., Grube, J.W., Leventhal, A.M., Luseno, W., Aramburu, C. The Impact of Flavored ENDS Use Among Adolescents on Daily Use Occasions and Number of Puffs, and Next Day Intentions and Willingness to Vape. Addict Behav. 2021;114:106773.

270. Kava, C.M., Soule, E.K., Seegmiller, L., Gold, E., Snipes, W., Westfield, T., Wick, N., Afifi, R. "Taking Up a New Problem": Context and Determinants of Pod-Mod Electronic Cigarette Use Among College Students. Qual Health Res. 2021;31(4):703–712. https://doi.org/10.1177/1049732320971236.

271. Chaffee, B.W., Halpern-Felsher, B., Croker, J.A., Werts, M., Couch, E.T., Cheng, J. Preferences, Use, and Perceived Access to Flavored E-Cigarettes Among United States Adolescents and Young Adults. Drug Alcohol Depend Rep. 2022;3:100068. https://doi.org/10.1016/j.dadr.2022.100068.

272. Lindpere, V., Winickoff, J.P., Khan, A.S., Dong, J., Michaud, T.L., Liu, J., Daisy, Dai, H. Reasons for E-cigarette Use, Vaping Patterns, and Cessation Behaviors Among US Adolescents. Nicotine Tob Res. May 2023;25(5):975–982. https://doi.org/10.1093/ntr/ntac278.

273. ASH. Use of E-cigarettes (Vapes) Among Young People in Great Britain, Action on Smoking and Health UK, 2022, available at: https://ash.org.uk/uploads/Use-of-e-cigarettes-among-young-people-in-Great-Britain-2022.pdf?v=1661866458.

274. Morean, M.E., Bold, K.W., Kong, G., Camenga, D.R., Simon, P., Jackson, A., Cavallo, D.A., Krishnan-Sarin, S. High School Students' Use of Flavored E-cigarette E-liquids for Appetite Control and Weight Loss. Addict Behav. 2020;102:106139. https://doi.org/10.1016/j.addbeh.2019.106139.

275. Sanchez, R., Ranjit, N., Kelder, S.H., Gill, M., Hoelscher, D.M. Intention to Lose Weight and Use of Electronic Cigarettes Among Adolescents. Prev Med Rep. 2021;23:101406. https://doi.org/10.1016/j.pmedr.2021.101406.

276. Holt, L.J., Ginley, M.K., Pingeon, C., Feinn, R. Primed for Positive Perceptions? Applying the Acquired Preparedness Model to Explain College Students' E-cigarette Use and Dependence. J Am Coll Health. 2022;11:1–11. https://doi.org/10.1080/07448481.2022.2089846.

277. Thanh, P.Q., Tuyet-Hanh, T.T., Khue, L.N., Hai, P.T., Van Can, P., Long, K.Q., Linh, N.T., Anh, D.T., Son, D.T., Tien, N.D., Quyen, B.T.T., Van Minh H. Perceptions and Use of Electronic Cigarettes Among Young Adults in Vietnam 2020. J Community Health. 2022;47(5):822–827. https://doi.org/10.1007/s10900-022-01113-4.

278. Maiya, S., Whiteman, S.D., Serang, S., Dayley, J.C., Maggs, J.L., Mustillo, S.A., Kelly, B.C. Associations Between Older Siblings' Substance Use and Younger Siblings' Substance Use Intentions: Indirect Effects Via Substance Use Expectations. Addict Behav. 2023;136:107493. https://doi.org/10.1016/j.addbeh.2022.107493.

279. Gentzke, A.S., Wang, T.W., Cornelius, M., Park-Lee, E., Ren, C., Sawdey, M.D., Cullen, K.A., Loretan, C., Jamal, A., Homa, D.M. Tobacco Product Use and Associated Factors Among Middle and High School Students—National Youth Tobacco Survey, United States, 2021. MMWR Surveill Summ. 2022 Mar 11;71(5):1–29. https://doi.org/10.15585/mmwr.ss7105a1.

280. Donaldson, C.D., Stupplebeen, D.A., Fecho, C.L., Ta, T., Zhang, X., Williams, R.J. Nicotine Vaping for Relaxation and Coping: Race/Ethnicity Differences and Social Connectedness Mechanisms. Addict Behav. 2022;132:107365. https://doi.org/10.1016/j.addbeh.2022.107365.

281. Gravely, S., Yong, H.H., Reid, J.L., East, K.A., Gartner, C.E., Levy, D.T., Cummings, K.M., Borland, R., Quah, A.C.K., Bansal-Travers, M., Ouimet, J., Fong, G.T. Do Current Smokers and Ex-smokers Who Use Nicotine Vaping Products Daily Versus Weekly Differ on Their Reasons for Vaping? Findings from the 2020 ITC Four Country Smoking and Vaping Survey. International Journal of Environmental Research and Public Health. 2022; 19(21):14130. https://doi.org/10.3390/ijerph192114130.

282. Notley, C., Ward, E., Dawkins, L., Holland, R. The Unique Contribution of E-cigarettes for Tobacco Harm Reduction in Supporting Smoking Relapse Prevention. Harm Reduct J. 2018;15:31. https://doi.org/10.1186/s12954-018-0237-7.

283. Hairi, F.M., Goh, K.T., Driezen, P., Nordin, A.S.A., Yee, A., Tajuddin, N.A.A., Hasan, S.I., Danaee, M., Kamaludin, I.S., Kaai, S.C., Yan, M., Grey, M., Quah, A.C.K., Thompson, M.E., Fong, G.T. Reasons for Using E-cigarettes and Support for E-cigarette Regulations: Findings from the 2020 ITC Malaysia Survey. Tob Induc Dis. 2022;20:33. https://doi.org/10.18332/tid/146364.

284. Barbeau, A.M., Burda, J., Siegel, M. Perceived Efficacy of E-cigarettes Versus Nicotine Replacement Therapy Among Successful E-cigarette Users: A Qualitative Approach. Addict Sci Clin Pract. 2013;8(1):5. https://doi.org/10.1186/1940-0640-8-5.

285. Pokhrel, P., Herzog, T.A., Muranaka, N., Fagan, P. Young Adult E-cigarette Users' Reasons for Liking and Not Liking E-cigarettes: A Qualitative Study. Psychol Health. 2015;30:12:1450–1469. https://doi.org/10.1080/08870446.2015.1061129.

286. Evans, A.T., Henderson, K.C., Geier, A., Weaver, S.R., Spears, C.A., Ashley, D.L., Fritz, M., John, L., Pechacek, T.F. What Motivates Smokers to Switch to ENDS? A Qualitative Study of Perceptions and Use. Int J Environ Res Public Health. 2020;17(23):8865. https://doi.org/10.3390/ijerph17238865.

287. McKeganey, N., Dickson, T. Why Don't More Smokers Switch to Using E-cigarettes: The Views of Confirmed Smokers. Int J Environ Res Public Health. 2017;14(6):647. https://doi.org/10.3390/ijerph14060647.

288. McKeganey, N., Barnard, M., Russell, C. Vapers and Vaping: E-cigarettes Users Views of Vaping and Smoking. Drugs Educ Prev Pol. 2018;25(1):13–20. https://doi.org/10.1080/09687637.2017.1296933.

289. Liu, J., Ramamurthi, D., Halpern-Felsher, B. Inside the Adolescent Voice: A Qualitative Analysis of the Appeal of Different Tobacco Products. Tob Induc Dis. 2021 Feb 26;19:15. https://doi.org/10.18332/tid/132856.

290. Katz, S.J., Erkinnen, M., Lindgren, B., Hatsukami, D. Beliefs About E-cigarettes: A Focus Group Study with College Students. American Journal of Health Behavior. 2019 Jan 1;43(1):76–87. https://doi.org/10.5993/AJHB.43.1.7.

291. Conklin, C.A., McClernon, F.J., Vella, E.J., Joyce, C.J., Salkeld, R.P., Parzynski, C.S., et al. Combined Smoking Cues Enhance Reactivity and Predict Immediate Subsequent Smoking. Nicotine & Tobacco Research. 2019 Jan 4;21(2):241–248. https://doi.org/10.1093/ntr/nty009.

292. Patwardhan, S., Rose, J.E. Overcoming Barriers to Disseminate Effective Smoking Cessation Treatments Globally. DAT. 2020 Jul 13;20(3):235–247. https://doi.org/10.1108/DAT-01-2020-0001.

293. DiPiazza, J., Caponnetto, P., Askin, G., Christos, P., Maglia, M.L.P., Gautam, R., et al. Sensory Experiences and Cues Among E-cigarette Users. Harm Reduct J. 2020 Dec;17(1):75. https://doi.org/10.1186/s12954-020-00420-0.

294. Van Heel, M., Van Gucht, D., Vanbrabant, K., Baeyens, F. The Importance of Conditioned Stimuli in Cigarette and E-Cigarette Craving Reduction by E-Cigarettes. Int J Environ Res Public Health. 2017 Feb;14(2):193. https://doi.org/10.3390/ijerph14020193.

295. Action on Smoking Health. Use of E-cigarettes (Vapes) Among Adults in Great Britain [Internet]. 2021 [cited 2022 May 23], available at: https://ash.org.uk/wp-content/uploads/2021/06/Use-of-e-cigarettes-vapes-among-adults-in-Great-Britain-2021.pdf.

296. Yong, H., Borland, R., Cummings, K.M., Gravely, S., Thrasher, J.F., McNeill, A., et al. Reasons for Regular Vaping and for Its Discontinuation Among Smokers and Recent Ex-Smokers: Findings from the 2016 ITC Four Country Smoking and Vaping

Survey. Addiction. 2019 Oct;114(S1):35–48. https://doi.org/10.1111/add.14593.

297. Wadsworth, E., Neale, J., McNeill, A., Hitchman, S. How and Why Do Smokers Start Using E-Cigarettes? Qualitative Study of Vapers in London, UK. IJERPH. 2016 Jun 30;13(7):661. https://doi.org/10.3390/ijerph13070661.

298. Pepper, J.K., Ribisl, K.M., Emery, S.L., Brewer, N.T. Reasons for Starting and Stopping Electronic Cigarette Use. Int J Environ Res Public Health. 2014;11, 10345–10361. https://doi.org/10.3390/ijerph111010345.

299. Bullen, C., Howe, C., Laugesen, M., McRobbie, H., Parag, V., Williman, J., et al. Electronic Cigarettes for Smoking Cessation: A Randomised Controlled Trial. The Lancet. 2013 Nov;382(9905):1629–37. https://doi.org/10.1016/S0140-6736(13)61842-5.

300. Kalkhoran, S., Glantz, S.A. E-cigarettes and Smoking Cessation in Real-World and Clinical Settings: A Systematic Review and Meta-Analysis. The Lancet Respiratory Medicine. 2016 Feb;4(2):116–128. https://doi.org/10.1016/S2213-2600(15)00521-4.

301. Farsalinos, K.E., Niaura, R. E-cigarettes and Smoking Cessation in the United States According to Frequency of E-cigarette Use and Quitting Duration: Analysis of the 2016 and 2017 National Health Interview Surveys. Nicotine & Tobacco Research. 2020 Apr 21;22(5):655–662. https://doi.org/10.1093/ntr/ntz025.

302. Hajek, P., Phillips-Waller, A., Przulj, D., Pesola, F., Myers Smith, K., Bisal, N., et al. A Randomized Trial of E-Cigarettes versus Nicotine-Replacement Therapy. N Engl J Med. 2019 Feb 14;380(7):629–637. https://doi.org/10.1056/NEJMoa1808779.

303. Biener, L., Hargraves, J.L. A Longitudinal Study of Electronic Cigarette Use Among a Population-Based Sample of Adult Smokers: Association with Smoking Cessation and Motivation to Quit. Nicotine Tob Res. 2015 Feb;17(2):127–133. https://doi.org/10.1093/ntr/ntu200.

304. Benowitz, N.L. Pharmacology of Nicotine: Addiction, Smoking-Induced Disease, and Therapeutics. Annu Rev Pharmacol Toxicol. 2009;49:57–71. https://doi.org/10.1146/annurev.pharmtox.48.113006.094742.

305. Mantey, D.S., Harrell, M.B., Case, K., Crook, B., Kelder, S.H., Perry, C.L. Subjective Experiences at First Use of Cigarette, E-cigarettes, Hookah, and Cigar Products Among Texas Adolescents. Drug Alcohol Depend. 2017;173:10–16. https://doi.org/10.1016/j.drugalcdep.2016.12.010.

306. Mantey, D.S., Case, K.R., Chen, B., Kelder, S., Loukas, A., Harrell, M.B. Subjective Experiences at E-cigarette Initiation: Implications for E-cigarette and Dual/Poly Tobacco Use Among Youth. Addict Behav. 2021;122:107028. https://doi.org/10.1016/j.addbeh.2021.107028.

307. Daniel, C., Haddad, C., McConaha, J.L., Lunney, P. Electronic Cigarettes: Their Role in the Lives of College Students. J Pharm Pract. 2021;36(217):089719002110268. https://doi.org/10.1177/08971900211026841.

308. Peraza, N., Bello, M.S., Schiff, S.J., Cho, J., Zhang, Y., Callahan, C., Tackett, A., Leventhal, A.M. Drug and Alcohol Dependence Acute Effects of Pod-Style E-cigarettes in Vaping-Naïve Smokers. Drug Alcohol Depend. 2021;228:109083. https://doi.org/10.1016/j.drugalcdep.2021.109083.

309. St. Helen, G., Nardone, N., Addo, N., Dempsey, D., Havel, C., Jacob, P. 3rd, Benowitz, N.L. Differences in Nicotine Intake and Effects from Electronic and Combustible Cigarettes Among Dual Users. Addiction. 2020;115(4):757–767. https://doi.org/10.1111/add.14884.

310. Simpson, K.A., Kechter, A., Schiff, SJ, Braymiller, J.L., Yamaguchi, N., Ceasar, R.C., Bluthenthal, R.N., Barrington-Trimis, J.L. Characterizing Symptoms of E-cigarette Dependence: A Qualitative Study of Young Adults. BMC Public Health. 2021;21(1):959. https://doi.org/10.1186/s12889-021-109 45-z.

311. Struik, L., Yang, Y. E-cigarette Cessation: Content Analysis of a Quit Vaping Community on Reddit J Med Internet Res 2021;23(10):e28303. https://doi.org/10.2196/28303.

312. Tsai, M., Byun, M.K., Shin, J., Crotty, Alexander, L.E. Effects of E-cigarettes and Vaping Devices on Cardiac and Pulmonary Physiology. J Physiol. 2020;598(22):5039–5062. https://doi.org/10.1113/JP279754.

313. Longitudinal studies are needed to define the long-term cardiopulmonary effects of e-cigarette use in humans.

314. Meng, X.C., Guo, X.X., Peng, Z.Y., Wang, C., Liu, R. Acute Effects of Electronic Cigarettes on Vascular Endothelial Function: A Systematic Review and Meta-analysis of Randomized Controlled Trials. Eur J Prev Cardiol. 2023;30(5):425-435. https://doi.org/10.1093/eurjpc/zwac248.

315. WHO. WHO Reports Progress in the Fight Against Tobacco Epidemic. World Health Organisation, 2021, available at: https://www.who.int/news/item/27-07-2021-who-reports-progress-in-the-fight-against-tobacco-epidemic.

316. INCCO. Bloomberg, the World Health Organisation & the Vaping Misinfodemic: A dossier produced by the International Networkof Nicotine Consumer Organisations (INNCO), INNCO, 2021, available at: https://innco.org/wp-content/uploads/2021/11/Innco-Dossier-Final-1.pdf.

317. INCCO. Bloomberg, the World Health Organisation & the Vaping Misinfodemic: A Dossier Produced by the International Network of Nicotine Consumer Organisations (INNCO), INNCO, 2021, available at: https://innco.org/wp-content/uploads/2021/11/Innco-Dossier-Final-1.pdf.

318. Global Tobacco Control (n.d.). Country Laws Regulating E-Cigarettes, Global Tobacco Control, available at: https://globaltobaccocontrol.org/en/policy-scan/e-cigarettes/sale.

319. Ministry of Health—Government of Brasil. Resolution No. 46 of 28 August 2009: Prohibits the Sale, Importation and Advertising of Any Electronic Devices for Smoking, Known as Electronic Cigarette, Ministry of Health, 2009, available at: https://bvsms.saude.gov.br/bvs/saudelegis/anvisa/2009/res0046_28_08_2009.html.

320. Soares, E. Brazil: National Health Surveillance Agency Maintains Ban on Electronic Cigarettes, Library of Congress, 2022, available at: https://www.loc.gov/item/global-legal-monitor/2022-07-25/brazil-national-health-surveillance-agency-maintains-ban-on-electronic-cigarettes/.

321. Indian Council of Medical Research White Paper on Electronic Nicotine Delivery System. Indian J Med Res. 2019;149:574–583. https://doi.org/10.4103/ijmr.IJMR_957_19.

322. Press Information Bureau Cabinet approves Promulgation of the Prohibition of Electronic Cigarettes Ordinance 18 Sep

2019, available at: https://pib.gov.in/PressReleseDetail.aspx? PRID=1585437.

323. Mendelsohn, D.C. *Stop Smoking Start Vaping: The Healthy Truth About Vaping*. Aurora house, 2021.

324. Department of Health and Aged Care. About E-cigarettes, Government of Australia, 2021, available at: https://www.hea lth.gov.au/topics/smoking-and-tobacco/about-smoking-and-tobacco/about-e-cigarettes.

325. Council Resolutions July 2009: E-Cigarettes. Pharmacia Dec 2009;17(3):8.

326. World Cigarette Prices (n.d.), Prices for Cigarettes in Isreal, World Cigarette Prices, available at: https://worldcigaretteprices.com/en/price-for-cigarettes-in-israel-101/.

327. NIDA. 2021, April 12. How Does Tobacco Deliver Its Effects? Retrieved from https://nida.nih.gov/publications/research-rep orts/tobacco-nicotine-e-cigarettes/how-does-tobacco-deliver-its-effects on 2023, May 25.

328. Ministry of Health and Welfare. E-cigarettes Are Not a Smoking Cessation Aid, Government of Korea, 2015, available at: https://www.mohw.go.kr/eng/nw/nw0101vw.jsp?PAR_MENU_ID=1007&MENU_ID=100701&page=19&CONT_SEQ=316042.

329. McNeill A, Brose LS, Calder R, Hitchman SC, Hajek P, McRobbie H. E-cigarettes: An Evidence Update A Report Commissioned by Public Health England, 2015, available at: https://assets.publishing.service.gov.uk/government/uploads/system/uploads/attachment_data/file/733022/Ecigarettes_an_evidence_update_A_report_commissioned_by_Public_Health_England_FINAL.pdf.

330. House of Commons Science and Technology Committee, E-cigarettes, UK House of Commons, 2018, available at: https://publications.parliament.uk/pa/cm201719/cmselect/cmsctech/505/505.pdf.

331. Committee on Toxicity of Chemicals in Food, Consumer Products and the Environment (COT) (2020), Statement on the Potential Toxicological Risks from Electronic Nicotine (and

Non-nicotine) Delivery Systems (E(N)NDS—e-cigarettes), UK Government, available at: https://cot.food.gov.uk/sites/def ault/files/2020-09/COT%20E%28N%29NDS%20statement% 202020-04.pdf.

332. PHE. E-cigarettes: A Developing Public Health Consensus Joint Statement on E-cigarettes by Public Health England and other UK Public Health Organisations, Public Health England, 2016, available at: https://assets.publishing.service.gov.uk/gov ernment/uploads/system/uploads/attachment_data/file/534 708/E-cigarettes_joint_consensus_statement_2016.pdf.

333. NHS (2021, November 24). Using E-cigarettes to Stop Smoking. National Health Services UK, available at: https://www.nhs.uk/ live-well/quit-smoking/using-e-cigarettes-to-stop-smoking/.

334. Torjesen, I. Stoptober Campaign Backs E-cigarettes for the First Time; The Pharmaceutical Journal. 2017. https://doi.org/10.1211/PJ.2017.20203620. Available at: https://pharmaceutical-journal.com/article/news/stoptober-campaign-backs-e-cigare ttes-for-the-first-time.

335. UK Department of Health and Social Care (April 11, 2023). Smokers Urged to Swap Cigarettes for Vapes in World First Scheme [Press release]. https://www.gov.uk/government/ news/smokers-urged-to-swap-cigarettes-for-vapes-in-world-first-scheme.

336. Ministry of Health (n.d.). Vaping Products: Information for Health Care Workers and Stop-Smoking Services, New Zealand Ministry of Health, available at: https://www.health.govt.nz/ our-work/preventative-health-wellness/tobacco-control/tob acco-control-information-practitioners/vaping-products-inform ation-health-care-workers-and-stop-smoking-services.

337. Ministry of Health (n.d.). Vaping Products: Information for Health Care Workers and Stop-Smoking Services, New Zealand Ministry of Health, available at: https://www.health.govt.nz/ our-work/preventative-health-wellness/tobacco-control/tob acco-control-information-practitioners/vaping-products-inform ation-health-care-workers-and-stop-smoking-services.

338. Ministry of Health (n.d.). Smokefree Aotearoa 2025 Action Plan, New Zealand Ministry of Health, available at: https://www.hea lth.govt.nz/our-work/preventative-health-wellness/tobacco-con trol/smokefree-aotearoa-2025-action-plan.

339. FDA. FDA Announces Comprehensive Regulatory Plan to Shift Trajectory of Tobacco-Related Disease, Death, Food and Drug Administration, 2017, available at: https://www.fda.gov/news-events/press-announcements/fda-announces-comprehensive-reg ulatory-plan-shift-trajectory-tobacco-related-disease-death.

340. FDA. FDA Announces Comprehensive Regulatory Plan to Shift Trajectory of Tobacco-Related Disease, Death, Food and Drug Administration, 2017, available at: https://www.fda.gov/news-events/press-announcements/fda-permits-marketing-e-cigarette-products-marking-first-authorization-its-kind-agency#:~:text= Today%2C%20the%20U.S.%20Food%20and,Product%20Applica tion%20(PMTA)%20pathway.

341. National Academies of Sciences, Engineering, and Medicine. (2018). *Public Health Consequences of E-Cigarettes.* Washington, DC: The National Academies Press. https://doi.org/10.17226/24952.

342. Legislative Review Secretariat, Tobacco Control Directorate, Controlled Substances and Cannabis Branch (2022), Tobacco and Vaping products actLegislative reviewDiscussion paper, Health Canada, available at: https://www.canada.ca/en/health-canada/programs/consultation-legislative-review-tobacco-vap ing-products-act/document.html.

343. Ministry of Health (n.d.). Position Statement on Vaping, New Zealand Ministry of Health, available at: https://www.health. govt.nz/our-work/preventative-health-wellness/tobacco-con trol/vaping-smokefree-environments-and-regulated-products/ position-statement-vaping.

344. National Institute for Public Health and the Environment. Assessment of Health Effects of Alternative Tobacco Products, The Netherlands Ministry of Health, Welfare and Sport, 2016, available at: https://www.rivm.nl/en/news/assessment-of-health-eff ects-of-alternative-tobacco-products.

INDEX

A

Action on Smoking and Health (ASH), 39, 58, 67, 170, 177, 180, 183, 196–198, 202, 209

Addiction, 10, 17, 21, 33, 88, 96, 153, 173, 202, 206, 207, 211

Additives (e-cigarettes), 23

Aerosol, 12, 13, 149–151, 153, 156, 157, 173, 203–205

Africa, 4, 48, 50–52, 59, 73, 109, 125, 148, 179, 183

Airway inflammation, 204

Airway resistance, 204

Alternative Nicotine Delivery Systems (ANDS), 151

Altria, 94, 161, 162, 165, 166

American Indians/Alaska Natives (AI/ANs), 66

American Vaping Association (AVA), 172

Anti-tobacco public health campaigns, 39

Asia, 47–54, 60, 67, 154, 166, 179

Asthma, 5, 75

Atomizer, 12, 150, 151, 157, 158, 205

B

Barriers to access, 62, 77

Behavioral scientists, 24

Behavioral therapy, 61, 62, 77, 80, 95

Big tobacco, 21, 162

Bio markers, 13

Blu, 159–161, 164, 166, 171

Brazil's National Health Surveillance Agency, 207

British American Tobacco (BAT), 156, 160–162

Bronchitis, 5, 37, 69

Brown & Williamson Tobacco Corp., 43

Bupropion (Zyban/Wellbutrin), 62, 78

C

Canadian Community Health Survey, 65

© The Editor(s) (if applicable) and The Author(s), under exclusive license to Springer Nature Switzerland AG 2024
S. C. Hampsher-Monk et al., *Tobacco Regulation, Economics, and Public Health, Volume I*, https://doi.org/10.1007/978-3-031-41312-4

255

256 INDEX

Canadian Student Tobacco Survey, 45
Canadian Tobacco and Nicotine Survey (CTNS), 45, 177, 181, 182
Cancer Research U.K., 83, 209
Cancers, 5, 8, 32–34, 36, 37, 39, 42, 69, 76, 85, 98–100, 107, 124, 125, 147, 148, 158, 207, 215, 216
Carbon monoxide (CO), 77
Carcinogens, 147, 196, 210
Cardiovascular disease, 8, 69
Cardiovascular health risks, 40
Cash-crop, 32
Cataracts, 5
Categorization (of e-cigarette users), 45, 154, 195
Centers for Disease Control (CDC), 6, 46, 66, 104, 169, 170, 173, 180, 199
Cessation aids, 13, 18, 61, 77, 78, 148, 203, 207
Cessation services, 11, 77, 78, 81, 106
Cessation, smoking, 1, 8, 11–13, 15–20, 22–25, 58, 61–65, 68, 74, 77–79, 84, 86, 89–91, 104, 149, 152, 189–191, 194–197, 199, 200, 202, 203, 210, 211
Chewing tobacco, 149
Chronic inflammation, 5
Cig-a-likes, 12, 157
Cigarillos, 149
Clearomizers, 157
CN Creative, 159, 160
College students, 172, 202
Combustible tobacco products, 8, 16, 44, 71, 147–150, 154, 171, 205
Competition, 19, 77
Compound annual growth rate (CAGR), 167
Confounding factors, 14

CONSTANCE (France), 46
Consumption (cigarettes), 34, 39, 44, 51, 59, 73, 84, 85, 92, 212
Consumption (e-cigarettes), 177
Consumption patterns, 19, 70, 154, 155, 178, 183
Continuum of risk, 154
Correlation, 14
Cotinine, 45, 156, 177
Counterfeit tobacco products, 92
Cross-sectional studies, 46

D
Demand, 2, 3, 11, 14, 17, 19, 21, 26, 33, 38, 57, 62, 72–74, 80, 81, 84, 86, 91–93, 134, 144, 159, 164, 166, 168–171, 179, 183
Diabetes, 5, 69
Differential MLSAs, 85
Dip, 149
Direct-Lung (DL), 205
Disinformation, 19
Disposable income, 4, 56, 57, 61, 62, 167
Dissolvable products, 149
Dose-dependency, 172
Dragonite International Limited, 159
Dry-hit, 215
Dual use, 20, 184, 186, 189, 190, 193, 194. *See also* Dual user
Dual users, 14, 186, 196, 197

E
E-cigarette-inclusive smoke-free (ESF) policies, 51
E-cigarette and vaping product associated lung injuries (EVALI), 22
Eclipse, 150, 156
Economic substitution, 14
Economies of scale, 34

INDEX 257

Educational attainment, 58, 63, 64, 191, 192
Education-based smoking disparities, 63
Electronic Nicotine Delivery Systems (ENDS), 47, 150, 152, 189, 205–207, 211, 212
Electronic Non-Nicotine Delivery Systems (EN&NDS/ENNDS), 152
Emissions tests, 13
Emphysema, 5, 69
Endothelial (dis)function, 204
Enforcement, 11, 62, 70, 77, 82, 85, 92–94, 144, 145, 221
Entrants (firms), 159
Environmental Impact Assessment (EA), 175
Epidemiological data, 23, 174
Epidemiological studies, 1, 69
Epidemiologists, 18. *See also* Epidemiology
Epidemiology, 206
Epilepsy, 33
Epistemic probabilism, 16
Ethnic and racial minorities, 58, 64, 189
Europe, 4, 26, 31, 32, 47, 48, 50–54, 60, 70, 87, 138, 140, 159, 166, 179
European Commission Special Eurobarometer report, 182
European Union (EU), 3, 22, 43, 51, 71, 75, 76, 80, 163, 174, 184, 185
Excise tax, 73, 81
Experimentation, 6, 23, 87, 88, 197, 203
External costs, 69. *See also* Externalities
Externalities, 2
Externalizing disorders, 193

F

Fatal flaw, 175
Federal legislation, 39
Federal Trade Commission (USA), 36
Feedback loops, 19
Food and Drug Administration (FDA), 10, 76, 78, 92, 128, 129, 153, 156, 164, 165, 169–171, 174–176, 211, 212, 215, 221–223, 226, 230, 231, 253
Framework Convention on Tobacco Control (FCTC), 46, 80–86, 133
Free-base nicotine, 12, 29, 163
Free market, 20
Free samples, 171, 172
Frequency of use, 14, 177

G

Gamucci, 159, 160
Gender disparities, 187
General Lifestyle Survey, 176
Glo, 150, 152, 156
Global Adult Tobacco Survey (GATS), 46, 104, 177, 182, 188
Global Health Professions Student Survey (GHPSS), 46
Global School Personnel Survey (GSPS), 46, 104
Global Tobacco Surveillance System (GTSS), 46
Graphic health warnings, 2, 3
Group-think, 63
Gums, 8, 148

H

Harm reduction, 16, 21, 30, 86, 139, 145, 194, 213, 216, 246
Health Canada, 185, 212
Health economists, 19, 24, 41
Health risks, 14, 40, 42, 66, 205, 207, 212

258 INDEX

Health Survey for England, 45
Health warnings, 3, 70–72, 81, 82
Healthy Ireland Survey, 177
Heated Tobacco Products (HTPs),
149, 150, 152, 156
Heterogeneity, 188
High-Income Countries (HICs), 47,
52, 56–58, 70, 82, 84, 179
Hookah, 149
Human-subject trials, 14

I
Illicit trade, 10, 11, 45, 62, 85, 92,
93
Immunological response, 5
Imperial Brands, 160
Incarceration, 68
Income disparities, 60, 62
Indian Council of Medical Research,
207
Indigenous populations, 34, 65, 66
Inequality, 68
Inflammation, 204
Innokin Technology, 159
Innovation, 19, 107, 158, 188, 198,
203, 210, 212
Internalizing disorders, 193
International Agency for Research, 73
Intersectionality, 68
Intervention, 3, 4, 16, 17, 19, 22, 24,
25, 31, 38, 45, 58, 68, 69, 72,
77, 78, 80, 82, 84, 91, 95, 121,
184, 195
Interventions, 107, 110, 121, 130,
131, 137
In vitro, 13
IQOS, 150, 152, 156, 161

J
Japan's Ministry of Health, Labor and
Welfare, 208

Japan Tobacco, 94
Joyetech, 159
Juul, 12, 152, 158, 161–166, 169,
171, 219–226, 229
Juul Labs Inc, 161, 162. *See also* Juul

K
KangerTech, 159
Korea Health and Nutritional
Examination Survey, 45
Korea Tobacco & Ginseng, 156

L
LGBTQ+ Disparities, 67
Longitudinal studies, 13, 46, 249
Lorillard Tobacco Co., 42, 43, 160
Lower-middle-income countries, 179
Low-income countries (LICs), 49,
179
Lozenges, 148
Lung diseases, 5, 147

M
Macular degeneration, 5
Malaysia's National E-Cigarette
Survey, 177
Marketing activity, 4
Marketing Denial Order (MDO),
165, 175, 176
Marketing practices, 163, 165
Market power, 72
Mass incarceration, 11, 93
Medicalized NRTs, 151
Medically-approved, 151
Medicines and Healthcare Products
Regulatory Agency (MHRA),
UK, 151
Medicines Control Council (MCC),
South Africa, 208
Meta-analysis, 68, 88

Microeconomics/Microeconomists, 69
Middle income, 49, 56
Minimum legal sale age (MLSA), 70, 76, 81, 164, 211
Ministry of Finance (Japan), 94
Ministry of Health and Welfare (Korea), 209
Ministry of Health and Welfare (MOWH), South Korea, 209
Ministry of Health, Labor and Welfare (Japan), 208
Ministry of Health (New Zealand), 210, 212
Ministry of Health (United Kingdom), 210
Minority ethnic groups, disparities, 68
Misinformation, 19, 191
Modern oral nicotine, 149, 152
Modified Risk Tobacco Product (MRTPs), 151
Mods, or "box mods", 157
Monitoring the Future (MTF) Survey, 177, 189
Monopoly, 33
Morbidity, 4, 7, 20, 25
Mortality, 4, 7, 20, 25, 54, 67, 69, 75, 83, 147, 211
Motivation, 8, 61, 62, 71, 72, 89, 90, 95, 194–196, 201
Mouth to Lung (MTL), 204, 205

N
Nasal cancer, 33
National Aboriginal and Torres Strait Islander Health Survey, 65
National Academy of Science, Medicine and Engineering (NASEM), USA, 212
National Adult Tobacco Survey (NATS), 45, 177

National Drug Strategy Household Survey (Australia), 45, 47, 104, 177
National Health Interview Survey (NHIS), 45, 46
National Health Surveillance Agency (Brazil), 207
National Institute for Public Health and the Environment (RIVM, Netherlands), 212
National Survey on Drug Use and Health (NSDUH), 180
National Youth Tobacco Survey (NYTS), 45, 169, 177, 180, 186, 198
New Zealand Health Survey, 45, 66, 116, 232
Nicolite, 159, 161
Nicotine addiction, 15, 18, 23, 61, 88, 209
Nicotine chewing gum, 7
Nicotine replacement therapies (NRTs), 7–9, 12, 13, 62, 71, 77–80, 90, 91, 95, 148, 153–155, 202
Nicotine salts, 12, 152, 229
Nicotinic acetylcholine receptors (nAChRs), 89
Nitrosamines, 154
NJOY, 159, 166, 176, 212, 224
Non-combustible alternatives (NCAs), 86, 149, 151, 211
Non-Communicable Diseases Global Action Plan (NCD GAP), 82
Non-smoker's rights groups, 40
North America, 32, 48, 51, 158, 179, 224
Nudge, 17. *See also* Nudge mechanism
Nudge mechanism, 194

260 INDEX

O
Oceania, 51
Odds ratio (OR), 64, 189
Office of Criminal Investigations (United States), 92
Office of National Statistics (ONS) (UK), 181
Online sales restrictions (e-cigarettes), 172
Oral cancer, 34, 154
Overseas trade, 32
Overshifting (a taxation subtopic), 72

P
Passive smoking, 41. *See also* Second-hand smoke
Pass-through, 124
Pax, 150
Pesquisa Nacional de Saúde (National Health Survey), 45
Pharmacotherapies, 7, 77–80, 132
Phillip Morris International (PMI), 156, 161, 162
Physiological addiction, 9, 91, 148
Pictographic health warnings, 3
Plain-pack rules, 2, 72
Ploom, 152, 156
Pod devices, 12
Point of sale (POS) scanner data, 177
Polarization, 17, 21
Policy framework, 4
Policy sharing, 3, 22, 79, 80
Population Assessment of Tobacco and Health (PATH), 46
Population-effect models, 18, 24, 82, 173
Premarket Tobacco Product Authorization (PMTA), 165–167, 170, 174–176, 212
Prevalence (adult use, smoking), 3, 4, 49–55, 71
Prevalence (youth, e-cigarettes), 15

Prevalence (youth, smoking), 23
Price elasticity, 73
Principle of proportionality, 16
Product placement, 36, 75, 76, 171, 198
Product standards, 76
Prohibition, 10, 11, 18, 20, 23, 34, 75, 77, 86, 144, 179, 206
Propylene glycol (PG), 12, 150
Public Health England (PHE), 13, 148, 209
Public use bans/laws/legislation (e-cigarettes), 83. *See also* e-cigarette-inclusive smoke-free (ESF) policies
PuffBar, 169
Pyrolysis, 215

Q
Quitting behaviors, 63

R
Racketeer Influenced and Corrupt Organizations Act (RICO), 44
Randomized controlled trials (RCTs), 90, 175
Reduced harm products (RHPs), 151
Reduced risk products (RRPs), 151
Refuse To File (RFT), 175
Regional disparities, 187
Regressivity, 74
Regulatory scientists, 24
Relative risk, 38, 154
Relative safety, 153, 209
Restaurant restrictions, 41
Reynolds American, 94, 161
Reynolds, R.J., 36, 42, 43, 156, 160, 161, 176, 212
Reynolds Vapor Company, 161, 176
Rhetoric, 20
Rheumatoid arthritis, 5

Risk-free, 13, 16, 17
Risk proportionality, 212. *See also*
    Risk-proportionate regulation
Risk-proportionate regulation, 213
Risk ratio (RR), 191
Risky behaviors, 87
Roll-your-own (RYO), 149
Royal College of Physicians (RCP), 1,
    13, 37–40, 206, 209
Ruyan, 161. *See also* Dragonite
    International Limited; Ruyan
    Group Holdings Limited

S
Safeguards, 17
Safer nicotine products (SNPs), 151
San Francisco Cancer Survey, 37
Second-hand smoke, 2, 17, 27, 39,
    40, 42, 44, 54, 59, 69, 75, 83,
    87, 156
Selection bias, 15
Side-stream smoke, 5, 27, 196
Skycig, 159, 160
Smoke-free laws, 2, 40, 41, 75, 81,
    83, 194, 197
Smokeless tobacco, 47, 48, 105, 149,
    154
Smoking abstinence rate, 203
Smoking and Alcohol Toolkit Study
    (United Kingdom), 46
Smoking cessation, 1, 8, 11, 13,
    15–20, 22–25, 58, 61–65, 68,
    74, 77–79, 84, 86, 89–91, 149,
    152, 189–191, 194–197, 199,
    200, 202, 203, 207, 210, 211
Smoking frequency, 64
Smoking history, 182, 185
Smoking initiation, 15, 58, 63, 85, 88
Smoking prevalence, 4, 41, 47–58,
    60, 63, 64, 66–68, 72, 75, 78,
    81–84, 86, 89, 92, 191, 210
Smoking prevalence gap, 63

Smoking rates, 1, 4, 15, 23, 35, 40,
    42, 46, 48, 50, 52, 56, 57, 59,
    62, 64–67, 82, 85, 87, 181, 186,
    191
Smoking-related harms, 16, 32,
    56–58, 62, 65, 69, 85, 87, 88,
    148, 156, 190, 196, 200, 205,
    209
Smoking-related health risks, 32
Smoking-related illnesses, 5, 6, 83
Smoking-related morbidity, 54, 67,
    69, 211
Smoking-related mortality, 42, 83, 87
Smoking Toolkit Study (STS), 75
Smoore Technology Limited, 159
Snus, 47, 149
Social justice, 68
Social media, 163, 164, 171, 172,
    220
Social scientists, 19, 24
Socio-economically disadvantaged, 2
Socioeconomic groups, 58, 63, 83,
    188, 189
Socioeconomic Status (SES), 57,
    59–63, 74, 88, 188–190
SoFIE-Health, 46
South African Pharmacy Council, 208
South America, 34
STEPs, 177
Stigma (of smoking), 6
Stigma (of vaping), 3
Subsidy, 91
Substitute, substitution, 11, 14, 16,
    19, 20, 86, 89, 90, 95, 157, 176,
    195, 203, 206, 210, 212, 216
Sudden Infant Death Syndrome
    (SIDS), 6
Supply-side response, 73
Surgeon General's report, 39, 159,
    218
Swap to Stop, 154, 210
Synthetic nicotine, 153, 169

262 INDEX

Systemic marginalization, 65

T
Tar, 7, 147
Taxation, 2, 6, 10, 11, 33, 35, 52, 61, 62, 72–74, 81, 82, 92, 94, 242
Taxes, 2, 3, 6, 7, 11, 16, 23, 33, 38, 62, 66, 70, 72–74, 81–83, 91, 92, 242
Temptation goods, 10, 23, 29, 179
Ten Motives Ltd, 159
The Premier, 156
Throat cancer, 37
Tobacco advertising, 3, 39, 76, 82, 84, 171
Tobacco harm reduction (THR), 7, 16, 21, 86, 211
Tobacco prevention programs, 43
Tobacco Products Directive (TPD), 80
Tobacco-specific nitrosamines (TSNAs), 153
Toxicant, 7, 13, 147, 210
Toxicological studies, 13
Trade-offs (may also be spelled tradeoffs?), 21
Traditional tobacco control, 7, 91, 94
Transnational Tobacco Companies (TTCs), 18, 160, 167

U
UN Framework Convention on Tobacco Control ("FCTC"), 3
Unintended consequences, 11, 17, 21, 23, 79, 94
Unregulated products, 11
Upper-middle-income countries, 179

U.S. Centers for Disease Control, 46, 67, 184
U.S. Supreme Court, 43
U.S. Surgeon General, 1, 37, 39, 71

V
Value judgment, 18
Varenicline (Chantix/Champix), 62, 78
Vegetable glycerin (VG), 12, 150
Vending-machine sales, 2, 70
Vuse, 12, 152, 160, 161, 164, 166, 169, 212, 225

W
Warning labels, 2, 3, 39, 71, 80, 84, 211
War on drugs, 93
Wick, 12, 150, 151, 157, 215
Withdrawal symptoms, 61, 91, 204
World Bank World Development Indicators, 50
World Economic Forum, 187
World Health Organization (WHO), 3, 22, 31, 46–50, 53, 54, 65, 69, 74, 80, 82, 83, 86, 104, 148, 152, 179, 205
World Health Organization (WHO) STEPs data collection system, 205

Y
Youth Risk Behavioral Surveillance (YRBS), 177
Youth vaping, 22, 23, 164, 165, 211